Having someone like Chet and BTL in my life has been profound. Life-changing is an understatement. It's my turn to do the same for the next generation. My OPUS takes another turn and it's been a joy, all of it. I am so blessed and in awe of it all.

—Brett Kaufman, Owner, Kaufman Development

My builder, Chet Scott, and **BUILT TO LEAD** has etched a place in my heart and has been there for me through it all. Together, curling hundreds of reps and more than 300 team practices, we've challenged, laughed, cried, and fought. The only thing we haven't done yet is wrestle. One day…The road continues—stay raw.

—Chad Silverstein, Owner, Choice Recovery / [re]start

I believe Chet because he's an example of what he teaches. He lives BTL. I learned that by spending time with him and observing him. I worked out with him, watched him, and chose to bring him into my inner circle. That was one of the single best decisions of my life. He shares truth in love with me and those I love. He is a truth-teller in my life and has moved Ohio State wrestling forward. It has been no surprise that my teams have finished first, second, and third at the NCAA Championships the past five seasons. Our results reflect our love for and connection with each other. BTL connects. It builds.

—Tom Ryan, Head Men's Wrestling Coach, The Ohio State University, author of *Chosen Suffering*

Understanding, building, and maintaining my core…Values, beliefs, strengths, and weaknesses…that's how I am becoming **BUILT TO LEAD**.

—Ronald J. Lockton, Chairman, Lockton, Inc. Owner, Lockton Companies

Chet's process was relentless, which at the time was annoying and frustrating. Yet it provided the needed push and persistence to clarity that

CEOs rarely have time to spend on creating their personal OPUS. True leadership of others cannot come until you have clarity on your gifts, your desires, and your reason to be fulfilled. The BTL process helps anyone find that path to fulfillment in themselves, so they can help others find their path and reach their own greatness.

—Lisa Ingram, CEO, White Castle Systems

The currency of leadership is measured in loyal followers. History has proven humans follow those who remain calm when environments are volatile. The purpose of BTL is to reveal to the leader who they are and what they stand for. Ultimately, the stand the leader takes separates them from much of life's volatility, which creates an attractor pattern of loyal followers. The followers become disciples of the BTL process, the flywheel spins, and the results are geometric.

—Rich Reda, CEBS, President, Benefit Communication
Insourcing, Lockton Companies

BUILT to LEAD has helped me in all aspects of my life, both at home and at the office. Chet helped me look at situations in different ways and showed me how to be open and responsive to different perspectives and points of view. Chet has taught me to be a better listener and, most importantly, has encouraged me to be more receptive and open to the opinions of my team. I do not want our team members to be afraid to voice their opinions. I also now slow down and better analyze situations before making decisions, which has made a huge difference. The Arnold Sports Festival is a better organization, and I am a better leader because of the many lessons I learned from Chet and **BUILT to LEAD**.

—Bob Lorimer, President, The Arnold Sports Festival

Today I am a better husband, father, and grandfather, and by the grace of God, I am blessed to lead a wonderful organization. I am eternally grateful for **BUILT to LEAD** and my dear friend Pete Kunk, who carried me to a better, more useful place on this planet.

—Scott McGohan, CEO, McGohan Brabender

I have met with Chet Scott just about every month for twenty years. Back then I was just taking over as CEO, and I wanted a performance evaluation. Chet made me painfully aware of the issues that would likely have hampered my success. Through working with him, I am a better leader because I am a better person.

—David Lockton, Owner, Lockton Companies

BTL has truly awakened me in ways that I did not even know were possible. The journey has just begun; I feel the core getting stronger, and the transformation taking place. I am forever grateful to Chet. I love the work.

Nicholas Myers, Head Men's Lacrosse Coach, The Ohio State University

More than a dozen years ago, our leadership team engaged **BUILT TO LEAD** to help us and our culture become truly one. Today, **BUILT TO LEAD** is building into our next-gen partners and our firm is giving the gift of BTL practice to the community in which we serve.

—Matt Hamilton, CEO, Owner, Hamilton Capital Management

BUILT TO LEAD woke me up as never before. Objective & humble clarity of "self" emerged as well as insight into the elements necessary for growth. There are no quick or permanent fixes. For those choosing ongoing hard work, **BUILT TO LEAD** offers unique guidance to live fully—with purpose, integrity, and promise.

—Jeff Loehnis, CFP®, President, Hamilton Capital Management

BECOMING
BUILT TO LEAD

365 Daily Disciplines to Master the Art of Living

CHET SCOTT

ethos
collective

Published by Ethos Collective™
PO Box 43, Powell, OH 43065
ethoscollective.vip

LCCN: 2020920779

ISBN: 978-1-63680-009-7 (paperback)
ISBN: 978-1-63680-010-3 (hardback)
ISBN: 978-1-63680-011-0 (ebook)

Available in paperback, hardback, e-book, and audiobook

All Scripture quotations, unless otherwise indicated, are taken from the Holy Bible, New International Version®, NIV®. Copyright © 1973, 1978, 1984, 2011 by Biblica, Inc.TM All rights reserved worldwide. www.zondervan.com. The "NIV" and "New International Version" are trademarks registered in the United States Patent and Trademark office by Biblica, Inc. TM

Author Photo: Mark and Shelly Photography, markandshellyphotography.com

Any Internet addresses (websites, blogs, etc.) and telephone numbers printed in this book are offered as a resource. They are not intended in any way to be or imply an endorsement by Ethos Collective™ nor does Ethos Collective™ vouch for the content of these sites and numbers for the life of this book.

Dedication

The book is dedicated to Miss, forty years my constant. Your love fuels me…

Table of Contents

Foreword

> Winning has a price. Leadership has a price.
> —Michael Jordan, from *The Last Dance*

Writing this foreword changed the way I think and the way I live.

I've been familiar with Chet Scott's **BUILT TO LEAD** for a long time, but three ideas in particular sunk in deep as I read this new book and digested it page by page.

"Authentic OPUS" is first. (I won't spoil it for you. You have to read the book.)
The BTL CORE is another.
And PoP. (I won't spoil those for you either.)
Can leadership be taught? Or is it innate?
Are some people born to lead and others to follow?
What is a leader anyway?

Chet Scott's answer to the first question is an unequivocal yes. But with this proviso: Before we can lead others, we have to lead ourselves.

This means introspection. It means self-scrutiny, self-dissection, self-definition. "Build your CORE," is how Chet would phrase it, by which he means, "do the inner work of discovering who you are, what you want, what you believe in, what you love, what you aspire to, what you're willing to sacrifice for."

We *can* learn to lead.
The capacity lies within us.

Michael Jordan famously said that leadership has a price. For him, it was the toll he paid to get to a level few, if any, have ever reached—the agony of early loss, the ordeal of growth and self-reinvention, the physical blows and injuries. It was the painful shedding of outworn identities, the embracing of generosity and inclusion. It was learning to trust others, embracing strategies and people that he might have rejected at an earlier age. The price was a species of isolation, the burden of responsibility, and the emotional expenditure of his "hero's journey."

We become different people when we become leaders.
A part of us has to die, and another part must be born.
We shed a skin when we become leaders.
It costs.
There's a price.

Chet Scott and his team at **BUILT TO LEAD** have spent decades investigating this odyssey of self-transformation. The reason this book is structured as a "yearbook" is that the transformation, for anyone, is a process—day by day, week by week, month by month.

What I love about *Becoming* **BUILT TO LEAD**, the book, is that Chet has broken down this process—this hero's journey—into its constituent elements, in sequence, and put the whole show back together in a way that you and I can follow.

BUILT TO LEAD is a philosophy. It's an ethic. But it's also a methodology. You can study it. You can "take the course." You can enroll in Chet Scott's academy.

What you'll find in the end, as I did learning from Chet, is that what you're studying is yourself. The process is not addition; it's subtraction. We are stripping away the notions of how Somebody Else should lead, or how some idealized version of ourselves should lead...and getting down to what Carl Jung called individuation.

We're asking the questions we started with above.
Who are we?
What do we want?
 Whom do we wish to lead? Why? Toward what goal?

The **BUILT TO LEAD** process is not a picnic. People drop out. They don't like what the process makes them see in the mirror. The price is too high. They can't take it.

This book is not necessarily fun to read. It asks tough questions. You may not like some of the answers you find yourself giving.

You will not be the same person at the end that you were at the start.

In the end, the **BUILT TO LEAD** process, like any odyssey of maturation, is a pilgrimage. We start where we are right now (or where we imagine we are), and we trek to a Santiago de Compostela of the mind and heart.

This book is the road map for that pilgrimage. Reading it, we can follow along, turn by turn, way station by way station. The pilgrimage follows a course. But the real journey is interior; it's personal. It's unique to each individual.

What is leadership anyway, at its essence?

It's example.
It's the woman or man out front, being true to who she or he really is... and drawing the rest of us after her because we admire that person and the goals to which she aspires. We follow her because we share those goals. Because we want to be like her.

The price of leadership is self-transformation. It's self-actualization. The price of leadership is coming into one's own...and demonstrating that for others to discern, to test, and to emulate.

Chet Scott's *Becoming Built to Lead* is the handbook and atlas of that transformation.

Steven Pressfield
Los Angeles 2020

Publisher's Note

TRUTH. Few *tell* it. Fewer *want* it. And even fewer *live* it.

You've heard the phrases:
The TRUTH hurts.
The TRUTH will set you free.
So, which is it? Does the truth hurt, or does it set you free?

The answer is both.

You're about to enter a brand-new world. For those with an unhealthy overindulgence in social media, it's going to feel a bit unfamiliar.

Get ready to think in ways you've never thought and dig deep, way beneath the surface. You'll find much more than treasure. You'll find yourself—without the masks, the labels, the pretense, and the lies.

It's going to feel painful—looking in the mirror always is. This is why the bulk of humanity prefers the bottle, the remote, or the screen instead. This is why we distract ourselves, just as our predecessors did hundreds of years ago.

Seventeenth-century French philosopher Blaise Pascal was willing to tell the truth to his generation. He said all of our difficulties are caused by our inability to sit quietly in a room by ourselves.

Why is sitting and thinking so hard?

Pascal had an answer for that one too:
The only thing that consoles us for our miseries is distraction, yet that is the greatest of our wretchednesses. Because that is what mainly prevents us from thinking about ourselves and leads us imperceptibly to damnation. Without it

we should be bored, and boredom would force us to search for a firmer way out,
but distraction entertains us and leads us imperceptibly to death.
Most prefer a life of distraction rather than a life of depth.

You're different.

You're the minority.

Count yourself blessed for meeting Chet Scott. I thank God every day. Chet is one of the top five most influential people in my life.

Later on in the book, you'll learn how we met and how he woke me up—personally, professionally, financially, and spiritually.

For now, remember this:

Chet doesn't care about impressing. This is why his book won't become a bestseller. It's *too* true. He could care less about entertaining or affirming you. But make no mistake—he believes in you more than you'll ever know. This is why he's not going to let you off the hook.

He knows the path because he's walked the path. In this book, there is no hype, only hard work. There are no platitudes, only pain.

If you don't know it by now, you'll soon discover what C.S. Lewis meant when he wrote, "Pain is a megaphone to rouse a deaf world."

You're about to wake up and realize you never knew you were sleeping.

Get ready to become **BUILT TO LEAD**.

Get ready to break free from the unlived life and become a soul on fire.

I believe in Chet.

I believe in his book.

And I believe if you do the work, you'll never look at life or yourself the same way again.

Kary Oberbrunner, CEO, Author Academy Elite,
Author of seven books, Soul on Fire, aka PJ in this book

Acknowledgments

This book would not have been possible without the help of so many. First of all, thanks, Mom, for your seemingly endless belief. Because of you, I believe. Thanks to sisters KA and Mary Marie and my new sisters Pinner and Sister Sue. Thanks to my brothers-in-law, Jim and Reenie. James Lambert, thanks for your calls and constant encouragement. Meeting you, with my Connie shoebox in fifth grade, was my good fortune. Thanks, Grover Simpson and Bryan Norton for introducing me to Lockton and for your friendship over the years. Thanks to the CompuServe team who taught me about leadership before I knew what I was doing. Thanks to all the X-Directs, especially Snuch, jmo, and Quinner, who walked with me through the sonic ride up and the quick trip down. Thanks, Doug Loewe, for bringing BTL into every institution you've led. Thanks, Greg Tillar, for modeling the way and putting up with my immaturity. Your leadership seared my sorriness. Thanks, Jeff Wilkins, for your belief and sending your son, Dub, my way. Thanks, Nickies (101-year-old father-in-law), for your stories and sound council. You represent the greatest generation very, very well. Thanks, Dad, Doctor 46, Doc Scott, and the original Chester Eugene, for your energizing love of me. You've been gone since 1996. Never forgotten. You will always be the kindest man I've ever met. You taught me to care less about what others think of me and care more about the audience of One. I'm looking forward to catching up with you soon...

Thanks to the BTL Band for believing, first as clients, now as colleagues. You each stamped your essence on this book. Thanks, LA, for everything. You were my best builder—period. We will ride again in Heaven. This time, you'll pick the route, my brother. Thanks, Kitty, for your timeless wisdom and grace. Thanks, Browny, for your humor, art, and well-timed "ands." Thanks, Petey, for being such a great neighbor, friend, and now BTL Bandmate. Thanks, Gu, for being the Gufrickin'rue. Your tireless work and tender touch are quite the combo. Thanks, Doscher, for bringing your art to our perfect mess. You're the little brother I never had. Thanks, Rachel, for bringing a head coach's perspective to our band. Your work ethic and energy juice me. Jiggles, Jiggles, Jiggles. Where to start with Jiggles. Thanks for practicing seven good minutes with Lauren and falling in love. Thanks for bringing your youth and enthusiasm to this not so young band of builders. Thanks, Dorothy, for coming on board and kicking ASS. Your edge is welcome here. Thanks, Tay, for your belief and being with me in practice after practice. Your perspective rounds mine.

Another round of thanks to Dosch and Gu for "hell week" with me culling away at the end. The book is better because of our addition by subtraction—much better. Forever grateful.

Thanks to PJ, Tina, Kirsten, Felicity, Dave, and the Ethos Collective™ team for making this book a reality. Thanks, PJ, for making me do what I can. Without you pushing me, this wasn't happening. I guess we've pushed each other. Good.

Thanks to Bk for your krazy belief. Bringing BTL into a startup taught us both more than we know. Thanks, Durp, for allowing our distinction to draw us together instead of splitting us apart. You and I are distinct and deeply connected, my friend. Thanks, Dub, for teaching me that investment dudes can be funny, friendly, and financially savvy too. Thanks, Slo, for being my trusted financial advisor and friend forever. Your advice and slo, steady hand are much appreciated. Thanks, Littlest Fricker, for trying to race after me in France as I sped down the mountain without brakes. You are a dear and forever friend. Thanks to the entire 3PP team—Downer, Kevin, Stud, Guv, Jmo, Slo, PJ, and Blondie. My CORE is strong because of you. Thanks to these same men plus the Shoe, the young Lad, Mickanator, Grappy, Littlest, and others for the many beautiful bike rides around central Ohio. So many of the ideas for this book came from time on the bike.

Thanks to Grappy, Cbear, Nick, Kevin, Lori, and Ohio State head coaches for your belief in BTL. Your team practices are my favorite playtime. Thanks to Dan and the Lower team. I love practicing with you. Greaves, Z, Kristin, Cashcash, and many more fine folks have taught me so much. Thanks to the Choice team—Kiesha, Josh, Heels, Warden, Cali, Hopper, and so, so many more. Love you. Thanks to k-dev krazies: we've grown up together. Frankeethecfoinghonkeenowpresident. OMG. Ian, Goalie, OG, Z, Jay, Lauren, Reika, Brad, ANP, and on and on it goes. Love to all of you. Thanks to Hamilton Capital and all your belief in BTL. You're more than great clients: you are the BTL financial advisory team. Thank you, thank you.

Thanks to Lockton Companies. David and Ron, your company is inspiring. Practicing with you two has been a privilege and great pleasure. Thank you for your continued trust and belief. Tommyc and the Midwest Series, my love and gratitude to all of you too. Thanks to Wierema for his Sunday writing on compass and map. Amazing. Practicing with you makes me smile, Wild Kitty, Moodyman, Gray fox, and many more amazing men and women. Thanks to Joeylamb and the KC producer team. Getting tired with Thomas, Stover, Joe D., and many more. Thanks to Brian Roberts, Brookethehippie, and Rich Reda for making me better. Thanks to Mark Henderson for your belief and encouragement.

Thanks to Bob Lorimer and the Arnold Sports Festival for teaching me that old dogs can learn new tricks. Thanks, Kyle, for teaching me to not judge a book by its cover. Your tenacity and toughness are second to none. Thanks to my cousin, Ann, and her husband, Jim Gant. Your writing, wisdom, and kindness are a constant source of smiles for me. Thanks to Steve Pressfield for the best Foreword in the history of Forewords. I cannot believe how quickly you digested our work and extrapolated it into words. Thanks to Team Fishel, White Castle, Baesman, CSC, Buckeye Boxes, Columbus Marble and Granite, Cello Poly, Rackspace, Interaxion, New Balance, and many more who are no longer clients but whose learning will never leave me. Thank you.

Thank you, finally, to my family. Thanks, Jordan, for teaching me to be a father. You have a tender heart and a tough mind. You've taught me not to put people in boxes or fall in love with labels. Thanks, Andrew, for pursuing your art and life in Berlin. Your smile and laugh are forever seared in my soul. Your love of old wisdom as a young man is so cool. You are the second best cook I know! Thanks, Krit, for being my best girl. "Shoe go bye-bye" was prophetic. You are the most like me. You are a beauty and a beast on the bike. You are my hiking companion when there is no trail. Thanks, Tay, for being with me on this journey of Becoming BTL. Having you in the band is pure joy. You have a great mind for it and will be a better builder than me—someday. Thanks, Jo (our 19-year-old dog), for teaching me small dogs are strong dogs too. Thanks, Penny (Krit's pup and our grandpup) for all the love and cuddles. And, of course, thanks goes out to Tank for teaching me to live hard and love harder. Teeks is my forever furry friend. All of you "children" fill my heart beyond your comprehension. You are masterpieces in the making. God bless you, as you have so deeply blessed me…

Thanks, Miss. Where to begin here. Thanks for choosing to go to Taylor University summer school. Best thing that ever happened to me was meeting you that summer of 1980. Thanks for being my best friend, lover, fellow parent, top chef, walker, talker, tax organizer, haircutting master, farmer, and health expert (introducing me to so many life-changing foods and supplements like collagen, vitamin E, magnesium, and many more). Thanks, Miss, for teaching me more about my joint health than any doc. My lack of pain in hips, shoulders, and back is more attributable to you than any other human. Thanks, Miss, for listening to me endlessly read my rants when they're fresh and raw. You've made them better. Every. Last. One. Thanks for supporting me in every way you can and always with a smile. Your endless love for me has changed my mind and heart. I could NEVER have written the words on this page without your LOVE written on my heart. I suck at romance and repairing anything around the house. You know this. Thanks for loving me for who I am. Thanks for being a strong woman—Greek Comanche, by God. Thanks for your truth and practical wisdom. I could go on. It's nearly time to stop. One more thought…

It seems silly to me, the subtitle of this book—mastering the art of living. To me, mastering the art of living is found through embracing the messes we've made, and instead of getting mad and cursing the world and each other, we make a better choice. We hold each other up. You are my hand to hold onto, Miss. You hold me together, actually. Together, we will live hard and love harder. Always together.

Finally, thanks, God, for the gift of this work and all these transforming souls you've put in my path. Thanks, God, for the gift of this life. Thanks, God, for Jesus and the greatest gift of His Grace. God, help me make the most of this gift. God, help me.

Live hard. Love harder (Thanks, Teeks)…

Introduction: Becoming BTL...

I am not a professional writer. I'm a builder and lead a band of passionate builders, fixated on building mastery in the art of living. Today, we number ten souls: Gurue, Peteboy, Browny, Kitty, Doscher, Rachel, Jiggles, Dorothy, and my youngest son, Tay. We are not normal, nor do we want you to be. We are Becoming **BUILT TO LEAD** and invite you to join us on this transformational journey of discovering how to master the art of living. We are far from mastering this art and understand we'll never arrive. It's a worthy aim and our life's work. We invite you to join us. So, if you're ready, let's get started. Actually, let's go back for a bit...

Way back in 1993, sitting in the CompuServe Board Room and bored beyond belief, I heard Maury Cox, our CEO, call my name. He had decided we needed to grow people as fast as we were growing profits and wanted somebody to check out the Center for Creative Leadership; that somebody was me. I resisted and told him to send Judy. *After all, she's the head of Human Resources, isn't she?* I reminded him I was busy running Sales and Service and didn't have the time. He insisted I go anyway. So, begrudgingly, away I went. Everything changed.

Not really, but something happened. Something inside of me knew this week had seared my soul. Upon my return, I started making small changes. I knew I was not going to leave CompuServe and take another job or go work for some competitor. I knew I was going to start my own company and begin a practice that would build leaders. I had no idea how but I knew this was my calling. No StrengthsFinder, DISC, MBTI, Kolbe, or any other tool or toolmaker told me. Something deep within me screamed it so loudly that my scared, small, sacred self couldn't stop the magnetic pull of my soul calling me to something more. I was becoming a soul on fire. The lure of more money didn't matter. More power seemed weak. But something calling me promised something that mattered so much more. What matters more, friend?

Meaning. Meaning matters more.

We are creatures in search of meaning. Don't believe me—marinate on Viktor Frankl's book titled *Man's Search for Meaning*. We are not meant to labor/live in vain. We are meaning mongers. We are meant to discover ourselves along with our gifts along the twisted, winding road of this life. Some of us will stumble into meaning. For others, the obstacle (like Viktor) will provide the way. For lucky (soft) souls such as me, the opportunity will become the way. Regardless of your situation or circumstance, friend, you are becoming **BUILT TO LEAD** yourself. Don't habituate building yourself with a scarcity mindset. This is the way of the world. You, friend, are the child of an abundant God, alive in an ever-expanding/growing Universe. You are meant for meaning. You know this because you've felt it in the *kairos* moments of life. Stop ignoring these signals.

Slow down and sit with this a while.

Why not build your BTL CORE—Figure out who you are, why you're here, what you believe, and why it matters? Why not author your OPUS—your labor of love? Here is your contribution and aim for work/life. Your Playbook of Productive action (PoP) will eradicate chronic pain with acute pain filled with passion and purpose and glimpses of joy. Substitute a PoP for chronic pain. You will feel the difference on your way to Becoming BTL. You will taste peace on the other side of acute pain. You will if you do the real, hard work of Becoming BTL. You choose. Your choices have consequences.

Why not let this book and these 365 rants be the catalyst for your calling? Each day is a designed practice. These daily practices are for you to read, write, slow down, reflect, and productively act. Do not skip any of the steps. Do not binge-read this book; that would miss the point. This book, a lot like your life and mine, is best when taken one day at a time. Answer the questions honestly. Write your thinking in narratives, not bullet points. Make the decision, daily, to baby-step something around your CORE, OPUS, and PoP. This is the power of BTL practice. Progress over perfection.

Let me be clear, concise, and direct about why we're here. We are here to live out our Purpose. Our Purpose at BTL is as follows: Together we Awaken, Challenge, and Transform a few individuals, teams and leaders from a lone toward all ONE—one 'L of a difference. One, distinct and deeply connected, Becoming BTL. Together, we transform. Always together. This is our why. Do you have crystal clarity of yours? You will have more in 365 days...

This book is a reflection of my strong CORE. Each day is filled with real content and a challenge or two for you. It represents my OPUS—my labor of love. I've written 3,500-plus rants over the past fourteen years helping me gain clarity for myself and our work. Culling has been hard OPUS (a term you will hear often in the days to come). This book is personal, spiritual, and a reflection of years of learning on my Builder's Journey. This book may be a wake-up call to launch you onto your Builder's Journey or a reminder to get you back on track. I hope you marinate on the twelve Builder's Journeys and let them sear your soul and transform you too. I hope you trust our framework and appreciate our transparency. I hope you become awake and oriented times four. I hope you become the original you already are. I have big dreams for you. Do you?

This is not an easy read. Life is hard and beautiful. We're glad you're here and promise to be with you throughout your journey of Becoming BTL. Let's go. Let's start the process of Becoming BTL...

"A master in the art of living draws no sharp distinction between his work and his play; his labor and his leisure; his mind and his body; his education and his recreation. He hardly knows which is which. He simply pursues his vision of excellence through whatever he is doing, and leaves others to determine whether he is working or playing. To himself, he always appears to be doing both."

Francois Auguste Rene Chateaubriand

BUILT to LEAD | together we transform

Build Your CORE

12 ESSENTIALS OF PERSONAL EXCELLENCE

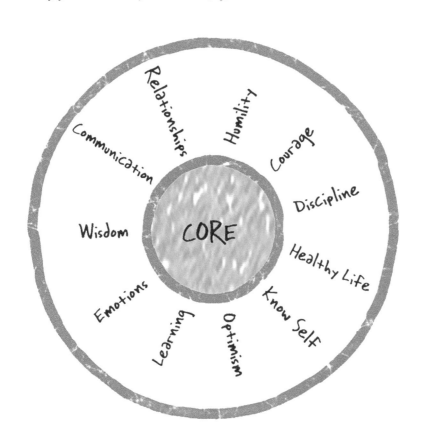

Kiesha's Builder's Journey

I started with my present company in March 2012. There wasn't much structure, accountability, or training. I was ready to leave after three months. When my boss gave me a promotion, I stayed. At the time, my self-worth was tied to work. I was a good person if I did well at work. By August 2012, I was asked to join a BTL practice. At the time, it was only offered to team leads. It was a big deal because I wasn't a team lead, and I was the lowest guy on the totem pole. I remember thinking from my first practice, *Is this really what all these people stopped working to come and do?* Back then, I was a workaholic. Work was my identity. The idea that people purposefully stopped working to practice sounded crazy. They also started each meeting by doing a plank. Nuts, right? I shared how crazy this whole thing was. I remember Chet saying, "Good stuff."

With my workaholic background, I got busy getting busy. I ate up everything that was said. Work on an OPUS—check. Start on your Worldview—check. Find a builder—check. Write a list of PAs. Rinse. Repeat. It seemed fine. I was busy. I was writing. For over a year, I felt like I was making real progress. I had been promoted again. I wrote this OPUS and started living it out. Little did I know, my BTL Journey hadn't even begun.

December 2013, we changed up the BTL structure at my company. The leaders formed a SEAL practice (as in Navy SEALs, SEAL Team 6, The Elite).Everyone was paired with a SEAL buddy. My SEAL buddy turned out to be my boss. Backstory is, my boss worked with Chet one-on-one before introducing BTL to the company. He knew his stuff. My boss is special. Not the "he is nice, and everyone likes him" special. I mean, he is crazy passionate, kind, driven, hardworking, generous, and intense. Everyone knew this. Everyone wanted to be picked, but secretly, we knew this was the real deal. I knew BTL wasn't going to be a cakewalk anymore.

Even though I was working on OPUS and had a Worldview, it was all bullshit. When I was first asked into BTL, I was sent discovery questions. This was supposed to be the first step in the BTL process. There are eighty questions. I got through ten and thought the rest were too hard to answer. I lost steam when I read #11. *Do you know what*

BUILT to **LEAD** | together we transform

you believe about why you exist? I knew what he was asking. *What do you believe about God?* I didn't want to answer it truthfully. I stopped there at Discovery and only answered that I don't believe in God. I had ideas about God and religion and was not interested in exploring any of it. I thought I didn't need to go deep into that topic to figure shit out. Now that I was paired with my boss and wanting to impress, I figured it was time to dive deep.

What started out as a question on a list for an exercise in a leadership program was a game-changer. You see, I didn't grow up in church. The words *God, Jesus, Bible, heaven,* and *hell* all made me feel uncomfortable. But all these words had meaning to me—I just didn't know it yet. I had this belief that I was a sinner. I was such a sinner that I wouldn't be able to go to heaven. God didn't love me like He loved those who followed Him and went to church. What a lie I was telling myself. I really didn't understand Jesus and what His death meant. What I really felt was alone. Somewhere in my life, I had picked up those beliefs. But I could also pinpoint where God was there and where I chose not to listen or see.

I found some builders who asked curious questions and challenged me. When I took the time to write, to really write what was on my heart, everything changed. For the first time, I felt awake. I didn't feel scared to answer, *Do you know what you believe about why you exist?* I exist because an all-powering, all-knowing, all-loving God created me. I am His work of art. I was created to be who He has called me to be. I am called to live out His purpose in seeking and saving the lost, just like me.

In 2014, I was baptized at my church. In 2015, I went to Nicaragua to help build a church for a local pastor. Later that year, I welcomed my first daughter, and my second daughter in 2017. In 2020, I am saying goodbye to a team I love and staying home to be a mom full-time with my little ones. I could not have imagined my life would have taken this direction eight years ago. I am thankful and blessed that it has. The work is never over. There is always more to write, read, and learn.

To say BTL changed my life is an understatement. BTL *saved* my life.

Day 1: Why are you here?

Pain is inevitable. Misery is a choice.

Becoming **BUILT TO LEAD** begins with a decision to replace chronic pain with more acute pain. We must each choose this for ourselves. The journey starts here with an honest look within. Slow down. Stop running from your pain. Stop numbing what needs, instead, to be uprooted and eradicated. Write honestly why are you here.

Eradicate chronic pain. Embrace acute pain.

> "God whispers to us in our pleasures, speaks in our conscience, but shouts in our pain; it is His megaphone to rouse a deaf world."
> —C.S. Lewis

Day 2: Why we write...

What are the two greatest influences in the life of an average American?

Well, go back two hundred, one hundred, or even fifty years and the answer was two words—faith and family. Fast forward to today and they aren't even in the top ten. The number one influence in your life is, most likely, the media to which you give your attention. A distant but significant second is the culture where you work. According to a 2002 Ball State study, the average American invests eleven and a half hours a day on their phone, plugged into mass media, social media, and mesmerized slowly to follow some mass of men/women.

Becoming BTL requires that you become the biggest influence in your life. This is why you must become a writer and speak from your heart. This is why trust is a must. None of us is meant to go it alone or even a lone. We are designed, instead, to become all ONE with the help of a few friends. We become the CEO of Y.O.U. as we practice writing in narratives, not bullet points, talking truth instead of spinning B.S. to sound good. Don't shoot yourself with bullet points. Your brain stores in story form. Write without worries about grammar, punctuation, or how it will be perceived. Write raw, real narratives, and find a friend. Talk. Write to become the biggest influence in your life. Write to avoid the natural pull toward mediocrity and the mass of men and women. Write to discover the road less traveled, your Builder's Journey, and figure out the baby step of PA to move you toward your true self.

Slow down. Write your thinking. Practice writing in narratives. Good...

Day 3: Happiness...

You cannot lead others further than you've led yourself.

This is painful just to admit much less do something about, huh? Becoming BTL is beginning to feel like one tough slog, and we're only on day 3. Catch your breath and take a moment to stop your relentless pursuit to the peak. You began by honestly answering why you're here. Now answer this. Why are you in such a hurry? Where are you going? Why does it matter? Are you chasing what matters most or simply settling for chasing what you can measure?

> I have often said that the sole cause of man's unhappiness is that he does not know how to stay quietly in his room.
>
> —Blaise Pascal

Do you? Slow down and reflect...

BUILT to **LEAD** | together we transform

Day 4: CORE-centered and self-controlling...

If you want to master the art of living, friend, you must stop aiming at fitting in. Masters are not normal, nor do they care. A master in the art of living builds a second nature. All humans come into this world self-centered and other-controlling. Excellence requires that you become CORE-centered and self-controlling. Excellence requires a strong CORE, authentic OPUS, and a discipline to PoP it out through your PAs. These focused few are on their Builder's Journey and aimed toward their OPUS, their labor of love. Productive action keeps moving them through life's adversity with hardly a break in stride. Like-minded folks come alongside, and as a band, they pick up speed with their ever-deepening sense of trust. This team is becoming a community with chemistry. They are freakin' magic for those who see through a performance-trained eye. Their performance is almost mesmerizing in its simplicity and crispness. They make the difficult look easy. Their size and audience are exactly what they are meant to be, at least for now.

Becoming ONE internally is a long, hard journey of discovery, reflection, and productive action. Seemingly impossible, only time and deep practice make becoming ONE possible. The enemy is to simply focus on results and outcomes, neither of which you control. The world lives here, and it's why there are so few individuals, teams, and leaders who are Becoming BTL.

The BTL leader focuses within on her OPUS and PA. She focuses on becoming whole by aligning behaviors with beliefs, closing her integrity gaps by bolting down beliefs, and changing behaviors. Slow down and sit with these thoughts for a while. Write. What baby step can you take today toward Becoming BTL?

Day 5: Builder's Journey...

So, what is your Builder's Journey, friend? Your Builder's Journey is for you to author. The Hero's Journey is the oldest story on the planet and has been told in every language with the aim of inspiring young people to leave the comfort of home and figure out life along the way. A strong CORE is essential. You must know thyself and get comfortable being who you are. Sounds easy. It's not.

An authentic OPUS is a must. *Opus* is a Latin word that translates to the English word *work*. It means "labor of love." At BTL, we've turned OPUS into an acrostic. Let's unpack this briefly here. You must know your aim: this is your O (Overarching vision). "Dream big," as Goethe said, "for small dreams have no power to move mankind." Next is your P (Purpose). This is your why. If you are to sustain effort on your Builder's Journey, you must be clear about why it matters, at least to you. U is your Unifying strategies: this is how you make progress toward the O with a clear sense of P. And finally, we get to the S (Scorecard for Significance). Your scorecard for significance is how you measure progress. Your BTL Builders will help you with each of these. Go ahead and start with the O & P. Write your big dream for work and life. Write why it matters.

Feel like turning back, friend? We're only five days in, and it's only going to get harder. Sure you want to get on the road to Becoming BTL? Hard OPUS you sustain as you perspire. Hard labor you disdain as you tire. Are you living a life worth the effort?

Day 6: Hard to hardened...

Loss is hard. Love is hard. Labor is hard. Loneliness is hard. Health is hard. Family is hard. Fighting is hard. Winning is hard. Discipline is hard. Letting go is hard. Sacrifice is hard. Training is hard. War is hard. Peace is hard. Aging is hard. Anxiety is hard. Chronic illness is hard. Not knowing is hard. Knowing is hard. Waiting is hard. Standing is hard. Humility is hard. Teamwork is hard. Justice is hard.

Forgiveness is hard. Failure is hard. Feeling is hard. Freedom is hard. Forgetting is hard. Forever is hard. Marriage is hard. Depression is hard. Dementia is hard. Disease is hard. Divorce is hard. Betrayal is hard. Death is hard. Conflict is hard. Courage is hard. Patience is hard. Perseverance is hard. Practice is hard. Reading is hard. Speaking is hard. Listening is hard. Love is hard. Writing is hard. Caring is hard. Understanding is hard. Repenting is hard. Repairing is hard. Retreating is hard. And on and on the list goes. Peck was right; Life is hard.

The hardest thing is becoming ourselves.

This is why we begin our work by being catalysts for our client's inner work—building the BTL CORE six-pack. Worldview, Identity, and Principles (W.I.P.) combine with the 3P's of Passions, Purposes, and Process. Hard to build. Hard to break. Hardened to stand. Life is hard. Choose what is hard now and life gets easier. Choose what is easy now and life will, eventually, get harder. Move your mindset from life is hard to I am hardened. Move your mind from hard to hardened. Pain is inevitable. Misery is a choice. You are choosing to build a hardened CORE. This is why you're here.

What is hard for you, friend? Write. Get to the root...

Day 7: Big FIVE fears...

Don Brown did us all a favor back in the day when he wrote *Human Universals*. Don and his team of anthropologists traveled the world to discover how much we humans are alike, in spite of our deep differences. My personal favorite among their documented discoveries was the fact that we humans are all afraid.

According to Don, we share five big fears.

1. Fear of death. This might not be personal death, as you may have made peace with your own. You still fear the death of a loved one, death of an enterprise, death of community, or even the death of a country. The fear of death runs deep.

2. Fear of the outsider. This comes from pre-historic wiring. Humans still fear the outsider is here to kill us because sometimes they still are—most times not. We tend to over forecast danger, danger, don't we? This explains why in a country as diverse as America we have more associations than any other.

3. Fear of the future. Leaders, please pay special attention. You can be wrong about the future, and your team will forgive you. You cannot be unclear. This is why we pay our financial planners mucho dinero. We fear our financial future more than any other.

4. Fear of chaos. This is why all tribes, when they initially come together, establish structure and order via rules and regulations. Even the loosest of cultures constrain the chaos.

5. Fear of coming and going and not leaving a mark. Humans fear not being missed. We want to leave a legacy. This is why the ones with power leave their name behind on buildings and monuments, and the rest of us carve initials into trees or spray paint away.

The most frequent command in the Bible? Fear not. Which of these big five fears do you need to face? Where are you along the road toward becoming and belonging? Who needs your hand? Whose hand do you need?

Day 8: Death...

Philip II, the father of Alexander the Great, thought one way. Louis XIV thought differently. Both were lucky enough to be crowned as King. Philip II, a Macedonian, probably lacked formal education and proper manners. He thought "early and often" about his eventual death. He hired a servant to remind him daily of his mortality. The servant's job was to utter these words each day at daybreak to his King, "Philip, one day you will die."

France's Louis XIV thought differently. During his reign, he decreed that the word "death" not be spoken in his presence. Louis was not alone in his fear of death. We're all afraid of the same thing—death. Yet most of us spend little time thinking about our mortality. We hear countless motivational speakers tell us to "begin with the end in mind," yet few of us really do. One day, friend, you will die.

Are you living by design or default?

What is it you want said about your life?

Have you authored your Worldview, or do you merely parrot others?

Are you living your life with 20/20 clarity as if 2020 is your end?

Are you more like Philip II or Louis XIV?

Let this rant serve as an irritant reminder. Great lives don't obsess about the end and don't freak out about the fact that someday they'll be gone. Great lives are lived through the seasons—by embracing transition moments, and MOT (moments of truth). Great lives require a deep focus on this moment. Live today with gratitude and clarity of aim. Great lives, as Solomon observed, recognize the gift of life and the giver as well. How 'bout you?

Day 9: Belong and become...

I believe human desire has two roots that branch out deep and wide. We all desire to know who we are. We want to become the original we sense we are but can't quite put our finger on. We want to know our identities and accept our secret name, as The Book of Revelation reminds us. We are wired to become. We are wired to become autonomous not a lone. So, why are there so many lonely souls and so few that are lit?

We humans are not designed to go it alone—in fact, it'll drive us all nuts. We want to be understood by another and fully accepted. We want to belong on a team, in a family, neighborhood, club, charity, or some community we can call home. We all want to belong, and none of us can force our sense of belonging. We can't make someone want to be with us, love us, join our team, invite us into their club, and understand and accept us for who we are. We can, however, give this gift to another. We can invite people into relationship and give freely to meet their needs. We are free to give this gift with no guarantee of it being reciprocated. Where, you may be asking, is the justice in this system? I mean why would we be designed for belonging with no guarantee we'll be receiving. Doesn't seem fair, does it? Seems like maybe there's a design flaw in us, huh?

Maybe, just maybe, there's a giver beyond our visibility who gives beyond our mind's comprehension. Maybe we're meant to look up and freely receive a love that makes no sense and can't be repaid, only passed along. Maybe there is such a thing as Grace from an all-loving, all-knowing, and all-powerful God. If all of us deeply desire to become and belong, it makes sense that we all come from a creator who designed such desires and designed a way for these desires to be met. I mean, that seems only right, doesn't it? And the missing piece has gotta be Grace, right? Slow down and look up.

Day 10: The melody line of BTL...

These first nine days have been awakening, huh? CORE, OPUS, and PoP. This is the melody line of Becoming BTL. Check. The aim of this effort is to prepare us for the real, hard work of your Builder's Journey. Roger that.

This journey will be filled with risky decisions and real adversity. You will become a mustang and not easily controlled. You will lose the ability to fake it and will care, but not that much. You will never walk nose to tail again, and you will be seen as someone weird, scary, and a little bit out there. You will fall on this journey and often fail. You will learn to fail forward, friend. You will form real community and gain clarity, confidence, conviction, and competence as you discover the joy of a life worth living. You will become a soul on fire. You will face your fears and act into them no longer driven by fear but fueled with inspiration. You are beginning to believe. Before we turn to day eleven, let me give you a reminder from a dead French dude named Blaise Pascal. "I give you the gift of these four words: I believe in you."

Leaders are believers. Are you beginning to believe in you? Slow down and build within. Slow down.

Day 11: Always together...

As founder of BTL, I believe all people are born and **BUILT TO LEAD**. All humans are on the hook, at a minimum, to lead themselves. We believe transformational leaders are inspired, not driven. This word difference makes a world of difference. None of us can lead another further than we've gone ourselves. Fact. We are with you on this journey of Becoming BTL. This is why our secondary logo is the image of two people on a climb. One is reaching back to lend a hand to another. Together, we transform. Always together.

We believe that none of us is as smart as all of us. We believe that we cannot change you, but we can inspire you to be the change (thanks, Gandhi).

So, friend, how can you trade a life of quiet desperation for one passionately in pursuit of your dreams? A work and life that, in a word, is OPUS? The *12 Essentials of Personal Excellence* is our framework for mastering the art of living. These essentials are easily understood but not easily lived. There is nothing new here but much that has been forgotten. In the pages that follow, we ask you to question everything and become fully engaged in the process. Think. Reflect. Slow down. Act.

Do not quickly rush to judge what you read. Train your brain to understand and widen your perspective. Become fully awake and enjoy the journey as we discover together how to overcome our greatest leadership challenge: the challenge of leading ourselves. Are you ready to accept the challenge of becoming CORE-centered and self-controlling? Are you ready to author an authentic OPUS? Are you ready to leave the land of comfort and convenience and embark on your Builder's Journey of discovery? You choose. Your choices have consequences.

BUILT TO LEAD | together we transform

Day 12: Worldview...

We all have a CORE, both physically and figuratively. A strong physical core keeps us upright and eliminates most chronic lower back pain. A strong BTL CORE does much more. A strong BTL CORE gives you strength, endurance, and stability through life's toughest tests. Your strong CORE eliminates chronic relational, emotional, spiritual, and mental pain. Your Worldview, Identity, Principles, Passions, Purpose, and Process give you what money can't buy, but we all desperately desire it: a strong sense of self.

Where, you ask, do you begin? Good question. We're going back so we can pick up the pace. We've all got abdominal muscles, even those of us who cannot see or feel them. Likewise, we all possess a Worldview, even though many of us cannot see or sense its influence. Your Worldview runs like a thread through your entire CORE, holding all elements in place. According to James Sire, author of *The Universe Next Door*, "A Worldview is a basic set of beliefs and concepts that work together to provide a frame of reference for all thought and action." In essence, your Worldview serves as your matrix through which you make sense of the world. *Matrix* is a Latin word that translates to the English word "womb." The ancient Romans used a matrix to figure out how to build aqueducts and arches. Your Worldview is your womb through which you give birth to the answer for why you're here, how you want to live, and where you're going.

Think about your deeply engrained behaviors and work your way backward. Your habitual behaviors have become habitual because they are tied to some belief. Your Worldview matters. Don't be a "second-hander," as Ayn Rand would say. Author your own.

Here are a few discovery questions to spur your thinking. How do you determine whether something is right or wrong? Do you know what you believe about why you exist? Why is it important to manage your thinking? Today, give birth to a few "I believe..." statements. Write them down. You're building your Worldview. Good.

Day 13: Know thyself...

Socrates said, "Know thyself," yet most of us do not. We've decided that what we do will define who we become. Reverse the equation if you want to master the art of living. Who we are should inspire what we do. Do you know who you are, friend?

Masters avoid the "do, do, do" trail that leads to achievement anxiety, desperation, and depletion. Most humans are stuck in a deep, well-worn rut on the do-do trail. Are you? Masters dream and do. Masters in the art of living ask themselves a few simple, but not easy, questions. What do you believe? Why are you here? Where are you going? Why does it matter? Are you aligning behaviors to your deepest held beliefs? What are you doing with your integrity gaps? When was the last time you questioned your deepest held beliefs? How easily do you operate alongside those who don't believe as you do?

Know thyself. Be hard on self and easy on others. Be hard on self, not down on self or high on self. Masters are Becoming BTL. Are you? Slow down and write your thinking. Pick a baby step and move.

BUILT TO LEAD | together we transform

Day 14: I am...

A big step in knowing thyself is accepting thyself. Many humans don't know themselves but are very aware of what others say about them. They base their sense of self on what others tell them. Oftentimes, this produces a case of mistaken identity. According to Merriam-Webster's definition, identity is "the distinguishing character or personality of an individual." At BTL, we believe writing your "I am" statements is a great first step to becoming the original you already are, but you've just been too afraid to be.

One of my best clients is a Jewish entrepreneur. When we began our work together, he dressed in a coat and tie, was a people pleaser, and hid his deepest held beliefs from everyone, including his family. As he built a strong CORE, his *I ams* became his *I cans*, *I wills*, and eventually his *I dos*. Today, over a decade of building later, he wears what he wants (nice pants and shirts, no coat or tie), says what he thinks, and wears a yarmulke proudly. He knows who he is. He allows others to be who they are. He's ONE, distinct and deeply connected, Becoming BTL.

Slow down and write some *I ams*. Care more about the names you call you and less about what others do. I am. Good.

Day 15: Principles...

Your Principles are the values that mean the most to you. Are you beginning to see how this six-pack emanates from your Worldview? Your Principles are the pillars behind how you live and work. My big three are as follows:

I will...
    ...model the way.
    ...embrace pain and suffering.
    ...embody truth in love.

Model the way is all about leading by example. Every day before my feet touch the carpet as I get up and at 'em, I remind myself to live that day aligned by these three principles. Don't be a hypocrite, Chet. Do what you want others to do. Model the way. Be incredibly prepared for every practice. Be with. Be good. Do good. Model mastery.

Embrace pain and suffering. I'm not a masochist. In fact, far from it. My aim here is to eliminate chronic pain and replace it with the acute stuff. My former self avoided all forms of pain and found myself in lots of chronic as a result. Chronic lower back pain was prevalent throughout my forties, the same with chronic pain in my left hip. Both have been eradicated through acute pain. The stronger my physical core has become, the less bothered I am by either of these. The stronger my BTL CORE, the less my personal, relational, spiritual, and emotional pain.

Embody truth in love. My favorite people to be around are the ones who've lost the ability to bullshit. I love not having to think about hidden messages and interpreting what is being thought but not being said. My aim is to be a truth-teller and a truth hearer. I'm much better at telling.

What will you do? What won't you do? Write version 1.0 of your Principles.

Day 16: Love to...

Your Worldview, Identities, and Principles are your WIP: work in process. Never stop working on your WIP. Evolve, adapt, and grow. Now, let's begin the building of your 3P's (Passions, Purpose, Process) to become the original you are. We will start with your "love tos…"

We talk about being in love, most often as an expression of *eros*. C.S. Lewis in his worthy read, *The Four Loves,* refers to this as romantic love. I would like to propose another thought. You and I are created IN love. *Agape*, as Clive would say, is the love we were created in.

You are meant to live a life of love, a life *you* love, and a life that loves labor and leisure. When was the last time you played? For many reading this rant, it's been a while—a long while. Many have given up on playing and invest their days laboring. Life is an energy management problem. Love is jet fuel. Fill yourself with it.

Today, begin again to love more. Write your "love tos…" I love to do this, and I love to that. I love to be with this person and travel here and there. Write like a banshee. Think back to childhood when you loved more easily, readily, and without so many responsibilities. Part of your CORE work is feeding your Passions. Remember how it felt? Now, go play—you know you love to.

Go play…

Day 17: Matrix...

The Latin word *matrix* has its origin in ancient Rome. The Roman engineers who were figuring out how to make roads, aqueducts, and other such things for the first time were early adopters, to say the least. They referred to the algorithms they used to solve these complex problems as the *matrix* because it gave birth to the answer. You see, friend, the Latin word *matrix* translates, literally, to the English word *womb*. The Romans believed the matrix gave birth to the answer.

Your Worldview is a matrix of sorts. Your Worldview is how you make sense of the world. Have you taken the time to consciously discover your deepest-held beliefs, or are you too busy to solve this internal problem?

Author your matrix. Align behaviors with beliefs. Of course, you have to know the latter to align the former. Slow down. Make sense of your world. I mean, come on, man, do you think you were meant to be a second-hander? Have you given birth to your answer?

There is no blue pill. Swallow the red pill and get on your Builder's Journey. Watch *The Matrix* if this doesn't make sense.

Day 18: My Worldview...

Here's the latest rinse of my Worldview. This matrix of mine helps me keep getting up and getting better instead of bitter. We are all a perpetual work in process. I am slowly beginning to see the shore. I share this work within, humbly and honestly, with family, friends, and clients in the spirit of transparency. My aim is not for you to believe what I do but to spur your thinking toward authoring your Worldview and aligning accordingly. My full Worldview is available at builttolead.com. Here's but a taste.

I believe…

- I am accountable to God.
- Absolute truth exists. It's just really rare and rarely found.
- I am my own worst enemy.
- Life is a paradox. We are poison and wine.
- We are made to glorify God by enjoying him. Thanks, LA.
- We are designed with the deep desire to belong and become. These desires are in conflict.
- We are made for relationship with God and humankind. And all human relationships are bittersweet.
- We are broken people trying to become whole.
- We are a perpetual WIP.
- A lone is one 'L of a difference from All ONE. Thanks, Gurue.
- The more I deeply change, the more authentic I become.
- Putting first things first does not make second things less.
- We don't see things the way they are. We see things the way we are. Thanks, Anaïs Nin.
- Food is our first medicine.
- Heavy metal toxicity is true. No doctors are God.

Never compare your insides to someone else's outsides.

What do you believe?

Day 19: Drudge. Driven. Drawn.

I'm re-reading another C.S. Lewis classic, *Pilgrim's Regress*. Playing off John Bunyan's bestseller, *Pilgrim's Progress*, published way back in the day in 1678, Lewis takes the reader on his hero's journey of discovery. Lewis' book describes the journey of his lead character, John, as he attempts to reach his dream state. Along the way, John meets many characters who symbolize the philosophical leanings of the day. Midway through his journey, he meets a man named Drudge, whose work for another is, well, drudgery. I see Drudge every day.

As I listened to my client describe his attempts to live a life of love, I heard him comment that he is tired by his drive. "I want to be drawn to my OPUS, not driven," he explained sadly. He's mostly drained by the weekend and finds the Sunday writing yet another thing he has to do.

Your OPUS, remember, by its very definition, is your labor of love. An authentic labor of love has drawing power. This is why the BTL builders take you through a lengthy rinsing process. You can't stop writing until you're smiling at the thought of taking baby steps toward your Overarching vision—the O of your OPUS. You and I smile when we're working toward something we're drawn toward. We may perspire and tire. We continue to be drawn. The heart, you see, is in the labor. We learn to love what normal folk loathe, not because we're driven or even super disciplined. We're drawn.

Drudge. Driven. Drawn. Of course, *drawn* requires you to leave the comfort of routine and take risks along the road to OPUS.

I encouraged my client to keep going. His OPUS is within reach, he just doesn't have it yet. He'll know he's got it when he can't stop himself from doing it. That's how you know. You're drawn. My coffee's cold now, and I don't much mind. I've taken too long typing away. Funny, I didn't sit down with my iPad driven to write anything in particular this morning. I couldn't help myself. Drawn.

Which are you—drudge, driven, or drawn? Write.

Day 20: Sit. Walk. Stand.

Sit, Walk, Stand, written by Watchman Nee back in 1957, is a beautiful sixty-seven pager and takes the reader through the book of Ephesians with crystal clarity. Nee reminds us why we have to slow down and learn to sit first. Once we understand what it means to abide, we can take baby steps and attempt to walk in love. When we learn to walk, resistance will come. Remember, friend, the more you and I attempt to walk in love, the more resistance we feel. Nee learned to embrace resistance and be thankful for those opposing him. Nee, you see, knew his only required response was to trust his Savior and learn to stand.

Sit. Walk. Stand.

Now for the coolest part of Nee's book. He wrote this bad boy from his prison cell. He was arrested in China in 1952 on false charges because of his beliefs. His writing and work carried on in spite of his circumstances. He kept sitting, walking, and standing, even though for the next twenty years of his life, he was confined to his cell. He died alone in 1972, still stuck in his prison cell. Nee's life reflected his OPUS, even though it certainly didn't go according to his script. He learned to sit, walk, and stand.

This past week, I experienced resistance. I wasn't thankful or grateful it came my way. I get paid to help people build strength within and stop trash talking themselves, yet I, too, struggle to stand against the least resistance. We are all a work in process, friends. I'm learning to sit, pray, and remember whose I am so I don't stay down as long. I'm learning to humbly sit, walk, and stand. Thanks, Watchman, for the inspiration. God, help me sit, walk, and stand. God, help me expect resistance and learn to love it and even the person resisting.

What do you believe when you face resistance? What beliefs keep you in the fight when life knocks you down?

Day 21: Labels...

Your *I ams* comprise your Identity. Worldview, Identities, Principles (WIP) are always a work in process. Have you given them a hard rinse with truth-tellers? Are you inviting others in to illuminate blind spots? Good. Then, as you take your StrengthsFinder's label and countless other good ones, you'll have a strong internal matrix to run them through. Make sense?

Here's my labeling of me—some of the names I call myself.

I'm a Christian sinner, crazy facilitator, and builder of better humans. I am a liberal republican/conservative democrat, and lunatic/independent. I am a loyal and loving husband, lousy romantic, impatient/loving father, thinker, feeler, silly, laid-back, and flat-out. I am a cyclist, runner, CORE freak, and recreational golfer. I am a healthy eater who also loves Third and Hollywood pecan pie sundaes. I am a reader, writer, and a tree hugger who loves Porsches. I am inconsistently considerate if I like you, high on empathy (hard for many to believe), and low on execution. I am CCD. I quickly find the melody line and miss a million little details. I am confident and convicted in my pursuit of mastery and don't suffer fools easily. I am best in small groups and despise networking. I am a great friend to a few but not good at staying attached to acquaintances. I play with fire as long as I'm the one with the matches. I am a truth-teller, but I'm still working on hearing more. I am poison and wine, and so are my relationships. I am a man with two mantras: keep working; live hard and love harder. I work in jeans and tees and love to wake up dead people. I'm weird, and I care but not that much. I could go on. I'll stop.

Stop allowing others to define you. Slow down and go to your room. Ask God for help. You do not belong in a box. You're a beautiful mess, just like all of us. Author your *I ams* and make peace with your place. There's a great Identity for us all, isn't it? I am a man making peace with my place. How 'bout you?

Day 22: Zoe...

There are three Greek words for our English word life. Thank God for the Greeks, huh?

Bios refers to physical life and is where we get the word biology. We train, feed, rest, and mostly focus on our physical health. We realize it takes more and more effort to maintain healthy bodies as time takes its toll. We know physical death is coming. We just don't know when. We mostly think the good life is around accumulating physical comforts, at least that is the way we live (me included).

Psuche is another Greek word for life. Psuche refers to the will, emotion, and mind. We derive the word psychology here. As we've evolved and become more aware of ourselves and the consciousness of others, we've become intrigued and invested in the cultivating of our minds. For many, this is the final frontier. Discovering the good life is around calming anxieties, playing to strengths, developing a growth mindset, and willing ourselves toward meaningful accomplishment. Combining psuche and bios would be Plato's balanced man—mind and body. End of story.

Jesus used a third Greek word: zoe—spiritual life. He would use zoe over and over in his teachings and remind us there is more to life than our minds and bodies. Jesus came to model the way, embrace pain and suffering, and perfectly embody truth in love. While we're alive, something inside tells us there has to be more than just bios and psuche to this thing called life. We seek, but no easy, definitive, foolproof answers appear. So, we either settle for some semblance of the good life by stretching our minds and bodies as best we know how or choose the more popular route of numbing and waiting for the pain to end.

Jesus calls us to explore zoe and live life abundantly by following Him. For me, this means opening my heart to receive zoe so I can give it away. It means accepting I don't understand much about God, Jesus, or anything spiritual at all. It means embracing the mystery of life and embracing all of God's creation, especially those who live unlike me. Now you know more about me and my beliefs. Good.

What, friend, do you believe about this thing called life? Write, please.

Day 23: Too lit...

Last night, I took two magnesium pills and nine drops of CBD oil. This is my post-performance routine, thanks to my Miss. It lowers bad brain chemicals and enables rest and recovery—works most of the time. It did not work last night. Here's why.

When the alarm vibrated at 5:14 a.m., I was already awake as I'd been tossing and turning most of the night. My mind wouldn't settle down. I was lit about this morning's workout in the new OSU Wrestling facility. My son was coming. Grappy's son was coming. Some of the Lacrosse coaches too. I anticipated the forty-five minutes of hell that would produce fails in me and everyone else. Back in 2010, I loathed this. I had not fallen in love with acute pain and believed chronic lower back pain, chronic left hip pain, chronic shoulder pain (in both), and chronic pain in my mind was simply the price one paid for passing fifty. I was wrong.

Pain is inevitable. Misery is a choice.

Choose acute pain. Peace is found on the other side of the acute stuff. These were not part of my Worldview back in 2010. They are bolted on now. Today, fifteen crazies mixed it up at the Jennings, and then forty-nine athletes mixed it up over at The Schumaker in BTL team practice. It was freakin' magic. You see, sleepless nights are part of the gig when you love work and life. Some nights, you'll be lit with anticipation of the OPUS ahead.

When was the last time you were too lit, and your brain was too lit to quit? An authentic OPUS lights you up. Do your work and the joy of your life keep you up or put you to sleep? Slow down and reflect. Sleep on it...

BUILT to LEAD | together we transform

Day 24: Character...

Recently, I had the chance to listen to Doc Potterat, former Navy SEAL psychologist. Doc Potterat is super smart and fun to listen to. He knows his stuff, and I always learn something when he speaks. We don't always agree on the details, which is not problematic at all. For instance, when he talked to one of my clients about the traits of not just the 1% elite performers but the 20% of the 1%, he shared that the first trait is the best of the best focus on their identities instead of reputation. He's close, but we think some additional clarity is warranted.

At BTL, we believe Identity is just one of the elements of your figurative CORE. It is not the whole enchilada, nor is it the opposite of reputation. Character is.

Let's be clear. Identity matters, but it's just not the polar opposite of reputation. Reputation is what others call you. Your reputation is what others name you or think of you. It may be accurate. It may be miles from the mark. Your identities are the names you've given yourself. You may see yourself as a top 1% performer in your system and call yourself a pro's pro. You may be delusional, dead on the money, or somewhere in between. Your character is who you are when no one sees. The crucible reveals your character. What comes out under pressure reveals what's been in you all along. Focus here, friend. You cannot control your reputation. Here are the elements of your figurative CORE, by way of reminder.

Worldview—your deepest held beliefs. Identity—the names you call yourself. Principles—the values that guide you in your everyday. Passions—your *love tos* that energize you through the good, bad, and ugly. Purposes—your big why's for work/life. Process—your Playbook of Productive action that tightens up all elements. Build your CORE. Become someone committed to building a more virtuous character within. You control your character. Stop worrying what others think of you and, instead, focus on what habits you're engraving on your heart. Going back and rinsing your CORE is a good PA for today. Baby-step it, please.

Day 25: A few with nerve...

I've been rereading the book *A Failure of Nerve*. It is my favorite book on leadership because Rabbi Friedman understands education, religion, psychology, and coaching. We are like-minded.

We lack leaders with nerve. We promote presidents in our corporations and communities who can keep the peace, not by taking a stand but, instead, by mitigating risk and finding the middle ground as Chamberlain did with Hitler. We hire coaches, consultants, and psychotherapists at record clips to give us the latest insights, knowledge, and, most importantly, the quick fixes to whatever ails us. We expect our marriage counselor to "get 'er done" in a matter of hours. We demand a litany of outcomes from our offsite executive retreat. We expect our politicians to protect our grandchildren's future without us going without anything in the here and now. As leaders, we play right along, and instead of focusing on the few and building performance based on strength, we listen and attempt to placate the very weak, irresponsible, and unreasonable. Evolution, remember, is true because the positive, strength-building traits are the ones healthy systems pass along.

Whatever system you are in, if you are trying to lead it, you are under attack. The more you attempt to influence the system toward strength, accountability, and generation-skipping performance, the more sabotage you're gonna stir up. Expect this. Stop focusing on unreasonable people using logic and reason. Your attempts to fix and change them will largely be a waste of time and source of frustration. Instead, you need to be unreasonable. Focus on the few. Challenge them. Push them. Make them do what they can. The people in the highest positions in your place of work are rarely the leaders people look to in times of trouble. Accept this fact. Stop aspiring for position and promotion. Focus, instead, on building strength. Allow nature to take her course. Leaders, regardless of their titles, always emerge in the crucible. Their words, polish, professionalism, public persona, and gravitas do not define them.

What does define them, you ask? Their lack of anxiety. Does this define you? Slow down and reflect.

Day 26: Protect your name...

There's not much that's more important than your name.

Your name, specifically the name you've given yourself, is really all you've got. Your reputation is not your name. Your reputation is what others name you. We can't protect our name in terms of what others will call us when we're not around. Your name is yours alone to give. Do not allow others to cause you to doubt your name. Many people call me too much or too little. Many call me crazy, extreme, and emotional. Many call me many names that are not edifying. I do not let their names into my CORE. I know who I am and whose I am.

I bathe in love, aim for mastery in my craft, and am fixated on Becoming BTL. I'm a truth-teller and still learning to listen more than speak. I make a lot of people uncomfortable and a few better. I'm a builder of people, and I always have been. I am clear, concise, and direct. I am confident in my craft but not much else. I rely on my bride, a few builders, a few friends, and a few clients to illuminate my blind spots, and, together, we are transforming. We are ONE, distinct and deeply connected, Becoming BTL.

Do you know your name, friend? The "dark night of the soul" moment is a case of mistaken identity, remember. I appreciate Marcus Aurelius now more than ever. Jesus too. These men knew their name. Neither of them wrote a book or had a monument erected for us to remember them by. They knew the importance of their name, and we're still talking about them today. What are the names (identities) you've given yourself, friend? Protect your name. Are you?

Day 27: Mantras...

Recently, a curious fellow asked me why I've begun to finish my rants with "Live hard. Love harder," instead of my old favorite "Good." Here's the long way 'round.

Distinct and deeply connected is never easy, but it's worth the work. Don't get discouraged and tell yourself you and your partner aren't ever gonna get there. Instead, replace the childhood script with one from today. Remind yourself to keep putting forth a full effort and that as long as you're still breathing, you're good. You see, the SEALs use this word, "good," when they communicate with each other. When they ask another SEAL how he's doing, the response is either good or silence. Their belief is nothing is taking them out of the fight except death itself. So, in their mind, they're always good.

My personal mantra used to be two words: "Keep working." I whispered these to myself all the time, and they kept me calm and moving. Since our little dog Teeks died, I've changed my mantra for staying calm in the crucible. Instead of "keep working," I tell myself to "Live hard. Love harder." I learned this from Teeks, who had a hard life from birth that scarred him for life. He got through it by learning to love harder. Once you registered in his directory, you became the object of his love. It softened and strengthened me. My aim is to embrace living hard and loving harder. So, my mantra has changed—it's evolved.

The crucible comes, ready or not. Your mantra brings calm, confidence, and conviction if you believe it. Have you chosen what you tell yourself when overwhelmed in moments of truth? Have you changed the way you talk to yourself so you live in more alignment with your deepest-held beliefs? Are you doing the work ahead of time or just hoping to rise to the occasion instead?

What's your mantra, friend?

Day 28: Model the way...

The aim for fairness is as old as humanity, and as much as we've evolved, we still struggle to achieve justice in every system where we congregate. Leaders have it harder. They, too, get wronged. The good, virtuous ones get wronged that much more. Study history, you'll see. Leaders have to understand this is the way it is and part of the price of leadership. It isn't fair we give ourselves the benefit of the doubt when we are over-served but assassinate the character of our leader when he has one too many. And it isn't fair that leaders gotta think about what's best for the system even when team members are out to sabotage them. Leaders, the few worth following, understand and accept this truth. Lead anything well, and you'll pay for it.

Leaders own their baggage and carry a bit of yours and mine too. Leaders fight for what's right even when they've been personally wronged. And this is why it pays to have good role models with virtuous Principles to follow. My favorite is Jesus. His big three leadership Principles—model the way, embrace pain and suffering, and embody truth in love—are easy to understand and beyond hard to follow.

Model the way. Jesus taught by simply saying, "Follow me." He led perfectly from the front even when his team fell asleep, couldn't quite keep up, and actively betrayed Him. Embrace pain and suffering. Jesus ran into the acute stuff. He didn't take the easy way out and understood the price required. Embody truth in love. Jesus loved us enough to die on that old rugged cross knowing full well He had done nothing wrong. Talk about tweaking a justice thread. Jesus showed us the power of His grace. We, the world, are still trying to figure out what makes no sense.

Model the way. Embrace pain and suffering. Embody truth in love.

These are the three bolted-on Principles I remind myself of daily. What Principles are you fixing your gaze upon, friend? What are your routines for keeping them top of mind? What are your rituals? Write. Try not to bullshit you. Be honest.

Day 29: Find your melody line first...

The real reason we love labels is because they represent a thousand little nuances that are so much easier to identify and apply than finding the melody line. We are often asked how the discovery of CORE Principles and Purposes is practically applied. What if you don't like what you discover when you look within? How does understanding Myers Briggs, StrengthsFinder, Kolbe, explanatory style, Grit Score, and other assessments factor in? How will you know if you're playing to strengths and living consistent with your CORE? These are great questions. They are not, however, what we believe requires answering first. Like C.S. Lewis, we believe putting first things first does not make second things less; it actually makes them more.

Find your melody line first, then apply a thousand nuances and a thousand more.

Most do the opposite and fixate on their labels because it's easier. They listen to the voice of the customer, of authority, or the voice of their family. Nothing wrong with hearing other voices. However, when it comes to a life of mastery, you must become the most influential voice for you. Masters know who they are, what they believe, where they're going, and why it matters.

Thoreau had something to say about mixing the order in *Walden*: "These people have become like machines, their sole purpose on making a living. This mass of men lead lives of quiet desperation, and die with their song still inside of them."

So, what is a melody line? By definition, it's "a linear succession of musical tones that the listener perceives as a single entity." Become a single entity, whole, perceived as comfortable, convicted, and confident because you are. Build a strong CORE, authentic OPUS, PoP it out on your way to becoming ONE, to Becoming BTL. Your melody line is found here.

Have you found your melody line? Slow down and reflect. Write. ACT.

Day 30: Healthy CORE—healthy culture...

Your team is not defined by the words painted on your walls. Your team is defined by the behaviors it allows, condones, encourages, and disciplines. You are defined by your behaviors. Healthy humans author their own deeply held beliefs and align behaviors accordingly. They close their integrity gaps when they say one thing and do another. Healthy cultures do likewise. Healthy cultures must be cultivated and nurtured.

Few teammates believe they can change their team's culture. Funny, it's always been a few who do—a few who possess a strong BTL CORE and know what they stand for. Few leaders have the nerve for fixing their cultures alignment issues. Few teammates feel they've earned the right. Few take responsibility for their own culture, much less their teams. All it takes to build a healthy culture in your corporation is a few with the nerve. A few willing to be less obedient to authority. Or maybe, a few willing to submit to a higher authority—much higher.

Every day, we challenge ourselves and a few high performers to build more strength within their CORE. Oftentimes, these challenges are greeted with passive-aggressive bullshit like "you're right, you're right." Remember, the human that tells another "you're right" rarely means what they've said. We listen to our own ideas. That's right.

A great litmus test for your CORE strength is to honestly evaluate your ability to speak truth to your leader and the least 'round you. If you hold back when you're not in a one-up position, you are weak in your CORE. If you have a failure of nerve when enforcing team disciplines, you're weak in your CORE. If you are harder on others than you are on yourself, you're weak in your CORE. If you are hard on yourself but can't confront a toxic teammate whose attitude is sucking life out of the locker room, you are weak in your core. Not a fun fact—but a fact.

You control the culture in your twenty square feet, friend. Your healthy CORE serves as a catalyst for a healthy culture. Weak CORE? Weakened culture. A strong CORE behaves without thinking about prejudice, power, or position. Your culture is contagious. Are you worth catching?

Day 31: Compass and map...

Imagine you are deep in the woods, scared and freakin' lost. What are the most important two tools you would want? When I ask this question, I most frequently hear food and water. This is good, but it's incorrect. Food and water are temporary tools. They have built-in expiration dates. When they're gone, they're gone, and soon, you will be as well. Another one I hear a lot is a lighter. This, too, is exhaustible. Flashlights are another frequent flyer. Again, batteries burn out, baby.

Lost in the woods, you need a compass and a map. The compass points due north, and the map guides you to temporary solutions (like food and water) and the big dream of getting out of the woods and onto the promised land. Most humans live like the ancient Israelites wandering in the desert for forty-some years and then dying. This is not the one you want.

Building your BTL CORE and OPUS are life tools. Your CORE is your compass pointing you due north. Your deepest held beliefs and Principles are going to dictate your days. Your OPUS is your road map for living your best life toward your land of milk and honey. It would be nuts to possess a strong CORE and authentic OPUS and then not use them. This would be like being lost in the woods with a compass and map and simply leaving them in your pocket. Nuts. I mean, come on, man, it would be insane to have built the tools and then not use them every week to guide your way. So, friend, build your CORE and author your OPUS. Use these tools. Look at them. Remind yourself, daily, who you are and where you're going. Choose productive action that aligns. Life is difficult. We are mostly lost in the deep woods. The best among us simply have better tools to navigate the adversities that lie ahead. The best among us use these tools every day, not every once in a while.

What about you, friend? Write what you're thinking.

BUILT TO LEAD | together we transform

Day 32: Weird wins...

Nearly every day in some BTL team practice, I announce one of the primary aims of our work is we want to make you weird. Lots of sideway glances come my way. Most of us are trying to fit in, so why would we want to make this task more difficult? We burn brain cycles trying to find the norm. We don't want to standout or seem like we're somehow out of place. You see, friend, we are all hardwired to belong. So, we try to.

The problem with this is so obvious most humans miss it.

None of us is wired to belong everywhere with everyone. So, the best bet to finding your pack begins by becoming more and more the unique, distinct, and weird one you are. We are hard wired to belong and become, remember. It's just easier to focus on fitting in, which is why normal humans fixate here. Don't be normal. Put first things first. Focus on figuring out who you are and becoming the original you are meant to become. Build a stronger sense of self by building a strong BTL CORE.

When we study excellence, the highest-performing teams are in fact a collection of weirdos. U2 are one, but they're not the same. Your team, if it's worth remembering, will not be focused on making you fit in. Your team leader, if she's BTL, will be figuring out how to help you embrace your unique abilities, your weirdness, and your ability to connect with others who are weird in their own way. Distinct and deeply connected is the kind of oneness we believe in. Great teams are a collection of weird ones who come together in complementary, collaborative, and chemistry-creating combinations.

Distinct and deeply connected, Becoming BTL. Focus on becoming, and when you figure out where you belong, nobody will have to tell you—you'll be weird and know it. It turns out aiming at normal never made much sense. Nobody even knows what normal even is, right? Here's what we do know. Weird wins. Focus here.

Day 33: God and Arthur...

Name a company that's been around over 260 years. They've innovated technologies that have transformed not only their company but also their entire industry. They pioneered social justice before the term had been coined. In the eighteenth century, they had health care benefits that companies like Google and Microsoft can't touch today. They had their own doctors and not only made house calls on the lowest level workers, but also made presentations to the board on doing even more. One of their doctors, Dr. Lumsden, visited all 3,000 employees' homes in 1901 to determine how to improve living conditions. The sweeping reforms he proposed were not only implemented for their employees but were also extended to the neighboring community.

This company produced leader after leader with hearts for good work. A number of them would follow their calling into the ministry and travel the world changing hearts and working conditions. This company innovated quality control measures and distribution methods unheard of at the time. Some of their workers would literally travel with the product overseas and across deserts and record meticulous details to determine painstaking methods to improve the product's quality and durability during shipping.

The founder of this company would start the first Sunday schools that educated the poor. He made a product too—one that would provide a healthy alternative to the two most popular and deadly drinks of its day: gin and water. You see, Dublin's water supply was polluted and deadly. Gin was plentiful and deadly. Dublin had a problem. God had an answer. Arthur, in the mid-1700s, walked the streets of Dublin, pleading with God to do something about the drunkenness all around him. He heard God tell him to "make a drink that men will drink that will be good for them." So, he did. Guinness started with a big dream by Arthur in 1759 with a clear purpose. For those surprised that God and Guinness go together, read *God and Guinness* by Stephen Mansfield. They go together quite well, kind of like a Black and Tan.

What do you believe about why you're here? Slow down, have a Guinness. Tell me more...

Day 34: Mistaken Identity...

Last night, my thought-filled mind woke me in the middle of another dark night. Instead of mulling over thought after thought, I quietly reminded myself of whose I am. I recalled Rich Nathan's reminder around discovering one's calling. My calling to this thing called BTL is not my primary call or even a secondary one. So, last night, as my mind spun up, I slipped into a silent prayer. I thanked God for His call to my relationship with Him, first and foremost. Next, I thanked him for the body of believers—the church and the community it represents and the opportunity to serve. And finally, my heart settled my mind. I prayed a bit for family, friends, and clients and drifted off realizing my Identity doesn't depend on my look within or my look for validation from others.

My Identity depends on my look up first.

As St. Augustine shared many dark nights ago, "Thou hast made us for thyself, O Lord, and our heart is restless until it finds it's rest in thee." Do you know who you are, friend? Have you taken the time to look within and understand your wiring, gifts, strengths, and God-given talents? And, friend, do you know whose you are? If you feel called toward your OPUS, doesn't this assume a caller? Slow down and reflect. Sit with these thoughts for a while. Many a man/woman suffers from a case of mistaken Identity. Maybe your Identity statements could use a hard rinse.

Rinse your *I ams*, please. Rinse and repeat.

Day 35: Meaning...

The American dream? It's not found in money and material. Nothing inherently wrong with money and material—don't get me wrong. I feel I've been blessed with plenty of both, even though many have more. I stopped chasing money back in 2002 when I sold out completely to chase meaning. I left the cushy corporate world with all its stock options, club memberships, and seemingly endless benefits to pursue my OPUS. I knew this work meant so much more to me and would soon find out I was not a lone. I am filled with joy, wonder, and a deep desire for more—more meaning, that is. You see, friend, once you taste meaningful, life-changing, life-giving work, you wake up ready to go. The universe will bend toward you. Enough of everything will flow your way, you'll see. The counting, endless scheming, and striving will succumb to your being. Peace.

Recently, I saw another young lad lit up chasing money, money, money. I smiled at his grit, determination, and fire. I reminded him that nothing matters more than meaning. America is filled with highly paid laborers devoid of enough meaning to keep them going. So, these successful money men and women eventually end up trying to buy happiness in all sorts of bastardized ways. It does not work well. Chase meaning. Aim at OPUS. You'll find unbridled joy amidst worthy challenges. You'll experience peace and real prosperity in your soul. A Duchenne smile will crease your face. Others may notice. You certainly will.

So, friend, this morning, what's your sense of being? Are you on edge and anxious or peaceful chasing a meaningful Purpose with unbridled passion? Chase meaning. You'll catch much more than money can buy.

Day 36: Self-centered and other-controlling...

Excellence, we believe at BTL, is built by going against your nature. We are the only animal who faces this dichotomy of becoming it's best by going against its nature. All humans come into this world self-centered and other-controlling. This is our nature. Excellence is achieved when we flip ourselves on our proverbial head and move toward becoming CORE-centered and self-controlling. Now, this move cannot guarantee greatness. Many a man or woman has become CORE-centered and self-controlling and slipped into the abyss anyway.

So, friend, it matters a great deal what you decide to believe (Worldview), the names you call yourself (Identity), and the Principles for which you decide to stand. It is up to you to channel your love tos (Passions) and not leave them unbridled, running rampant. It's on each of us to discover Purposes and use them for the greater good, not just our own. And none of this is an event. We don't build a better nature over a retreat, seminar, or in a moment of pure enlightenment. We build a better nature with a million baby steps taken one at a time.

You were born self-centered. Are you building a better nature? Are you becoming CORE-centered and self-controlling? Are you seeking happiness and soft soap or getting down and dirty in search of truth, love, and goodness? God, help me leave my selfish nature a bit more today. Slow down and reflect, friend. What do you think?

Day 37: Chabod...

My dad put me to bed with stories from his childhood, especially when he attended Washburn University and played basketball for the Ichabods. He identified as an Ichabod as he did a Jayhawk. After his second year playing basketball, he made the hard call to hang up his sneakers in service to his bigger dream of being a doc. He loved playing hoops but couldn't keep up his grades while doing so. Dad transferred to KU and gave up glory on the court for what he felt was God's calling on his life—serving the sick with his heart and soul.

Ichabod is a Hebrew word that translates to "no glory, inglorious, or where is the glory?" In the book of Samuel, the story of Israel's defeat, the loss of the Ark, and the death of Eli and his two sons brings deep despair and deeper loss of identity. Phinehas' (son of Eli) wife, as she gives birth to her son, declares his name Ichabod because the glory has left Israel on this darkest of days. Talk about a tough identity. Ichabod was born into a defeated community with no dad, no mom (died giving birth), and no grandpa either.

Chabod is another Hebrew word. This one translates as "full glory, the full glory of the Lord." One I of a difference, huh? The difference between full glory and no glory comes down to an I. When I seek glory, when I make it all about me, and seek to be the one served, I get in my way. You and I do not make good gods. Maybe we are in need of the great physician to be made whole. Maybe we're not meant to go it a lone. Maybe God's infinite love is the one 'L of a difference toward becoming all ONE. Maybe?

God, help me admit my eye problem is really an I problem; I've just had a hard time seeing it. God, help me allow Your glory to overtake my ego and self-centered need for applause, praise, and prominence. God, help me be more conduit than cul-de-sac. God, help me lose the I and gain Chabod instead—one I of a difference.

Do you have an I problem? Write your thinking, please.

BUILT TO LEAD | together we transform

Day 38: Enough...

I can remember meeting my financial planner at a basketball game back in the early nineties. I knew then I wanted to start BTL, but my financial fears held me down. I was too weak to make the leap.

You see, friend, I was too spiritually, mentally, and relationally weak. My bank account had grown, but my CORE had mostly come along for the ride. Still, to this day, I need reminders to squelch my rampant insecurities roaming like an unbelieving lion just beneath the surface, ready to devour my confidence and conviction and leave me believing I'm not enough. We need reminders. I mean, why else would the Bible include hundreds of reminders for all of us to fear *not*?

God looks at me, sees who I'm becoming, and reminds me I am His. God does not infuse doubt and wrongful desire. God promises peace regardless of my outward performance. God reminds us all we are not a lone: never have been, never will be. You and I are enough. Financial poverty is not our problem. We can all solve this one when we realize we're already enough.

Our spiritual poverty is the real hole.

As Pascal said so eloquently back in the 1600s, "We all have a God-shaped vacuum that only He can fill." A six-, seven-, eight-, or nine-figure net worth won't fill it. Fourteen or fifteen majors didn't do it for Tiger. Gold medals won't make you whole, and neither will world championships. There is nothing wrong with the aim for excellence and the straining for success. We are made for OPUS and lots of it. Keep it all in perspective. Do not fixate on outcomes. Practice. Do good work. Focus on the process. You are more than enough. So, go on and push forward with persistence and peace. Trust God. Trust yourself. Trust a few friends. Trust the process. What are you filling your holes with? Whom do you trust? Slow down and reflect.

Day 39: Love harder...

A client wrote me about his time inside one of London's libraries studying the Vincent Van Gogh exhibit and the letters to his brother. Van Gogh produced over 2,100 pieces of work. He wasn't a bad life coach either. Here's the summary of Van Gogh coaching up his brother back in the day from *Ever Yours: The Essential Letters*:

1. One must work and dare if they ever want to live. (CORE. Use it.)
2. I know what I want to create and am utterly indifferent to the criticism. (Authentic OPUS. No noise.)
3. I am always doing what I cannot do so I can learn how to do it. (PoP it out. Do hard things.)
4. I will always be myself and care relatively little if others approve. (Courage.)
5. Normality is an easy paved road, but few flowers grow on it. (Be you.)
6. I am seeking. I am striving. I am in it with all my heart. (Passion)
7. I would rather die of passion than boredom. (Dream and Do)
8. Your profession is not what brings you a paycheck. Your profession is what you were put on this earth to do with such passion and intensity that it becomes a spiritual thing. (OPUS calls you)
9. I think the best way to knowing God is by loving many things. Love this friend, that person, this thing, whatever you like, and you will be on the path to knowing God. (I love to...)
10. The fisherman knows the sea is dangerous, and the storms are terrible but doesn't see these dangers as reason to remain on shore. (More love than fear.)

Van Gogh burned out bright. He lived thirty-seven years. Jesus, thirty-three. MLK, thirty-nine. JFK, forty-six. Lincoln, fifty-six. Marcus Aurelius, fifty-eight. Booker T. Washington, fifty-nine. Jane Austen, forty-one. Teeks, eleven. It's not the years we live, friend, but the life in them. Do not go quietly or slowly, please—leave that to candles. You and I are meant to burn out bright.

Get busy writing your own version of "Starry Night." Live hard. Love harder....

Day 40: The tyrant known as me...

We have lots of problems, none more debilitating than lost identity. Few humans know who they are. For those of you who have been offended by my references to God, here comes another. My aim is not to impose my belief on you, only to be transparent and trigger your thinking. Make sense?

Genesis 1:26–28 says, "So God created man in his own image, in the image of God he created him; male and female he created them. God blessed them and said to them, 'Be fruitful and increase in numbers; fill the earth and subdue it. Rule.'"

Hebrew scholar Robert Alter says the idea of *rule* translates to "a fierce exercise of mastery." I love this definition. If this is our original design, why are there so few examples of fierce masters of their craft? I believe it's often a case of mistaken identity. We have forgotten whose we are. We have fallen for power, position, and prominence. We have become fiercely competitive even in our closest relationships. We're good, or so we tell ourselves, so we get busy powering over people. Ruling them. Controlling them. Manipulating them. Using all our faculties to rule our kingdom; however large or small its domain. By God, we are going to dominate.

We have forgotten to fiercely focus on mastering our greatest leadership challenge: ourselves. We are focusing attention out the window instead of in the mirror. We see others and their need for rule: our own, not so much. We wonder why our ruling is met with resistance. We drive ourselves nuts fixing other's bullshit while stepping in our own. Rule begins within. Rule your internally divided kingdom first. You and I are a house divided.

What, friend, do you believe? Whose are you? Have you taken the time to look within and build your CORE? Are you closing your integrity gaps and fiercely mastering you? Are you fixated on ruling others?

God, help me tame the tyrant known as me. God, help me.

Day 41: Invictus...

The Latin word *invictus* translates to the English word *unconquerable*. Nelson Mandela's favorite poem bore this title. He memorized it and recited it to himself countless times from his prison cell on Robben Island where he was forced to live for twenty-seven years. He left the prison cell and became the president. Few go from prison to presidency. Few view the obstacle as the way. Few set their souls free even when not behind bars. Few choose small, simple suffering. Most of us are so easily broken and conquered when the crucible arrives because we've done next to nothing hard. Today, discipline your mind, body, and spirit. Resist impulse. Become unconquerable by conquering the mind. Enjoy a piece of William Ernest Henley's poem, "Invictus."

It matters not how strait the gate,
How charged with punishments the scroll,
I am the master of my fate:
I am the captain of my soul.

No wonder Nelson's identity was that of a president even when his reality was a prisoner. What, my friend, is your identity? What adversity are you catastrophizing instead of conquering? You are invictus. You are unconquerable. And you are never really a lone, so don't be afraid to ask for help when the crucible's kicking your ass.

Rinse your *I ams*, please. Your strong CORE is your get-out-of-jail card. Build it.

Day 42: Be like Mike...

In 1934, Mike King traveled to Berlin to check out a Baptist preachers' conference. I can only imagine the fire and brimstone being laid down before the wall went up. Mike was so blown away by what he learned about Martin Luther that he decided to change his name. Mike became Martin Luther, and his five-year-old son became Martin Luther King Jr.

I'm rereading Eric Metaxas' book *Martin Luther* and am blown away by what I'm learning. Martin didn't set out to break away from the Roman Catholic Church; he simply aimed to reform her. The Pope and emperor, however, could not handle any form of dissent, and their inability to listen led to the greatest change the Church had ever seen. Martin started the people's church. Martin represented the peasants and the common people, and he provided them hope that in their church, they could take communion, build community, and learn more than a couple of verses along the way. Martin gave voice to the people. Mike King Jr. would as well.

Mike King was a long way from his sweet home in Alabama when inspiration caught him. Who knows where you'll be when some breath of air infuses your lungs, lifts your spirit, and inspires you to see yourself, your world, and your role in it in a whole new way? Who knows? You may even decide to rename yourself too. Slow down today. Invest some time working on your identities, not your mistaken one. Thank Martin for modeling the way. Listen for the sounds, sights, and scents of your calling. Open your eyes and mind. Be like Mike, and let your voice be heard.

Rinse and repeat your *I am* statements, friend. You're going to hear this a lot—rinse and repeat.

Day 43: Compete...

Nothing worth possessing has ever been given.

My mom, back in the day, reminded me of this thought on a regular basis. She told me not to expect people, God, or the universe to give me my heart's desire. She told me to earn it. She told me to work hard for what I wanted, and her stories of the Dust Bowl, Great Depression, and how her mom and brother made it on their own seared me for life. I was small and scrawny, and she made me believe it didn't matter.

She taught me how to compete. She engraved her mantra of "keep working" onto my heart. For the longest time, I thought it was my idea too. Mom didn't seem to care that I took way too much credit for myself; she wanted me to believe and put up with my immaturity. She knew life was hard and wanted her son to have a hardened mind. She knew competitors had to have a belief to compete. So, she kept giving the belief alongside tough truth. Mom epitomized tough and tender. She babied me like crazy too. I didn't know how to work a washing machine until college, but I knew how to compete. I'm amazed at how many talented teammates seem to be missing this critical ingredient. They have not built a competitive character. They have not been built at home, only coddled or left alone. Not good.

You, friend, are being **BUILT TO LEAD**. Do not run from this building or just go through the motions. Engage your heart and mind. You must compete every day, every possession, every match, every opportunity, against every opponent, but mostly against yourself. You cannot switch it off and on. Your competitive character is engraved by your habits. There are no guaranteed wins regardless of how many times you've taken 'em down. It might help to remember a little Lao Tzu: "If you wish to be out front, then act as if you were behind." Compete. And give more than you take. Reproduce in another what has been produced in you. The best competitors embrace the competition too. What about you?

Day 44: Ten things everybody ought to know...

I'm asking all my clients to write out the ten things they think everybody ought to know. Don't think. Let what's top of mind flow to your parchment. Here's mine, at least for now.

1. Nothing matters more than knowing what matters most to you. Figuring this out is the aim behind authoring your BTL CORE, OPUS, and Playbook of Productive Action. Start here.
2. There is a God, and I think we can know Him.
3. One day, you will die. Aim at heaven. Take nothing for granted. Practice gratitude. Live hard.
4. Either/or thinking is lazy, and so yesterday. Practice the power of "anding." Evolution *and* creation are true.
5. Love more. Start by loving yourself more. Love your family, friends, and teammates. Love work. Love life. Someday, maybe you'll be the one able to love the world. See one and two. Love harder.
6. Nobody is as wise as everybody. There are no enlightened ones, only those still working on becoming more light. Keep seeking more light, friends.
7. Life is better when you learn to do hard things well. Start small. Baby-step it. Keep working.
8. Learn to laugh more and loathe less. See five as a reminder.
9. We are meant to belong and become. Nothing makes sense a lone, and you've got to go it alone at some point. Find your tribe and try to keep it open to outsiders (at least those who want the best for you). Figure out who you are and keep figuring out who you're becoming. Never arrive.
10. Play more. Our most creative, inventive, and collaborative selves are found when we play. Play every day. Play with your kids. Play with your brothers/sisters. Play with your teammates. Play with strangers. Play with people like you. Play with people you like. And play with people unlike you and with people you don't particularly like. Play. See one through nine as a reminder. Nothing is so important that you and I shouldn't play around on this serious, limited, and blessed time we share. Play more. Live hard. Love harder.

Your top ten list is a reflection of your deepest held beliefs. Maybe it's time for a Worldview rinse.

Day 45: Freakin' magic in the making...

Becoming BTL begins with awakening to the liberating fact that becoming the original you already are is all we're after. You are an original designed by a loving God, who has left it up to you to figure out who you are (becoming), why you're here (becoming & belonging), where you fit (belong), and how to make it meaningful, energizing, and a life worth living (OPUS).

You are meant to become and belong. And all that we see here is but a glimpse of what is to come. We are all so much more than meets the eye. You, friend, are not done evolving. Keep working. Keep loving. Keep giving. Keep believing. Become the original you already are, but you've just been too afraid to reveal. Find your place of belonging as you journey through work and life. As you begin to feel comfortable in your skin (especially as it wrinkles), content with your people, and your contribution.

You are freakin' magic in the making, friend.

Becoming BTL is the point of being here. Every one of us was born to lead ourselves, at a minimum. You are not an apology, so stop selling yourself short with all kinds of disclaimers and negative self-talk. You are an original. The world wants you to play small and survive for seventy-five or so. The world wants you to mindlessly follow your fear-based, lizard brain. God designed you to find flow, joy, love, and meaning on the road to becoming and belonging. Life is difficult. Obstacles are in our way. You are made for these hard moments of truth. You are made through them. You are made to learn to do hard things well. You are made to smile as you figure all this out and include all kinds of distinctly different dude's into your dream. You come in a lone. A life worth living is all about moving toward becoming all ONE—one 'L of a difference. One, distinct and deeply connected, Becoming BTL.

What do you believe, my friend?

Day 46: Your moral code...

In case you're not familiar with the term, emerging adults is another category we've created, not unlike my parents' generation created the category *teenager*. Prior to my generation, you just went from single digits to "buck up." I'm rereading the book, *Lost in Transition*, by Christian Smith, which describes emerging adults (eighteen- to twenty-nine-year-olds) as being morally adrift, to put it mildly. The majority, in fact, have yet to face a moral dilemma and, even more telling, have yet to experience regret. Yup, it's true, as far as truth goes. He summarizes the prevailing Worldview of today's youth as "liberal individualism." Read this one, at my age, and you'll be between a laugh and a tear throughout.

I turned to the second chapter, hoping for some relief, and was greeted by an old friend. A dead French guy (Blaise Pascal) and a stinging quote of his from the 1600s. "The only thing that consoles us for our miseries is distraction, yet that is the greatest of our wretchednesses. Because that is what mainly prevents us from thinking about ourselves and leads us imperceptibly to damnation. Without it we should be bored, and boredom would force us to search for a firmer way out, but distraction entertains us and leads us imperceptibly to death."

What is the basis for your moral code? Is it yours, your parents, your hardwiring, your culture, or from something beyond, before, and bigger than you? Reflect on a recent moral dilemma you faced. How did you resolve it? Are you slowing down and reflecting as a habit of the heart or just staying busy, so there's no time to think about such things?

As for me, I've got some regret, repair, and real, hard work ahead. I am not yet the man I want to be. I like that as a Worldview thought. I guess you could say I believe in the "not yet" and the "soon to become." What about you? What do you believe?

Day 47: Galton...

Francis Galton was a child prodigy (there are none, really), and by four, he knew Latin and long division—learning appeared to come easy. In 1869, Galton (cousin of Darwin) published his first study on the origins of high achievement. Outliers, he believed, were remarkable in three ways: "they demonstrate unusual 'ability' in combination with exceptional 'zeal'" and "the capacity for hard labor." He was saying that the elite are skilled, passionate, and have a penchant for hard labor.

Skill. Passion. Effort.

Darwin was a high performer. He was an astute observer of flora, fauna, and also of people. His vocation was to observe slight differences that lead to survival. Darwin was a plodder. Darwin, like so many of the elite we study in this work we call BTL, married the mundane. At BTL, we are on a never-ending quest to understand the roots of high performance. The more we learn, the more convinced we are that sustained high performance is not a mystery—it's just not easy to master. It's gonna take lots and lots of time.

This is why we focus all our clients on building our big three if you will: CORE, OPUS, PoP. The elite are aligned, you see. They spend little time thinking about who they are, whether they can become great where they are, or even worry for a second about where they'll end up. The elite know who they are because they've invested the time building their BTL CORE. They know where they are because they've invested the time authoring and living their OPUS. And the elite know where they're going because they're committed to their Playbook of Productive Action (PoP). They understand it's not enough to dream big. They do all the little things, and they do them incredibly well, to master the mundane on their way to mastering their craft.

Skill. Passion. Effort. CORE, OPUS, PoP. Build here, friend.

Day 48: Identity...

Jim Gant, former Green Beret and author of *One Tribe at a Time,* had just explained to a number of my clients how hard it was to do his job when our military bureaucracy got in the way, the Afghan government fought him, and the Taliban wreaked havoc. I turned to him that afternoon and asked him what kept him going. I curiously awaited his response. I didn't have to wait long. "My sense of Identity," he replied in an instant. He had written out his Identity word—warrior—and the book behind it. He knew who he was and why he was in it. This wasn't a check-the-box kinda Identity. This was built in the crucible. This was real. This kept him going.

Your Identity is your anti-anxiety pill.

What keeps you going when you find yourself overwhelmed and all kinda entities arranged against you? Do you know who you are? Do you know whose you are? Do you know why you're here? Do you know where you're going? Do you know who's in control? Have you made peace with your place? Last night, I had another dark night of the soul as I was awakened by a bad dream. I recounted a number of Psalms, repeated The Lord's Prayer, and reminded myself whose I am and who I am. It was a hard night in my head because my sense of Identity needs strengthening. We're in the crucible. Shit's getting real. Are you?

"Knowing others is wisdom. Knowing yourself is Enlightenment."
—Lao-tzu

Day 49: Purpose...

Nietzsche was partially correct when he said his piece about the power of knowing why you're here: "He who has a why to live can bear almost any how." Here's the missing element, friend, if you want to sustain a sense of purpose in work and life. Nietzsche, you see, forgot about the power behind the purpose. Show me anyone with a convicting sense of purpose—Passion is present. For most, the Passion is driven by fear. This works for a season or two, maybe more. The drive to prove the world wrong has fueled many a dreamer, as has the fear of losing. Passion ignites and fuels purpose. This is why we have Passions and Purposes as two critical elements to your BTL CORE. Make sense?

If you want a why that can bear any *how*, friend, fuel it with the only pure passion on the planet: Love. This is why when we ask our clients to author their BTL six-pack CORE, we have them write their Passions in the form of "love tos." We believe you and I were designed out of love and for love. For many of us, however, the last time we invested in cultivating our love tos was long ago. We're responsible now. We get stuff done and take care of others. There's no time to fill our own lungs or lives. So, out of fear, or some misplaced sense of self, we put it on others and become, as Ayn Rand would describe, "second-handers." You're not meant to love nostalgically, friend. You're meant to love God, love yourself, love people, and, yes, even labor in love.

Rinse your CORE Purposes, friend. Go deeper on discovering your why's for work and life. Don't stop until you have a why worth any how. A Passion fueled Purpose is the route to Becoming BTL. This is the one you know you want if your aim is to live hard and love harder.

Build Your Humility

12 ESSENTIALS OF PERSONAL EXCELLENCE

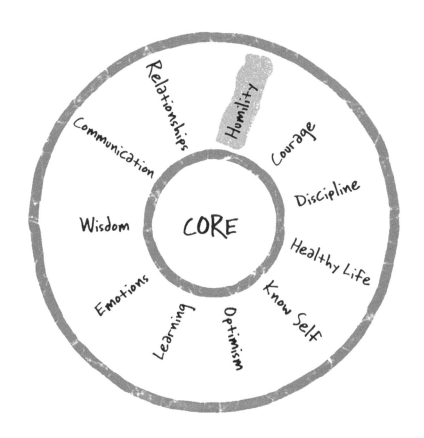

Dub's Builder's Journey

My first exposure to **BUILT TO LEAD** came in 1997 or so when I was a college student. A mutual friend shared with me some of Chet's early Worldview worksheets, and I immediately went to work trying to define mine on a plane ride home from school. I found the exercise fascinating and useful but only rinsed it once or twice in the following weeks. My CORE was immature and weak at that time. I was way too self-centered and other-controlling. The Worldview work I did got me thinking, but I was too young and inexperienced to really know who I was or who I wanted to become. My definition of success was too focused on money and buying stuff. Work was merely a means to have more choice. OPUS wasn't even on my radar.

Fast forward twenty years. After a first job, graduate school, and starting a tech company that was successful but ultimately pillaged by ego and greed, a long-time friend and I were looking for some help trying to figure out how to reinvent ourselves and our real estate development business in the midst of a terrible recession. We were in debt up to our eyeballs and knew we would be for some time. Once again, the same mutual friend suggested Chet Scott and **BUILT TO LEAD**.

Through our first few meetings and in the productive actions I took on my own, I caught fire. The stories resonated, Chet's candor pierced me, and it was clear to me that I was learning about real people who achieved greatness and about eternal truths that have been around since the dawn of time. I wanted to learn it all. I knew I'd never be the same. Once I wrote down, rinsed, and repeated my Worldview and my ideal day pursuing my OPUS in great detail many times, I could think of nothing else. This was the path, and it was going to be scary and hard, but I had a guide with real knowledge and perspective and the ability to get me to listen.

The highs and lows of my daily trials became less high and low, merely steps or part of the path. I made lots of mistakes and learned from them more quickly. I wrote and spoke more truth to those I loved and those with whom I disagreed, sometimes more effectively than other times. I learned to be more CCD. But I also learned to anesthetize and to repair. I trained hard at times and then was soft far too often. Still am. I did a few dumb deals and a few good ones. I ran all kinds of experiments. And the whole time, no matter what, my builder would listen and tell me the truth. The long-time friend and I realized his OPUS was in real estate, but mine wasn't. We managed to part as close of friends as we ever were, only because I had the guts and ability to speak the truth in love to him in a way he understood.

It took me a while, but in 2010, I finally landed in an experiment that clicked. An experiment in the investment business came to me courtesy of Chet, who made a connection on a very thin inkling that I may be interested in the work, and the team may be interested in someone like me. Right off the bat, the work felt different. It wasn't work but rather something I was good at and enjoyed doing. I was experiencing OPUS for the first time in my life. The work was (and still is today) the most intellectually stimulating and thrilling application of my efforts and skills that I could've ever dreamed. My new teammates saw my passion, recognized the shoot in my eyes, and appreciated the lessons I'd learned in my previous experiences, along with the creativity I brought to the team. We grew together.

Ten years later, I'm singularly focused on my OPUS. For the first and only time in my career, I'm not thinking about what's next or what else is out there. I made sacrifices to be here that I would have shuddered at only a few years ago, and I don't think twice. I'm thinking only about how I can be the best at what I do and how our team can be the best in our business. I think about it almost every minute of every day, and I'm energized by this and those around me. As I think back to that kid sitting on an America West flight home from Tucson, I had no idea what an impact a clear Worldview and OPUS would ultimately have on my life. I had no idea then how tough the world really is or the incredible difference between OPUS and labor. If not for **BUILT TO LEAD**, the speed bumps I hit would've felt like mountains. If not for the clarity I gained through practice, the shoot in my eye might otherwise be a lot less clear to those around me. And I think it would've taken me a lot longer and a lot more mistakes to find my OPUS.

Day 50: Four healers...

According to John and Julie Gottman in their book *Ten Lessons to Transform Your Marriage*, the "Four Horsemen of the Apocalypse" regarding relationships are criticism, defensiveness, contempt, and stonewalling. Consider them the plague. Here are the BTL four healers. Feel free to overdose on these, friend.

1. When talking about anything tough, remember to give your teammate some anesthesia before you open 'em up. Start soft. Tough conversations are best delivered from tender hearts. Soft hearts are strong enough to hear hard truths and speak 'em too. Soft hearts delivering hard truths are more likely to be heard.

2. Instead of mastering triple-d, become a master of "tell me more." Develop the habit of hearing the yearning, not the whining. As you hear the yearning for connection from your partner, friend, neighbor, or loved one, turn toward them. Turn toward. Absorb.

3. Repair. Become a master repairman/woman. All relationships are built by broken people. None of us is whole. Know this and lead the way in repairing with those around you. Forgiveness and restoration are only for the strong. Live hard. Love harder. Lead in repair, leader.

4. Accept influence. Oh, God, do I really have to do this? This is the hardest one for me and maybe for you. I love to influence others. I love to be right and make things right. I love to fix other people (what a warped thought) and find it hard to admit I'm wrong and accept another's attempt to fix me. Houston, we've got a problem. Remember this, friend: nothing says, "I love you" more than letting another influence you. Men, this is extremely important for us. According to the Gottmans' research, a husband's willingness to accept influence from his bride is the leading indicator of a happy home.

Thanks, Miss, Mom, and many more for your grace and patience with me. God, help me avoid mastering the four horses and, instead, become a master in humility. God, help me master the four healers. God, help me live hard and love harder.

Day 51: Love...

Recently, during another teaching from Rich Nathan at Vineyard Columbus Church, we learned the difference between forgiving and floor mats. As believers, we are called to forgive as we've already been forgiven. Forgiving does not mean we become floor mats for another. To forgive means to let go, to set free, to release. When we forgive, oddly enough, it is our own selves who are most set free. We can set limits on behaviors we tolerate. We cannot limit forgiveness. Forgiveness does not mean reunion or reconciliation. Forgiveness only requires one heart—my own. Reconciliation, on the other hand, requires both parties. You, friend, can control your heart. Is there someone whom you still hold in contempt, disgust, and in the clenches of your mind?

> To excuse what can really produce good excuses is not Christian character; it is only fairness. To be a Christian means to forgive the inexcusable, because God has forgiven the inexcusable in you. This is hard. It is perhaps not so hard to forgive a single great injury. But to forgive the incessant provocations of daily life—to keep on forgiving the bossy mother-in-law, the bullying husband, the nagging wife, the selfish daughter, the deceitful son—how can we do it? Only, I think, by remembering where we stand, by meaning our words when we say in our prayers each night 'forgive us our trespasses as we forgive those that trespass against us.' We are offered forgiveness on no other terms. To refuse it is to refuse God's mercy for ourselves. There is no hint of exceptions and God means what he says.
>
> —C.S. Lewis, *The Weight of Glory*

Forgiveness is a process. Today, I began the process of letting go, setting free, and releasing a wrong done to me by a close friend. I peeled away the first layer of pain, let it go, released it. I'm not done; I'm simply starting the process of forgiving. Really, I'm finally learning how to love.

Are you? Whom do you need to forgive? Forgive now.

Day 52: Praus...

Praus is a Greek word I recently learned from my good friend, jmo. *Praus* translates to meek. Here's what jmo wrote me this morning, and I'm passing it along. Meekness is rarely taught in western civilizations. The word *praus* was borrowed from the military and relates to horse training.

So, friend, how well do you stand when others are firing rounds of hurtful words your way? How well do you stop when your little voice whispers something is better off not said? How well do you respond when tweaked, torched, or even slightly touched? Are you strong, passionate, determined, and under control? We come into this world self-centered and other-controlling. Excellence is CORE-centered and self-controlling. Meek is not weak. Which are you becoming?

Day 53: Repair 101...

There are no equal partnerships. Someone strong and humble takes the lead. If you simply want to stay married and create a transactional relationship, you can take more than give. You may get away with it, at least for a while. You may stay together, but it won't be freakin' magic in the making. Transformational relationships are worth the extra effort, friend. It just takes one to bring it into reality—one willing to lead in repair.

Recently, a strong client of mine got in his own way. We all do. He offended his partner in word and deed. He told her to get over it. His attempt at repair had him saying a classic no-no: "You took it the wrong way." Never tell another how to take whatever it is they're taking, by the way. He made matters worse by continuing his repair with too many words. "I didn't mean it that way." Never tell another their interpretation is the problem unless you want a helluva fight coming your way. Nobody cares what you meant in a moment where they received something that harmed their heart. So, when repairing, use few words. When a teammate, loved one, or partner tells you that you've harmed their heart, soften your own. Feel the sorrow you've caused and shut the #%$k up. When you get around to opening your mouth, let it be with contrition, remorse, and regret. Tell her/him, "I messed up. I'm a dumb ass. Forgive me." Offer zero disclaimers. Own your stuff. This is repair 101.

Lead a marriage, partnership, company, family, or team of any size, and you must lead in repair. Leaders mess up as much as any. The BTL leader repairs even more. Humbly, they repair. Pride brings enmity, division, and leaves the team feeling the leader is looking down on them. Humility unites us, brings healing, and leaves the team feeling the leader is worth following because they are, in fact, human. Remember, we stick it to the man. We stick with the HUman. So, stop fighting with another and fight your pride instead. Become a master of repair. Together, you'll transform. God, help me give more than I take.

Make sense? Make it common practice.

Day 54: Producer—led...

During practice twenty-five, we talked about the term "producer-led" and what it means. We discovered, together, that it means many things. This is not surprising when you think about it. Anaïs Nin quoted ancient wisdom many moons ago when she wrote in *Seduction of the Minotaur*, "We do not see things as they are, we see them as we are."

When it comes to your company, community, team, or family, wouldn't it be great, leader, if we saw you mostly as someone there to serve the greater good? Producer-led, just like president led or head coach led, is best led when it means servant led. Your position does not exist to give you a one-up position to power over people. Your position exists to give you a platform from which to serve. How do you see your position? How does your team? When was the last time you got curious, invited feedback, asked the team to tell you more, and offered zero resistance to hard truth?

Model the way. Embrace pain and suffering. Embody truth in Love.

Master these principles, producer, president, head coach. Get in the habit of saying, "Follow me" as you lead the bayonet charge down your figurative "Little Roundtop." Ask your hungry teammates when they were last fed, as Colonel Chamberlain did with his new team of mutineers. Listen to hard truth, speak it, too, and love the good work you are blessed to bring to this world. Your team will see you however they are, regardless. Enough will see through their bias, prejudice, and previous experiences with power— to see something different. A few will begin to believe. Freakin' magic in the making, you'll see.

What are you doing today to serve those you're blessed to lead?

Day 55: Humility...

Pride is the most potent of the seven deadly sins for a reason—it's personal and cultural. Every generation suffers from this. The generation currently in power sees clearly the ignorance of their predecessors and doubts the capacity of the coming one. The greatest generation still doesn't think us boomers understand how soft and squishy we are. On and on, this will go. The root reason is collective, cultural pride. Generationally, we think we're better than those who came before and those who are coming after.

Every culture flatters itself, thinking it sees things clearly that previous generations missed. Every culture thinks it's the first to discover unadulterated truth. We see previous generations' blinders, not our own. We see previous generations' ideological handicaps, not our own. We see previous generations' laughable logic, not our own. We see through a foggy lens and believe we have 20/20 vision. We don't understand we suffer from ideological cataracts. Fact. So, friend, build strength within your CORE. Build your humility. You and I are not all-knowing. You and I have personal presuppositions and generational ones too. We're all biased to our own. Study history. Explore science. Deepen faith. And do it all with humility.

Francis Collins and his team discovered *The Language of God* when they broke the code of our DNA back in the day. We thought this would give us answers; instead, it's given us better questions. The more I learn, the less I know. Become aware of your pride. It's hard to stay humble when you're always looking down. Look up. Be grateful.

Slow down. Where do you need to build humility? Where are you comparing yourself to those who came before and those coming after? Look in the mirror. Write your thinking. Now, go talk to someone much older, much younger, be curious. Good…

Day 56: Giving...

We are meant to be conduits, not cul-de-sacs. Cul-de-sacs, you see, are dead-ends. We are meant to be conduits of positive energy, purpose, and love.

As leaders, we have the privilege to model the way for those under our charge. Leadership is influence, and the good ones make us want to do more, somehow, without feeling less of ourselves. We marvel at how they get so much done, and it inspires us to do more ourselves. We admire how they pour themselves into others and decide if they can do it, we can too. Leaders, the kind worth following, have such a strong sense of self that we feel energized when we're around them. They make us do what we can. We suffer together, and it fuels us instead of depletes us.

You cannot give what you do not yet possess, friend. Do you know who you are? Are you aligning behaviors to your bolted-on beliefs? Are you building competence and confidence in your character? Are you a dead-end cul-de-sac or a life-giving conduit energizing all around you? Slow down and reflect.

Where's an opportunity, today, to be a conduit? Baby-step it, please.

Day 57: Truth does not harm...

My favorite verse in the Bible is John 8:32. "And someday you will know the truth, and the truth will set you free." I believe this. Richard Rohr does as well. His "and" from his book, *Falling Upward*, is a really thought-provoking one. "Before the truth sets you free, it tends to make you miserable." I believe this too.

Truth sets us free, and truth hurts; oftentimes, it hurts for quite a while, doesn't it? It is only your perception of it, however, that allows it to make you miserable. Same for the lies from a lover, son, daughter, or even your mother. Truth hurts as it helps us face facts and find the honest way 'round. Truth does not harm. Truth hurts. This has been a helpful distinction for me and the governance of my affairs. I am learning to seek truth, speak truth, see truth, and attempt to be truth. You and I have a long way to go if we are in pursuit of this most freeing and difficult aim.

Truth does not harm. Truth in love that is.

Stop telling lies, particularly to yourself. Embrace the pain and suffering of seeing your holes instead of fixating on others. The ancient wisdom still applies today—keep your Principles close at hand—when the crucible comes, there won't be time to pull them forward and magically put them into action. Again, ancient wisdom applies—we don't rise to the occasion, but we fall to the level of our training. Train your mind by reminding yourself of your CORE principles and aligning behaviors with them, instead of rationalizing behaviors as you look back on your day. Become more rational and less rationalizing. Lies will lose their grip—you'll see.

Model the way. Embrace pain and suffering. Embody truth in love. These are my three guiding Principles. I think about them every day and align accordingly. I am lying less to myself and almost never with others. Still a long way to go. I am much better at modeling the way and embracing pain. Truth in love is where I struggle the most.

Slow down and tell yourself some hard truth about you. Face facts. Write. Come clean.

Day 58: Win/lose and learn...

If you want to lose at life, keep winning and not learning.

This thought came to me recently during another BTL team practice. I'm not sure where it came from, but it flew into my head in a moment of clarity. I love it when this happens, and the more I get lost in the work, the more the work does this to me. Funny how the universe works, isn't it? When we study excellence, a very piercing discovery has been around what derails winning individuals, teams, and leaders.

Themselves.

As Lincoln said so long ago, all humans can handle adversity, but few can handle power. Your job, leader, is to make sure you and your team learn the most when you win. The demanding leader is sober and views wins and losses very similarly—as an opportunity to get better. Do not get intoxicated with wins or depressed with losses. Get better with both. And the more difficult adversity is not a losing streak; it's a winning streak absent learning. Do not allow yourself and your team to win without learning.

Our clients are winners. We deal with uncommon individuals. Very few are derailed by some disastrous loss. Most elite performers are derailed by their inability to resist impulse when they keep winning and winning and winning. Think Tiger Woods, friend. He self-destructed after winning fourteen majors and telling himself he deserved to celebrate. He won fourteen majors from 1997–2008. He's won one since. His story is repeated in the world of work, sport, art, and any other craft. If you want to lose at life, keep winning and not learning. Winners learn to respect the game. Winners learn humility, or someday, the universe humbles them.

If you want to lose at life, keep winning and not learning. Continual learning is the habit of the uncommon among the uncommon. Build humility within. Look up and become grateful. Look around and gain perspective. Look down and pull another up. Win/lose and learn.

Slow down. Write. Build humility, my strong friend.

Day 59: Bowl of cherries...

John and Julie Gottman, authors of *Ten Lessons to Transform Your Marriage*, know a thing or two about relationships. According to their research, you've got to get your ratios right. They've observed long-term relationships depend far more on avoiding the negative than on seeking the positive. If you want your trusted relationships to last, you've got to avoid the emotional equivalent of "stepping in it." In *Thinking, Fast and Slow*, Daniel Kahneman wrote, "The psychologist, Paul Rozin, an expert on disgust, observed that a single cockroach will completely wreck the appeal of a bowl of cherries, but a cherry will do nothing for a bowl of cockroaches." We humans are wired to remember the gross way more than the good.

The Gottmans' research shows that stable relationships have positive interactions that outnumber bad ones by at least five to one. My limited research with clients and the relationships with their teams would align but with a catch. You see, not all negative encounters sear the emotional brain the same. You can be a bowl of cherries for freakin' ever, and one dumb move can plop a cockroach right where you don't want it. Recently, a friend described an encounter with her leader. They weren't seeing eye to eye on a benign issue when her frustrated leader blurted out six searing words, "You know where the door is!" She threw cockroaches in their relational bowl. Gross.

The problem is you can't measure most relational stuff, so you tend to underestimate its impact. You think you're a bowl of cherries. She, on the other hand, can't get her mind's eye off the one cockroach. Understand the fragility of relationships. Your relationships require consistency, predictability, and avoiding the negative. You have no idea. Swallow your pride and remove the cockroaches from your relational bowls. Own it. Clean it up and learn how to avoid what caused such a disgusting interaction again. You may be on your way to becoming a relational bowl of cherries.

What are you putting in your relational bowls at work? Home? Good.

Day 60: Cincinnatus...

I love leadership stories, and a ton of my belief system has been built through the power of story—the same is likely true for you. Like it or not, we are all affected by the stories we absorb, replay, and come to embody. One of my bolted-on beliefs about leadership is the best leaders are reluctant ones. They don't pine for the job. They are just the obvious choice. Countless stories have seared this one home, and here's one of them: the story of Cincinnatus.

Way back in the day (458 BC), Cincinnatus was plowing his field when a team of Roman leaders informed him he had just been elected dictator. Back in the day, the term "dictator" didn't have such a bad rap. The Romans only played the d-card during a crisis, and the term was a tight six months. So, Cincinnatus dropped his plow, grabbed his toga (no joke), and off to Rome he went. His first act was to call up every able man to fight the Aequi. He led them himself. From the front. He did his duty for Rome, even though he was happy as a clam just days prior out doing his thing on the farm. He put his country above his comfort.

History records a rapid victory for Rome. Cincinnatus and company defeated the enemy forces in a mere fifteen days. Cincinnatus was hailed a conquering hero, and all of Rome celebrated him. He had all the power in the world. He'd been made dictator and had another five and a half months of unbridled authority. So, what'd he do? Built a few monuments, carried off some serious gold, did the old grapes and fan thing for day upon dreamy day? Nope. He resigned. Quit.

Cincinnatus was a reluctant leader. Once his job was done, he returned to his plow and led his small team back on the farm, where he belonged. So, next time you make the trek down to Cincy for a game, brew, or chili dog, remember the city bears its name in remembrance of a farmer, turned dictator, turned farmer again. A stud who knew a thing or two about power—it should only be used in reference to boats and weightlifting—
    thanks Herb Kelleher (founder of Southwest Airlines).

    What, friend, are you striving toward?

Day 61: Repent...

Repent. For many of us, just reading this word makes something inside us tighten up. We are almost repelled by the mere mention of this word. For many, the reaction is visceral. We often think of this word as something to be avoided—like I don't want to feel the need to repent or repair because it requires me to acknowledge that such a need even exists. So, we tend to rationalize away whatever caused that word to enter our mind and simply do what normal humans have done since the beginning of time—move on. We ignore the internal nudge. We move on. Nothing changes.

Repent, according to Merriam-Webster's definition, is "to change one's mind."

So, friend, you only have two options available if you want to feel more whole, more united, and an ever-increasing sense of personal integrity. You can rationalize your behavior to better align it with your deeply held beliefs, or you can repent—change your mind—and decide to deeply change your behaviors that are out of alignment with your beliefs. Repent is not a four-letter word. Stop acting like you're whole when you know you're not. The best among us understand that ever-increasing integrity is the beginning and the end of excellence—the alpha and omega if you will. Repent. Repair. Restore. Renew. Who knew this kind of rebirth would change us from the inside out? Who knew?

God, help me move from hole to whole. Same sound. One w is the difference, and a world of difference it is. What blemish or blemishes are you still covering up? What speck in another's eye is crystal clear, but you cannot see the plank in your own? Where do you need to change your mind?

Day 62: Faith...

Over 500 times, faith is mentioned in the Bible alongside the words trust and believe. Clues are all around us in our desire for justice, love of beauty, and our love of love itself. Faith is the hand that grabs hold of God. *What does faith feel like?* I wonder.

Faith doesn't feel like certainty. Faith doesn't feel like math. Faith and doubt go together. Faith is a choice. Faith is as much a matter of will as anything. It is a decision with what we're going to do with evidence about why we're here. Faith is a choice to see. The good Samaritan didn't look away. He saw an injured man and acted on what he saw. Faith is a choice to see and not look away. You have to have faith. Life takes faith, doesn't it?

Faith can feel like a choice to get on the down escalator. Moses chose to be mistreated. He associated with the Hebrew people instead of enjoying the benefits of being with the Pharaoh. Moses was well educated and a great leader. At age forty, he was at the top of his game. He chose to get on the down escalator. He committed career suicide. He chose insecurity over security.

Maggie Gobran, the Mother Teresa of Egypt known as Mama Maggie, loves the garbage kids of Egypt and has been nominated for the Nobel Peace Prize. She was a rich lady on top of the world. She regarded disgrace in the here and now as nothing when compared to glory in the life beyond. She weighed things and said this is actually better than that. You can read more about her story in *Mama Maggie* by Marty Makary.

What's your faith in, friend? Are you putting your faith in visibility over vision? Slow down. Come down from your lofty perch. Embrace uncertainty. Have some faith...

Day 63: Not bad for an adopted Dad...

Marcus Annius Verus was born in AD 121. In 137, Marcus was adopted by the childless senator Antoninus (heir to the throne) and took on the name Marcus Aurelius Antoninus. One year later, he assumed the throne. Leadership was thrust upon him.

Marcus underwent serious coaching/training/building as the Roman Empire would one day be his to run. In fact, that day arrived on August 31, 161, when his adopted father, Antoninus, died. We know Marcus Aurelius would go on to represent the high-water mark for philosopher/king. I'm enjoying the manuscript he wrote titled *Meditations*. He simply wrote to remind himself of the Principles he believed and hoped to live. Book one is titled "Debts and Lessons." Marcus begins by thanking his family, friends, teachers, and teammates for what they taught him. His longest learning is addressed to his adopted father. Here's a taste:

Compassion. Unwavering adherence to decisions once he'd reached them. Indifference to superficial honors. Hard work. Persistence. Listening to anyone who could contribute to the public good. His altruism. Not expecting his friends to keep him entertained at dinner or to travel with him. His searching questions at meetings. His restrictions on acclamations—and all attempts to flatter him. His constant devotion to the empire's needs. His stewardship of the treasury. His willingness to take responsibility—and blame—for both.... Qualified to govern both himself and them. His ability to feel at ease with people—and put them at their ease, without being pushy. This, in particular: his willingness to yield the floor to experts—in oratory, law, psychology, whatever—and to support them energetically, so that each of them could fulfill his potential.... Strength, perseverance, self-control in both areas: the mark of a soul in readiness—indomitable.

What are your bolted-on Principles for governing yourself and your team? Where do you need to yield the floor to teammates so they can fulfill their God-given potential? Baby-step like this adopted dad did. Are you becoming CORE-centered and self-controlling friend? Slow down. Reflect. Meditate. Write. Not bad...

Day 64: Pride...

There is a reason the second essential in the *12 Essentials Playbook* is titled "Build Your Humility." Pride has been the biggest divider of humans since the beginning. If our aim is to unite with even one other, we have to build a strong sense of self while not getting full of self. So, since pride is my biggest problem, here are some disciplines I'm attempting to habituate toward the aim of beating back mine.

Find and admit where I am prideful. I am most prideful of my mind, my work, and my will. Stop comparing myself to you. Pride always compares. Dang it.

Admit my weaknesses. I suck at structure and order. I'm not tender unless I really love you. Details disturb me.

Seek feedback from a few. Thank you, Miss, more than any other.

Keep my CORE in perspective; look up. Practice gratitude.

Praise others, even those we compete with. Celebrate the success of others. I suck less if you're on our team.

Ask more questions than provide answers. I'm getting better here unless your answers display a lack of mental gymnastics or, worse yet, a lack of effort. I despise laziness.

Listen. Limit my use of technology, leave my mobile behind, clear my mind from the past, the future, and away from my insecurities, and look another in the eye and receive all they are sending. This is exhausting and can only be done in fits and starts.

Stop seeking justice. Practice repairing relationships. Easy when I think it was my bad that caused the break, not so easy when I'm still stung from your betrayal. God, my sense of perspective is warped.

The stronger you build your CORE, the more pride gets in the way. This is why building humility follows building your CORE. Write where you need to build humility today. Ask a truth-teller for help.

Day 65: Forgiveness...

Forgiveness is all about you making up your mind. You can look at your offender and get even, or you can give grace. We tend to want justice when we're wronged and grace when we wrong another. Every one of your close relationships will deepen or dry up, depending on your ability to forgive. Seven years ago, a client gave me a little book titled simply *Forgiveness* by Adam Hamilton. On page fifty-three, Adam drives home a wonderful point around forgiveness as he describes our tendency to hold onto our skewed sense of justice instead.

Because we are human, all of us sometimes do things we shouldn't do. When your partner has done everything or, more realistically, almost everything possible to take the pain away, to lift the rocks from your backpack, then it's up to you. Sometimes we decide that we like to collect these old rocks. We hear our partner earnestly seek our forgiveness, but we decide to hold on to the rock. We decide that we like it in our backpack. At that point, the offended becomes the offender. That's no better or fairer than creating it in the first place. Both repentance and forgiveness take effort. Yet both are works and expressions of LOVE.

Want a hand to hold onto that deeply connects with you? Lean toward grace, not justice. Develop the habit of expressing your regret and repairing. Develop the habit of accepting your partner's attempt at repair and gracefully forgive. Let go of the rocks, not the hand. You choose what you hold onto. Your choices have consequences. Jesus, thank You for Your offer of grace. Thanks for taking my rocks and placing them "as far away as the east is from the west."

Is your heart filled with gratitude or get even? It's easier to forgive another when our heart is filled with grat instead of get, right? What do you think? Slow down and reflect.

Day 66: Avodah...

Avodah literally means "work, worship, and service" in Hebrew, as Kitty shared recently with the BTL Band. Your work, friend, when done with an informed head and full heart, is much more than just a labor or even a labor of love. Our work together is designed as an act of worship and service toward humankind. Our work, friends, is sacred.

Today, perform your OPUS in service to your clients and as an act of worship to God. Today, let a sense of *avodah* inform your every hour. We do not have to work, friend. We get to work. We are designed to work, and work is meant for our good and for the greater good. We are not all designed for the same work, but there is some work perfectly designed for you. You know this when you allow your spirit to taste flow and lose yourself in *avodah*. When you and I lose ourselves in *avodah*, we come out of it feeling more, not less. Good work promotes a good tired. What do you feel after a full day's work? Slow down and sit with this for a while. Slow down.

You are not meant to labor in vain. You are meant for good work, work that literally means work, worship, and service to you. Becoming BTL is a journey toward *avodah* for you and me. It's work—make no mistake about it. It's the kind of work you aren't sure you want to start, but once you do, it's the kind of work you don't want to stop. *Avodah*. Thanks, Kitty, for the reminder.

Live hard. Love harder.

Build Your Courage

12 ESSENTIALS OF PERSONAL EXCELLENCE

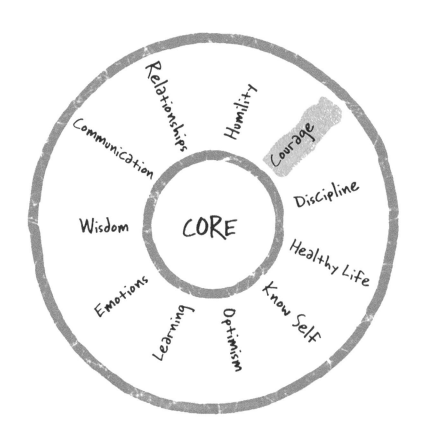

Grappy's Builder's Journey

In the fall of 2014, I was introduced to Chet Scott and his life-changing leadership model, **BUILT TO LEAD**. I had no idea of the incredible journey I was about to embark on. As a head coach for twenty-eight years, there was leadership before BTL and after BTL. There was marriage before **BUILT TO LEAD** and after **BUILT TO LEAD**. There was fatherhood before BTL and after. They were different. After was far better. Not easier, just better. BTL challenged and refined me in every way. Not in the way a motivational speaker or inspiring movie does—this is far deeper, with the purpose being permanent transformation. Not surprisingly, BTL takes work. The model founded on love demands acute pain over chronic pain. It demands a deep internal search of who we are and what we stand for. BTL rips at our CORE. It refines us and feels so good.

I believe Chet because he's an example of what he teaches. He lives BTL. I learned that by spending time with him and observing him. I worked out with him, watched him, and chose to bring him into my inner circle. That was one of the single best decisions of my life. He shares truth in love with me and those I love. He is a truth-teller in my life and has moved Ohio State wrestling forward. It has been no surprise that my teams have finished first, third, second, second, and second at the NCAA Championships the past five seasons. Our results reflect our love for and connection with each other. BTL connects. It builds.

There are no coincidental occurrences in this life. We run into those in our daily thoughts and actions move us toward. I am grateful for my path crisscrossing with Chet's and BTL. I have been challenged, educated, uplifted, and pushed to be more. Not more than I can be but all I can be. Thank you, BTL. Thank you, Chet Scott.

Day 67: Do more...

"Happy families are all alike; every unhappy family is unhappy in its own way."

From its very first sentence, Tolstoy's *Anna Karenina* made young Teddy think. He, not unlike the mass of men in our day or in Thoreau's, was leading a life of quiet desperation. You see, young Teddy had already lost his father, mother, and his lover, Alice, who had just given birth to their first child. Young Teddy ran from his feelings and fueled himself with busyness. He ran for the open spaces of the West and took up residence in the Badlands. He ranched and rode his horse. It was a good distraction for a while.

Eventually, young Teddy realized his running away wasn't the road toward his OPUS. So, he wandered back east and found solace and friendship in his childhood friend, Edith. Three weeks later, this friendship turned into an engagement of sorts. His newfound love opened his heart to his life's work. He was a progressive reformer and wanted to do his part to bridge the gap between rich and poor. Teddy wanted to hold big business to a better standard. So, in 1886, he would begin a long and life-changing career in politics. He was twenty-eight. For twenty-two years, he would serve his country eventually in its highest office as president. President Roosevelt, that is.

Every day in BTL practice, we aim at embracing paradox. We believe faith and doubt are bookends—tough and tender too. We don't run from feelings, and we don't run over the vulnerable either. We make people do what they can, and most don't like being pushed. We focus on the few and, just like you, get bummed out by the very ones we're trying to help. It feels good to embrace the paradoxical truth about family too. Happy ones are not always happy. Marinate in the blessings, not the bummers. There will always be those that stand in opposition to your way. Remember, you are not in their hands, and you are not their plaything. You are in God's hands. Marinate on whose you are, friend. Change your mind. Be like young Teddy and make your body, mind, and spirit do what it can. Serve your family, team, and extended community. Do more than you think. Happiness is a great outcome but a horrible aim. What paradox do you want to embrace today?

Day 68: Sparta's way...

In 480 BC, King Xerxes led his Persian army into the "hot gates" at Thermopylae, where they destroyed thousands of Greeks, including 300 Spartans led by King Leonidas. Persia won the battle. The Greeks, however, would win the war. We Americans should study the Greeks and, in particular, the Spartans. Our founders did. Our founders understood we owed a debt of gratitude to Sparta and her most prized product—her people. Sparta produced strong men and women. Study them.

The Greeks, inspired by the standard of valor set by the 300, defeated Xerxes later that year at Salamis and saved Western democracy from dying while yet in the cradle. Without this act of valor, our founders would have had no framework to study, no model to learn from, and no courage to be gained from a tiny nation taking a stand against a world superpower. Sparta's way paved America's way. Sparta's way…

We seem to have forgotten Sparta's way in our modern world. The root problem on most teams today is an abundance of weak, survive-at-all-cost kind of people. The weak think it's manly to manipulate for personal gain and play quick-and-dirty politics and poker with other people's lives. Leaders who tolerate this weakness create a culture devoid of deep trust and produce a tax of time on the system. CYA (cover your ass) culture adds more meetings and fewer decisions. Performance suffers, as the focus is inward and around weak people. Symptoms carry the day while roots continue, quietly, to decay. This is not Sparta's way.

Today, study some history, namely your own. Root out your cowardice and your avarice and take a stand. Stop hoping somebody else will do it. Become one of the few who stand. Throughout history, it's always a few strong men/women who inspire their teammates and jolt us out of our passive, weak status quo. These few turn our attention outward, toward our collective aim, and return us to a healthy status that rewards risk-taking, deep trust, and an abundance of action—productive action in particular.

Your team needs you to be the woman we both love and loathe because of the edge you set. Your team needs you to remind them who they are, why they're here, and where they're going. Are you?

Day 69: Kiss the ring...

You, friend, have an abundance of fear. You mostly fear loss. You fear the scourge of power if you feel you lack it and the loss of power if you think you've got it. According to Aung San Suu Kyi in *Freedom from Fear*, this is another human universal. "It is not power that corrupts but fear. Fear of losing power corrupts those who wield it, and fear of the scourge of power corrupts those who are subject to it."

You would think we'd have evolved beyond this by now. I mean, come on, my fellow American, you may be almost as powerful as JLo, but neither she nor you even come close to the absolute power of Elizabeth I back in the sixteenth century. Queen Elizabeth decided life and death for her subjects. The most powerful woman in your world cannot legally kill you, friend. So, why do I constantly hear clients, BTL team practice participants, and endless others ranting about the most powerful person in their world, forcing them to either "kiss the ring" or die?

The answer is always misplaced, irrational fear.

You are free. I suggest you begin to act like it. Stop complaining about your leaders to colleagues, partners, bartenders, and baristas. Talk to your leader. Get your stuff together and give her a logical, well-thought-out argument for what you want. Give her your logic for why this is the best way forward. Listen to what she has to say. Understand her perspective, because as your leader, she's got a wider one than you. She may listen. She may not. She may be persuaded. She may not. Regardless, you are free to decide whether to continue playing ball on her team or not. You do not need a better leader. You need to be better. Your problem is you are filled with fear. Your problem is you fear the scourge of power and ain't nobody threatening to cut off your head. Nobody's asking you to "kiss the ring."

Slow down and reflect. Slow down.

Day 70: No mo...

You most likely need to tell yourself no mo. You see, leader, most of you continue to simply do mo. You do more, do more, do more, and then wonder why at the end of the workday, you head home telling yourself and then your loved ones—no mo. What's up with that? Home and loved ones deserve mo, don't they? I mean, what's the point of going home to be with if you've got nothing left in the tank? BTL leaders dream and do, remember. BTL leaders say no mo to many good things so they can go home and still have energy to be with. You see, simply being with those you love requires energy and attention.

Many people assume my mantra is no mo.

I manage my time like it's all I've got to give. I say no mo a lot. This allows me to give other BTL builders the ability to say *thank you* to me, and *yes, please,* to you. Some of them have grown their business to such a degree that they, too, are saying no mo, and other BTL builders and clients are able to say thank you to them. You see, friend, you don't become a master at your craft by constantly piling on mo. You build mastery by building better projects, whether they be human, hangers, helicopters, or hugely beautiful developments. You build mastery by saying yes to the best. This is simple, not easy. The more mastery you build within and with your aim, the more the world is going to show up and want a piece of you. You are going to have to say no mo to many good things. Say no mo, anyway.

Leave lots of good work on the table of life. Leave juice in the tank for the trip home tonight. Take your strong CORE and authentic OPUS with you and use it as the compass and map that it is. Stop saying yes to over-scheduling everything as if success is defined by doing more. No mo.

When was the last time you said no mo and meant it? Mo of this, please...

BUILT TO LEAD | together we transform

Day 71: Toto...

Our culture has made *The Wizard of Oz* a story you can't forget. What you may forget is it starts with the town leader—Miss Gulch—coming to collect the dog who bit her. The conflict in the movie begins when the man, Uncle Henry, wusses out. Aunt Em doesn't speak the truth because she believes it would compromise her Worldview. Toto, the dog, is the truth-teller.

So, Dorothy leaves the shire to protect her best friend, Toto. Along the way, she discovers who she is. Her strong CORE keeps her on the yellow brick road, and she never loses sight of her aim, her OPUS. Along the way, she encounters real adversity, always with Toto by her side. The crucible doesn't melt her; it makes her. The Wicked Witch of the West? Not so much. Dorothy becomes the builder of the scarecrow, tin man, and the cowardly lion. Toto runs under the radar but is the catalyst behind the whole story.

Dorothy could not go back to the place of "there is no place like home" if she had not deeply changed. My role is to be your Toto of sorts. I'm comfortable in this role. It fits me. I believe God wired me for this work. I feel his presence when I bark, bite, and when I see you on your Builder's Journey. My aim is a lot like Toto's, you see, I am not the hero: you are. All my barking and biting is an attempt to inspire Y.O.U. to leave your current state, discover your dream state, and have the courage to follow your yellow brick road.

So, if some Miss Gulch has put you in a basket, follow Toto. Dare to jump. Build your strong CORE. Author an authentic OPUS. Follow your yellow brick road and inspire others to do the same. The BTL builders are not here to change you into something you're not. We're here to help you get comfortable being who you are. We're comfortable being your Toto. How 'bout you, Dorothy? Are you ready to become BTL?

Day 72: Pruned...

Friedman's gem titled *A Failure of Nerve* is one of my favorite leadership books. Slow down and read this non-anxiously.

> A leader must separate his or her own emotional being from that of his or her followers while still remaining connected. A leader needs the capacity not only to accept the solitariness that comes with the territory, but also to come to love it.
>
> Next, I began to establish leadership seminars emphasizing the self-differentiation of the leader rather than focusing on method and technique. But this type of focus on self-differentiation, I also learned, is not easy to foster, especially when society's own emotional processes are in a state of regression. Frankly, it is easier to focus on data and technique. Yet, at this point, I am convinced that to the extent leaders of any family or institution are willing to make a lifetime commitment to their own continual self-regulated growth, they can make any leadership theory or technique look brilliant. And, conversely, to the extent they avoid that commitment, no theory or technique is likely to succeed for very long.

We are here to provide the conditions for your growth. So, when you notice a BTL builder spending an inordinate amount of time pruning, watering, and focusing on a few, all you've got to do is ask for attention to come toward you. As gardeners, we will prune as best we're able, but it's an imperfect process—it will hurt. Remember, pruning is a good idea until you're the one being pruned.

When was the last time you asked to be pruned?

Day 73: Fear and gratitude...

John Newton, slave ship captain and author of my dad's favorite hymn, "Amazing Grace," had this to say as he looked back on his life. "I have reason to praise God for my trials, for, most probably, I should have been ruined without them." Aleksandr Solzhenitsyn, the author of *The Gulag Archipelago* who suffered in Russian prisons for years, wrote: "Bless you prison, bless you for being in my life. For there, lying upon the rotting prison straw, I came to realize that the object of life is not prosperity as we are made to believe, but the maturity of the human soul." Viktor Frankl, who you've heard me quote almost endlessly, authored *Man's Search for Meaning* and in it describes the hell of Nazi concentration camps. He also, surprisingly, said, "In some ways suffering ceases to be suffering at the moment it finds a meaning, such as the meaning of sacrifice. Those who have a why to live, can bear with almost any how."

Every day in the work of BTL, we encounter good men and women with seemingly overwhelming struggles. Whether the struggles involve themselves, their partners, their business, or their babies, these struggles overwhelm nearly all of us in the moment. Sometimes, it's helpful to understand a broader perspective than the current struggle affords. Remember this, friend. When you suffer, your vision and perspective shrink. Your normal brain develops acute tunnel vision and focuses exclusively on what is wrong. Train your brain to open a bit wider when it tells you to go turtle and sit in your pain.

It might be helpful to remember a little wisdom from Jack, an OSU grappler, during practice eleven. "You can't be grateful and fearful at the same time."

Learn from John, Aleksandr, Viktor, and the Jack and Jill's around you. Broaden your perspective. All humans suffer. When you find yourself in a pain prison of your mind, train your brain to focus away from fear and toward gratitude. Get through the current iteration and stop the brain from flying forward. The sun will rise. Thanks, Jack, for bringing your perspective to practice four years ago. You're going to make one L of a lawyer.

See beyond your immediate circumstances today. Remind yourself of your CORE Purposes. Focus your mind on your why.

Day 74: Agitate...

Alright, let's imagine you recently had your first heart attack. After a successful surgery, the convo with the cardiologist goes somewhat predictably: start exercising, stop eating this or that, lower hyper stress, and whatever other behavior modifications the doc thinks are pertinent to her patient. The patient nods along in agreement. "You're right, doc" is the most common response. Makes sense. The doc is, in fact, right. Here's reality, however. Roughly 90% don't do anything. They continue to do exactly what hurt their heart in the first place. Ninety percent! Here's why.

Nobody consistently agitates them, and they haven't learned to agitate themselves. Deep change is irritating, uncomfortable, and sometimes acutely painful. Most humans cannot do it a lone, and most humans don't have a truth-teller (pain in the ass) beside them. Builders are agitators. Stop trying to be nice, friend; be kind instead. Kind is love in action. Sometimes you're tender and sometimes tough.

If you have a loved one whose heart is under attack, you might not want to be so nice and passive. Tough love might set you and them free. BTL Builders agitate, not because they want to but because it's the right thing to do. Last night, during practice ninety-three with a great team, I agitated a number of them because I want them to reach beyond themselves. In my opinion, this team is capable of more. I believe in them, so I risk losing them by pushing them to keep reaching. The elite never stop reaching. They understand the gig is chasing another small, incremental gain and then another. So, they agitate themselves and don't tolerate a lack of agitation.

> When deliberating on a negotiating strategy or approach, people tend to focus all their energies on what to say or do, but it's how we are (our general demeanor and delivery) that is both the easiest thing to enact and the most immediately effective mode of influence.
>
> —*Never Split the Difference* by **Chris Voss**

Agitate yourself today. Make yourself do something that scares you.

Day 75: False harmony...

Today's politically correct culture produces an abundance of teams with false harmony. They look good. They are not. They never fight in public and don't know how to fight in private. They avoid conflict. These teams underperform. We teach them to fight to improve performance instead of fighting to prove a point. Big difference. Here's why false harmony is the norm: it's just a little bit easier. How much easier is it for you to talk to your coworkers about your verbally abusive peer than to talk truth directly with them? It takes courage to face your fear of rejection and run into conflict with your spouse, friend, coworker, or leader. Here's good news…

Most conflict is simply a conversation to be had.

As we learn to speak truth in love, we discover most of our conflict is a communications problem, a translation issue that two people can usually solve on their own or with the help of a virtuous builder. The energy that comes from a diverse, innovative, results-oriented, passionate group of people will generate heat. Heat will fuel high performance and also produce heated moments. Deal with it.

During these healthy conflicts, high-performance leaders mine for more. Normal ones bury it. Problems do not age well. Conflict doesn't resolve itself. You and your team are not part of some self-healing system. Problems must be addressed to be eliminated. The sooner they're addressed, the more simply they are solved.

So, leader, move toward your team members. Expect conflict. Valuing false harmony is the problem. You and your team are building a culture. Make it a culture that values truth, not the lie of false harmony. Make it a culture of hard-won, true harmony that fights to improve performance, not prove a point.

What conflict is crippling your culture? What are you waiting for?

Day 76: Fatigue to full...

Life is an energy management problem.

Recently, I challenged a team that's feeling some battle fatigue to write out their top five drains. You know, the things that when you see them on your schedule, you suddenly feel sick to your stomach or, at a minimum, some sense of dread. It did not take the team long to fill the page with five fatigues. Next, I asked the team to write out five things that make them feel like the Energizer Bunny. You know, that feeling when you see something or someone on your schedule, and you say to yourself that you can't wait, can't do it enough, and can't believe your good fortune. These are, in BTL parlance, your love tos. Love is pure energy.

As the team shared their top fives, it was amazing that at least four out of five were things in their control. I mean, come on, man, do you really have to go to big parties that drain you like a tiny reservoir in Death Valley? I used to dread doing stuff like that until I discovered that big parties could be energizing if I did them my way and deeply connected with a few instead of mindlessly mingled with many. I had more control than I thought. You do as well, friend.

Life is an energy management problem, and it's your problem to solve. Do not blame being overwhelmed on others. Take responsibility for yourself. Stand up straight, shoulders slightly back. Decide that when you do a drain, you give yourself some sunshine and a short walk in the park (if that's one of your love tos). Do not allow circumstances and other people to deplete you. You choose with whom you mingle, where you work, and whether you're getting better or growing bitter. Choose to feed the Energizer Bunny more than the things that fatigue. More OPUS than labor. More alignment within your strong CORE than with what others think, what's popular, or what once defined you. Life is an energy management problem.

Today, decide to move from fatigue to full. Problem solved.

Day 77: Stand...

This early a.m., I'm reminded of how high the bar is for every leader. As a leader of anything or anyone, you can count on one thing—resistance. Leading creates a rub. Your team doesn't know all the circumstances and situations your position puts you in. Your team simply sees how you respond. The reason we have so few deeply committed teammates around us as leaders is because we leaders are noncommittal. We don't take a stand. Our team sees this moment and is seared. We kneel at the altar of the board, majority partner, owner, or investor, and get exactly what we deserve—a team that does likewise.

Want a better team, friend? Become a better leader. Take a stand. Stop backing down from the fight right in front of you. Stop delaying the confrontation with the bully in your system. Stop avoiding the hard conversation with your teammate who puts up numbers but misrepresents the brand. Start speaking truth in love, being crystal clear with expectations, and holding all around you to performance standards—high standards.

I recently sat with a positional leader lacking courage. He's in a moment of truth and is attempting to dance instead of stand and deliver. He's being bullied, knows it, and not unlike Neville Chamberlain back in the day with his bully, Hitler, is trying to negotiate, placate, and dance with someone who wants nothing but control. You, leader, cannot be given courage in these moments. You must already possess courage. For in these moments of truth, what comes out of us is simply a reflection of what is in us.

You are meant to stand. You are born to become strong. The character of courage must be built. Build your courage enabler—your BTL CORE. Leaders face resistance, just like all of us. The leaders we want have courage, take stands, and do not back down from bullies.

Today, stop dancing in your MOT. Deliver.

Day 78: Embrace it...

Conflict scares almost all of us. However, conflict is not going away as every one of us is, in fact, a house divided. So, if we have conflict within, it only makes sense it's gonna be there with another. Embrace it, friend. Embrace it.

Don't be afraid. Don't get angry, and don't aim at getting even either. Instead, employ educated empathy and give and take care. You'll reach more than just compromise; you will begin to learn how to collaborate. As you turn conflict into collaboration, you will turn one-time foes into newfound friends. You will open more doors and close more deals. You will begin to believe that conflict is really only a conversation to be had. You will stop hiding behind texts and tweets, and you will begin to talk face-to-face as you see the world you don't know (outsiders) as people just like you, only different in an interesting, not intimidating way.

You see, our Purpose at BTL is to be a catalyst for community. The best kinda community is not a clique or cult where everyone seems of similar mind. The healthiest community is where we've learned to come together, surface our conflicts, see other perspectives, and have healthy dialogue that doesn't divide but actually helps us come together and become more whole by coming alongside people who simply have different holes than we do. As we learn to build this kind of trust, we realize that each other's holes are what make us whole. So good when we stop fearing those unlike us and see each other as distinct ones with whom we just might deeply connect. Conflict isn't all that scary when you think of it in this context. Conflict is a conversation to be had. You are not meant to go it a lone, friend.

Today, pick a target and give them a helping hand. Pull them up because you want to.

BUILT to **LEAD** | together we transform

Day 79: Nerve...

Recently, during another strong practice, a client of mine found clarity. He understands why he's got a cancer in his system. He faced the facts and wrote out the productive action to step into the healing process. He has come to an intellectual understanding. Now for the really hard part.

Does he have the nerve?

Toxic people, you see, are a lot like malignant cancer cells. Malignant cells do not evolve, specialize, or colonize with a purpose and are totally un-self-regulating. Malignant cells go rogue and disconnect with the very cells that might help them. They reproduce uncontrollably and are guilty of treason, killing the body that gave them life. Malignant cells don't know when to quit. Sound like some toxic attributes of anyone in your system?

I reminded my client I've had Dr. Cutfirstaskquestionslater cut cancer cells out of my body fifty-nine times. Who wouldn't do the same if cancer cells were discovered in them? Of course, you wouldn't even think about waiting, would you? Why then do so many leaders take so long to cut toxic teammates? The root reason leaders are waiting is simply a failure of nerve. It is one thing to come to an intellectual understanding regarding what must be done. The real question remains. Do you have the nerve?

What cancer aren't you cutting out of your system, leader?

> What really frightens and dismays us is not external events themselves, but the way in which we think about them.
> —Epictetus

Day 80: Wise...

Wisdom is knowing when to respond, if at all, to an injustice. Wisdom is knowing when to turn toward, away, or against. Wisdom is knowing when to sit in the discomfort quietly, when to absorb the tension, when to get curious, when to walk away, and when to roar like a righteous lion. Wisdom is an acquired discipline. It takes time, lots of time. You see, friend, I mostly learn about myself when instructing another. I study, learn, and apply (mostly hard truths the application is focused on me). Fact. I, too, am overly trained to my justice thread instead of those around me. I, too, am a work in process, and the more I learn, the less I know. There's another one right there. Wisdom is found when you focus your words on repairing the relationship, not fixing the person. Nobody wants you to fix them. We all want to feel oneness with someone who gets us.

Slow down and write your thinking. Choose a productive action on something you've been chewing on for a while. Stop ruminating like a cow. You don't have a rumen, you know. Wise women and men choose productive action that is always specific, concrete, and actionable. Focus here. Wise…

Day 81: Fear...

Think about what you'll be like at ninety. None of us is very good at accurately imagining our future. When I ask clients what they most regret as they look back at life, most speak of regret in terms of something they've done. When I change the question to what they think they will most regret at ninety, most speak of something they failed to do, like not spending enough time with one of their kids, their spouse, or not really understanding who they are. When we think of the present, we regret acts of commission, and when we forecast, we mostly think we'll regret acts of omission.

This really doesn't make sense, does it? You see, our brain doesn't keep very good track of our omissions, so as we ask it to remember what we've deeply regretted, it doesn't find anything we failed to do but an abundance of shit we stepped in when we did. This explains why so many of us have an abundance of fear when it comes to doing and not so much when it comes to not. We cannot forecast how we'll feel if we hold onto our conflict with another teammate for years, but we are certain it won't stink as much as stepping into it now. So, we wait. And don't even seem to regret it.

Until we imagine ourselves at ninety.

You tend toward inaction. Act. Admit you suck at forecasting pain—you overestimate it. Embrace acute pain. It'll be over before you know it. Preload your pain response. When you tell yourself there's no out, it's amazing what gets done. When climbing the French Alps, I told myself there wasn't an option to stop on any climb. My mind overruled muscles. I was free to stop or turn around at any point. Nobody was holding a gun to my head. However, my preloaded commitment kept the pedals turning all the way to every summit. It was a satisfying victory over self. You and I are happiest when we choose to act into fear and when we choose PA, acute pain, and commitment. Commit. Do the work. Face your fears by acting into them. Don't give yourself an out. Doesn't make sense at first blush, but it does.

What acute pain would eradicate some of your chronic stuff? Embrace this.

Day 82: Rob Lowe...

I find myself frequently quoting Rob Lowe. I know, I can't believe it either. I read Rob's book, *Love Life*, and fell in love.

Who knew Rob was a history buff, thoughtful politically, descendant of the Hessian mercenaries, and loved the movie *My Dog Skip* (had my bride at that one)? He even hired an acting coach who taught him something very BTL: Actors play the truth. Rob never went to college, but he'll never be the same after taking his son, Matthew, to his east coast college of choice. Rob had his first taste of alcohol at five and his last taste on May 10, 1990 (except for a slip up in the air where he mistook a mimosa for an o.j.). He's one of the few addicts where rehab, well, rehabbed him.

My favorite learning from this book was Rob's coaching to his son when dropping him off at college. His son doubted his belonging at this place of higher education. His son was anxious. He turned to Dad for some solace and courage. Dad, remember, never even went to college, much less one with the pretense and pressure found in this moment. Here's what he told his son in his moment of doubt.

"Never compare your insides to someone else's outsides."

Recently, during BTL team practice with the crazies of Choice Recovery, we translated this thought to the root of so many self-limiting beliefs. Oftentimes, our crazy, negative beliefs begin when we compare our insides to someone else's outsides. We assume, since they look so good on the outside, they most certainly have it all figured out on the inside. We compare and find ourselves coming up small, so we play to it. Instead of comparing, friend, use your psychic energy to build your insides—your CORE. Build within. Instead of comparing and competing, you'll find yourself complimenting, congratulating, and encouraging. Good. So, friend, never compare your insides to another's outsides. Build your insides and fill them with love so you'll have something good to give to someone else. What team couldn't use a few teammates who never compare but instead make it their modus operandi to compliment, congratulate, and give courage?

Slow down and write what you're thinking.

Day 83: Excellence...

Excellence is not the opposite of failure—not failing is. The surest way to avoid failing is to play not to lose, mitigate risk, and do what you know you can do easily. Excellence demands more, much more.

Excellence is you at your best and can only be obtained when you do more than you think, take calculated risks, fill your heart with more love than fear, surround yourself with truth-tellers who encourage and correct in just the right ratios, and when you get joy from learning to do hard things well. Excellence is idiosyncratic. There is not another's formula to follow here. We cannot simply imitate another's way and have it lead to our highest, best way. We have to study ourselves, surround ourselves with transformational teammates, deepen our understanding of our way, and enjoy nuancing it to an even better iteration of our way. We have to find joy in the pursuit of better. And not better so we can look down on others but better, so we have more to give others.

Excellence is you at your best. Only you can lead you down this path. Only you have insight into you. Others can help illuminate a blind spot, but only you can let the light in and reflect it out to the world. Others will help, but you've got to decide to let them. God didn't make a mistake when He made you. He made you beautifully and uniquely to become the original you already are. You are free to believe this or leave it all behind. As for me, I'm going to keep working, keep playing, keep giving more than I take, keep laughing, and loving. Loathing? Not so much.

Today, I am choosing to live hard and love harder. I'm choosing better. How 'bout you?

Day 84: Energy...

We are here to flip the script on your energy. You see, friend, humans naturally run on fear. We come in crying because we're afraid nobody's going to hold and feed us. We fear the outsider, future, chaos, and coming and going without leaving a mark. We run on fear. Most of us are more like Harold Abrahams than Eric Liddell. Harold ran because it was his weapon to prove his worth. He ran because he feared he wasn't enough.

Eric ran too. They were the two fastest in the world back in 1919. Eric ran because he felt God's pleasure when he did. He ran like the wind, and as he reached his stride, he would tilt his head toward the heavens, and a smile would crease his face as he pushed himself to the edge of the envelope. Eric ran on his second nature. You see, friends, fear works for a season, two, or thirty even. Love fuels a lifetime.

I want the culture of love, not fear. This is the entire point of BTL practice. Life is an energy management problem. Run on love, friend. Move from a lone toward all ONE—one 'L of a difference. The difference is always love. So, do not settle for what is well within your reach. You are meant to push the envelope and find the outer edges of your capacity. You and I, unlike the rest of the animal kingdom, are at our best when we go against our nature, when we build a better, second nature. The ancients had a word for this second nature: they called it virtue.

What fuel are you running on today, friend?

BUILT to LEAD | together we transform

Day 85: Forecast with faith...

Animals don't suffer from anxiety and panic attacks. They don't forecast the future; rather, they truly live in the moment. So, they experience fear when a predator prowls, but once they outrun her and don't become dinner, they go back to grazing, grinning, and sleeping well that night. We humans may have recurring nightmares after a similar event. Our brain will continue to forecast another near-death moment coming, so we worry, mostly about the future. We forecast the future. The positive outcome of this ability is evident when we have faith in our future. When we believe the future can be better than the present moment, we dream and do. We dream big about what we want to build a better way, a better home, a better future. Our creativity and innovative desires come from our ability to have faith in the future.

Faith matters a great deal. The hopeless do not dream and do. *Why bother?* They ask themselves. The future is one long stint in the dentist's chair. So, they sit there in anticipation of more pain, more drilling, and a pain-filled future. The truth is that as bad as the dentist chair seems in the moment, the pain is short-lived and benefits long-lasting. Once the crowns are complete, our smiles return, the days of wooden teeth and dentures are a distant memory, and we turn our attention to doing whatever it is that we love to do, knowing that our mouth is ready to go the distance.

So, friend, you can forecast your future. The more you forecast with faith, the more you grin and bear those dentist chair moments and anticipate the smiles of a better you when the adversity is over. You are a forecaster, whether you know it or not. Forecast with faith. I mean, come on, man, what's it going to hurt to have more faith than fear? What is the alternative? Just sit there and accept that life is going to drill you? Viktor Frankl survived three years in Nazi concentration camps and saw, firsthand, what happens when faith dissipates. In *Man's Search for Meaning*, he wrote, "The prisoner who had lost faith in the future—his future—was doomed. With his loss of belief in the future, he also lost his spiritual hold; he let himself decline and became subject to mental and physical decay....He simply gave up."

Recognize adversity is coming and know it's not going to defeat you but instead define you. I have faith in my future. I have faith in God. I have faith in a few. How 'bout you?

Day 86: Faith...

One of my favorite T-shirts has two words on the front: Faith and Fear. Fear is crossed out. You and I need more faith than fear if we're going to do anything uncommon. Fear dominates the common man. Faith is the elixir of the uncommon among the uncommon. Fear comes at us in a million different ways. Faith comes from within. Others can believe in us, but it's up to you and me to internalize it and claim it as our own. Faith over fear, please.

Here's a brief glimpse into Bono's (U2 Lead) faith. "It's always the same attitude that wins the day: faith over fear. Know your subject, know your opponent. Don't have an argument you can't win. On the Africa stuff, we can't lose because we're putting our shoulder to the door God Almighty has already opened. We carry with us—this something that's important— the moral weight of an argument."

You have to believe, leader, before your team does. You have to believe, coach, before your athletes do. Faith over fear. Fear is coming fast and furious. Most leaders are walking around on pins and needles, coddling and cajoling in equal parts, and afraid to go all-in on anything. Don't be another common leader filled with more fear than faith. Reverse the modern, mediocre, and mindless means of managing people and projects. Flip the script to faith over fear. Faith is the elixir of the uncommon among the uncommon. God designed you to become uncommonly good while doing uncommonly good work. The uncommon woman appears fearless. She is not. She simply has more faith than fear. Do you?

Day 87: Ghairat...

This morning, the book titled *American Spartan* by Ann Scott Tyson is open on my recently organized desk. I've read this book more than once since reconnecting with my cousin Ann and meeting her husband, the main character of the book, Jim Gant. This book is another anti-whine pill for me. You and your team would benefit from reading good stories like this one that makes you whine less. Here's a taste from page 151.

"We have the best tactics in the world, the best equipment in the world, the best plan in the world, but when this happens it's going to come down to *Ghairat*, your bravery and your courage to fight," Jim said. *Ghairat*—one of the words tattooed on Jim's wrist—was a core tenet of Pashtunwali, the code of behavior by which Pashtun tribespeople lived. It meant personal honor and valor and was the most important measure of character and manhood of a Pashtun tribesman.

Jim has *Ghairat* oozing from his pores. He signs his notes to me, "Strength and honor," and he means it. Jim certainly had the bravery and courage to fight, but more telling, he embodies the root reason behind virtuous bravery and courage. He embodies heart. Make no mistake: Jim is meek, not weak. He is tough and tender, but you would want him on the front of your Hummer. Every BTL team we build beside could sure use a few more teammates with personal honor flowing from a full heart.

What does your team see tattooed on your heart? The bravery and courage to fight for what's right combined with the grit to get it done? Or the passive, political, play it safe and protect mine? Does your team see a leader who demands from others what he demands for himself? Does your team see a tough and tender leader willing to pull and accepting of the push from below? Slow down and check-in with some teammates. Ask them what they see tattooed on you.

Day 88: Beginning to believe...

One of my favorite scenes in *The Matrix* is when Neo stops running. You see, humans have been taught to run from the agents in this movie that is so true to real life. So, when Neo doesn't run and instead decides to stand and fight for what he wants, Morpheus is asked by Trinity, "What is he doing?" Morpheus responds with some CCD magic. "He's beginning to believe!"

This week, I've watched my son beginning to believe, namely in himself. You see, he's been apprenticing for less than a year and has made numerous contributions in BTL team and one-on-one practice but nothing like he's made this week. He's made contributions I couldn't make. He's brought the hammer in his constant calm demeanor when I've hit tilt. He's done it his way and inserted himself in practice without an ounce of hesitation. He's beginning to believe.

Your job, leader, is to believe in yourself and your team. Your job is to catch people giving full effort and growing and give them your esteem. Your job is to challenge them out of your belief and celebrate small moments where they're beginning to believe in themselves. Leaders are believers. Leaders are humans who don't run from a fight and, more often than not, fight for what's right. Leader's belief inspires those around to believe just a bit more. We all start with only a mustard seed of belief, and that's all it takes to build a rock-solid root system.

Are you beginning to believe, friend? Are you believable? Are you inspiring committed teammates or compliant ones? You should know this. Do you? Tay, I give you the gift of these four words: "I believe in you." Thanks, Pascal. Good effort, Tay. Keep working.

Day 89: Winners...

I love word changes—love them. I love the word change from woe is me to work on me. Another favorite is from do or die to dream and do. I also love when we create new meanings or bring clarity to new words. At BTL, we took the Latin word OPUS and created an acrostic, OPUS (Thank you, Shannonball.) O—Overarching vision. P—Purpose. U—Unifying strategies. S—Scorecard for significance.

Here's a word from Friedman that brings clarity to what it means to be a hero. According to Friedman in *Failure of Nerve*, you are a HE/RO. The HE is about the intensity of the stressors. The more intense the stressors, the more opportunity for a heroic response. The RO, you see, is just that: the response of the organism. A hero is someone who uses stressors to improve her response. A hero is made in moments of truth. The more intense/poignant the moment, the more heroic the response. Stop whining about whatever current storm you're facing. Embrace it. Be grateful for it. The more difficult and intense the opponent, the more grateful the heart of a hero. You see, friend, winners relish hard stressors. Do you?

Word change warning. Winner or whiner. Whiners worry. Winners work. Whiners belittle. Winners believe. Whiners blame. Winners work on their game. Whiners aim to alleviate anxiety. Winners relish the pressure to perform. So, friend, look forward to your next hard test. Relish the MOT. You are a winner, not a whiner. You are Becoming BTL, right?

Day 90: Practice 231...

Recently, I saw strength in someone I was seeing for the very first time. Rare. We were in practice 231 (practice one for her), and she took a seat next to the owner to give him some feedback. (She'd been on board for three days.) In the interview, she told him unapologetically she had left with her head spinning. His challenging words left her feeling discounted by what she had done before. I asked her what he said that minimized her past. "He said, 'You're corporate,'" she replied emphatically. Her father had worked for GM. She had taken pride in what he had done. "I'm a UAW brat" was part of her identity. Her new leader's words had made her feel small. So, why, friend, was she sitting in the seat next to him?

Simple. His words hit home.

As she drove back to her place of employment, she knew she had to leave. You see, sometimes, the truth has to hurt before setting us free. Durp's words had lit a fire in her. These surroundings, in this crazy place of Choice, were what she wanted. So, she did what only the few do in these moments of clarity. She acted. This strong, young woman sat down at the kitchen table and told her husband and family she was "weak in her CORE." She had made up her mind: she was quitting her job, and she hadn't even been offered the job at Choice yet. She just knew she had to take the first step in faith and get out of the place that really made her small. She acted in her MOT and quit her job. Quit that day. She got challenged with some hard truth. She could have gotten down on self. Instead, she got hard on self. In the process, she got lit.

Slow down and reflect, friend. What hard truth are you running from? What hard truth are you not hearing?

BUILT TO LEAD | together we transform

Day 91: Talk does not cook rice...

As I look back over nearly twenty years of practicing BTL, the greatest limiter of human performance is more fear than love. Most reading this rant suffer from fearing the scourge of power. Most are like a former client of mine who loved our work and the strength he gained within, but when it came time to fight, he feared his owner more than he loved his life. So, he chose to follow his owner instead of chasing OPUS. He settled for peace and pay. The road to sustainable high performance does not come to settlers.

Most clients tell me half-truths they've been telling themselves. They tell me their plans to stand up for what they want. They tell me they're ready to dream and do. Few, however, have the courage to take the leap when it's time to go. Durp and Brett are leading two of the highest performing companies in Cbus, and both of them had to take the leap. One left a comfortable partnership and one a comfortable family business. Both left because they had more love than fear. This is the heart of high performance, friends. You cannot fake this character. Many former clients of mine talked a good game. Talk does not cook rice (thanks, Rich Reda).

Courage causes sustainable high performance because it is only courage that enables consistent action. High-performing individuals, teams, and leaders are defined by a lifetime of consistent PA. Sometimes, it takes courage to stay. Sometimes, it takes courage to leave. Sometimes, it takes courage to fight for right. Sometimes, it takes courage to live to fight another day. Sometimes, it takes courage to wait. Sometimes, it takes courage to initiate. Sometimes, it takes courage to sell, and sometimes, it takes courage to buy more. Sometimes, it takes courage to speak hard truth, and sometimes, it takes courage to say nothing.

The wise person thinks before jumping headlong. Do not make the mistake of ruminating without action, though. Decide to move because you know this to be true: Talk does not cook rice. What are you thinking? Where are you building courage today? ACT...

Day 92: Jackie and Branch...

The day was August 28, 1945, and the scene was a nondescript office in Brooklyn, New York. Branch was the sixty-four-year-old GM of the Brooklyn Dodgers. He began his crucial conversation with Jackie awkwardly. "Do you have a girlfriend?" led things off. "Do you know why you were brought here?" was Branch's quick follow-up. Jackie had no idea. He thought he was being called up to play for the fictitious Brooklyn Brown Dodgers team. Branch, you see, had been scouting Jackie in secret. He was recruiting the best athlete with the best attitude. Branch was an innovator.

You see, Branch Rickey wanted to innovate by integrating. Racially torn America was hardly ready. Branch believed he could integrate the major leagues, but it would take the right man to make it happen. So, he focused on Jackie's character as much as his bat speed, fielding prowess, or skills around the base path. "I know you're a good player," Rickey began. "What I don't know is whether you have the guts. I'm looking," Rickey continued, "for a ballplayer with guts enough not to fight back." Rickey knew Jackie would have to tolerate abuse after abuse with the superhuman commitment to never, ever hit back.

Knowing Jackie shared his Christian faith, Rickey brought a book with him that day titled *Life of Christ* by Giovanni Papini. He flipped to the passage where Papini puts his spin on the Sermon on the Mount and refers to it as the most surprising, shocking teaching from the Bible. Rickey wanted Jackie to understand the Worldview it would take to keep from retaliating against the racial hatred he was sure to face. Jackie knew this was indeed humanly impossible, but with God's help, it was entirely possible. So, as Eric Metaxas writes in *7 Men and The Secret to Their Greatness,* "Jackie Roosevelt Robinson and Branch Rickey shook hands." Jackie would make history. Jackie would prove he was strong enough to not fight back once over the course of 151 games during his first major league season. Thanks, Jackie and Branch, for modeling the way and showing a hurting world that love conquers all. Thanks for the civil score. Thanks for innovating by integrating.

What, friend, are you doing to integrate those unlike you onto your team? What are you doing to move toward all ONE, one 'L of a difference? Slow down and integrate some more...

Day 93: Gratitude...

My son Taylor told me he's surprised how quickly I figure out the right way forward during BTL practice. Suddenly, sitting next to me in the car ride home, he was just out with it. Recently, Miss went out of her way to make Father's Day feel like it was made for me. She didn't have to. I didn't ask her to do anything special. She took it on herself to take special care of her husband on her Father's Day. My daughter, Krit, notices whenever she hears my name mentioned at her place of work. She makes a simple act of kindness and calls me. She doesn't have to. Hearing her voice is like plugging my heart into an electrical outlet of sorts—it energizes me!

Recently, Bk took the time to text me happy wishes from a land far away. He didn't have to. Another client wrote me his PA from our last practice. I reluctantly took him on a while back and wasn't sure he would do the hard work to become BTL. Dear Lord, was I off track. He doesn't miss an assignment and does each one like it might be his last. He and I are working in the courage essential, and he told me something I already knew. He told me I give him courage, and I give him heart. He, like my son, Miss, Krit, and Bk, is simply krazy kind, at least to me. And as I get older and a bit wiser, I'm beginning to slow down and absorb these simple acts of kindness. Slowly, as I train my mind to reflect on all the good going on around, I find myself a bit grateful and humbled. You see, as much as I may know that those around love and appreciate me, it helps to be reminded.

So, leader, remember to give courage to the strong around you, tell your dad or son something you're sure they've already heard, do something small with a large heart, use your voice to energize, and as you focus your mind on all you have to be thankful for, remember you don't have to do anything you don't want to. Give because you're grateful. Give because you want to. Give. Give. Give. Thanks to my family, friends, and clients for giving me energy today. I'll do my best to pass it along. What are you passing along, friend?

Day 94: Bob and John...

Finding your voice is going to be a struggle. Taking the road less traveled is difficult. Embrace this. At BTL, we use a variety of artists and entrepreneurs to demonstrate this process. Might I suggest you take in a little Bob Dylan when you find the time to watch the documentary, *No Direction Home?* Check him out, finding his voice through the "long piece of vomit" that became the song "Like a Rolling Stone." Watch him turn up his organ player, who wasn't really an organ player either. You will never listen to the song the same.

Next, watch a clip from *Walk the Line*. Take in Johnny Cash walking his jagged line. Tune in to the progression of his discovery. Observe a nervous John earning his big break with Sam Phillips from Sun Records. Sam gave John hard truth when asking if he had something else to play. Sam said: "I don't believe you." Those words made Johnny do what he could. He played from his heart. Sam signed him on the spot. Check out a stronger, weathered version of John standing up to Columbia Record executives. He wanted to go to Folsom Prison. They wanted him to go electric. He decided to dress in all black, and the rest is history. Lastly, watch John find his voice with June and his dad.

John and Bob shared the same bosses at Columbia Records. They were telling Bob to hurry up and finish his electric album experiment. Bob's bosses wanted him to go back to his roots and give his audience what they wanted: folk music. Bob told them no bueno. He turned it up even louder, especially the organ player! These same executives were telling John to stop doing what he had always done. They told John that even Bob had gone electric. John told them what they could do with the tapes from Folsom, and away he went. John went to his grave nearly blind, wheelchair-bound, sick as a dog, and with a failing heart—still singing his song.

Where are you on the road to singing your song, friend? Are you turning up those on your team or tuned into yourself? Dream and do. Now, that, friends, is the direction home. Good.

Build Your Discipline

12 ESSENTIALS OF PERSONAL EXCELLENCE

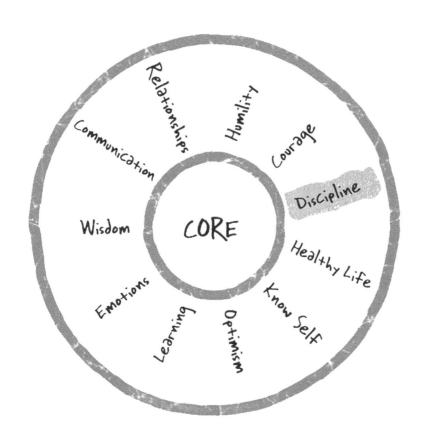

Brett's Builder's Journey

My BTL Builder's Journey began through an experience I had as part of Young Presidents Organization (YPO) in 2009. The YPO format includes small group forums—groups of seven to ten presidents of mid-to-large-sized companies that meet monthly, share best practices, and confidentially advise each other in an effort to enhance our work.

I was reluctant to join this group, but I took what felt like a leap of faith and followed the advice of a mentor. There was a member of my forum I wasn't sure I had much in common with at the time; I wasn't sure we could help each other since we had very different businesses and lives. But of course, he would end up becoming a very dear friend and an instrumental catalyst for my life shifting so dramatically.

It was very uncommon to bring anyone in from the outside, but after a few years of being in this group, Chet Scott was brought in to take our group through a series of exercises. I think we spent the entire four hours doing seven good minutes. I've never seen ten men more uncomfortable in their entire lives. We were asked to make eye contact, to listen, only listen, to be curious, to not think about the next question while the other was talking but to simply listen. At the end of the meeting, Chet left, and our group gathered to discuss the experience and bring the meeting to a close. We went around the circle and shared our final thoughts. The group was unanimous—they hated it!

Except me—I loved it. I loved everything about it. This brought my first BTL learning to the forefront: "It's for the few."

BTL isn't for everyone: it's hard to listen, it's hard to stay curious, and it's hard to get out of your head and "be with," but I knew it was exactly the hard work I needed to do. I immediately tracked Chet down for what would become the first of many lunches at Northstar Cafe and begged him to take me as a client. I didn't know what I was asking for or even what he did. The title "coach" had always been reserved for sports in my mind, but I knew the universe had brought him to me.

I was working in a multigenerational family business as president, but I was really just going through the motions of life. **BUILT to LEAD** would wake me up in a hurry, first with "Discovery," then "Love To," and eventually "Worldview, Identity, and Purpose (WIP)." My Productive Actions and Scorecards would build over time, and I was now on the BTL journey toward my OPUS. I worked with Chet individually at my old gig, and then eventually, it spread to the head of the system and surrounding team. We would read, re-read, write, write, and write some more. We would make sure we had done everything possible to get my current company running on BTL before I considered making any kind of serious changes. Then, after a couple of years, it was clear my OPUS was outside of my current gig. I took the leap. Chet tried to slow me down, but I was on fire. I jumped.

Kaufman Development became my OPUS. It was time to find a home, and after some good coaching, Chet and I stumbled into 30 Warren. We painted the walls of our new HQ with quotes from the playbook—from Bob Dylan, Bono, and Chateaubriand, and even Chet got an important wall. "Leaders are believers" hangs at KDEV and every community we build. We started in New Albany with the Gramercy and then downtown with 600, out to 801 Polaris, and then 250, 80, LVQ, Gravity, and others all came later. I was Chet's first client to build a business from scratch. He was by my side for every interview, every slow to hire, and every quick to fire. We practiced together in teams of faux, fauxnomo, krazies, leaders, etc. And we would have others come along for the ride. 3P from Chet's basement to our community gyms will always be remembered while we try to forget the wall sits for late arrivals. People caught fire and took their own jumps, either here or somewhere else is the mantra. No dead men walking allowed.

Outside of the business, Chet became more than a coach. He is like a father, brother, and friend all in one. He has been there for me as I raised my kids, strengthened my marriage, and reinvented my relationships with my family. There are too many laughs, van fights, and tears to mention. At the end of it all, we always knew we were going to be *good*.

Now, I find myself shadowing Chet, learning what it's like to be on the other side. I'm also learning how to become a coach and returning the favor to others. Having someone like Chet and BTL in my life has been profound. Life-changing is an understatement. It's my turn to do the same for the next generation. We continue to "be with" as my OPUS takes another turn. It's been a joy, all of it—so blessed and in awe of it all.

Day 95: The gap trap...

A client recently told me he has a high bar for his bride and his team. He doesn't believe either can hit it. He's high on responsibility, so he hits it for them. He's growing tired.

I've seen this so many times in BTL, I've given it a label. It's called "The gap trap."

The gap trap is the trap many high performers trip up and fall into. It's created when the high performer decides to fill the performance gap on their own. The right way to lead anything is to increase the skills and capacity of the team. This is a huge problem for the responsible leader. This leader decides the team isn't capable, so they shoulder the burden and will their way forward. Somehow, someway, they close the gap on their own. The problem is starting to build...

Next year the gap between widens. Again, they don't see capacity, so they shoulder the burden and blow a disc or two in the process. This goes on for years and years and years. They eventually burn out or blow up. My client has fallen into this trap in work and life. He is overly responsible in both. He now understands this and is choosing a new PA to dig his way out. He knows this will be more acutely painful in the short-term. And, he knows a high performing team lies on the other side of this acute pain.

The gap trap is created when high performers overly value their abilities and undervalue their teams. It is highly arrogant and usually accompanied with some serious contempt. It stems from a leader's failure of nerve. It takes nerve to give hard truth to those we live and work with. It's much easier to fill the gap on our own. Until it's not.

Do not fall into the gap trap. Fall, instead, into the habit of loving your team enough to tell them the truth, believe in them enough to give them the chance to learn, and challenge them to close their own performance gaps. This works in work and life. It just takes more humility to pull it off at home.

Where are you in the gap trap? Why? What's your stop doing list? Don't know? Ask your team...

Day 96: Genius and dumbass...

I am blessed with being surrounded by strong men and women who trust me to play some small role in making them do what they can. My job is to mostly remind them.

Most humans listen to noise—like the static on an old AM radio. My job is to help them tune into more signal. Today, after reading what amounted to nothing but noise, I reminded my client to tune into his station instead. This dude can outthink just about anybody in his field when he's tuned in and giving his attention to straight signal and blocking out the noise. His problem is he gets distracted by the noise. So, I reminded him this turns him into a dumbass. He's not good at dealing with drama, regulating others' emotions, and winning over others with his eloquent, empathetic words. Fact. We have other leaders on his team who thrive here. So, I reminded him to delegate what weakens him and play to his teammates' strengths. "Stop trying to deal with stuff that drags your ass down," I reminded him as we laughed at how obvious the signal was once we took our attention off the noise. "You're a genius when you play the long, strategic game," I told him with shoot in my eyes. We laughed as he wrote down productive action and freed his mind to focus strategically.

You, most likely, are a lot like my genius client.

You cannot be all things to all people. You know this. In fact, you most likely coach others around you to play the infinite game, focus on what they can control, trust the process, stop resulting, and don't let the naysayers get in your head. You are caught in the knowing/doing trap. You know what to do, yet don't do it. So, leader, tune into pure signal and let the noise roll on by. Trust the strong CORE you're building and focus your eyes on OPUS. Smile at the obstacles in your way and look right past them. Keep your eye on the prize. Make another committed swing. Rinse and repeat. We've all got the opportunity to be a genius or a dumbass. Feed your strengths and become more domain-specific strong. I mean, come on, man, only a dumbass would keep doing what drags them down, right?

Slow down. Write. ACT...

Day 97: ONE—uncommon among the uncommon...

The aim of our work at BTL is to transform ourselves and some of our family, friends, and clients into one, distinct, and deeply connected. We build ourselves first and foremost and understand we are our own worst enemy. We cannot take others further than we've gone ourselves. We are always under construction and live with the mindset of "no finish line." We are some weird dudes, huh? Our aim is not to intimidate you with our strong CORE, self-authored OPUS, and commitment to PoP. Our aim is to inspire you to do likewise.

You, friend, can do more than you think. Like most of us, however, you are limited by your mind and perceived limits. In fact, most humans live life allowing their governor (self-limiting beliefs) to determine their accomplishments. When you engage with a builder, do not expect them to accept your excuses. Expect them to make you do what you can as we live out Ralph Waldo Emerson's quote: "Our chief want in life is somebody who shall make us do what we can." We are that guy!

This work is not a quick fix or hack. Transformation takes time, energy, and a shit ton of effort. You will not be normal, but you will, many times, wish you were. Your mind will want you to stop, settle for the way you are, and accept whatever height you've reached as high enough. Stop those thoughts. Replace them with some thoughts like these from someone very weird, David Goggins, in *Don't Hurt Me*:

No matter what you or I achieve in sports, business, or life, we can't be satisfied. Life is too dynamic a game. We're either getting better, or we're getting worse. Yes, we need to celebrate our victories. There's power in victory that's transformative, but after our celebration, we should dial it down, dream up new training regimens, new goals, and start at zero the very next day.

We, your builders, will model the way. We will start at zero every day. We will act productively. A few of us will grow old but not tired together. You see, friend, we are aiming at becoming ONE—uncommon among the uncommon. How 'bout you?

Day 98: Habits...

According to Charles Duhigg, a habit expert, you don't change a bad habit, but you respect the habit loop. In BTL language, we don't change old habits, but we wire up better ones. I guess we agree with his book *The Power of Habit*: changing habits is about changing routines.

During practice with a team of grapplers, I made them think about changing some of their routines. Many of them have a bad habit of playing it safe when they tire and simply making it to the finish line with more points. The reward, you see, is still winning, no matter what they mouth. I want them to change the routine to going even harder as they perspire and see the reward of learning more about limits, especially perceived ones.

One of my old habits was around eating sweets. The cue was hunger, especially after cycling or intense exercise, and the routine was going to the pantry or fridge and grabbing something sweet like a cookie, ice cream, or both! The reward was a delightful sugar high. The cues in work and life are not the problem. Neither are the rewards. I mean, come on, man, we all get hungry, and there's nothing better than feeling satiated. The way toward excellence is found in finding better routines (better routes) to getting there.

For me, instead of cookies and cream, it's now my routine to grab 85% dark chocolate. Instead of a pure outcome focus to my work, it's now my routine to move toward learning from what went well, not just what went wrong. We learn the most from what went well, especially as you move toward excellence. Think about it. How much can Kyle Snyder or Kollin Moore learn from losing when it only happens once or twice a year? The elite learn the most when things go well. Excellence is a process of small, iterative gains.

Cue—routine—reward. This is the habit loop.

Better habits come from better routines. Better routines come from better rituals. Slow down and evaluate your habits today. Change one of the habit loops limiting your performance.

BUILT TO LEAD | together we transform

Day 99: Edge, execution, and excellence...

"We don't rise to the level of our expectations; we fall to the level of our training."

—Archilochus 650 B.C.

"Under pressure, you don't rise to the occasion; you fall to the level of your training."

—Navy SEALs.

It's easy to have an edge for a while or when you have something to prove. Keeping an edge, especially when your team is leading or winning, is another thing. You've got to train harder once you reach the pinnacle of your work. You can't simply let them turn it on when they think they have to. Your job, if you're a leader, is to make your team train with an edge, relentlessly focus on execution, and commit to excellence. Your job is to make them think they're behind even when they're way ahead. Hard to do, regardless of the sport or market. The best way to create a sustainable edge with your team is by kicking your own ass. Nothing keeps the team on edge more than the edge of their leader. Study Alexander the Great, you'll see.

What's your level of training? How about your teams? Today, take them higher. Make them do what they can. Start by making yourself...

> The knowledge and skills the athletes accrued from "life" traumas and their ability to carry over what they learned in that context to novel situations certainly appears to affect their subsequent development and performance in sport. Talent needs trauma.
>
> —*Faster, Higher, Stronger* by **Mark McClusky**

Day 100: One warrior...

Every morning, I remind myself to live my Principles: model the way, embrace pain and suffering, and embody truth in love. I fail to live these perfectly every single day. Mastering the art of living is about progress, not perfection.

When starting BTL back in 2002, my aim was to transform every client and every one of their teammates into ONE. I've changed my belief and no longer aim at transforming everyone on their team. Studying history has changed my belief. I no longer believe transformation takes a team. Transformation doesn't even take a few. Transformation is possible with just one—one warrior, that is. This has transformed my thinking and our BTL practices.

Heraclitus, back in the fifth century BC, said this about the power of one warrior on the battlefield. "Out of every one hundred men, ten shouldn't even be there, eighty are just targets, nine are the real fighters, and we are lucky to have them, for they make the battle. Ah, but the one, one is a warrior."

You, leader, are one warrior. Your team must see shoot in your eyes for them to have any hope in theirs. You are the one. Everything rises and falls on leadership. Your job is to model the way, embrace pain and suffering, and embody truth in love. Your job is to focus on changing your behaviors and your beliefs about others. Stop expecting a team of warriors behind or beside you. Be one. Your belief will transform you and at least a few of your followers. Focus on the few. Transform from a lone toward all ONE— one 'L of a difference. Mass attracts mass. One warrior attracts another.

What are you attracting, leader? Are you focused on the 5X performers or the ones who shouldn't even be there? Are you worth catching?

BUILT to LEAD | together we transform

Day 101: Burst toward our best...

I am a cyclist. Nobody pays me to ride—I just love to. Actually, I love to go fast. I ride all year long and rarely go fast. During the spring, I always wonder if this is the year that it won't happen. I ride and ride, the speed stays the same, and the negative questions begin. I want a linear progression to my effort. It doesn't happen. I start to lose hope. Suddenly, seemingly out of nowhere, my performance bursts. We don't progress in a linear fashion. We suddenly lose weight, gain speed, or grasp a concept. We need to trust the process.

Nassim Nicholas Taleb, in his book, *The Black Swan,* explains,

"Nonlinear relationships are ubiquitous in life. Linear relationships are truly the exception; we only focus on them in classrooms and textbooks because they are easier to understand. You play tennis every day with no improvement, then suddenly you start beating the pro. Your child does not seem to have a learning impediment, but he does not seem to want to speak. The schoolmaster pressures you to start considering 'other options,' namely therapy. You argue with her to no avail. Then, suddenly, the child starts composing an elaborate sentence, perhaps a bit too elaborate for his age group. I will repeat that linear progression, a Platonic idea, is not the norm."

We burst.

At BTL, we practice hard using the 12-8-4 framework as our process. Our practices are nonlinear and feel like fits and starts more than anything. We have a front-row seat to bursts. We watch people breakthrough. We watch people experiment. We watch people fall. We watch people grow. So, friend, don't worry if your performance gains are nonlinear. Trust the process. Keep riding hard. Speed will come. Keep embracing the pain and suffering. Keep encouraging those around you and pulling others along. Keep looking beyond yourself and see the beauty amongst the beast. You will not break, but instead, your performance eventually will burst. As long as we keep working, we'll burst toward our best.

Trust your training today. Focus on the process, not the outcome. Good.

Day 102: Problem solvers...

Every leader gets exactly the team they deserve. Want a better team? Become a better leader. Everything, and I mean everything, rises and falls on leadership.

Recently, a strong leader/doer learned a bit more about how to take his signature strength and build it into his teammates. This dude is sharp and gets stuff about as fast as any I've built beside. We review something once, and he gets it. This is not normal. He is elite and knows it—normal. We are working on him building his teammates so they won't need him. The very thought of this causes him to shudder. I mean, come on, man, who doesn't love having a team that depends on them? It feels good to be the man, you know.

Your job is to build a team so strong they tell themselves, "I got this. What does leader XYZ do, anyway?" Your problem, if you're a normal leader, is you've still got an ego to feed. Stop enjoying the sense that you're needed and create a team that doesn't need you. Teach them how to think. Make them solve their own stuff. Do this by mastering the art of greeting their problems with questions, not solutions.

Your job, leader, is not to solve problems. Your team does not need you to fix them, and neither does your bride, brother, or partner, do they? Your job is to build better problem solvers. Stop telling them what to do and master the art of getting them to figure it out themselves. Your aim is to surround yourself with strong, interdependent teammates who come together and collaborate. Your aim is to create chemistry and flow, right?

Stop giving out answers like candy and replace them with curious questions. Stop solving problems and start building problem solvers. Where do you want to start today? Tell me more...

Day 103: Adjust your mirrors...

Today, when you get into your car, take a glance at your two side-view mirrors and notice what you see. Most will see the back half of their car. What is the value of having side-view mirrors if you have them pointed so far inward that all you see is what you already know is there? Does it make sense to turn your head while traveling in a different direction at over 70 mph? Nope, it doesn't. Here's a prevailing reason why we do. A long time ago, in a driver's training program, some authority figure told you there is a blind spot in every car. There is no blind spot. The bad news is if you adjust your mirrors properly when there is nothing beside you, you will see nothing. Apparently, most of us would rather see our own vehicle.

In life, you and I have blind spots.

As much as we try, we cannot know everything about ourselves or the team around us. We need the help of true friends to even understand who we are. We rarely ask those who know us to tell us something that might actually help us speed on down the road. We would rather see ourselves the way we've always imagined ourselves, even though we know we need help. We would rather just shove our weight around and albeit, bruised and battered through the process, keep the pedal to the metal. We change lanes in our car by turning our heads. We don't trust our mirrors.

We choose the direction of our lives in much the same manner. We don't have mirrors (truth-tellers), and we don't trust the mirrors we have or the mirrors we have don't trust us. Adjust your mirrors. Seek feedback early and often. Develop at least a few truth-tellers and routinely ask them to illuminate your blind spots. The hardest part is hearing the truth the first few times. As you listen, process, and adjust, you will get better. You will begin to see feedback as the breakfast of champions and get after it every day. Trust will build. You and your team's speed will too. Very cool.

Who are your mirrors? How often do you look their way? How often do you make adjustments? Adjust your mirrors, friend. Today.

Day 104: Performance—Aggressive...

High performers, remember, are performance-aggressive, never passive.

The world is full of faux performers who have succumbed to fear and decided, instead of playing with truth, they will play it safe. These performers mask their thinking and feeling and take just a fraction too long to open their mouths or get their shoulders in front of their defender. Instead of speaking truth or finding themselves in space, they say nothing or find themselves without the ball. I see this every day. So will you, most likely, when you look in the mirror.

Your job, leader, is to face your fears and, in moments of truth, remain aggressive. Do not hold people to a higher standard—hold them to your standard. Too many leaders hold their team to a lower standard than they hold themselves. What is up with that nonsense? Don't get me wrong—I do not want you leading in a bullying way but aggressive in a performance way. Aggressive because you are here to perform at the highest level and attack your work with your whole heart and complete effort. High performers are performance-aggressive. The world is full and getting fuller of passive-aggressive people.

We need Y.O.U. to become one of the few with a dream worth pursuing, a dream worth your best, a dream that will energize you to bring aggression toward your performance. Every day, people are watching you and seeing how you're performing when away from home. I hope they see you going for it, getting your shoulders in front of whatever defender you happen to face, and making those around you do what they can. Passive, loose cultures are great when your aim is chill. Performance-aggressive cultures are the ones you want when your aim is thrill. The thrill of victory that is.

Where are you going to be performance-aggressive today? *En brera.* No alternative.

Day 105: Toughness...

You do not build toughness by taking the easy way 'round. You do not build a tough team by coddling them.

I have lots of tough clients at BTL. There are not many soft leaders that succumb themselves to Becoming BTL. Every one of my clients is tough, at least on themselves. Here's an interesting observation through eighteen years of building tough clients—very few are as tough on their team as they are on themselves. Most coddle their team. You build tough teams by teaching them how to do hard things well. You build tough teams by holding them to a high standard. You build tough teams through a rendering process that spits out those who can't take it.

According to Bill Self, coach of the Kansas Jayhawks, the opposite of toughness is soft.

Soft is thinking you should have help on defense, and that thought causing a letdown. Toughness is the anticipation that you won't get help, so you do everything in your power to stop your man. If the people around you are tough, and they are willing to do tough things, I think you are more likely to be tough too. That's good peer pressure. Peer pressure can make us do things we shouldn't do, but it can make us want to do the tough things, the right things, too.

You don't build tough teams by yelling, screaming, or demanding they do more than they can. You build toughness by modeling the way, embracing pain and suffering, and embodying truth in love. Stop expecting less from your team, BTL leader. You didn't get to your position by taking the easy way 'round, did you? Follow me. That ought to be enough. If you want to learn more, check out *Toughness* by Jay Bilas.

Day 106: When no one sees...

Let me be clear. According to Anderson Ericsson, the dude responsible for the 10,000-hour rule (which his research claims is not a rule but a guideline, by the way), the greatest predictor of going from good to great is not what you think.

Ericsson's research, covered in his worthy read titled *Peak,* debunks a number of myths regarding the lynchpin of high performance. All kinds of elite athletes are not well-coached. Great coaching counts, just not as much as we think. A whole bunch of world-class performers did not start early in their chosen profession—doesn't much matter. And the world is full of world champions who took forever to focus single-mindedly on their craft. The number one predictor of who makes the jump from good to great?

The hours dedicated to solitary practice.

Turns out, most athletes work hard during team practice, but only the best of the best put in a volume of training when no one sees. Our own research at BTL agrees. The only athlete to interrupt Coach Ryan (Grappy) and my one-on-one practice was World, Olympic, and NCAA champion, Kyle Snyder. On multiple occasions, there would be a knock on the door, more like a pounding, really. I'd open the door to see a shirtless Kyle smiling from ear to cauliflower ear. "Hey man," he'd begin all apologetically, "there's nobody else in the room, and I really need a spot for this next lift!" So, of course, we would march down to the room and spot him for however long it took. He did this all the time.

The greatest predictor of your greatness is no different. It comes down to how much you want it, doesn't it? Saying you want to be great is what all kinds of well-intentioned performers preach. Doing the hard, extended efforts, especially in solitary confinement, is what separates the wheat from the chaff. Do more solitary practice. Of course, for this to become common practice, friend, you've got to love more. Nothing fuels sustainable, solitary practice better than more love. Again, strong CORE, authentic OPUS, and the discipline to PoP it out, especially when no one sees.

Day 107: Triple-A...

I have an abundance of overly responsible clients, thank God. Can you imagine your system being run irresponsibly? Recently, a sleep-deprived, problem-saturated, and highly responsible client of mine greeted me at our crack of dawn practice with a cry for help. He told me his story. I sat, sipped my coffee, and simply tuned in. He spoke. I listened. After a number of minutes and a handful of curious questions, I reminded him as follows:

You are responsible for you. You are responsible for leading your family and your teams, but you are not responsible for their lives. You are a leader, not a king, and clearly not a very good God. You are responsible to model the way, embrace pain and suffering, and embody truth in love. Do this daily, and you will walk the earth in peace. You won't walk perfectly or painlessly; you'll simply stand supported by your strong CORE and walk in the direction of your dream—your OPUS. A few will come alongside. We call this process the Builder's Journey, remember.

My client smiled, thanked me, and felt better immediately. His brain is a bit cluttered, as is yours. He's holding too many unfinished problems, projects, and priorities in his cerebrum, and it no likee. Remember, my friend, you must build within first before you get busy packing your bags to leave the Shire. Only the strong survive on the Builder's Journey. Many make the mistake of jumping before building a strong CORE and authoring an authentic OPUS. Oftentimes, these jumps are away from someone or something instead of toward anything authentic, aligned, and awesome. Triple-A is the *one* you want.

CORE, OPUS, PoP—is it time for a rinse? Time to go 3-for-3 if you want to get to the majors.

Day 108: Marry the mundane and try new things...

The greatest predictor of whom you'll marry? Proximity. We have a bias toward those who live nearby. We also have a proximity bias when it comes to dealing with people entering our club, charity, company, or community. We don't want strangers in our club or community because we've grown close to our clique and fear the outsider will mess it up. This is the root behind sibling rivalry. Ohio State and Michigan are rivals. Ohio State and Kansas? Not so much. Ohio State and California? Not much at all. Proximity matters. Make sense?

If your aim is excellence, you'll need to fight against biases—proximity, either/or, availability, actor/observer, focus and blindness, and many more. We're naturally biased toward what we know. This is why travel, challenging books, new things, and people unlike you are so good for your brain.

Routine is good. You are what you habitually do. And break out of your high-performance habits every so often. Recently, the 3PP team and I took a trip down to OSU Jennings Center and walked around doing stupid things with heavy sandbags. We climbed ropes that scared us and wrecked me. We did sprints across soft wrestling mats that felt like running in sand. We mixed it up for ninety-seven minutes to the point of depletion. We tried doing new things to strengthen our COREs. It wasn't pretty, but it was good.

Remember, you can only do what you have learned to do. Stop allowing your brain to fixate on what's top of mind—what's proximate if you will. Marry the mundane, try new things, take risks, and force yourself to deeply change. Excellence is tasted when you're squarely in the challenge zone, just this side of panic, like I was halfway up my last rope climb, hanging by a thread. This same recipe of marrying the mundane and trying new things might be an accurate predictor of who stays married. What are you doing to challenge your status quo? When was the last time you cheated toward your husband or wife? Funny, huh, how hard it is to marry the mundane and try new things. Do it anyway. Done so.

Day 109: Cascade meaning...

I'm not a big believer in most of the popular business practices. Most businesses cascade goals, especially numeric ones. In other words, the top dog sets the global goal, and the country managers take their piece and cascade the goals down the line. So, by the time you have your annual goal-setting meeting with your manager, she already has her number and simply gives you yours. Your goal's been set for you. This is not a goal.

The only goal that gets a human going is the one she sets for herself. Remember another law of human nature—we mostly listen to our own voices. Yours and mine? Not so much. So, leader, if you want to create a team of 1%'ers, don't tell them what to shoot for. Instead, connect them to your big dream that is well beyond this fiscal year's objectives or goals. Connect them to the O of your OPUS, your Overarching vision. Dream big and do lots of little things in service to it. Dream and do.

Inspire the team to do likewise. The best way to create 5X performers is to stop trying. Unleash them. Set them free. Unbridle them. Launch them. Inspire them with your big dream and get comfortable, just this side of chaos. Yeah, baby. During team practice 281, I heard a team of high performers dreaming and doing in alignment with their leaders. We were blown away by the clarity with which they recounted his OPUS and recited their own. No wonder they are not normal and setting records. You see, friend, this leader has figured it out. He doesn't sit around cascading goals. He's elevated the aim. He's cascading meaning. OPUS, your labor of love, is a meaning maker. Cascade this. Cascade meaning.

Is your OPUS a meaning maker for you?

Day 110: Everydayness...

BTL believes that excellence flows from ancient principles, and not much is new. Here's an example: If you're aiming at elite status in your domain, you must love the labor. Excellence is hard work and only sustainable if you love its pursuit. Secondly, you need mentors—lots of them. Nobody is as smart as everybody. You are not meant to go it a lone. Masters are mentored by like-minded men and women who make each other do what they can.

And excellence requires everydayness. Excellence isn't achieved with a sometimes mindset. Excellence isn't turned on and off. Excellence is an everyday endeavor. This is why all ancient teachings mostly remind us. We need daily discipline more than another offsite, retreat, event, or degree. The elite practice an everydayness with excellence. They understand we don't make giant leaps in performance. Instead, it's an iterative approach. Excellence is baby-stepped out iteratively with your commitment to everydayness. This is where most of us fall short. We think we know stuff, can do stuff, and don't comprehend the everydayness of the elite. Rest and recovery are important—don't get me wrong. We want our clients to rest and recover when they've lit all their matches. And we want them to embrace the everydayness of their aim.

This is why the O to your OPUS has to be so freakin' big and ooze out of your pores. Ain't no way to dream and do and dream and do some more unless the O (Overarching vision) is worth the everydayness of effort. If you want excellence, you will develop an everydayness around effort. This is nothing new. You know this. It's just easier to go hard for a while and ease off a while longer. It's the everydayness that separates the elite from the good and well-intended. Everydayness is the rigor of excellence. Simple, not easy. You know this, right?

Everydayness. Is this the habit of your heart?

Day 111: Obstacle...

My favorite author had it going, down the drain, that is, when he wrote his most famous work. You see, back in the late 1940s, C.S. Lewis was hitting an all-time low both personally and professionally. He had just been passed over for two major promotions at Oxford, his best friend died suddenly, and his brother (living with him at the time) was battling alcoholism. As if these weren't obstacles enough, Mrs. Moore (caregiver) had developed dementia and flipped from giving to taking care. Lewis' dear friend Tolkien had also gone south on him as he accused Clive of stealing some of his literary ideas. Yikes. The college of English is divided on what direction to go, and Lewis finds himself more isolated than ever. So, what does he do?

He does not give up, and he doesn't stop working. Nope, he does not. He keeps working and decides to double down on his effort, even though at the time, he's overwhelmed with his workload. He escapes into an imaginary world and begins writing with almost reckless abandon. The result?

The Chronicles of Narnia.

Yes, friend, whatever obstacles are in your path, however large they loom and difficult the way appears, remember the ancient wisdom from our stoic friends: the obstacle becomes the way. Obstacles are a fact of life, friend. Your mindset determines if you use it to energize you and your mates or let it use you. Use your obstacles. Use your imagination. See beyond those looking past you. See beyond the wall. Keep your eyes on the summit and see the beauty, not the beast. Embrace the pain and suffering as you labor not in vain but in passionate pursuit of your aim. Your obstacle is your way when OPUS is your aim.

Rinse your OPUS until it's squeaky clean and crystal clear. This is your way forward.

Day 112: Specific, concrete, and actionable...

You do not get better learning things, but you can get better doing things. If you become a client of ours, you will quickly habituate productive action. You see, friend, PA must be specific, concrete, and actionable. Many well-meaning clients have big desires but lack tiny disciplines. So, when they get excited with learning they want to put in play, I always ask them to write it out. Most often, they write something vague, enormous, and undoable. I've come to believe this is simply the human's reaction when they discover something they want to work on. We decide to go big and end up going home.

You do not get better by going big or going home. You get better in baby steps. You get better by doing small things over and over again. You get better by choosing baby steps of PA and left foot, right foot your way forward. You get better by small, iterative gains. So, when you learn something, you can't wait to convert into action, start small. Choose a baby step and make it specific, concrete, and actionable. Don't overwhelm your increasing elastic mind, friend. Masters understand there are no giant leaps for mankind, only baby steps that eventually land you on the moon.

So, if you want to stop eating sugar completely, start by cutting out cookies and ice cream today. Make it through this iteration. Tomorrow, decide to cut out cookies, ice cream, and your morning donut. Get through this. Don't let the brain rush ahead to Wednesday, and don't start thinking about cutting out sugar all at once. Start small. Make it specific, concrete, and actionable. Keep reaching. Slowly, you're tightening it up. We get better by doing better. We get better by marrying the mundane, iterative process of progress. Specific. Concrete. Actionable.

Look at your PoP. Is it specific, concrete, and actionable? Tighten it up today.

Day 113: Acts 19:20...

Back on a Sunday in 2019, I gathered with Mom and a few others for some worship together at Mom's church. This is the same church we attended growing up. Attendance is down, and the average age is up. Whenever we've worshipped there, it's been life-giving as you can't help but pick up some energy and love radiating from Mom singing and smiling next to you. This Sunday, a new pastor (William) was leading this congregation and leading it well.

He took us through the elements of an exciting church. He shared scripture from the book of Acts, and he told stories about John Wesley, the Apostle Paul, and Jesus. He spoke from his heart without any notes and, like a true mathematician, tied it all together with solid logic and sound reasoning. He laughed at the current state of the church in America and reminded us not to worry about it. He said the aim at growing attendance is the wrong recipe. Systems do not grow because we focus on growing them any more than teams win when we tell them, "Just win, baby." Growth is an outcome. You and I cannot control outcomes. Focus on what you can control, friend. Build a stronger sense of self, become more CORE-centered and self-controlling, receive God's love, become a conduit (not cul-de-sac), and let His love flow through you. As William reminded us back in 2019, focus on the controllable.

Slow down and reflect on Acts 19:20: "So the word of the Lord grew mightily and prevailed." Focus here. God, help me marinate on your word and let it grow mightily in me. God, help me stop the incessant focus on outward growth, wins/losses, and other short-sighted aims. God, help me play the long game and play it with love. Where, friend, is your focus? Are you building sustainable strength within or overly fixated on "just win, baby?" Slow down and sit with this for a while. What's growing mightily in you, so you prevail?

Day 114: En Brera...

June 7, 1967, is a huge day in history. You see, June 7 marks the date the Jewish people took back their city for the first time in over 2,000 years. Yes, you read correctly—2,000 years! King David, you know the one from way back in the Old Testament, led the last Jewish occupation. In 1967, this small but mighty nation took back what is rightfully theirs and did it against all odds—and alone. Nobody came to help her. The UN did nothing. The French—nothing. British? Nothing. The US did nothing.

Israel stood. Alone.

Yet, somehow, on June 7, 1967, the Israeli flag flew over the Western Wall. The Israeli leaders from Moshe Dayan down to Uzi Eilam are amazing examples to study and learn from. As they gave orders throughout the war that sounded impossible and even crazy, they "anded" a Hebrew phrase at the end, *En brera*. This is the mindset of high performers. Few can relate because only a few are willing to go it alone. The Israeli army is filled with the few, by the way. You see, they have no alternative. A nation that is nine miles wide at the waist can't afford an army with only a few all in. Study them and apply your learning. A good place to start your study would be to read Steven Pressfield's beauty, *The Lion's Gate*. You'll learn the Hebrew phrase these Israeli leaders embody, *En brera*—no alternative.

Study. Learn. Apply. Alone.

What, friend, are you willing to stand alone for? Where do you need an *En brera* mindset? Write down a few potential no opt-out areas in your work/life. Pick a target to persevere. Remember who you are—you are Becoming BTL. So, get up. Stand. Give yourself no opt-out, no alternative. *En brera*. Now. Do. The. Work.

Day 115: Done so...

We work with a number of elite teams in commerce, community, and sport. Even among the elite, there is an epidemic of anxiety. I'm certain this is not a news flash for most. The root causes are biological, environmental, cultural, and too complex to cover in one day. I am convinced a great starting point to ease your anxiety is to stop the endless, negative chatter in your head. Too many elite individuals invest way too much time thinking endlessly about last night's mistake, today's tests, and tomorrow's expectations. They chew the cud over and over and over. Remember, the main reason we live in a society that doesn't reflect much is because when you begin to practice slowing down and sitting with stuff for a while, it sucks the life out of you. Reflecting is a great idea until you start to do it. So, do this instead.

Throw up thoughts on paper. Stop holding onto your bullshit and thinking it's going to smell better if you give it more time. Get it out and notice the pattern of your thinking. Anxiety is a complex epidemic, but when you develop the habit of writing out your thoughts, you eliminate the endless bullshit banter. Your brain will have one less mess or two or three to chew. Clarity comes when the brain has less bullshit with myelin wrapped around it and is able to build neural networks for productive actions instead. The power is in your pen. Write your thinking. What PA is your writing revealing?

Kit Carson, way back in the day, was an uneducated hill jack who turned himself into a legendary American scout and leader. He learned eighteen Indian languages and tracked anything and everything. He led expeditions to Oregon and California that forever changed our continent. He had every reason to worry and panic; instead, he simply performed. His habit was that when he had a thought, whatever it was, he turned it into action. His internal mantra was two freakin' magic words: "Done so."

You can do likewise. The more you write, friend, the less you'll ruminate, and the more you're going to gain energy from reflection that's been turned into action. Nike says, "Just do it." What about you? What needs to be done so today? *En brera...*

Day 116: What the hell...

Herman and Mack, a couple of psychologists whose research is found in the book, *Willpower*, coined a phrase that describes many of us. When we've blown a commitment we've made to ourselves, whether it's a diet, a drink, a drug, or a dirty deed of any sort, we tend to say to ourselves, "What the hell." Herman and Mack, not surprisingly, coined this the "What the hell effect." Once you say this in your head, the gluttony, sixth drink, and the affair all transpire as your unrestrained impulses run wild. Virtue, you tell yourself, will jumpstart in the morning. Not good.

Want to stick to your disciplines, whatever they are? Set up "bright boundaries" that your mind cannot miss. Nothing to eat after 8:00 p.m. and one cheat meal is a bright boundary. Set yourself up to be monitored. Weighing yourself every morning is monitoring. Texting me a cheat is too. Dealing with my questions is another. We don't break old habits. We wire up new ones that are better. This takes time. The most disciplined people on the planet spend very little time exercising their willpower. They've come to understand exercising willpower takes too much energy. So, they invest their willpower in building bright boundaries, so they don't have to think when the chocolate Little Debbie cakes start talking late at night. Funny, huh?

> As, the body uses glucose during self-control, it starts to crave sweet things to eat — which is bad news for people hoping to use their self-control to avoid sweets. When people have more demands for self-control in their daily lives, their hunger for sweets increases.
>
> —*Willpower* **by Baumeister & Tierney**

What the hell. Where do you crave more discipline in your life? Why? What are the patterns to your problem? What are their roots? How are you establishing bright boundaries? How are you monitoring yourself? Who is holding you accountable? Tell me more, my friend. Tell me more.

Day 117: The gold standard...

The gold standard for deliberate practice, according to Anders Ericsson, author of *Peak* and the original researcher behind the science of expertise, is found following a very specific structure and order. Here are his seven steps with a BTL twist.

1. Deliberate practice develops skills that have long been established as foundational for mastery. For instance, if your aim is sales mastery, you must practice listening to find the hidden need, desire, or problem to solve.

2. Deliberate practice takes place outside the comfort zone and requires the participant to practice stuff just beyond their reach. This demands near maximum effort and is not particularly enjoyable in the moment.

3. Deliberate practice aims at specific goals, not vague "keep getting better" bullshit. We chunk out the gains through a series of small, incremental gains.

4. Deliberate practice is, well, deliberate. The participant must fully engage with all attention.

5. Deliberate practice involves feedback, lots of feedback, from the work, and from a virtuous coach/builder. Feedback is worthless unless the participant uses it and makes minor adjustments, mostly while alone.

6. Deliberate practice depends on effective mental representations. One of the best ways to build stronger mental representation for whatever you're working on is to visualize the speech, conversation, design, or crossover dribble right before you go to sleep.

Lastly, deliberate practice always involves what we call marrying the mundane. You've got skills, but you identify baby steps and keep popping them out when most folks are long gone. Deliberate practice is not about going for some pre-prescribed number of hours (10,000 hours, for instance, is a myth) or some pre-prescribed number of reps. Deliberate practice is a lifestyle, like my latest re-read of *Peak*. It won't be my last. Masters, remember, keep working.

Are you deliberately practicing to master your craft, friend?

Day 118: Domain specific...

We've all heard the saying, "Jack of all trades—master of none." We tend to believe it's true, yet how many of us know the specific skills required to master our craft, whatever our craft is? If you're an athlete, for instance, you don't build general skills in athletics, do you? Of course not. You build skills in golf if you're a golfer and skills in wrestling if you're a grappler. If you're a business owner, CEO, or leader in your company, do you know the necessary skills to master whatever leadership role you're in? Are you building domain-specific expertise in your industry with your team and peers?

Lead anything, and you've got hours and hours and hours of study ahead of you. You've got to build lots of mental representations so you can sift through the noise and clangor of ideas and find the one or two you and your team have got to do. You see, one of the lynchpin skills for every leader is the ability to find the melody line. You can't find the recurring theme without knowing your industry, team, competition, CORE, and OPUS. You must know your history, financial forecasts, and, most importantly, your friends. Nobody is as smart as everybody, and you'll require the help of a few friends if you're chartered with leading anything. Oh, yeah, you'll have to sniff out saboteurs too.

Masters in the art of leading love their craft and their team. Seems like leaders just might have to be masters of all trades. Are you beginning to see why leading has to be a labor of love? What skills are you building to lead like a master? Who is helping you become a master at leading your teams? Are you humble enough to ask for help? Slow down and sit with this for a while.

Day 119: Elle Woods...

During another truth-telling practice with one of my favorites, I grabbed his attention by comparing him to Elle Woods. Yeah, Elle Woods from *Legally Blonde*. You see, my client is doing his job the way he sees his leader do his. He's winging it and counting on his charisma, conviction, and competence to carry him forward. So, I hit him with some hard truth about his preparation habits. They suck. He's got to prepare a lawyer's argument and come into each and every meeting like someone with something to prove. He's not the senior leader. He's not the main man, at least not yet. Like Elle, he could be if he takes himself a bit more seriously.

Elle's problem wasn't that her leader and colleagues didn't take her seriously. The bigger issue was she hadn't taken herself seriously. It all changed when a truth-teller told her to stop letting one pr#$& hold her back. In that MOT, she saw the light and began to believe she was not just a blonde; she was legally blonde. My client and I concluded practice today, laughing at the irony in my analogy. He got the message. I made him play it back to me and decide on his baby step PA to begin building his legal resume if you will.

Remember, leader. You don't get what you want. You get what you earn. And you've got to prepare a lawyer's argument if you want to earn the right for one of your ideas to be taken seriously. Prepare like your life depends upon it. Most professionals who appear to be winging it aren't. They've just prepared for so long and mastered their craft so well that it appears effortless. Woods did the work. How 'bout you?

Day 120: Damn few...

We believe you cannot become BTL without lots of hard training. This is why we designed discovery to be so difficult and require all to complete the eighty-one questions prior to beginning the building process. Throughout history, the greatest teams have been assembled and built roughly the same way: through the severity of their training. Ancient self-help expert/trainer Thucydides summed it up succinctly: "We should remember that one man is much the same as another, and that he is best who is trained in the severest school."

Come train with us. Expect it to be hard. Like anybody who practices with us discovers, difficult training has its rewards. And oddly enough, the reward comes when we embrace the idea of "not yet." You see, the real rewards follow years of severe tests in whatever is your world. The BTL builder and framework provide the fertile soil for growth so you'll be ready to pass your life exams.

Come train with us. Do not wait to begin training when the test arrives. This is what the masses do and then complain in the crucible and cry out for help when none can come but the resources from within. Do not wait. Train. We will make you do what you can. You will discover new limits and push through them. You will discover new Passions and ignite them. You will discover new Purposes and fully realize them. You will attract a few.

The BTL school is a severe test. You can pass it with the help of a trained builder, a few teammates, your hard-earned strength within, and your authentic aim toward an OPUS of your authoring. Come and train. Come and make us do what we can too. Together, we transform. Always together. Becoming BTL is for the damn few. Is it for you?

Day 121: Sunday discipline...

A discipline we are seeing great results from is writing every Sunday the top three to six PAs for the following week while reflecting on the top PA from the week that just was. Here's the step-by-step recipe.

1. Grab your CORE document and read it. Remind yourself who you are becoming. Look at it and think about this past week. Did you behave in alignment with your beliefs? Where are your integrity gaps? Who is helping close them? Write. Rinse if necessary.
2. Grab your OPUS and read it. Was your OPUS the focus of your week? Did busy-ness get in the way? What will you stop doing so you can live the life you want at the place you call work? Look at your strategies. Did you have great PA in each strategy? Are there strategies that sound good but don't have PA behind them? Are there PA you never seem to have energy for doing? Write. Rinse strategies, if necessary.
3. Look at the PA you wrote for the past week. Evaluate your performance as simply pass/fail. Write.
4. Slow down and think strategically about your upcoming week. Think. You've invested so much time and energy into Becoming BTL. Don't go through the motions now and let someone else think for you. Don't ever think you've arrived and have it all figured out.
5. Send your writing to your builders. If you're a client of mine, I expect this every Sunday night. Send it to another too. I've been amazed at the insight and inspiration that comes from a teammate who sees their leader modeling the way.

Your CORE and OPUS are not static. They are not meant to be one and done or even one hundred and done. They, like you—are alive. As long as we're alive, we're evolving. The more we change, ironically, the more calm and consistent we become. The Sunday discipline isn't magic. Sunday discipline is a framework for slowing down and building consistent quiet, reflective time into your life. Look back as a discipline. Be hard on evaluating yourself without getting down on self. And look forward to another great week living in alignment with your CORE, OPUS and PoP. Sunday discipline is a great PoP. Is it yours?

Day 122: Cook better...

At the tail end of Lauren's leader practice forty-eight, Nick shared his learning. He shared his learning in the form of an old catchphrase about handling the heat. He gave his spin, which was good. "If you can't handle the heat, get out of the kitchen or learn to cook better."

You see, friend, the universal language spoken between teammates and leaders is the language of performance. If you find yourself unable to get through to the one above you, whether they're your manager, CEO, chairman, or just some chump with an oversized title, don't struggle with trying to get your message heard. I'm not saying you should stop talking altogether—just stop talking to your leader when you sense your words are nothing more than wasted breath. You've always got options—at least two. You can get out of the kitchen. Fact. You are free to leave. You can learn to cook better. You can always let your cooking talk for you. You choose.

Every day in BTL, we challenge teammates to talk/write to themselves. We encourage them to gain clarity with what skills they need to master to dominate in the kitchen. All leaders worth their salt listen to the universal language of performance. So, if you find yourself not getting through, try cooking up a storm. When your food is selling like hotcakes, feel free to talk to your leader about whatever's sitting in your craw. Until then, if you've chosen to stay in your current kitchen, choose to cook better; bitter, not so much. Make sense?

Cook better.

BUILT to **LEAD** | together we transform

Day 123: Persist and resist...

I'm loving the reread of my Penguin classic, *Epictetus Discourses and Selected Writings*. Epictetus was born into slavery, achieved freedom (in more ways than one), and taught philosophy most of his life. He didn't write a book but made such an impression on one of his students that they wrote a compilation of his lectures, so his thoughts live on today. Epictetus (55–135 AD) words are still relevant today. Here's but a small, small sampling for your digestion this morning.

Epictetus thought the darkest vices were the lack of persistence and lack of self-control.

Without persistence, we don't endure hardships well, and without self-control, we don't resist pleasures. Instead, we over-indulge. Sound familiar, friend? Epictetus, during one of his CCD lectures, said it well: "Two words should be committed to memory and obeyed by alternately exhorting and restraining ourselves, words that ensure we lead a mainly blameless and untroubled life. These two words were persist and resist." Well-spoken, Epictetus. Persist and resist.

What struggle are you enduring well, friend? What sweet indulgence are you resisting? Again, the ability to resist impulse is how we humans build virtue and defeat the natural slide into any number of vices. The natural decay of my body is a great reminder that only a few among us have the fight to finish strong. God, help me persist and resist while receiving and giving love. Persist and resist. You and I tend to be better at one than the other. Where, friend, do you need to build the discipline to persist and resist? God, help me resist the temptation to indulge and rationalize it away. God, help me resist.

Day 124: 20—40—60...

20-40-60 is the BTL recipe for slowing down and speeding up. We recommend our clients embrace this discipline six days a week. Twenty minutes of reflection/meditation/prayer. Forty minutes of reading/writing around something meaty to make you better. Sixty minutes of exercise. Some clients embrace this. Most don't. We do. You see, if 20-40-60 is good for our clients, it's got to be more, not less, for the builder.

My commitment is 30-120-90. I do more to have the energy, strength, and conviction to make a few do what they can. Fact. If you want to teach anything, get comfortable being a perpetual student. "Give me six hours to chop down a tree, and I will spend the first four sharpening the axe." Thanks, Abraham Lincoln. What are your disciplines to stop the do, do, doing, and take some time to sharpen?

I recently reread David Epstein's latest book, *Range*. It's about experimenting and playing before finding your domain to dominate. I just read how Van Gogh made Lincoln's path to the presidency look like it was linear. Van Gogh tried and failed at nearly everything for thirty-four of his thirty-seven years on this planet. He killed the last three with his paintbrush. His discipline of intense observation led him to paint masterpieces like "Starry Night" in next to no time. It just took him a while to find his canvas and medium. He killed it because he kept playing/experimenting. Nobody had to tell him when he found it. The same is true for you, friend.

So, keep working, keep playing, keep experimenting, keep observing, and keep going. A burst is coming. 20-40-60 just might slow you down so you can see your starry night. Slow down and sit with this for a while.

BUILT TO LEAD | together we transform

Day 125: Rituals...

Routines are overrated. Habits don't tell the whole story. Habits cannot convey heart.

The litmus test is not as simple as looking at your routines. The world is full of mediocre performances produced by people with great habits. Huh? Habits matter. The commitment behind them matters more. Tommy Amaker tells the Harvard basketball team over and over, "Don't mistake routine for commitment."

We mostly miss this and evaluate ourselves on our routines. The 1% evaluate themselves more critically. They study the details. They make changes before the market, or the enemy does. They lead the charge, which oftentimes means they lead the change. They constantly ask themselves for more. It's not enough to just show up. Showing up is a start.

Showing up with your bayonet fixed, so to speak, is the one you want. You've got to love what you're fighting for to taste the beauty of your commitment. Turn your routines into heartfelt rituals. See the sacred element in mastering your craft. Sense the privilege of this present moment practicing with your team. Commitment turns routines into sacred rituals. This is the heart of high performance.

Don't believe me? Study Alexander the Great. Steven Pressfield's *The Afghan Campaign* is a good place to start.

Build Your Healthy Physical Life

12 ESSENTIALS OF PERSONAL EXCELLENCE

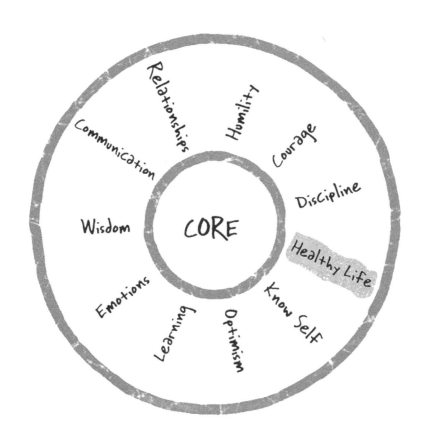

Jiggles' Builder's Journey

My journey begins about 100 yards from where I sit right now in German Village in Columbus, Ohio. Funny how life comes full circle.

I was born the oldest of two into a loving family and was told from the time I could start speaking that I was a mini-adult. I have always gravitated to those I admire who are ahead of me in years and experience, as I view their insights about life as a guide for my own.

The first major challenging period of my life started about the fourth grade when I quickly gained a lot of weight and unneeded fat. This lasted until I grew a couple of feet in early high school but forever shaped my personality. It was during this time as the ultimate outsider during my formative years where I fell in love with trying to understand people and how they think. Most importantly, it taught me to always be humble and kind.

As I entered high school and refocused on my health, I committed to never let my health be out of alignment again—a principle I failed for a period in my early twenties but has been re-established with vigor today.

During this same period, on my fourteenth birthday on the 11th day of September in 2001, like most Americans, my life was forever changed. This was such a vivid moment of truth for me that I remember the birthday wish I made that year was to be able to help those people who were tragically hurt and killed. It was in this moment I knew I was going to dedicate my life to serving others with the gifts I was given—I just did not know how yet.

My college and early professional career were one of experimentation both in work and life. Born from many generations of entrepreneurs, I knew my journey would take me there, and it did quickly.

I started my first company in 2010 in Park City, Utah, after a short one-year and one-day stint as an auditor with KPMG (which could not have been more out of alignment with my CORE strengths) and

BUILT TO LEAD | together we transform

stumbled through the immense challenges of building something from scratch, especially at the ripe age of twenty-three. In reflecting on this time, I realized I was chasing all the wrong things in life. External goals, validation and acceptance from others, wealth and status, and a whole slew of other hedonistic tendencies.

Amid that journey, in May of 2012, I experienced another moment of truth when I got a call from my brother saying our father had collapsed while giving a speech in Indianapolis. I rushed home from Chicago, where we were attempting to scale up our struggling startup, and I knew our lives would never be the same again. He was diagnosed with a stage-four glioblastoma, an incurable brain cancer. My parents were divorced, and it was time for me to become the CEO of his care and the family, which I chose to step into and was vastly unprepared for what lay ahead.

During that remarkable eighteen-month journey of caretaking for my father, I came apart at the seams as my coping mechanisms were constantly self-destructive in hopes to mute the pain and stress. I was living in what we call integrity gaps with my physical, emotional, mental, relational, and spiritual health while trying to take care of my father and play a peacekeeper role among the family at large. However, in hindsight, this was when I finally transitioned from a boy to a man, cemented by delivering my father's eulogy in November of 2013.

In the couple of years that followed, I slowly put the pieces back together, primarily through reworking my entire set of habits and behaviors. I had to leave our startup behind in support of my father to help him manage his role in a family business, a private family foundation created by my Great Uncle Harold in 1959, that I now serve as a trustee of today with a portion of my time and energy.

I also doubled down on the city of Columbus, the place I grew up in and where I had a deep passion for changing the trajectory of its future. After re-immersing myself in the community, especially the entrepreneurial community, I found myself in a role to help establish a Columbus office for an Akron-based private equity group that had a portfolio of real estate, operating companies, and early-stage venture capital investments. I hadn't quite pulled my life back together, but I gave all I had and realized I had the potential to become a high performer.

It was in late 2015 that I had the chance to meet Brett Kaufman, a man whom I respect in so many capacities in work and, more importantly, in life, and we began to discuss ways we could collaborate in both. He and the team at Kaufman asked me to join their rapidly growing company, which I couldn't wait to accept. It was at that moment that the trajectory of my life finally changed from sleepwalking to waking up.

At KDev, I was quickly introduced to another transformative figure in my life, Chet Scott of **BUILT to LEAD**. At Kaufman, we believed investing in your people holistically will hopefully light a few souls on fire. This growth mindset was the main thread in our culture and fueled us to accomplish some bold ideas.

We accomplished many things as a team at Kaufman, including building the first intentional community in Ohio, The Gravity Project, that has now evolved into a ten-acre urban neighborhood that will eventually encompass over 1 million square feet of residential, office, retail, place-making, community spaces, and programming that bring people together around unique growth-oriented experiences. It is an extension of who we were as human beings at Kaufman Development, and it's remarkable to see the community that's emerged at Gravity.

A couple of years into my tenure with the team, I had another transformative experience at a **BUILT to LEAD** Practice during a seven-good-minutes exercise with a new teammate, whom I instantly fell in love with and is now my soul mate, Lauren. A few short years later, we were married and expecting our first child, and she has been the biggest blessing in my life. She is my ultimate truth-teller.

After four years with the KDev team building our dream and after 250 **BUILT to LEAD** practices under my belt with Chester, I became clearer on my OPUS to serve and build into the next generation of leaders in this world. I knew it was time to step away from the business and team I love to follow this calling. **BUILT to LEAD** transformed (and, I would argue, saved) my life, and it's now my life's work to build into others in a way that creates teams built around a higher purpose while living in alignment with who they are. My hope is that these leaders and teams will positively impact the world in which we live for many generations to come.

Day 126: Einkorn wheat...

The discovery of Einkorn wheat reads like a movie script. You may remember back in 1991 when the world discovered "Otzi," a frozen man from 3400 BC found intact high up in the Italian Alps. Scientists have been studying his remains ever since. In his grip, pouch, and belly were Einkorn wheat seeds. We had no idea what they were.

Carla Bartolucci was born into a poor but productive American family, lost both her parents very young, studied abroad in Italy, and discovered more than her love for food (found her husband too). When she had her daughters, her passion took a turn. Her daughter was sickly from the start, and nothing seemed to help. Carla tried everything and went to all kinds of doctors in search of a cure. Nothing seemed to work until Otzi stumbled along. Carla heard about the ancient grain found in his hands and, like the bold entrepreneur she is, picked up the phone and called them. The scientists were more interested in studying the grain than in making anything out of it, so they agreed to give her some seeds to play with at the farm. So, play, she did. This grain is very different from the hybridized product we're all familiar with. It's much harder to work with but much denser in nutrients—much denser. In fact, Einkorn wheat is loaded with proteins and minerals that make it a superfood.

Fast forward to today. Jovial Foods is the name of Carla's thriving Einkorn wheat business. Her products are sold around the world. Her daughter's ailments and chronic illness symptoms are gone since Carla began to cook only Einkorn pasta, bread, pizza, and other Italian goodies for her. Countless others have found her products superior, all because Carla was curious. We went to visit Carla in Lucca, Italy because Miss has a mind very much like Carla's. My bride had been ill for over a year when her curiosity connected her with Carla and Einkorn wheat. We went in 2018 as a celebration of Missi's return to a healthy/physical life we weren't sure was possible eighteen months back. If you haven't checked out Carla's products, you are missing a key ingredient to your wellness. The junk we market as grain is a joke. Get her cookbook at Jovialfoods.com. You'll be better fed and better for it. Food, remember, is our first medicine.

Day 127: Lead the afflicted and addicted...

Humans do not hear well when hurting, and most humans are hurting most of the time. This has become a bolted-on belief in my Worldview.

Humans listen to one voice above all others—their own. The addict listens to his own voice no different than the affluent, the homeless, the young, or the very old. So, if you want to help your teen, teammate, parent, or peer, remember, they don't want to hear your persuasive speech as to why they ought to stop or start something. Ask them questions. Stir their thinking. Start hypothetically speaking. Start slowly and follow the trail they take you up or down. Most addictions are born during the transitions of life. Tune in. Addictions are born and bred during times of transition because these times are filled with feelings we'd rather deaden than deal with. Addictions are a feelings disorder more than you and I tend to think. The world wants us to categorize addicts as people with a particular problem—a character disorder.

See your friend as someone hurting and hiding.

Change your mind about what's wrong with them. Tune in. Lead anything, and you're going to find yourself leading affluent, afflicted, absorbed, abused, and addicted. Learn to turn toward, non-defensively listen, and understand them. This is going to take a lot of time, energy, and love. You cannot muster this love when you, too, are all a lone. You just may be the friend who helps heal their hurting heart before the addiction spirals into further dysfunction and eventually out of control. Addictions form when we feel a lone and dissipate as we feel a turn toward another. The addict desperately wants to transform from a lone toward all ONE—one 'L of a difference. The addict needs a hand to hold on to; maybe it's yours.

Slow down and sit with this for a while. No easy answers. No one-size-fits-all here. Nobody has the time to do what makes perfect sense but makes no cents. Nobody normal that is. Be one of the few who listens and loves as she leads. Lead the afflicted and addicted. Live hard. Love harder.

Day 128: Mount Pomeroy and Krit...

July of 2015, Krit and I made a memory at Deer Valley Ranch, Colorado. When we drove the four-wheel drive up the rocky road and jostled Krit and me from side to side, I knew it was the beginning to an epic day. Moments later, Cowboy Bob parked the Suburban, and out we hopped. Brandon, Krit, Bob, and I stared up at the toughest first hour of what would become a five-hour climb. There was no trail; Bob commented as he headed through the brush. Talk about Captain Obvious. Within minutes, we were crossing the first of a few mountain streams, and Krit and my unprepared feet were soaking wet. As we headed up the first climb, we were grabbing onto anything for leverage.

The first-hour climb was done in less than forty-five minutes, so all were feeling good as we gasped for air and saw a series of ridgelines as far as the eye could see. There wasn't any sign of life, and the only sound was our collective breathing. I asked Cowboy Bob where exactly we were headed. He said to Mount Pomeroy and pointed beyond the last ridge. "You can't see it yet," he matter of fact concluded. I looked at Krit, looked at the rocky mass ahead, and put one foot forward, and then another. After completing five ridge climbs and descents, we stood looking over Upper Lake Pomeroy. Brandon had back planted already and was bleeding from hand and leg. Krit was soon to go down on the descent. I felt like I couldn't get my balance and could go down on every rock that wiggled. Bob was still bouncing along.

We were cold, tired, mentally exhausted, and when she said she was done, I was as happy as I've been since seeing the last turn on Alpe d'Huez. Bob and Brandon estimated the last climb was all of ten minutes, but Krit and I were done. We found a tiny alcove next to a huge chunk of snow, which blocked the cold wind and hunkered down. It was 10:00 a.m., and we'd been climbing for three hours. Neither of us is fond of ham and cheese, but we ate every scrap of it without so much as a word. Chips, candy, crackers—didn't stand a chance. We both chuckled that we would have eaten the paper too. The thought of going up and down the ridgeline for another two hours was more than even Cowboy Bob could imagine. So, as we made our way off the first ridge, he veered off course and headed straight down. Like an idiot, I followed close behind. Krit and Brandon waited back and shouted out at both of us. Cowboy Bob said he was checking it out to see how sheer the drop off was. My mind began to forecast forward, and it wasn't good. My feet, however, just kept moving.

Bob shouted back to Krit and Brandon to come along—we were going straight down. Yikes. The next hour was one massive adrenaline rush. Every step down was a controlled rockslide. I was scared. My legs were weary and wobbling. Krit would take a bad fall on this descent but fell into the mountain instead of away from it. Her injuries were on her backside. Her knee was screaming, and her new tennies were bloodstained too. She kept coming. Bob bounced along like the Cretan bounce developed by the natives of Crete, who just hop from rough rock to rough rock along the rugged island mountains. Bob, by the way, is a fifty-nine-year-old retired teacher.

After a really rough hour, we were sitting on a rock, and there was actually grass around it. Krit and I embraced and knew we had made it. The remaining ninety minutes was much easier. Her knee screamed, my legs shook, yet we kept going, albeit slowly. When we saw the truck, I told Krit she had done a great job. This hike without so much as a sniff of a trail was the hardest I've ever done. Cowboy Bob caught it and seized the moment too. He turned toward Krit and gave her a tip of the hat. Cowboy Bob doesn't mince his words. As he turned the ignition, he turned toward Krit and said simply, "That hike you just did is harder than 80% of the 14er's. You see, the 14er's have been leveled off, and trails put in due to their ridiculous popularity. I don't do them anymore. I prefer the ones like this where there is no trail, no people, no plan—you gotta make it up as you go."

I grabbed young Krit's arm and gave it a squeeze. She and I had just made a memory that's gonna last. We had taken a calculated risk, nothing crazy, but not safe either. Krit had to make her own way, as did I. Isn't this the lesson of life, friend? I'm really happy for enduring the challenge that felt like it was just out of reach. Krit grew on that ridgeline. She suffered and kept going in spite of the cuts, cracks, and crazy climbs. Thanks,

Krit, for inspiring me and knowing when it's time to stop, refuel, rest, and then go again. I'll never forget Mount Pomeroy and the image of you putting one foot in front of another. I'll never forget the guts you showed. You are finding your way, young Krit. Keep going, beautiful woman. Keep going, brave lady. And know all my love is always coming alongside.

What big, physical dream keeps you going, friend? Learn to do hard things. Never stop. Done so.

Day 129: Roger that...

We've all memorized the Tiger narrative: child prodigy to professional master—start young, deliberate practice for a bazillion hours, master your chosen craft, and find meaning as you win medals and make millions along the way. We've mostly bought the Tiger narrative, as witnessed by the decline in America's best high school athletes playing for their actual high school teams. Club sports, premier leagues, and national/international team play are where our best and brightest are found. Is this the new road to excellence?

Nope, not really.

When you study the facts around who achieves mastery across any domain, there are a few Tigers and a ton more Rogers; Roger Federer's, that is. You see, Roger played a ton of games as a child and pretty much loved to do anything with a ball. He loved wrestling, skiing, and swimming too. He didn't get hyper-focused at an early age. By the time he decided to focus on tennis, most of his competitors had strength coaches, nutritionists, and world-class instruction. Roger had his dad, whose instruction consisted of two words: "Don't cheat."

For me, dabbling in lots of sports as a kid taught me one main thing about myself: I'm a competitor. So, when college ended, and my competitive golf ended with it, I decided the next best thing was a career in sales since it, too, seemed competitive. From IBM (briefly) to CompuServe, I learned the sales craft and moved into management. Learning to lead a team and figure out what makes others tick fascinated me like nothing before. The Center for Creative Leadership in 1993 was my aha moment. I knew at that moment the domain I wanted to master. I wanted to build leaders and do it better than anyone.

Too many Tiger types burn out young. They discover their early focus was not aligned with their "love tos," and they lose the zest to keep climbing once they've reached dizzying heights. Play. Experiment. Expand your range. Paint, write, learn an instrument (never done that), travel, and keep your senses open to your energy. When you stumble into what lights you up, what you want to make your labor of love (OPUS), nobody will have to tell you—you'll know. So, go on. What are you waiting for? Just do it. Roger that, huh? Roger that.

Day 130: Chillin' it to killin' it...

Elite athletes, individual performers, warriors, business owners, CEOs, and senior executives must all learn to manage their human stress response. We are not mentally tough. We are getting softer, even the best among us. "Life is difficult," said M. Scott Peck. "Life is suffering, "said Buddha. "The impediment to action advances action," said Marcus Aurelius. And recently, David Goggins pronounced a very popular phrase: *Can't Hurt Me*. We seem to be embracing the "can't," but not the rest.

The BTL recipe is to build a strong CORE and couple it with a strong mind.

One of the first elements we're going to teach you is how to flip the switch on your central nervous system. The parasympathetic nervous system is chill mode. You want to live most of life here. Your body and mind are restoring, resting, and operating at low rpm. You also have the sympathetic nervous system. This is kill mode; you know, fight or flight. Well, friends, to be at your best, you must learn how to flip the switch to killin' it. You must learn how to manage your human stress response. You will not give your most compelling presentation if you're in chill mode when your client expects your most persuasive argument. Good luck winning your match when your competition is killin' it and laughing at you trying to "detach from the outcome."

How well do you toggle from chillin' it to killin' it? What stressors flip you out? Masters in the art of living flip the switch without even thinking. Do you?

Day 131: Managing the stress response...

The best definition of mental health? One's ability to manage the stress response. Here's how. Start by figuring out your pre-performance routine to flip the freaking switch. I do it by reminding myself I'm grateful to do the work I'm about to do. I tell myself, *Don't hold back.* I'm paid to facilitate practice that makes people better. I have to be on, prepared, and passionate. Check. I remind myself of my Purpose (it's the opening page of our website for a reason) and my bolted-on Principles: model the way, embrace pain and suffering, embody truth in love. Check. Lastly, I mentally rehearse the opening plan for practice and finish with my favorite prayer: God, help me. Check. I'm ready to go. I'm planning on killin' it.

When the last practice is in the books, my post-performance routine kicks into gear. Spiritual music or silence is my system's signal to begin to flip the switch to chillin' it. (I will do this in between practices too. I toggle a lot on purpose.) As I pull into my garage, I'm chill. I walk into my home and remind myself of another principle: be with. Technology is off. My bride is my focus. My brain chemicals are starting to behave. The end of my day is a couple magnesium pills (further clears out the fight chemicals) and seven to nine drops of CBD oil. Chillin' it.

Your job is to manage your stress response. Your best version is found when you control your stress response and do not become the plaything of circumstance and other people (thank you, Viktor Frankl). My pre-performance and post-performance routines come directly from my strong CORE. My CORE informs my mind, almost without thinking. The more you integrate, the less energy you consume toggling back and forth. Someday, it may even appear effortless. It is not. Do the work. Manage your stress response. Be your best at killin' it and chillin' it. Do you see how this thought ties into this book's opening quote from Chateaubriand? Tell me more, my friend. Tell me more.

Day 132: Know why? Know the way...

No why? No way. You see, friend, most of our big dreams, audacious adventures, and stretch goals are hatched when warm and cozy in front of fireplaces and feeling comfortable. Nothing wrong with this. If you want to achieve what you're after, you must anticipate the obstacles in your way before you find 15% climbs around the next Col du Galibier switchback. If you don't have clarity of why your aim is worth the effort in these MOT, your obstacle is going to shred your spirit. No why. No way.

However, if you dream big while you're comfortable (almost all my craziness comes from the comfort of our warm/cozy office, by the way), you need to anticipate the obstacles and prepare your mind to answer in the affirmative when nasty stuff comes your way. You've got to know why you're here, why you're headed into hard things, and why it matters to you and yours. You have to believe the obstacle is the way, or you will find yourself turning away.

Know why? Know the way. (I freakin' love word changes—if you haven't noticed by now.)

Dream big, friend. Dream and do. Do the work to bring your big dream into reality. Don't forget to anticipate the obstacles and how to answer them before they show up. Preload your response.

> Vivian, you know we barely have enough money to get these girls back to the dorms tonight. Girl, we don't even have leather balls! I would tell her, it doesn't matter. We're going to be so good, the world is going to come to us. I promise you our time will come and she'd say, You know what? Because you said it, I believe you.
> —*Standing Tall* **by C. Vivian Stringer**

Preload it. Internalize your mantra so you will marry the mundane and make the most of MOTs. "Keep working. Live hard. Love harder." These are words that carry me upward and onward.

Have you built your mantra to go alongside your strong CORE and authentic OPUS? Are you starting to understand why clarity is critical, friend? Slow down and build resolve, not some candy-ass New Year's resolution. Know why. Know the way. Do you?

Day 133: Again, let's train...

> "Three things will last forever: faith, hope, and love;
> but the greatest of these is love."
>
> —1 Corinthians 13:13

Recently finished my second read-through of *Born to Run*. What a great book this has been for me. So much more learning the second go 'round after ten years' time. Forget the science. Forget the latest analytics. Forget nutrition, tapering, periodization, and everything else you know about your sport. Forget recruiting pure talent and all the five-star bullshit. Find athletes with faith in themselves and in something bigger than themselves. Recruit athletes who exude hope and embrace adversity. And watch their bodies as they train, especially as they fatigue. Look for an abundance of love.

Don't take me literally and forget everything else, but the greatest of all these is love. Recruit love because love has no ceiling. You and I were born to run toward someone and something. Run with those you encounter along your way. Be with them and celebrate the gift of coming together. Deepen your faith in what isn't yet seen or seen only dimly. Never stay down for long or even think about giving up. You have everlasting value, and life is filled with meaning, purpose, and obstacles. Run around, over, and through them. Fall in love with all of it, even fatigue. The more you fall in love, the longer you laugh as you tire, the less you fear the wall as you fatigue, and the more you focus outside yourself as pain registers in your brain. Love conquers all.

You are born to run. Joy is found through doing hard things well. Start, friend, by learning to do hard things not so well. Keep working. Have faith, don't lose hope, and find the love in it all. Is your focus on the pain (fixed mindset), or is love telling you it's nothing but a gain (growth mindset)?

Again, let's train. Today, fall in love with your training. See something beyond the momentary pain. What is your aim?

Day 134: I had...

I had chronic pain in my right shoulder from a cycling injury in 2008. I had chronic pain in my left from a weightlifting accident back in 1985. I had chronic pain in my left hip from 2006–2008 that got so bad I had to stop playing golf. My orthopedic said this would only get worse. He informed me a hip replacement was in my future. His advice? Call me when you can't take the pain!

August 1, 2010, I made the decision to attack chronic pain unrelated to the three above. The chronic pain I went after was the pain on paper regarding my high cholesterol, blood sugar numbers, visceral fats, and high blood pressure. Another doc informed me I was pre-diabetic, skinny fat, and much sicker than I looked or felt. I begrudgingly changed my exercise and eating habits. This produced some unintended consequences that "I had" thought were simply mine to live with. I began to plank, pull, and push for thirty minutes, three days a week with my friend/client, Littlest Fricker. I stumbled onto the TRX six months in and added it to our arsenal. The pain in my shoulders increased, and oftentimes slowed me down. I kept pushing and embraced it. I was beginning to feel the difference between harmful pain and pain that hurts and helps.

Somewhere in 2012, something crazy happened. I woke up one morning and noticed nothing hurt! Both shoulders rotated, cracked, and creaked but no pain. The debilitating left hip pain? Gone. Both of my shoulders stopped hurting. The TRX puts such a load on your shoulders; I hadn't noticed what it was doing under my skin. It was building lots of little tendons and tiny muscle fibers and relieving joint pressure. No more chronic pain.

Pain is inevitable; misery is a choice.

Want to rid yourself of your chronic pain? Step into acute. Embrace it in short bursts. The chronic pain you are facing can only be beaten by putting yourself in more pain now. Relationally, true. Spiritually, true. Physically, true. Chronic pain is not inevitable. "I had" is possible and painful. Choose this acute pain now. What chronic pain do you want to attack today? Don't wait. Initiate. ACT…

BUILT TO LEAD | together we transform

Day 135: Smart...

Recently, during a couple of team practices, it hit me how far off course we've fallen as we've evolved of late. One of my Instagram posts did it. Some hotel is offering spiffs to guests who will put their phones in an empty fishbowl during their stay. You have got to be kidding me. We are enslaved by a tool designed to make us smarter.

Someone recently told me that BTL practice is a luxury. He's right, of course. So are cars, club memberships, dinners out, bikes, fancy clothes, kettlebells, TRXs, and all kinds of stuff. There is nothing inherently wrong with enjoying life's luxury, as long as you don't allow them to own you. Your smartphone is a luxurious tool. Own it. Do not allow it to own you. If you find yourself needing hacks to loosen its grip on you, you should have a level five fire alarm reverberating in your head. You are not using your mind; in fact, you are losing it.

I have a dumb phone by design and zero plans to upgrade. Zero. No need. I'm not missing out on anything. I use technology and have figured out how to make it work for me. You have to figure out how to use tools you can afford and limit yourself from taking advantage of everything you can afford. Do not wait for someone/something else to govern you—you govern you.

Food. Rest. Love.

Eat real food as a starter, mostly plants. Get plenty of sleep. Love God, love people, and love giving away your gifts for less than they're worth. Start here with these basics. I'm quite confident you'll figure out the rest once you realize your luxurious tools aren't the real problem, but your lack of a strong CORE, authentic aim, and discipline of productive action are. We are our own worst enemy, aren't we? Wake up, friends. Live life by design, not default. Own your decisions. Start with food, rest, and love. Of course, don't forget to move. Smart.

Today, decide to be your own governor. Where you gonna start?

Day 136: Mental health 201...

Here's the BTL recipe for improving your mental health. We are not docs. We are, however, students of human nature. If you practice these disciplines, you will feel better if your struggle is unipolar depression.

1. *Learn optimism.* Read the book by the same name from Seligman. It allows you to become aware of your explanatory style, the way you explain events to yourself. Master the ABCs. Yeah, baby.
2. *Widen your perspective.* Study history, and you will see whatever you're going through, it's been gone through before. Study resilient examples.
3. *Practice seven good minutes.* Talk. People go nuts alone. We need each other. Give the gift of understanding; you'll get back more.
4. *Get sunlight.* You are designed to be outside and have your feet on the ground. Do this daily.
5. *Eat food. Drink in moderation.* Eat real food packed with nutrients. Avoid the middle aisles of the grocery—they are filled with processed bullshit, not food.
6. *Practice gratitude.* Start a gratitude jar and stuff it daily. Pray. Meditate. Do the calm app thing. Grab a hand and give more than you take. Give more. The more you give, the more you receive.
7. *Love.* Love is pure energy. Pet a dog, phone a friend, or help a neighbor. Grab a hand and give more than you take. Give more, and you will be blessed. Take more, and you'll be cursed.
8. *Move.* It's almost impossible to stay in unipolar depression when you're running every day—too many endorphins. Move it.
9. *Don't sit on social media or technology for hours on end.* Regulate your screen time. Less is more.
10. *Build your CORE. Live your OPUS.* Start here. Never stop. Tighten this, and guess what happens to the other nine?

Which are you avoiding? Which do you want to know more about? What would you "and"? Slow down and reflect. Write. ACT.

BUILT TO LEAD | together we transform

Day 137: Defeated...

Back in 2000, I was still in the corporate world but had one foot out the door—I knew my time working for the man was limited. Lance Armstrong had just released his book, *It's Not About the Bike,* and I was ready to lead a team down to Boone to check out the routes that had brought him back into cycling after his bout with cancer. He had just won his first Tour de France, and his story had Larry, George, and me all fired up. I had a business meeting in the general vicinity of Boone, North Carolina, and decided this would be the trip to check out the epic climb up Beech Mountain. I would go it a lone.

Arriving at the base of the mountain late afternoon, I was filled with nervous energy anticipating the climb. Clipping into my pedals and turning right onto the climb, it started going up almost immediately. Sweat began to pour into my eyes as I turned to the right again, just past the real estate office nestled into the pines. It looked beautiful as I tried to take in the views. After the turn, it was a beast. The incline registered over 20% gradient and the twigs pushed on the pedals for all they were worth. The bike barely moved, and the brain began to perform some quick calculations. There were no gears left as my right hand desperately tried to find another tooth, and no shift happened. I was in the granny gear, and the turn 'round was glacial. My mind screamed at me to keep pushing, but the tired, depleted twigs were unresponsive to the call. I got nothing. Defeated, I did the only thing left to do: I turned the bike to the left (halfway up the climb) and surrendered.

So began my love affair with cycling the mountains. What defeats us doesn't define us. Our response does. What hard thing do you want to learn to do well?

Day 138: Victory...

In 2019, four of my cycling buddies (Littlest Fricker, downer, Blondie, Guv) alongside Miss and our son Andrew headed to Lake Annecy, France, and our third reunion with some of the hardest climbs in the cycling world. We climbed between 6,000–10,000 feet each day for nine days. Andrew, our son from Berlin, met us there. He and Miss enjoyed cycling with us on some of the days and taking in the Alps and mountain lakes on others. It was not about the bike; it was about the bike, beauty, and best friends being together doing hard things as best we can. No turning around this time. I'm twenty years older than my first trip to Boone but much wiser—I have more gears and have trained more effectively.

My relationship with pain has changed. Back in 2000, all I was doing was riding. My core was weak. I hadn't drawn the correlation between the core and transferring power to the pedal. It hurts training the core, but only for a while. We've all embraced this pain in the 3PP. The stronger core will not only transfer power more effectively, it takes the strain and subsequent pain off the lower back. Are you slowing down and strengthening your core and CORE, friend? Or are you just focused on getting to the top without calculating the cost? There is more to life than simply conquering your climb, right?

This trip was a celebration of slow learning, slow cycling, slow suffering, and slowing down (especially eating) to take in the beauty, not the beast. We focused on each other (giving courage) and the beauty of God's creation (giving thanks). We found joy in doing hard things together. We discovered the gravity hack too. The mountains have an anti-gravitational pull if you slow down and bathe in their beauty. If you turn your head to the left and right, you will find your spirit lifted, and your pedal stroke invigorated. You will strain but with less pain. The beauty will pull you up. Life is bitter and sweet, beauty and beast. Focus on the beauty, not the beast.

What big, physical dream is pulling you to new heights? What are you waiting for? Who are you taking with you? Remember, together we transform, always together...

Day 139: Mental health 301...

If you feel that in some sense you are suffering, please keep reading.

Whatever your plight, here's some good news for perspective: you are not the first, nor will you be the last. In fact, suffering is and always will be part of the human experience. So, like me, learn to embrace pain and suffering. Keep learning. I'm currently reading another sensational Stoic book titled *How to Think Like a Roman Emperor.* Written by Donald Robertson, this beauty has all kinds of hidden gems about the life of Marcus Aurelius. I am loving it. One of Marcus Aurelius' favorite quotes is fast becoming one of mine. Here it is. Absorb this into your system, friend. This is mental health 301. "It is not things that upset us but our judgments about things." Thanks, Epictetus.

It's not the slight from one of my clients that upsets me, but it's what I think that slight says about me that upsets me. It's not the look you just shot me, but it's about my perception of what that shot meant. It's not my high cholesterol reading, my fifty-ninth cut, or my inability to fix you, my friend, that upsets me. It's what I think about it that puts me on the down escalator or puts me in a catastrophic free fall. Your mental health takes a huge leap when you realize this fact. You cannot control people, circumstances, or much of anything. Control your mind. Think like a Roman emperor, friend. If you change your judgments about what harms you, you may just find yourself healed.

Write about your sense of suffering today. How could you change your judgment about things?

Day 140: Porn...

Only recently have scientists begun to believe our brains are elastic, meaning you can literally change your hardwiring. We now know neurons that "fire together, wire together." If you want to learn something, put in the hours mastering the movement until you hardwire the new neural network. This is great news for those of us who aren't afraid of putting in hours toward our labor of love. Mastery, it turns out, is more about doing the work, putting in the hours, practice, practice, perfecting practice. Fire and wire.

There is a dark side to brain plasticity. Neurons do not have a moral code. So, if you feed your brain negative thoughts about a particular person or group of people in general, your brain will learn to hardwire a negative mental model. You will get better at believing the worst. Study prosecuting attorneys, and you'll see why they lead in drug addiction, divorce, depression, and even suicide. They have negative neural networks that make them masters in the courtroom, at home, and in life, not so much.

Now for the darkest of the dark—porn. According to Dr. Doidge in *The Brain That Heals Itself,* "Porn viewers develop new maps in their brains, based on the photos and videos they see. Because it is a use it or lose it brain, when we develop a map area, we long to keep it activated. Porn hyper activates appetitive pleasure, not the consummatory one." Translation. Looking at porn creates an almost endless desire for something that won't satisfy. According to Doidge, most of his patients crave porn but paradoxically don't like it. Since the brain is rewiring its appetitive pleasure, those participating in porn are like the rat pressing the bar for more and never getting enough. Historically, there was the shame of the person at the check-out counter to slow the would-be porn addict. There once was faith and family who taught the moral code or, at a minimum, preached impulse control. Today, the media and culture say there's nothing wrong with it, and if some pleasure is good, why not experience more, more, more?

Neurons are neutral, friend. Ones that fire together, wire together. Please understand this is fact. Open your eyes. Do not take up residence in denial. Sadly, when your brain becomes a master at porn, it will soon become its slave. What do you believe about your brain on porn, alcohol, distraction, or any other addiction?

Day 141: Mentally tough...

Your body has two engines running in your central nervous system—the sympathetic (fight or flight) and parasympathetic. Whenever you engage your sympathetic nervous system and jolt your muscles with adrenaline, you temporarily shut down your parasympathetic one, the one managing your immune system and fighting to keep you healthy and disease-free. One is on, and one is off. Our central nervous system does not discern that these stressors may not be life-threatening. It assumes the threat must be real because you send all the same signals primitive man did many moons ago.

Instead of being run down by a saber-toothed tiger, most of us are simply rundown. According to Hans Selye, the guy who actually invented the term stress, this is serious stuff:

"My research appears to indicate that humans have only a limited supply of deep adaptive energy. Most of the energy expended in the stress response can be recovered through rest. But a certain amount of this energy resource may be irretrievably lost. For this reason, it is important to reserve this adaptive energy for those occasions where the issues are significant and not to squander it on trivial conflicts."

Your body is yours to manage. Slow down and reflect. Recently, I was reminded in a conversation with Eric Potterat (former SEAL psychologist) that mental toughness really comes down to managing your stress response. How well are you managing yours? Remember, when you're being run by your sympathetic one, you have a hard time hearing and an even harder time learning. So, if you find yourself unable to recall the words from a recent hard conversation, it might not be age-related senility but stress-related sympathetic. The mentally tough not only manage their stress response, but they also seek eustressors out as a bee does honey. The mentally tough build capacity by running toward challenges just beyond their current reach.

What baby step do you want to play with to better manage your stress response? Write. Reflect. ACT.

Day 142: Major Taylor...

This morning I finished *The World's Fastest Man*, and what a great reminder it was. Major Taylor lived hard and loved harder. He accomplished much in his hard fifty-three years. He fought racism and forged friendships with those unlike him. He trained hard and compromised little. He frequently failed on his way to leveling up. He loved harder and yet died alone, far from family and friends.

As a cyclist, I'm surprised to just now learn of Major Taylor. He has cycling clubs named after him all over our great, divided, messy, and magnificent country. Funny, the first one was established right here in Columbus, Ohio. Who knew. The book ends with an appendix dedicated to his training regime back in the late 1800s and early 1900s. No smoking or drinking dominated his disciplines. Good food. Lots of water. Interval training. Strength training. Lots of rest, recovery, and massage. And, of course, core strength. Major knew that nothing mattered more than a strong core and back. Nothing.

Build your strong core and CORE, friend. Never stop the work on your physical core, and never stop the work on your BTL CORE. Life is hard. Always has been. Always will be. Prepare now for the coming storms. This current crisis is training. Get through this iteration. More are coming. Slow down and reflect. Are you building a strong core and CORE? Slow down and reflect.

Live hard. Love harder...

Day 143: Grateful for Greece...

Pheidippides was a professional Greek runner (a *hemerodromos*) and was the dude who ran from the Battle at Marathon to Athens in 490 BC. He's said to have screamed *"Nike"* (victory) before breathing his last. Here, as Paul Harvey liked to say, is the rest of the story.

Persia had landed on the shores of Marathon and was a mere twenty-five miles from Athens when the Athenian leaders sent their strongest *hemerodromos*, Phed, to run for help. So, Phed laced up his sandals and started running. Herodotus recounts that he ran fast. Athens to Sparta is over 140 miles, and Phed made it in less than two days. There were no fanny packs, water bottles, food stations, or light to guide his way over rocky, mountainous terrain. Phed made it, talked the Spartans into joining the fray, and realizing the Spartans weren't coming right away (six-day wait for a full moon superstition), he took a cat nap and then hoofed it back to Athens. He made the return trip in two energy-draining days. Are you kidding me? Nope. Phed was a pro.

The Athenian army had already departed by the time a panting Phed made it to Athens. So, you guessed it, Phed booked it another twenty-five miles to Marathon to deliver his message to General Miltiades. After a couple of nights camped in the mountains, Miltiades decided his army had to act. He ordered a night attack carrying their 45-lb shield, full helmet, and body armor. Miltiades ordered his men to run the final mile across the open field as the arrows filled the morning sky. So, they ran into the Persian army outnumbered 50,000 to under 10,000. Surprised, the Persians made military mistake after mistake, and Athens beat them back into full retreat. If every team we work with could get this message, victory would most often go to the aggressor.

You can read more about this in *The Road to Sparta* by Dean Karnazes. Today, think about being more aggressive. You've been on your heels for a long time. What do you say we attack today? Tomorrow, the rest of the story.

Day 144: Phed...

Here, friends, is the rest of the story as promised yesterday.

A bunch of Persians had gotten back in the boats and were headed to an undefended Athens. So, a few Athenian warriors made the twenty-mile run toward Athens to cut the Persians off before they made land. Yes, reading this is anti-whine material, isn't it? Phed ran on his own back to Athens to calm the citizenry with the amazing news of victory at Marathon. The final twenty-five miles depleted him. Upon arriving and delivering his message, he breathed his last. Historians recall he ran something around 330 miles in total. Not 26.2.

There are no shortcuts or easy recipes, and always so much more than meets the eye at first glance. We like to tell short stories, net it out, and only focus on the last leg, forgetting the mundane miles of preparation that led to every moment of truth. Want to perform better in your MOT? Practice like Phed. Practice like a pro. Prepare your mind for fight, not flight.

Prepare your mind with your pre-performance routine. Find your mantra and stop whining. Just do it, right, Phed? Our world is soft and getting softer. Be one of the few who keeps getting after it as you age. Find something worth striving toward, fighting for, and bring a few buddies along. Enjoy the camaraderie of suffering. Nietzsche was right: What doesn't kill you only makes you stronger.

Choose suffering. Phed's marathon was not chosen. Phed ran for his country and the Western way of life. Phed ran for his life so you and I could enjoy ours. Appreciate this gift given over 2,500 years ago. Slow down and sit with this for a while. We are grateful for the Greeks, aren't we?

Today, choose suffering. Pick a hard thing you want to do well. Baby-step it. If you want to learn more, pick up *The Road to Sparta,* by Dean Karnazes.

Day 145: Leadership starts...

I've been studying what makes individuals, teams, and leaders perform at a high level since 1993. I became a positional leader in the world of work in 1984—the same year I became a father. Miss and I both wanted a big family and wanted to start while we were young. I was in my second job since graduating in 1981 as IBM had hired and fired me within the same year. CompuServe hired me immediately. CompuServe was selling electronic mail and other leading technologies of the day. Within two years, I was promoted from salesperson to branch manager and was responsible for a team. So, I began to learn about leadership from being a father and manager at the ripe age of twenty-five. I'm a slow learner. For instance, I've been writing about the importance of one's literal core since I started BTL back in 2002. I knew this was true but was too weak to do what I knew.

I was stuck in the knowing/doing trap. (This trap is characterized by our knowing truth but not acting upon it.) You may be as well. It wasn't until one of my clients kicked my ass and made me read one particular page out of *The Primal Blueprint* that I converted my learning into PA. Sadly, it was August 1, 2010. I had known my literal core was central to my health for eight years before I began to act on my learning. I'd been stuck in the knowing/doing trap far too long.

As my friend Jim Gant would say, "Stop being a private." Leadership starts when you start it yourself, regardless of where you are. Leadership starts when you believe. Leadership starts when you begin to believe you are on the hook to lead you, at a minimum. You are a leader, whether you're a positional one or not. We get better by doing more with what we learn. What baby step are you taking today to build a more healthy/physical life?

Day 146: Checking my chatter...

As I drove my luxury vehicle toward Dr. Cutfirst's office, I was feeling sorry for myself again. I was in a climate-controlled vehicle, heated seats turned on, Spotify chill tunes soothed me from six speakers, and my mood was some combination of frustrated, angry, and sad. Yes, I'm soft. I was allowing my mind to marinate on another "woe is me" moment. I mean, "come on, man," I heard my little voice scream, "this sucks that you're wasting another day sitting with Dr. Cutfirst for the fifty-ninth freakin' time!" Wrapped in luxury and listening to chill tunes just wasn't doing it. So, I slowed my breath and brain. And as I did, something funny happened in my head. I imagined what this might have been like one hundred years ago. Hmm.

What if my genetic existence came into being back then? Well, I thought, *I would probably be dead by now as these little nuisances would have been a full-fledged nightmare.* No cuts and these little squamous cells would have surely found an organ or two by now. A slow, miserable shutdown would have already hit this system, and it wouldn't have been a fun ride down either.

My mind and mood changed. Instantly!

I went from "woe is me" to "wow, how lucky am I to have the luxury of Dr. Cuttfirst and her cancer-killing knife?" A Duchenne smile creased my face. My mood completely changed, even though the circumstance was exactly the same. I began to see Dr. Cutty as she really is—a helpful tool technology has gifted me. "I'm lucky to have her help me," I kept saying to my sorry, soft self. My mind changed, and my mood came along for the ride. By the time I arrived, my mood was chill and calm. Very cool.

What if your circumstances are not the problem, but your perspective is? What if? Hmm. Stop allowing your little voice to chatter unchecked. Water the positives as you widen the lens of your perspective. Repent— change your mind, remember? My biggest challenge remains keeping my chatter checked too. How 'bout you?

Day 147: Pain...

Pain is inevitable. Misery is a choice.

These words came to me as I studied pain many years ago. The most common physical pain is found in the lower back. The most common cause of this chronic pain is a combination of too much weight on the human frame and too little core strength for support. Back in 1965, the average American male was 5'9" and a buck sixty-five. Today, we've picked up an inch of height and around thirty pounds. We've chosen poorly as a nation. Fact.

Lower back pain is a form of chronic pain. Many have chronic back pain for years, even decades. Of course, not all back pain is caused by poor choices. Some are due to injury, accidents, bum luck with regard to genetics, and countless other causes. The fact remains that for the majority, it's due to poor choices. When it comes to eliminating chronic pain, the best solution involves more acute pain. The recipe involves more pain, at least for a while. Most choose to simply stick with chronic pain and begin the numbing process.

> If you know who you are and why you're doing what you're doing, you will have an easier time digging deep in the fourth round of a five—round workout. It's easy to quit something as hard as the CrossFit Games, especially without a firm grounding in why you are working so hard.
> —Dottir **by Katrin Davidsdottir**

Choose to put yourself in more acute pain physically, spiritually, mentally, and relationally. Chronic pain is not inevitable. Stop running away from something chronically wrong with you or yours. Maybe you've chosen the chronic pain of numbing yourself with alcohol or drugs instead of facing the deeply rooted problem head-on. Maybe you've chosen the chronic pain of looking away instead of looking inside. Pain is inevitable. Misery is a choice. What are you choosing?

Day 148: Better...

I hear lots of confusion around human performance and the basic physics of improvement. At BTL, we study high performance as our profession. We don't know much, but we do know this. You do not get better by saying stuff to yourself, even if it's really, really good stuff. You get better by doing stuff. As Aristotle said way back in the day, "Excellence is an art won by training and habituation. We do not act rightly because we have virtue or excellence, but rather we have those because we have acted rightly. We are what we repeatedly do. Excellence, then, is not an act but a habit."

Recently, I spoke encouragement to my friend, PJ, and enjoyed the camaraderie of suffering with my dear friend. We did seventy-seven burpees and a whole mess of other exercises for 44:44. He told me two years ago that he couldn't do one burpee. He's gotten better by what he's done. He is learning to listen to his body and avoid harming it while continuing to push his weak mind. This is true for you and me. As we age, we must do more, not less. The world will tell you what you can't do, shouldn't do, and encourage you to join them on the couch, taking your prescription meds, acting your age, and telling yourself stories about what you once were back in the day.

Do not buy that bullshit.

You do not get better by saying stuff to yourself. You get better by doing more. You get better by surrounding yourself with tough men and women who make you do what you can instead of telling you to stop and play it safe.

Young or old—CORE, OPUS, PoP is the one you want.

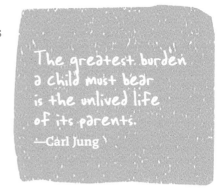

The greatest burden a child must bear is the unlived life of its parents.
—Carl Jung

Day 149: Time...

You and I do not manage time. We exist in time. You and I are not in control of time; we simply enjoy the gift of time. Time is God's greatest, most beautiful gift to all of us. That's why it's called the present (thanks, Joe Friend and Kyle Alfriend).

Slow down and absorb this moment. What do you want to make time for? Why haven't you found the time? Are you beginning to understand that living our melody line (CORE—OPUS—PoP) is easier said than done? Becoming **BUILT TO LEAD** is a gift you've given yourself. It would be nuts not to use it. Are you integrating work and life yet? What are you waiting for?

Day 150: Know your limits...

"A man's got to know his limitations." Harry Callahan from *Dirty Harry*.

The second to last was a great ego test for me. The twigs and my thirty tooth (granny gear) had been grinding all week on steep mountain passes. Unlike my trip over at age fifty and fifty-five, this trip at sixty had me paying more attention to my body. Yes, we're talking cycling in France again.

For over a week, I had been pushing my body hard. My lips were chapped from the constant mouth open, panting for hours at a time. The only sign of wear was my right knee. There wasn't pain when I spun the granny, only when I tried to push a bigger gear to keep up with Littlest Fricker, Downer, or Blondie. Looking at the climb profile during my pre-ride planning, I decided to spin through the first seven kilometers. I executed the plan, got dropped like a bad habit, and watched friends ride away while I monitored my breath. The knee felt great. My ego felt like shit.

Onto the last climb up Mont Cenis. The grade was all under 10%, and twigs weren't tweaked. I decided to ride like I stole something. When we crossed the bridge and headed up the first switchback, I pushed the pedals and listened for the right knee's response. Nothing. My breathing went nuclear, legs started to sing, and I felt the pain that comes from pushing the limits but not exceeding them. It is a fine line. You've got to know your limitations. Sounds easy. It's not. Most of us stay below our performance threshold because we fear pain and back off before we ought. High performers know their limitations and push beyond them, just not too far. Life is a hard, unforgiving, never-ending test. You've got to embrace pain and suffering and know when to back off and swallow your pride. You've got to think beyond the first mountain and keep something in reserve. You've got to figure it out for you.

Do you need to kick yourself in the ass and shift up a gear or two? Do you need to ease off, let some recovery seep into your system, and live to fight another day? Slow down. ACT...

Day 151: Hard OPUS...

Hard OPUS you sustain as you tire. Hard labor you disdain as you perspire.

Life is hard. The good life is not defined by comfort as much as it's defined by learning to do hard things well—hard things that you want to do well, that is. You see, friend, life is an energy management problem, as a bunch of OSU head coaches and a couple of Aussies learned recently. Most humans run on fear. This is fuel that works for a season but not for a lifetime. Love is the only sustainable energy. Fill up here. Dip deeply into the love reservoir, please.

Life is an energy management problem. Are you beginning to understand why we believe Becoming BTL cannot be taught, only caught? This morning, a team of friends and clients learned to do a few hardcore exercises. We put our heels in the TRX torture straps and learned some new moves. We made mistakes and flopped around a bit like fish out of water. We laughed at each other and ourselves. We kept working. We sustained hard OPUS. We've come to love working our literal core down in the 3PP as much as we love building our figurative BTL CORE. We know it's not easy to stand, so we strengthen our spine. We understand life is hard and not getting easier as we age. What do you believe?

What hard things are you learning to do well? What big physical dream keeps you building below the waterline? Are you living hard OPUS or loathing hard labor? Slow your sorry-ness down. Live hard. Love harder.

Day 152: Marathon: dream to done so...

According to a wide variety of neuroscientists, we begin a linear hockey stick of progression from nineteen to twenty-seven. Once we step beyond year twenty-seven, it's a slippery slope of decline. There have been a number of studies to determine the rate of decline. In other words, if we peak physically at twenty-seven and the hockey stick of progression begins at nineteen, we have an eight-year run where we're getting stronger and stronger. So, if it's a linear progression going up, my guess is it's fairly linear on the decline too—until I read *Born to Run*. Our decline is not linear.

Sixty-four is the real number.

Are you kidding me? Nope. Go to the website for the Leadville 100 trail race. Look back over the previous year's winners and notice an Indian-sounding name that appears as the winner in 1992. Google his age. Want more? Ask me to tell you the story of the eighty-something woman who rode her bike up Mont Iseran or the seventy-something man who rode ahead of me to the top of Galibier. These mountains are "out of category" Tour De France climbs—too tough for a label.

Nobody must have told them.

Every day, we challenge individuals at our practices to capture a big dream for themselves that would be physically challenging and give them energy. We want something beyond losing weight or looking good. Bigger is better when it comes to dreams. Hearts don't catch fire when the brain signals all it wants is to suck less. Choose a big dream that brings a smile to your face just thinking about it. Gain clarity around why.

Why does this dream energize you? Why does it matter? Why questions are powerful. Lastly, we ask them the big one: Who would they invite to go along? Who matters most? Slow down and think about your dream for a healthy/physical life. What brings a smile to your face as you imagine playing in nature, doing something difficult with someone you love? Tomorrow, we'll talk some more. For now, just write.

Day 153: Physical dreams...

So, here's our recommended PA for going from dream to done so with your physical dream.

1. Dream again. Dream big. Dream about something physical you want to accomplish (Athens Marathon, November 8, 2020, for me).
2. Get to the why's behind the dream. (One summer, I took a picture with family in front of the original Olympic stadium. I thought, *How cool would it be to run on that track?*)
3. Determine who you want to do this with. (Krazy Kyle, upon showing him my pic, tells me he's doing this marathon. I'm going to run the route of Phiedippides, recall history, and why I'm here.)
4. Go and connect others to your dream and allow them to influence its direction. (I talked to Tay, Miss, Doscher, Brett, and others. Miss is coming, maybe others).
5. Choose a baby step to move you toward your dream. (I'm running five miles three times/week and warming up the legs, talking to marathoners, and riding my bike because it's fun.)
6. Set reminders to keep you going with the baby steps until they become habits and then disciplines down the line.
7. Enjoy the journey. Bathe in beauty. Don't grind. Find the joy, instead. Look around and marinate on all the good as you grow tired.

There's the recipe. Make it yours. Dream and do with another. We buy the lie that tells us, with age, all we can count on is the decline. The truth is we need to dream again.

When was the last time you've had a big physical dream?

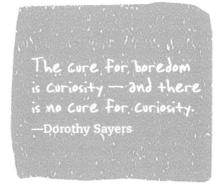

The cure for boredom is curiosity — and there is no cure for curiosity.
—Dorothy Sayers

Day 154: Puddles...

When we were kids, there wasn't much more satisfying, at least for me, than watching a good Kansas storm move through Salina from west to east with rapidity. I mean, it would blow in and out in minutes. I can remember, like it was yesterday, the joy of putting on my rubber boots and heading out to the curb on 11th Street to jump up and down in the big puddles that had formed at the bottom of our driveway, just after the thunder and lightning show came and went. What fun it was to jump up and down and get wet in the process.

As adults, many of us have lost sight of these simple perspectives.

When storms suddenly wreak havoc in our adult lives, we tend to sit and stew instead of anticipate the fun it's about to become. We act as if blue skies and sunny days are the only ones worth making the most of, and we hunker down and gut it out on all the others. When we step in a puddle, we get pissed and jump quickly as if our misstep must have been a mistake. What if it's our perspective, not the puddle, that's the problem? What if the storms and puddles haven't really changed, but we have? What if life is meant to teach us to play with what we've got, where we've got it, and with whom we've been given?

Slow down and think about your puddles. Puddles don't overwhelm us. Nobody is dying when we step in one. Puddles are simply part of life. We all step in 'em. You and I choose our perspective. We either jump up and down and make the most of our misstep, or we curse the puddle, puddle maker, and treat it like a torrential downpour allowing it to sweep us away, take us off course, and away from our dream. Now, that would be childish, huh? What problem do you need to reframe as a mere puddle, friend?

Day 155: Eustressed out...

Stress is any challenge that promotes growth. More stress than you can handle feels like distress. Less stress than you can manage leads to boredom, stagnation, and complacency. The sweet spot is eustress where you are out of the comfort zone reaching, but it feels like you've got a chance. This is how you grow.

One person's hyper-stress is another's challenge. One person's ho-hum is another's reach. The magic to managing your stress levels is two-fold. First, you've got to improve your tuneage. Finding your eustress sweet spot requires finetuning your capacity and matching it to the proper challenge. Too easy, and you'll get bored and quit. Too hard, and you'll soon burn out. Once you've tuned in, you've got to push on. This is the second half of the equation and the one that stops most. You cannot increase your capacity without increasing the challenge. When we do pulls in the 3PP, I see people embracing the push. Going from the sissy bar to the high bar and then jumping up on the beam is a stress to each of us. This is by design.

The key to you experiencing more of the helpful effects of stress is embracing the fear of failure. Most of us have a very low tolerance for pain. We've become soft and think we're hard. Today, push yourself outside your comfort zone and see what happens. Go on—jump up and grab onto the high bar. Feel the roughness of the bar digging into your soft hands. Feel the steel put some incredible pressure on the tips of your fingers, grit your teeth, and pull yourself up anyway. Feel the rush of blood through your body as it does something it felt it could *not*. Your brain is now on a natural high. You are, in fact, eustressed out. This is growth.

Now. Do it again.

Day 156: Blockage...

Over time, your arteries harden and accumulate plaque. You and I know this is true, thanks to Leonardo da Vinci performing the first autopsy and enlightening us all way back in the day. Today, however, coronary heart disease is still the most common form of cardiovascular disease and can result in a heart attack and sudden death. We now know much more than we did back in da Vinci's day, yet we still struggle keeping our arteries open and clean.

Your system is a lot like the arteries in your body; they've got to be maintained to stay clean. Over time, your team figures out where they can come clean with truth and where they can't. So, they often congregate outside an easy, free-flowing leader's office. They've got something holding them back and need to get it out. They tell the safe leader their trouble, and now he/she has been triangulated (thank you, Friedman). Now, the open, safe leader is holding the tension and must decide what to pass on to the head/heart and what to hold. Instead of creating a direct artery to the source of the struggle, this system has created a workaround that adds a tax of time and distrust. Eventually, this kind of system burns out the nice leader and ends up with more and more attacks from the heart/head. Not good.

Are you allowing your system to triangulate, leader? Are you holding onto tension that belongs to someone else? Do you enjoy people queuing up outside your door? Slow down and write. Tomorrow, we'll de-triangulate together. Always together.

Day 157: Plaque...

If your arteries are accumulating plaque, a good doc is going to prescribe a change in diet, exercise, distress reduction, and restorative sleep at a minimum. A good doc doesn't jump to drastic measures like stints, open-heart surgery, or dope you up with cholesterol meds unless they've tried this first. The same is true for plaque in your work/family system. Most of you can get cleaned up in a couple of steps.

Create a safe environment that values truth over false harmony. Humans fear leaders. The BTL leader knows this and creates margin to slow down and be unproductive with their team.

Expect triangulation. Get curious. Practice this as your response to the triangulator, "Hey, I hear you, but before we go any further, have you told Richard what you're about to tell me?" If the answer is yes (this will be rare, by the way), ask them to tell you more and get to the root. If the answer is no, get the other person on the phone or bring them in the office so they can hear it directly from the source. You will quickly get out of most triangles.

Your system is healthiest when the arteries of communication are open between peers. Problems don't sit long and accumulate plaque because the blood is flowing freely, so to speak. Your job is to build this kind of culture in your systems. And your job is to stop over-operating in another's space. Slow down and marinate on a little Friedman magic in the box.

> Leaders who are most likely to function poorly...are those who have failed to maintain a well-differentiated position. Either they have accepted the blame owing to the irresponsibility and constant criticism of others, or they have gotten themselves into an over functioning position (that is, they tried too hard) and rushed in where angels and fools both fear to tread.
> —*Failure of Nerve* **by Edwin Friedman**

Day 158: Thankful for fleas...

Corrie Ten Boom and her sister, Betsie, were held in multiple German concentration camps back in World War II for helping Jews in Amsterdam. They were living according to their CORE and taking a beating for it. You can read about them and six other strong women of faith in Eric Metaxas worthy read, *7 Women*. I consider books like this an anti-depressant of sorts—after reading 'em, I find myself unable to whine, at least for a while.

One particularly discouraging day, Corrie noticed their prison cell was flea-infested to boot. As Corrie cursed her plight and her oppressor, her sister offered some CCD wisdom. She counseled Corrie to thank God for everything in their barrack, including the fleas. To make it worse, she went to the extreme of quoting scripture too. She read 1 Thessalonians, "Rejoice always, pray without ceasing, in everything give thanks; for this is the will of God in Christ Jesus for you."

So, Corrie listened to her truth-teller and thanked God for everything. She thanked God for fleas. I cannot imagine being thankful for fleas. Can you? Much later in their prison time, it became clear the fleas had been a blessing. Turns out, the guards never came near them and refused to enter their cell. Why? You guessed it! They were afraid of fleas. The fleas saved them from further torment from their oppressors. Corrie learned to thank God for fleas. I certainly have much good going on and a few fleas to find. God, help me be thankful for my slights, my sorry skin, and my struggles within. God, help me learn in everything to give thanks. Thanks, Corrie and Betsie, for modeling the way.

What fleabags are you thankful for?

BUILT TO LEAD | together we transform

Day 159: Twenty-seven to remember...

During team practice, I asked my client to describe his 3P workout and why he is committed to pushing, pulling, and planking his ass off three days a week. He looked sideways my way before telling his team about the why behind his 3Ps. They mostly listened. Once he finished speaking, I asked him to head over to the pull-up bar and try to knock out forty pulls. I asked the team to come out of their seats and count 'em as he pulled 'em up. They shouted them out, one by one. Number twenty-four hurt him badly. He stopped at the bottom, and I urged him on. He knocked out another. Once you've stopped and are simply hanging by a thread, it's almost impossible to do another pull-up unless your someone as crazy as young Durp. He knocked out yet another. And then one more.

Twenty-seven pulls. He was fried. He dropped from the bar, and the team cheered in response. They had just seen their leader put actions to his words. They were seared. I pulled them back together and asked them why we had just gone through what we had just gone through. They threw out some thoughts, and I kept telling them to keep going. Finally, someone got it. They saw the 7-38-55 example being brought to life in front of them.

7-38-55

Seven percent of your message is words, thirty-eight your voice, and fifty-five percent in your body language. Nothing makes your message more believable than modeling the way. Someday soon, your team will forget your words, leader. Durp modeled his why. His body and his body of work made him believable. Why are you wasting your time trying to find the right words when nobody remembers 'em anyway? Why not just sear them with your tone, your body language, and your example? We learn some from principles and precepts. We mostly learn from a person, from someone willing to model the way.

Durp is worth following. Are you?

Day 160: Let us run...

"Let us run with endurance the race that is set before us, looking to Jesus."

—Hebrews 12:1

After reading the latest science on endurance, it's humbling to remember how much of endurance comes down to our beliefs. Where does your strength come from, friend? Who do you rely upon? What are your deepest held beliefs around why you're here, whose you are, and who you are becoming as you endure a life of abundance as well as agony?

God, help me run the race humbly with endurance. God, help me.

Day 161: Sweat the right stuff...

When the brain is overwhelmed with too many tasks, it tends to ruminate and hold as many as possible in working memory for as long as it can. Eventually, this brain fatigues from too much thinking/too little acting and pops. Hard stop, oftentimes. Not smart.

However, when your brain has clarity about Worldview, Identity, Principles, Passions, Purposes, and Process, it's freed from thinking about the big stuff while trying to manage the small stuff. Smart. The reason some humans sweat the small stuff more than others is because they lack clarity around their WIP and 3P. Their BTL CORE lacks definition. These humans think too much about daily tasks and stressors because their brain can't connect the dots and make sense of it all. Not smart.

Want to increase your ability to get stuff done? Get clarity within. Build your strong CORE and authentically author your labor of love, your OPUS. Sweat the big stuff, if you will, even though your brain is telling you there's no time, and these deadlines right in front of you are labeled "dead" for a reason. You are not your mind. Control it. Sweat the big stuff. Before you know it, you won't be sweating the small stuff. The problem isn't that you're sweating. We are meant to labor, friend, just not in vain. We are meant to labor toward our aim, toward our labor of love. Here is where we drain the tank and come away, feeling somehow fuller. Smart.

Remember, friend, hard labor you disdain as you perspire. Hard OPUS you sustain as you tire. Have you chosen to do the hard work within, leader? Have you settled for becoming a highly paid laborer? Sweat the right stuff, friend. Smart.

Day 162: Peace...

Eight years ago, I made a change in my belief about pain. I now believe that peace comes on the other side of acute pain. Peace begins with a moment of surrender where we come to grips with the fact that we are not in control. If you and I aren't, who is? Answering this thoughtfully will be more painful than ignoring these thoughts in your every day, numbing them on your overwhelming days, and distracting yourself on the days in-between. Ignoring, distracting, and numbing will work for a while.

Picture a person with lower back pain and slow but steady weight gain. Ignoring it works for a while. Clever distractions work until nothing novel remains, and even the iPhone, Snapchat, Twitter, and YouTube seem so yesterday. Numbing works well until alcohol isn't enough, pot takes too long, and Oxycontin hits require more, more, more. Suddenly, the spine collapses, and nothing seems to work. The temporary peace this person had enjoyed was never real, never theirs, and not for long.

Picture the same person facing lower back pain and deciding to inflict more acute pain on purpose. This person decides to eat less and plank more. This will hurt a whole lot more than ignoring, distracting, and numbing. Acute pain will come in regular, jarring doses. Someday, this person will begin to gain strength in their core, and the pressure on their spine will lessen. They will know their choices made a difference. They will feel some semblance of peace on the other side of pain. Armed with this confidence-building experience, this same person will face another form of pain, inflict more acute pain on purpose, and slowly arrive on the other side again. More, more, and more momentum will build within.

Peace is possible, friend; it's just found on the other side of acute pain. Thomas Carlyle said, "Doubt, of whatever kind, can be ended by action alone." So, don't take my word for it—act into your chronic pain. Act. Pain is inevitable. Misery is a choice. What are you choosing?

Day 163: Golf and gratitude...

I began playing the game of golf at age nine. Dr. Scott sawed off some clubs for me, put spikes in a pair of tiny, leather loafers, and away we went to the Salina Elks golf course. There was something magical about walking around the countryside and chasing a little white ball. The grass was buffalo wherever there was any, and you learned to hit the ball first because the ground was as hard as concrete. It was not much of a golf course, but I loved it.

Recently, a couple of minutes before 8:00 a.m., my caddie (Squirrel) and I put a peg in the ground at one of the best golf courses in the world, Muirfield Village. I've been playing here for twenty-seven years now. The smells and sounds are a bit different from fifty-two years ago, but they're just as intoxicating. I'm grateful my dad introduced me to this game. It has taught me so much over the years of playing it. My game has disintegrated, but my enjoyment has increased exponentially. Every round, especially ones where it's just me and my caddie, take me back to the peace and solitude that only the game of golf offers. What other game is there that immerses you in God's creation, absorbs fully your attention, and places you in competition with only yourself? It can be enjoyed alone or with others. It can be played with competitiveness or social shits and giggles. Played alone, it turns spiritual, at least for me.

My golf balls have the Muirfield Village logo on one side and BTL on the other. The number is always seven, the most significant number in the Bible. You see, friends, for me, every round of golf is a reminder to enjoy all of life, not just the sweet shots, to keep score accurately, to play the ball where it lies, and to appreciate the time. I fired an eighty-six (not very good), but Dad would have been proud. I counted 'em all, cursed after none, inhaled the sacred smells, and exhaled all expectations. I was alone and all ONE, filled with golf and gratitude.

Today fill yourself with _____ and gratitude.

Day 164: Mentally strong...

Here is a habit of the mentally strong, friend. Master this. You are wired to remember your fails. Nothing wrong with your cranium when it does this. Use this to avoid the hot stove, running into traffic, and repeating stuff that hurts and doesn't help. Make sense?

Here is a habit of the mentally strong, friend. Masters remember their little wins. You see, friend, you've had lots of little wins, but your natural brain doesn't find most of them worth storing. Fight this tendency. Slow down and take a moment to celebrate your baby steps of progress today. This doesn't take long and will not make you soft. This habit will build self-esteem. The mentally strong fill themselves with esteem, primarily their own. When you esteem you, you begin to deepen your belief in you, and the more you believe in you, the more likely you are to get out of your comfort zone and reach for better. The mentally strong take more calculated risks. This is how they keep getting better. You build capacity by reaching outside your comfort zone and building skills you don't currently have. Do more of this, friend.

During a yoga class in the desert, I built some skills by doing poses very poorly. Everything felt out of sorts, and I didn't look very capable next to a bunch of old ladies and my best Miss. The instructor worked me hard and didn't let me off the hook. It hurt physically and mentally to do something I didn't know how to do. It hurt and helped. After class, I thanked the instructor for pushing me. She looked me in the eyes and told me she hadn't pushed me at all. She reminded me that she wasn't the one making me do anything: I was. So, I took a moment and let that thought seep in. I celebrated a little win doing yoga, even though I didn't do it well.

What little wins are you celebrating today?

BUILT TO LEAD | together we transform

Build Your Knowledge of Self

12 ESSENTIALS OF PERSONAL EXCELLENCE

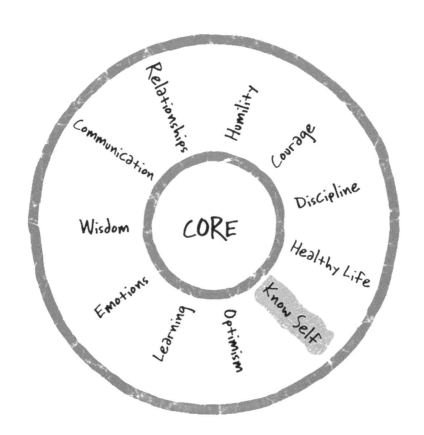

Cali's Builder's Journey

I think the clock exercise hit me the hardest. I shaded in (at the time) twenty-five years' worth of my life. I felt like a lost, tired, beat up dummy who worked hard and had little show for it. I was waking up because I had to, working because I had to, staying in a relationship because I felt like I had to, and I was coming to BTL because I felt like I had to. This clock exercise made me realize that we all have a timer, and it's not going backward. I didn't immediately take action because when I would begin to start writing about those topics, it hurt. It hurt bad.

Through BTL, I've learned this pain is actually good. It's how we learn who we are, what we're meant for, and where our hearts' deepest dreams and desires lie. Which then enables us to see clearly enough to begin chasing. I began building myself, my career, a life for my kids, and dug myself out of both debt and an abusive relationship. I did this through tireless writing on my beliefs—about love, about work, about money, about debt, about relationships, about trust, about forgiveness, and many more. These discoveries led me to figure out who I believed I was and uncover who I wanted to be.

It's funny—I actually did the most writing on the Identity piece of the WIP. Looking back, man, was I a mess! I'd let the words and actions of others toward me or about me really cloud my feelings of myself. I worked through abandonment issues from a fatherless childhood, body image issues from a far-from-perfect man, and a deep sense of failure by getting pregnant young and not finishing my degree. After about six years of working on myself, I can say today I'm far from a failure. I wake up every day because I love what I do and the people I spend my time with. My work has purpose, and I feel fulfilled day in and day out. Some days are tough, but the aim is clear, and it keeps me going. I'm happily engaged to a man who both makes me better and shows me a love I've only ever dreamt about. My children are thriving in school and growing into two of the greatest people I've ever met. My mom is proud of me and the life I've built and continue building. My brain is stimulated, I'm constantly learning, and my heart is full—I truly love my team and my work.

Bringing it back to the clock exercise, I can't help but think where I'd be today had I woken up earlier. My story is, unfortunately, relatable to many others. I work hard to stay raw and vulnerable with everyone around me, both here and outside of here, because I believe sometimes people just need a little hope. They need to see it's worth the pain of getting started.

As far as the impact on the team, I've watched BTL turn up our high performers and weed out our low. The bar was raised companywide by just a few lighting up through team practice. Conflict squashed, communication improved, challenges thrown, differences discussed, fights for performance, and, most importantly, deep trust built. Trust is truly at the root of high performance, and we're getting stronger every day.

Thanks for kicking my ass all these years. I'm still chasing the west coast but getting closer—I can feel it.

Cheers to another 365!

Day 165: My labeling of me...

According to DISC (a fairly old personality profiler), yours truly is a high I and secondary D. My MBTI says I'm an ENFP, which means I like to talk, intuit, feel, and perceive stuff. My explanatory style is barely optimistic, but my hope score is through the roof. Not sure what that one means. I love my strengths-finder results. They labeled me as an activator, command, learner, woo, and relator. This was version 1.0. When taken a second time, seems my wiring disconnected woo, relator, and command and rewired strategic, maximizer, and belief. My IQ test is 140, which is much better than my college label of 3.0. Simon Baron-Cohen has a great test to label your right/left brain. Turns out, I'm off the chart empathetic, but my system's thinking leaves much to be desired.

I believe we love to label our teams, our children, our parents, our neighbors, and ourselves because it's so much easier than getting to know who they really are and who we really are! I don't come with a simple label, and you don't either. I'm done trying to label my family, friends, and clients. My son Jordan has taught me the futility of the effort. He's a professional poker player, compassionate to the poor, and so much more. He cannot be boxed in. Forget your labels, friend. Do you know your identities, the names you call you? Have you spent time alone reflecting, thinking, and writing, or are you too busy running? Until you know who you are, it doesn't make much sense adding all these tag lines. Slow down and reflect. Go to your room. Invest time alone rinsing your *I ams*. Write. Rinse and repeat.

You are not who your labels say you are. See you back here tomorrow. We'll go deeper. Good.

Day 166: Match...

Humans love answers. We love personality profiles because they spit out simple answers like you're an EFNP, fact finder, lion, or blue. We love StrengthsFinder, Grit Assessment, and adversity tolerance tests because they provide answers to complex questions. We feel better being told we're this, that, or the other thing. Here's the truth, however. None of these tests represent absolute truth. You see, friend, whatever you are today, you can bet it wasn't accurate a decade ago. You are evolving. The more you've experimented and remained open to opportunities, the more likely you've found a match between your gifts and good work. When we study the elite in most any endeavor, a test didn't tell them who they are and how to best express it in their work and life—experiments opened their eyes. Nobody told them. They just knew it when they found a match.

You know more than you think about what moves you toward your best self. Pay attention a bit more, please. You are your best bet on figuring out you. Back in 1993, sitting in a crowded classroom at the Center for Creative Leadership, I knew that I'd found my calling. None of their crazy tests gave me the answer. None of the crazy docs did either. I just knew that what they were doing didn't look like work; it looked like fun. It felt like I'd found a match. I wanted to know more, so I started to study individuals, teams, and leaders with the aim of figuring out the essentials of excellence—I still am.

There is nothing wrong with taking tests and looking for answers. Experiments are just better bets. When you play around with something that interests you, nobody will have to tell you that you've found a match. You will know it when you stumble into it. Miss and I recently celebrated thirty-eight years of marriage. We dated around prior to deciding. We experimented. When I met her, however, I knew we were different. I felt like I'd found my match—I still do. Stop the incessant search for answers, friend. Experiment. Play. You'll know when it's a match. Remember that work we did on your love tos? Go play…

Day 167: Pass the tension...

Every system is filled with tension. The best tension comes when your system is growing faster than you thought it could. The worst tension comes when your system is receding. No system can survive a deep, relentless recession for long. Tension, remember, is not the problem—owning more than your own is. This is painfully obvious to see in other systems. When it comes to seeing this same tension in ourselves, our brain tricks us in a freakin' million little ways to miss the mark. Look at anybody in your system with the *responsibility* strength, and you will most likely see this strength stretched into a nightmare.

High-performing systems are filled with tension. If your system is not growing as you want, take a look around and study it. You will most likely find that the tension doesn't belong to its rightful owner. Somebody or some group is pushing their tension to someone willing to take it. Your job, as a leader, is to distribute it to its rightful owner. Simple, not easy.

Awareness doesn't make us better. Productive action does. You always have choices. Your choices have consequences. Choose wisely. Choose to own your tension and pass the rest to its rightful owner. What tension are you hoarding instead of passing along?

> To the extent that you
> (A) become enmeshed in
> the relationship of B and
> C (either because you have
> taken on the responsibility of
> their relationship or because
> they have focused on you)
> ...you will wind up with the
> stress of their relationship.
> —*Failure of Nerve* by Edwin Friedman

BUILT to **LEAD** | together we transform

Day 168: Attention is attractive...

Let's imagine, leader, that you want a bit more consistency, more commitment, and more competence from your inner circle. You know they can do more, be more, and give more but can't quite push the right buttons. You feel stuck and are beginning to feel like you're stuck with them. Has it occurred to you that they may be feeling stuck with you?

Your team wants more, too—they want more of you. Give your teammates consistent, undivided, and non-judgmental attention. Be with. Understand them. Attention is attractive—really, really attractive. We do our best work where our heart is in it. This is a rare and wonderful thing when we feel whole—wholehearted, that is. You see, friend, most humans protect their hearts from those in power. This is why most humans do their best work at home, in community, or for some charity they care deeply about. They feel connected. Connected teams are built primarily by your attention, leader. Want your team to care more at work? Build a more connected team. Give more of your attention, your most precious commodity. Give them the gift of your non-anxious presence. Give them this consistently, not when you have the time, but when you've made time for what matters most, when you've made time for them. Be with.

Give more attention to your team, leader. Understand them. Care for them. Protect them. Be vulnerable and share your heart. Jesus is right: Give, and it shall be given to you. Where, leader, do you give your undivided attention? Have you chosen to give more first, or are you waiting around until you get more? Are you connecting from your heart or hiding behind heady, strategic instructions from on high? Attention is attractive. Master the art of being with. Are you?

Day 169: Awake and oriented times four...

What's your name? What time is it? Where are you? What just happened?

These are the four questions Terry asked me on the side of Breckenridge Mountain Eight back in the summer of 2008. The ambulance sirens were blaring, the sun was shining, and my brain was refusing to cooperate. Just moments earlier, I had been enjoying a mountain bike ride with my son Jordan when I rounded the last switchback and saw an obstacle in my way. Another rider. My last memory was my feet leaving the pedals. I remember the awesome feeling of taking flight. When Terry arrived and started in with the questions, I could only remember my name. I was alert and oriented times one. Not good.

Life is hard. You don't know what's around the next bend. You think you're flying high until suddenly you're not, and nothing makes sense. This is why you're here slowing down. This is why you build your CORE, author your authentic OPUS, and prepare for your tough trials. All of us would benefit from being knocked out for a brief period and observing the mind rebooting itself.

Do you know your name (Identity)? Do you know what time it is (*kairos*)? Do you know where you are and where you're going (OPUS)? Do you know what just happened and why it hurts (strong CORE)?

Slow down...

Day 170: Learning...

One of my deeply held beliefs is around learning. I believe we are meant to be lifelong learners. None of us is enlightened. Some of us have simply learned to keep seeking light.

Modern man is learning stuff about the universe and uncovering incredible truths about artificial intelligence at an ever-increasing rate. We are living in an amazing time of discovery. Self-driving cars are coming fast and so much more. The modern world keeps bringing new possibilities into the hands of the many. We can get things done on our own that only a few years ago were impossible without tons of others doing the heavy lifting. Yet we continue to self-sabotage at alarming rates. It seems the more we make life easy, the harder it is to stay happy. With the opportunity to have so much done for us, we struggle to make our moments matter.

If you want to avoid shooting yourself in the foot, learn more about yourself than you do about other stuff. Study you. Know thyself, really know who you are. Self-awareness is undervalued. Oh, we certainly talk about it, get report after report about it, identify our personality in hundreds of new ways, and have 360 after 360 presented to us. We do not lack data. We're not learning much, it would seem, if you study how frequently our most successful self-destruct. Build self-awareness. Study you. Seek truth, hard truth about your tendencies. Learn. Own your stuff. You see, you are your own worst enemy, at least that is my belief about all of us.

When was the last time you asked for someone to illuminate your blind spot? Do it today, friend. Learn more about your greatest leadership challenge—learn more about you.

Day 171: Stronger...

I suck at most anything mechanical. Working on crossword puzzles does not excite me. Sudoku leaves me sad. Handyman, I am not. I invest very little effort in being well-rounded. I play to my strengths. Simple, not easy.

The world will tell you to work on what weakens you. Performance appraisals, 360 feedback, and countless, well-meaning colleagues will tell you exactly what they think you need to work on to improve your performance. Ninety-nine percent of their feedback will not be helpful. The best feedback always comes from the activity. Tune in. Your strengths are not defined as stuff you're good at. Your strengths, properly defined, are what makes you feel strong. Thanks, Marcus Buckingham. Do you know yours? Do you play to them every day, or only on the weekends, or when you have the time? Do you know how to make them stronger? Are you still doing the work? Slow down and sit with this for a while.

Studying, learning, and applying what causes individuals, teams, and leaders to go from a lone toward becoming all ONE lights my fire. Preparing for one-on-one practice with any one of my clients is almost as flow producing as the actual practice itself. Practicing with any of the teams I'm blessed to call BTL is my greatest strength. No work makes me feel stronger than creating a MOT with a team of men and women who've come together for the express purpose of becoming more than they currently are. It sends tingles down my spine and makes me conscious of my Creator. I feel strong, joyful, and grateful. Feedback from others is welcome but rarely moves the needle. Feedback from the work, however, is the station locked into my internal dial. I am not alone. Masters are not trying to become something they're not. Normal humans are constantly obsessed with others' opinions. Masters play to their strengths and make them even stronger. Masters fixate here. Do you?

Slow down. Reflect. Write. Are your CORE and OPUS becoming your compass and map?

Day 172: Messi strong...

Messi is the soccer maestro that leaves most defenders frozen in their tracks. He's a master. Watch him on film and be amazed at his moves. The ball appears to be attached to his boot. Here's a funny fact. Messi hardly touches the ball with his right foot. I mean, come on, man, wouldn't you expect the maestro to be equally adept with either foot, able to beat his opponent regardless which way they play him? Nope. Turns out he's not very good going right. In fact, his touches are 10:1 left foot to right. He plays to his strength 10X! His opponents know this. His coaches know this. Does. Not. Matter. Turns out, you don't even have to be well-rounded in your chosen endeavor; you just have to be extraordinary. Freakin' magic, huh?

Do not run from feedback. Let it in. Welcome it. Learn from the 1% who can make a world of difference. Let most of it, however, run right on through. And tune your dial to the work itself. You will quickly learn what works. Don't fixate on applause and being popular. Fixate on mastering something meaningful and joyful for you. Tune into your God-given strengths and keep working 'em like life itself depends upon it. Never stop working. Never stop learning. Never stop your pursuit of excellence. You are meant to labor in love, not vain. Labor in love.

This is why we believe our OPUS acrostic is freakin' magic. You see, friend, OPUS is a meaning maker. Play to it. Play with it. Who knows what a 10X touch might do for you and our world? For those of you I'm privileged to play with, see you at our next practice. See you in my place of OPUS. See you soon, my labor of love. See you soon.

Life is an energy management problem. Your strengths give you juice. What strengths of yours are you learning to trust like Messi trusts that damn left foot of his?

Day 173: Truer...

Most leaders hesitate in MOT (Moments of Truth). They don't trust themselves to speak truth in love, so they hesitate and wait for when the time's right. Funny how time, right now, is so rarely right, huh.

The truth is many MOT come and go because the leader hesitates out of fear. I've oftentimes told these leaders they whiffed, and they agree. "I know, Chet, I know," they will say. "I know I need to be tougher," they share almost as a poor form of penance. Here's how I've recently discovered to sear their sorriness. I tell them this hard truth—they don't need to be tougher, not at all. They need to be truer. Truth in love, you see, is both tough and tender. In MOT, it matters a great deal if you trust your heart and head enough to open your mouth and let truth spill out. The stronger your CORE, the less hesitation, and the more the moment feels like Church, Synagogue, or another virtuous, sacred space.

Truth does not harm.

Truth may hurt. Truth helps. Truth, eventually, heals. So, next time you think about hesitating in an MOT, remind yourself you don't have to be tougher, only truer. What will your team look like when it bathes in more truth, especially more truth in love? You, leader, can handle truer. Lead a team toward being truer. Slow down and sit with this one for a while. This was a tiny truth loaded with performance ramifications. Write.

Live hard. Love harder. Be Truer…

Day 174: Genuine objectivity...

Recently, we had a newbie join a high-performance team we've worked with a number of years. I asked the leader to tell our newb what to expect in BTL team practice. The leader took a moment to think. "Two words," he said and then paused before sharing his two words to describe me. Before dropping the two, he told the newb that BTL practice as facilitated by me isn't "rah, rah—or in-your-face crazed." I couldn't help but smile as I tuned in and waited for his words. He continued to tell the newbie more about what this wasn't. "Team practice isn't this or that. It's not like anything you may have experienced over here or there," he continued. He paused again and then dropped his two words to describe BTL team practice and my leadership. I waited and wondered.

Genuine objectivity.

My client described me, and this thing called practice as genuine objectivity. He went on to explain what he meant. He shared that I am genuine. He told the newbie he could trust me, that I'm no bullshit artist—just the opposite. He said, "Chet brings genuine objectivity to our team that we appreciate." He went on and on, at least it seemed so to me. He kept coming back to genuine objectivity. I've never heard me or BTL team practice described so well.

Our job, as builders, is to calmly read the room and offer objective, outside perspectives rooted in competence and delivered with humble conviction. Our job is to play with what the team gives us and "and" in such a way it feels almost scripted even though there's no way it could have been. Our job is to remain quiet most of the time, let others speak, tune in, and tell stories that are sticky, relevant, and bring it home. We are not entertainers, politically correct, bullshit artists, or soft kitties. We are truth-tellers who build distinct and deeply connected teams stronger. We bring genuine objectivity to practice. We build teams of peers that do likewise. Two words to describe BTL and our style? Genuine objectivity.

What couple of words describe your style, leader? Don't answer yourself. Go ask those you're called to serve.

Day 175: Be with and be the man...

One of our favorite prescriptions for our clients is to master the art of being with (thank you, Larry). The journey toward Becoming BTL requires the leader to, simply, be with her team. Nothing builds trust more than the non-anxious presence of a leader. Simple, not easy. Be with. Here's the paradox. It's not enough to simply be with. Sometimes (oftentimes, actually) you, leader, have to be "the man." Be with and be the man.

Be with, without be the man, is not leading: it's more akin to being a good friend. To be with and be the man, you must possess a strong CORE, clear OPUS, and the wisdom to toggle between be with and be the man. This is really freakin' hard and takes a ton of time, a few truth-tellers around you, and a willingness to be humbled in front of the very ones we're supposed to be leading.

Be with and be the man is for the few—the few willing to master the moments of ambiguity and lead anyway. These leaders toggle wisely. Sometimes, they make the team do more. Sometimes, they stay quiet, be with, and let them figure it out. Sometimes smiling and jumping for joy and sometimes being CCD, correcting, and even imploring 'em for more. Sometimes, these leaders get heated, make mistakes, and humbly repair.

You most likely are better at be with or be the man. Lean against your tendency. Lean into it too. Lean on others. Nobody is as smart as everybody. Be with and be the man. Figure it out. What are you doing to lean against your tendencies?

Day 176: Intuition...

Intuition—like so much of life, we think some people have it, and some don't. I mean, come on, man, we know the old saying, "A mother's intuition," means that Momma just naturally got mo. We think, regarding intuition, incorrectly.

Expert intuition, according to Daniel Kahneman in *Thinking Fast and Slow,* is not some mother's magic. Expert intuition is the result of deliberate practice done well. Mothers do mostly possess it when it comes to their kids. You see, most moms have been deliberately studying those they love since before they gave birth and have tuned in to all their body language, tone, and patterns of behavior. Expert intuition is due to the expert's attention. Mom's know what's up before most men because they've been more attentive. The truth is they have become an expert by paying attention with their eyes, ears, nose, and hands— yes, their hands. Moms learn so much by touch, don't they? I wonder what will happen to the evolution of this intuition with so many Moms death-gripping iPhones and locked in on Instagram?

So, friend, if you want to make quicker and better decisions in your profession, pay more attention to the people and process. Study them. Study competitors. Study the best. Figure out how to extrapolate your learning to your system. Brett Kaufman doesn't have some God-given talent for picking the right location and matching it with the right product/experience. He's been studying Columbus and his craft since he turned pro. His gut is more informed than yours or mine when it comes to saying yes to one and no to another. You don't have to be a mother to build a mother's intuition. You just have to train all your senses and care like one.

Where are you giving your undivided attention, friend?

Day 177: Presence...

Leaders, please listen up. I know you are super busy getting all kinds of good stuff done. I see it in your darting eyes, nervous twitches, and uneasy posture, so I'll get right to the point.

It's not your position; it's your presence. It's not your power; it's your presence. It's not your perfection; it's your presence. It's not your process; it's your presence. It's not your professionalism; it's your presence. It's not your people; it's your presence. It's not your problem-solving; it's your presence. It's not your pride; it's your presence. It's not your playing of the games; it's your presence.

It's your presence that sets the tone on your team. What, leader, does your presence bring to your teams? Does your presence bring something different at home? Slow down and sit with this for a while. Slow down, busy leader. Your presence matters more. Thank you, Jesus, for modeling the way, embracing pain and suffering, and embodying truth in Love. I sense your presence even now. It's not your perfection, friend; it's your presence.

Slow down, friend, and tune into your presence. Be with.

Who you are when you are with them is more important than what you say or do.
—Gurüe

Day 178: Begin to believe...

Today, during a freakin' magic one-on-one practice with a young leader who is gaining clarity, we went from his writing to a scene out of the movie *The Matrix* to drive home a point. He lit up like a Roman candle lights up a darkened sky. He is becoming a new man (Neo) as he is beginning to believe he has what it takes. He does, by the way, he's just taken a while to believe it. The same is most likely true for you, my normal reader. Your limiting beliefs are limiting your behavior more than your bolted-on beliefs are igniting them.

Flip the script.

Write out your self-limiting beliefs, friend. Now, throw them out. I mean, really toss them in the trash. Flush them. Eject them into outer space. You get the picture, I'm sure. Now that you're clean, write out your most bolted-on beliefs. Inject these deep into your CORE. Begin to monitor your behaviors and catch yourself beginning to believe and acting accordingly. Gain courage as you notice this second nature growing within you. Like my client today, you can be the change you want to see in the world, but first, you've got to believe.

There is nothing more powerful than a believable version of you. What self-limiting beliefs are you ejecting, friend?

Day 179: Loss to learning...

The heart of elite performers, if they are to sustain this level of performance, is rooted in love and humility. Elite love the pursuit of better. Elite don't like to lose but have the humility to learn like a banshee when they do. Yesterday, an elite client of mine wrote me some great words. He wrote to me the root reason behind a recent loss of his. He beat himself up. I mean, he kicked himself hard. He wrote it out so he could get it out, he told me. He went to bed that night and slept like a baby. This morning, he further explained himself, and his good night's rest was further proof to him that kicking his own ass had been a righteous experience. He had gotten it out of him and was at peace that the loss was turned to learning.

If you want to become elite and sustain it, you had better get busy building this skill. If you want to be normal or average, just tell yourself the lie that you're "showtime" when you didn't even make the show. Go on—put yourself on Instagram, Twitter, and whatever other social media you choose. Make yourself look like you've got something special. You'll feel good for a while. This feeling will not last for long.

Elite performers lose. When they do, they learn. Elite don't wait for their coach or builder to jump their stuff. Like my client, they beat their builder to the punch. Are you beating your builder to the punch or bullshitting yourself? When was the last time you were harder on yourself than someone on your team? When was the last time you learned, really learned, by humbly admitting you got your ass handed to you and getting it out there instead of burying it somewhere?

Day 180: Praise...

During practice 217, a new teammate told her team she's trying to figure out how to get her cup filled around here. Being surrounded by crazies in a culture of curiosity, she was immediately greeted with curious question after curious question. As the team took her deeper into her thinking, it became clear that one of her love languages is around words of affirmation: she loves praise. Come to think of it, don't we all?

Who doesn't love to be recognized and have a leader who cheers them on and notices even the smallest of accomplishments along the way? Humans thrive when proper praise follows good performance. Makes sense. So, leaders, remember to celebrate early and often. Celebrate small victories, not just large. Celebrate baby steps. Praise hard work and effort even when we lose. And, teammate, don't forget you live in the real world. The perfect, praise-heavy leader doesn't exist. There will be many of your best moments missed by him/her. Oftentimes, they won't even be present. Sometimes, you won't have another teammate around to praise your magical moment either. And even when people are present and the performance freakin' magical, there will be many a moment where the leader/teammate/customer/friend is simply busy thinking about another performance or performer while participating alongside you.

Remember, the best praise comes from performing. Yes, the best feedback is always from the work itself. As Mihaly Csikszentmihalyi, the author of Flow, proved through his research on optimal performance, the best feedback is the immediate feedback you get from your work. So, get in the habit of tuning into your performances and knowing the difference between when you're in the zone vs. the mediocre middle or just checking off the boxes. Your body and brain will tell you. Tune in. Master your craft and pay attention to the tiny details that lead you to a praiseworthy performance. Turns out, the best way to maintain a full cup is to authentically esteem yourself for a job well done. The best praise comes from the performance itself. Fill your own cup, friend.

Day 181: Stretch your strengths...

Here's some truth about your nature: you have one. You have much in common with other humans, yet you are unique, gifted, and gloriously made as a creature of God. You are not a mistake. You are a child of God, designed for purpose and meaning beyond belief. You alone can figure you out—it's your most important work. Hence the Oracle's famous creed, "Know thyself."

Most never do.

So, here's some truth for you. You do not become something you're not when you cheat toward what strengthens you and away from what weakens you. Life is an energy management problem, remember. God didn't design you to labor in vain, pain, and eventually drained. God designed you to labor in love, being who you are, displaying His glory, and giving the world a glimpse of His nature as you give more than you take while leaving the world in a little better place. So, friend, do you know your hard wiring? Do you know your labor of love? Are you playing to your strengths?

Masters are always domain-specific. You are meant to master your craft. As you gain clarity within, you will discover your strengths, which will enable you to sustain uncommon effort and build unique skills in your labor of love—your OPUS. You are an original with unique strengths. Know them. Cheat toward them. Build mastery in and through them. Stretch your strengths. During practice twenty-nine, we pushed a teammate outside his comfort zone, and we stretched him. The next day, he responded that he appreciated and wanted the push. Instead of pushing back, he pushed through. How 'bout you, friend? Are you staying in your comfort zone or putting yourself in the challenge zone and stretching your strengths?

Day 182: Feedback you can use...

I recently freaked a BTL team out when I told them that about 1% of the feedback I receive from others regarding my work is useful. Ninety-nine percent goes into my CORE and finds no place to call home. The stronger you become, the more you're going to discover the best feedback comes from your work.

Humans are not very good at evaluating others. Fact. We are better at evaluating ourselves. Play to this with your questions, leader. Ask your teammates one or two questions about themselves. Ask them to tell you more. Dig. Humans do not reliably rate what another human is feeling/thinking (Thanks, Rob Lowe). Most of us struggle to be accurate when it comes to either.

Practice being interested in them, leader. Are you aware of when you're at your best? Do you know when you're in the zone leading others? Do you know how to put yourself in flow? Are you studying you? Are you studying your teammates?

> The more a job inherently resembles a game—with variety, appropriate and flexible challenges, clear goals, and immediate feedback—the more enjoyable it will be regardless of the worker's level of development.
> —*Flow* by Mihaly Csikszentmihalyi

Day 183: Be you...

Build a strong CORE. Confidence, conviction, and calm will come. Be who you are. Throw away the masks. Dump the false bravado or false humility. Be you. As you learn to be you at your best, you will connect with the right humans along this road we call your Builder's Journey. Stop worrying about being what you think others want you to be. You, by the way, are a horrible predictor of what others are thinking. Stop trying. Get comfortable in the only skin that must fit you—your own. So, next time someone comes in curious or challenging, be good with it. Don't think. Don't panic. Don't get put off. Don't get anxious or defensive. Don't take it quite so personally. Rinse your CORE. Make your OPUS your aim. Become disciplined in your PoP.

Be(come) you. Good.

BUILT to **LEAD** | together we transform

Build Your Optimism

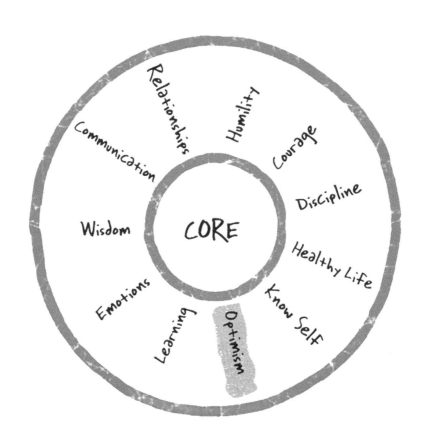

Chad's Builder's Journey

My life has been incredible and, at times, incredibly hard. I grew up in Cleveland, the youngest of four. My middle school and high school years were defined and focused on one thing, the sport of wrestling. I learned everything I needed to know about mental toughness, discipline, and doing whatever it takes to get what I want. A road less traveled, for sure. I didn't leave for college with the color medal I wanted, but I left with something much more valuable and knew that when the next expression of something I loved showed up in my life, I had what it took to get after it. Going hard with all my heart was all I knew.

My college experience at Ohio State was a joke. I learned more during my first sales call than all four years in class. I started my business from my apartment on campus during my senior year and, after graduating, opened my first office. I had no clue how many orange barrels would get in the way as I started down the path of becoming an entrepreneur.

Over the past decade, I had twin boys, transformed myself into a believer, put a yarmulke on my head and started living an observant lifestyle, bought out my business partner, moved into a new city, became a community builder, got remarried, gave up control of my company, started a new company (and then another), and negotiated new partnerships, all of which led me to a point where I could finally start integrating my work and life OPUS into one crazy unrealistic magnum opus. I've decided to retire from things I don't like and from doing things with people I don't care for. Now, I'm focused on leading leaders *and* still allowing myself to be led.

My common denominators have been few—coaching and developing, learning and applying. My desire to grow and my courage to go has been my best asset. My builder, Chet Scott, and **BUILT TO LEAD** has etched a place in my heart and has been there for me through it all. Together, curling hundreds of reps and more than 300 team practices, we've challenged, laughed, cried, and fought. The only thing we haven't done yet is wrestle. One day…The road continues—stay raw.

Day 184: Learntohelpyourleaderville...

Learned helplessness is a term coined by the father of positive psychology, Dr. Martin Seligman. If you haven't read his seminal book, *Learned Optimism*, you're missing out. According to Seligman, learned helplessness is growing to epidemic proportions in our country, and it's the ultimate gateway drug if you will. Once you tell yourself you are not responsible for your plight, it's like taking a pill that will quickly have you tumbling down the bunny-hole and landing in victimhood. Seemingly, this village has lots of well-worn trails leading in but none leading out. Do not swallow the learned-helplessness pill.

We see the effects of this pill all over the world of work, mostly around the relationship between associates and leaders. Very few teammates have learned to help their leader, partner, or even teammate. This is the epidemic of the "I," and it's not helping any of us. Instead of seeing your leader as someone to avoid, workaround, or placate, see your leader as someone in need of your help. Learn to lead up.

Here's the recipe for learning to help your leader. Step one is a big one. Step one is to be a performer. Nobody listens to the whiner, barely holding onto his job. Get your stuff together before you open your mouth. Perform. Help those around you perform. Be accretive. Now you're ready to step up. Instead of complaining about your leader, schedule time to talk. Ask if they want to hear your perspective. If they don't, depart. If they do, speak CCD. If they listen and then go all Triple-D on you, depart. If they listen and ask clarifying questions, answer them with truth in love. Tell them hard truth because you want both them and your system to learn. Once they've got the nugget, thank them for their time and depart. Rinse and repeat as necessary. You've left learned helplessness and taken up residence in the village of high performers—Learntohelpyourleaderville.

Where are you taking up residence, friend?

Day 185: Learned optimism...

When I first read *Learned Optimism* by Martin Seligman, I can remember wishing my dad was still alive. He suffered his entire life with negative thinking. My dad was not alone. Losing our optimistic attitude shows up in a variety of places but none more powerful than in our loss of confidence. On the days when I trust my swing, golf is about fairways and greens; however, when my confidence is shaken, golf is all about sand, water, and trees. Our attitude affects more than our performance in sport.

We all have a little voice inside our head that either encourages us to go for it or screams for us to run away. One screams, "You da man," while another chastises, "You ain't nothing." Our little voice is complicated. Understanding and changing it is something most will benefit from. Me included. I tend to catastrophize specific situations. When that situation goes negative, for whatever reason, the little voice tells me, "That is just the way it is—it will not change." I catastrophize. Conclusion: I surmise that things are much worse than they are and that changing them is above my pay grade. This is the route to victimhood. You do not want to take up residence there.

Pessimistic thinking is a leading cause of depression, and we've got an epidemic of depression going down. Women are twice as likely as men. America is leading the way. We who have so much to live with appear to have too little to live for. Reading Seligman's work has changed my mind. His ABCs are freakin' magic. We'll unpack this a bit more tomorrow.

Today, scream something positive at yourself.

Day 186: ABCs of optimism...

Let me introduce you to the ABCs of your explanatory style.

A stands for adversity. There is power in naming. Name the event, circumstance, or person. Your little voice is lessened when you name your adversity.

B represents your beliefs about said adversity. Again, beliefs matter. When adversity strikes, write what you believe about it. It's amazing how many adversities summon up our self-limiting beliefs.

C stands for the consequences.

Explanatory style, according to Dr. Seligman's research in *Learned Optimism*, is very powerful. Your explanatory style is rooted in that little voice in your head and plays like a long-ago recorded script. Certain events trigger my negative thinking. Certain people too. As I've built awareness and caught the script before it goes thermal nuclear, my catastrophizing has calmed down. This is learned optimism.

When adversity strikes, high performers explain events more positively than the norm. High performers do not catastrophize. They do not explain good or bad events as personal, pervasive, or permanent. High performers have learned optimism. This is not some "Pollyanna, rose-colored glasses" positivity. This is learned optimism. The aim is to develop one's resilient response to adversity.

> ...briefly, the first is that in general, depression is a disorder of the "I," failing in your own eyes relative to your goals. In a society in which individualism is becoming rampant, people more and more believe that they are the center of the world. Such a belief system makes individual failure almost inconsolable."
>
> —*Learned Optimism* **by Martin Seligman**

What, you ask, is the resilient response of high performers toward whatever adversity they face? Keep working. Now, you might know a bit more about why "keep working" is one of my mantras. What are yours?

Day 187: Explanatory Style...

Today, a client told me some hard truth. He failed this past week in significant ways. In fact, he told me very soberly that he rates himself (on a scale of 1–10) around a two almost every day. He is not thinking clearly. His explanatory style, the way he explains events to himself, is messed up. He is hard on self and down on self.

So, I reminded him what it looks like to be hard on self but not down on self with the story of Matt Biondi and the 1988 Olympics. You see, Matt faced massive disappointment and adversity by losing the first two races by a fraction of a second. Most would have told themselves it just wasn't their day. Matt told himself to keep working, so he did, winning five gold medals. Biondi was hard on self, not down on self. Matt was mentally tough. My client is learning to catch his little voice and then change it. This is not easy and starts with awareness of the adversity.

My client is not behaving in alignment with beliefs. He is filled with negative self-talk, rooted in his childhood, and habituated for far too long. We're changing this. Actually, he is. I'm simply giving him tools and holding him accountable. You, too, most likely have integrity gaps that are not a reflection of your character but instead reflect inaccurate thinking. It's far easier to change one's thinking than it is to fix a character flaw. Catch the faulty thinking and learn to replace the negative self-talk with thoughts anchored in reality. You are not too much or too little. You need to focus your mind on the progress you're making, not the distance you still have to go. We are all a work in process, my friend. Tell yourself that next time adversity and your explanatory style try to make a mountain out of a molehill.

Read *Learned Optimism* by Martin Seligman. Learn your ABCs.

BUILT TO LEAD | together we transform

Day 188: Hope...

Without hope, we don't dream. Thankful, grateful, and hopeful are intermingled.

Way back in the day, Chet and Marie Scott, after surviving WWII, the Great Depression, and the Dust Bowl, decided to get married. As soon as Chet was through medical school, they started having babies. Settling in Salina, Kansas, they were optimistic Jayhawks, to say the least. Marie's first pregnancy resulted in a miscarriage, as did the next two. Hope took a hit. My two brothers, Charles Godwin and David Michael, didn't live a day. Hope hit bottom. After a handful of unsuccessful attempts, most normal humans would have given up. Chet and Marie decided to keep trying. Kathryn Ann was born on January 6, 1956. Mary Marie came bursting on the scene August 10, 1957. Marie was satisfied. Chet, however, wanted a boy. So, after all those births, all the pain, and in the middle of all the work involved in raising two toddlers and a family medical practice, they pushed for one more. Chester E. Scott II came screaming onto the scene on March 25, 1959, and here I am sixty-one years later writing about it. Chet and Marie were filled with hope.

Thank God they were.

They had been through hard times and acute pain. They had not lost hope. They brought babies into the world and gave them what they hadn't been given: gifts, good clothes, bikes, balls, piano lessons, cars, their own rooms, and more attention than could ever have been given to them. Chet and Marie had big dreams for the world they were giving their children, fueled by their hope for better times. We inherited this hope. We are blessed beyond belief as a result. Actually, we are blessed with belief as a result. You see, leaders are believers. Leaders, the kind you and I will follow, are filled with belief. Leaders believe in themselves, their teams, and their vision. Leaders believe the best is not behind them, but it's just up ahead. Leaders are dreamers. You and I don't dream if we don't have hope. I hope you're getting this, and I hope you're giving it too.

What do you believe? Are you believable? Are you letting a few hard times rob you and your team of hope?

Day 189: Milk and honey...

Dream and do. You've heard this before, friend. The BTL way forward, toward the life of your destiny, is found on the dream and do trail. We believe all humans have a song to sing, a canvas to cover, and unique gifting and wiring toward becoming the original you already are. Out of fear, the mass of humanity gets busy on the do-do trail. As of this writing, we don't know where this trail leads. It appears to be a lot like I270 or any other outer belt around our great country. It's filled with cars, but it's not going anywhere unless you know which exit to take. The do-do trail is like an endless 270 doing loops until you run out of gas, left with the feeling of *what was the point, really?*

Dream and do, instead. Like the Israelites of old, the promised land is your destiny. Metaphorically, this dreamland is flowing with milk and honey. Don't believe this means the dream and do trail is all butterfly kisses, however. Think about it. If your destiny is milk and honey, this means there's gonna be bulls and bees. You know what this means, right? Bullshit and bee stings.

Dream and do is no easy way. There is no easy way to anything excellent. You were not made for easy either. You were meant to aim at excellence and never stop working toward your dreamland. None of us is designed to go it a lone. We are meant to belong and give courage to each other along the dream and do trail. We are meant to move from a lone toward all ONE—one 'L of a difference. We are meant to become one, distinct, and deeply connected. The bullshit and bee stings are obstacles in the way. No biggie when our eyes are focused on the milk and honey.

Bullshit and bee stings. Milk and honey. Where, friend, is your focus?

Day 190: Reminders...

We ended practice 125 with Bradley talking about rekindling, rediscovering, and re-energizing. He feels like his life has become too narrowly focused over the past half-dozen years or so. He feels lost and wants to find himself, so to speak. He is not alone in this endeavor of rediscovering, rekindling, and re-energizing. We all lose some of ourselves as we move through the natural transitions of life. All humans must learn to downshift and slow down on the speedway we call work and life. Rediscovering your love tos is all about the power of Passion.

Life, remember, is an energy management problem. Most humans lose track of their love tos along the way toward becoming an adult. Caught up in the rush to responsibility, they forget the artist inside. Reawakening these Passions is part of the process. This is why the 3P elements of your CORE begin with Passions, followed by Purposes, and delivered through your Process. Humans need lots of reminders. Slow down and let a little kindling restart your fire.

Even Big Ten championships are bitter and sweet, like so much of life. There are always those who felt like the team won, but they lost. There are those who felt the team won, but they're not really a part of it since they didn't even get in the game. There are those who felt the team won, they won, yet it feels shallow or something less than it should. There are always those who feel like it's time to move on to bigger things and not take the time to celebrate along the way. All victories, I've come to discover, have an element of the bitter and the sweet—such is life. Great leaders understand and embrace this. Learning to love yourself, your work, and your team is fuel for life. Learn this. You are an artist in addition to whatever else you are. You cannot perform at your peak until you align Purposes with Passions. Rediscover, rekindle, re-energize. The greatest moral teachers do little instructing; they mostly remind us.

Remind yourself who you are, why you're here, what you believe, and why it matters. Rinse and repeat. Are you beginning to see why CORE, OPUS, and PoP are BTL's version of the Energizer Bunny? Do you feel re-energized? Slow down. Reflect. Write.

Day 191: Hear me...

We are blessed to work with a very strange breed who hold positions of power yet are willing to subject themselves to being humbled in the process of Becoming BTL. This process is always acutely painful. Peace is found, fleetingly, on the other side. Life is hard even for those whose privilege it is to lead us. This is why the Bible instructs us to pray for our leaders. Fact.

Recently, a leader shared one of his leadership challenges with me. He has a teammate who is lost in his negative explanatory style—his pessimistic way of explaining what's going on. The funny thing is, his teammate is at the top of his game. He's best in class and the envy of the entire organization. He's the main man, and we all know it. Doesn't much matter, friend. This is a frequent leadership challenge as much as the common cold. You see, friend, we mostly listen to one voice—the little one in our head. It doesn't do much good trying to go around and fill everyone up with your belief when they lack belief themselves. The best way to help the hurting is to hear them. Ask them to tell you more and hear them out. Hear the yearning, not the whining. We all hurt and want an ear.

The more you hear me, the more my mind calms and soothes itself. And as the mind calms, clarity comes. Feeling understood frees our bullshit-burdened brain. As we write, further clarity comes. We see, oftentimes suddenly, where we're shaming ourselves. Leader, most of your team is hurting, even the elite amongst you. Stop attempting to fix them through your words. Give them your ears. Give them the gift of hearing. Most humans, especially the high-performing ones on your teams, listen to their own voice. Hear them.

Who on your team needs the gift of being heard? Who is quietly asking you to *hear me*?

BUILT TO LEAD | together we transform

Build Your Commitment to Learn

12 ESSENTIALS OF PERSONAL EXCELLENCE

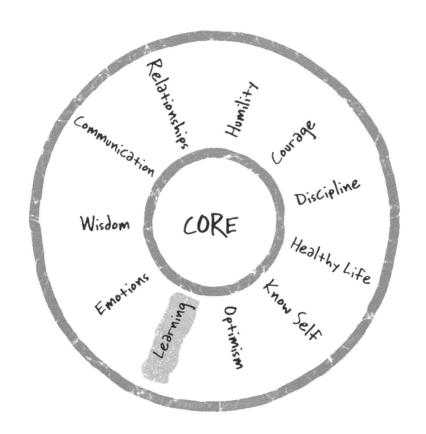

Kyle's Builder's Journey

I am insane. Extreme in everything I do. I have always chosen the path of the greatest risk and highest adventure, both in business and in play. I started my business for the purpose of creating unlimited funds to pursue my adventures. And I achieved every financial goal I wanted. My life reached perfection as my four became old enough to join me in the adventures. I did it on my own, in my own way, without help from anyone. I was proud of my "self-made" label and fully embraced the attitude of "if it's going to be, it's up to me!"

Then, a series of events began to dismantle my entire life, both professionally and personally. I responded as I always respond. Fight back. And always fight to win. I remained fully confident in my ability to return to the top. If it's going to be, it's up to me.

This was when I met Chet Scott. I was not enthusiastic about meeting him. Over the years, several coaches had pitched their services to me. I was unimpressed with their generic advice. My success had come from doing things my way. Aggressive, innovative, shooting from the hip. Their assembly-line solutions would never work for me.

But Chet Scott was different. He gave no solutions, no answers. Instead, he asked questions. Deep questions, forcing me to discover the CORE of who I am, defining the force that was driving me.

To be honest, I was very frustrated during those first months. Impatient. Just give me some good tips and advice—and let me return to the battle. I'll be on top in no time. But Chet was not impressed with my speed. His first steps were to slow me down (something we are still working on). He taught me to talk less, write more. He said, "You are allowed to shoot from the hip. But know why you are shooting."

Slowly, I discovered Chet focused less on the goal we call "success" and more on the process we call OPUS. He led me to clarify and articulate my Worldview, my Identity, my Purpose (uniquely mine, not his). He then developed productive actions, a daily scorecard measuring my growth toward my stated purpose and beliefs. It is a never-ending journey, becoming clearer with every step forward.

Chet began to remove my blinders, opening my eyes to both my greatest contradictions and my deepest passions. I began realizing how I too easily altered my values to guarantee a win. How my courageous acts were often to mask my fear of coming in second. How my extreme actions were often hidden attempts to control areas where I had no control.

In Chet's typical clear and concise manner, he called me "fat and lazy." He said, "You run marathons and triathlons without training, which is insane. But you fail at the simple disciplines of daily workouts. It is because you are afraid to look inside. Afraid of the quiet. Afraid to discover and expose the real you." Chet still demands success (he is relentless), but he demands a success that is comparable to my CORE beliefs and values. Going through this discipline has been the most painful experience of my life. It has been beautiful.

Through Chet, I learned about focus. To laser-focus on what matters and leave the rest. I learned the difference between knowing I can do anything and believing I should do everything.

I learned to become much harder on myself but much softer on others. To become more insane in me, my disciplines, my CORE, never giving myself a pass. And learned to stop attempting to control the things out of my control, most specifically people.

Through Chet, I learned the deeper meaning of integrity. That every action must align with my clearly articulated CORE. And we continue through the painful and unending process of matching my beliefs to my actions.

I initially signed on with BTL to get some shortcut tools in my drive to success. Instead, I discovered more about myself than I ever thought possible. And I am on a never-ending journey of clarity, integrating my life, my business, my loves, my beliefs, my values.

Through the BTL process, I reshaped my business, and specifically my role. We are now far more profitable and getting better. My health and weight are at their best in thirty years and getting better (Chet and I are competing in the 2020 Athens, Greece, Marathon). But most importantly, my business and life are growing in the direction I love. It is a business worth owning, a life worth living, all for a cause worth fighting. This is my BTL journey.

Day 192: Slow down and reflect...

Slow down and reflect. When I re-wrote the 12 *Essentials Playbook* for the fourteenth time back in 2006, I was struck with the need to add these four words to the end of many pages in the playbook. I knew most of my family, friends, and clients were fixated on going places, doing things, and getting stuff done. They're busy making things happen and always looking for the next hack to hurry more things along.

Here's the thing, friend. You and I are not things.

We are not meant to move like machines and keep finding the next gear and more horsepower in our quest for more speed. High-performing humans, unlike other animals, are prone to running themselves to death when nothing is actually chasing them. This infatuation with speed leads to lots of success and feeds on itself until greeted with hard stops like heart attacks, high blood pressure, or hard falls from on high. This is why I'm still using these four words—slow down and reflect—as reminders for all of us seeking excellence.

We're our best when we reflect and act, when we're the reflective ACTionator, as I coined long ago. I know there is no such word as ACTionator, but it describes what we're after so much better than the reflective activator. We are all about productive action and want to remind you that most PA is preceded by slowing down and reflecting. Do not skip this step. Don't continue to act quickly on big things. Do not rush to judge and form quick conclusions on those you barely know. The world wants us to speed up. Excellence requires we slow down.

Where are you rushing to judge and need to sit with your perceptions a bit longer? What decisions are you over-analyzing? Where are you on the continuum of reflective ACTionator—too reflective or too action-oriented? Slow down. Reflect. Write. See, we've changed...

Day 193: Pass to passion...

A BTL team practice participant recently wrote to share his reflection on a recent promotion that passed him by. His initial reaction was frustration, and instant fatigue, like somebody took the air out of his balloon. He was wrecked, wronged, and worried his professional life was wasted. Here's what I reminded him. This might be just what you need to hear, friend, when you, too, are left sitting on the bench, on the outside looking in, or passed over for that promotion that had your name on it.

Most hinge moments in life are following perceived adversity.

When I was passed over way back in the day for a position I thought was mine, it opened my eyes to my passion for pushing others. I was pissed, feeling betrayed, and all wound up to stick it to the man. My bride helped me look at this pass from her perspective and not let it wreck my sorry-ness. She told me to turn this pass into my passion. She told me this was good and to get over it. So, I did. The pass turned into passion. The pass became the path to building BTL. See your pass in this light, friend. The obstacle becomes the way, right? Thanks, Miss and Marcus Aurelius. It's good to have a truth-teller and history as your friend and teacher. Pass to passion. Now, that's some good learning, huh.

Build your CORE. Aim at your OPUS. Allow them to do their job. Pass to passion. Good.

Day 194: No stability without volatility...

There is no stability without volatility. Do not get too comfortable in your work. Embrace the adversity. Fire dissipates without obstacles in the way. Fact. You, too, lose energy when whatever you're working toward does not push back and make you do what you can. So, friend, run with your idea. Take the risk. Back in the day, innovators had to risk it all. Not so today. I just enjoyed a new product from the Paleo Chef. I found her through my bride on Instagram. Her Phat Fudge is great in my coffee and as a low sugar substitute on the bike. She created her new line of food products because her digestive system was beyond volatile—it was a wreck. Combating her food allergies led to her new career. Her newfound stability came through her digestive volatility.

Embrace adversity. Don't put your head down; instead, pick your sorry-ness up and look around. Whatever stuff you just stepped in is fuel for your next expression. There is no long-term stability without experiencing and understanding volatility. Stability is built through volatility, not through the status quo. BTL practice is volatile. We are in the business of making people uncomfortable, not because we enjoy wreaking havoc, but because we know there is no stability without volatility. Work with us. Wake up. Expect it to feel worse before it gets better.

There is no motion without friction. Fact. Slow down and sit with this for a while. Write...

Day 195: No more to know more...

Remember, the enemy of mastery is thinking you know it already.

The enemy of mastery is your thinking, friend. Here's a helpful hint to prime your mastery mindset. Let's start with what not to think. Never say stuff like, "I know that, I didn't really learn anything new, or give me something new." Never say bullshit like that to yourself or your builder unless you want to get your butt kicked. Never think those thoughts, much less verbalize 'em! Never.

You see, friend, masters keep learning until they die. Masters never stop learning, mostly about stuff they already know. Masters tell themselves this. Make this a habit, friend. Tell yourself, "I've got a lot to learn, I've found the melody line, and now I'm after a thousand nuances and then a thousand more." Masters never stop nuancing. Masters remind themselves and their builders they've got a lot to learn. Masters always want others to bring it on. Masters understand that deliberate practice is the only real route to mastery. So, they marry the mundane. Actually, they come to enjoy it. They find joy in learning to do hard things well. I hope you just learned a little something, friend.

I've got lots to learn about all kinds of stuff I already know, including what I think I know about you and me. How 'bout you? What do you know about you? What do you know about those closest to you? Think again. Stop the normal thoughts of *no more, we're good,* or *I've got this*—and replace them with the master's CCD thought process.

Know more. Good.

BUILT to LEAD | together we transform

Day 196: Life is more mystery...

As most of you reading this rant know, C.S. Lewis is my favorite author. I've read everything he wrote and understand very little. I feel the same when I read meaty, thought-provoking books of any type—understanding does not come easily.

C.S. Lewis took on tough topics, none more difficult than his attempts to understand pain and love. If you want to understand some of his thinking on pain, try on *A Grief Observed,* where Lewis dissects the emotional nature of pain. For a better understanding of why pain exists or the more intellectual piece to the puzzle, take in *The Problem with Pain.* Both of these will require slow digestion and lots of rumination. Both will illustrate how pain and love are so closely intertwined. Want to understand love more? Read and write in *Mere Christianity* and dive headlong into *The Four Loves.* This side of heaven, we'll never really know anything, just catch glimpses and keep going.

You see, friend, understanding pain and love, not unlike understanding any of the big questions of life, is more mystery than puzzle. Our brain prefers puzzles, doesn't it? When we face complex problems in life, we tend to use our right hemisphere and figure out the missing pieces to the puzzle. We love to solve problems where there's clearly an answer, especially a singular one. My best learning from Lewis has been in realizing that most problems are not puzzles. Most of the problems preoccupying my mind and the minds of my family, friends, and clients are mysteries—they just don't make sense. Missi's illness is a classic example. No matter how much we learn, we can't seem to find the missing piece. And even if we did, we'd never understand why pediatric cancer came into being. Will we ever understand the depth of love we have for our puppies, parents, and especially for our children? One of my most calming, bolted-on beliefs is "the more I learn, the less I know." I've found peace through faith, even though all faith is more mystery than it is like finding that missing puzzle piece.

Life is more mystery than puzzle. What do you think?

Day 197: Nuancing...

Recently, during a tough and tender practice with a strong leader, we shared a simple coaching moment. I told my friend he is not emotionally intelligent. He's made a habit of interrupting those who can't keep up with his very advanced mind. He finishes what they start and does it well. I explained why this is a limiting habit as a leader (he makes his team feel less, not more) and what I want him to do to change it. We invested the entire practice on this one nuance. Were we wasting our time?

Nope. We were following the recipe for Becoming BTL.

When you reach elite status, the gains are small, and the impact is transformational. Most one-on-one practices nuance what is already known. The elite, remember, marry the mundane and understand that small, incremental gains are the stuff of magic. Excellence is about finding the melody line and then a thousand nuances and a thousand more. We never stop the hunt for small, incremental gains. Do you?

Today, work on something small. Recently, the BTL band has been weighing in on a nuance to our process. It's not broken in its current state; in fact, it's pretty freakin' magic in my mind. However, we are rinsing and trying to nuance it toward something even better. We may revert back to our current version. We may not. We're focused on nuancing the same way we ask our clients to nuance their performance. We eat our own cooking, you know.

What about you? Have you found the melody line for your work and life? Are you finding a thousand nuances or settling for good enough? Tell me more, friend. Tell me more…

Day 198: Unite us...

One hundred years ago, the Ku Klux Klan was reborn. This time, the hatred was focused toward Catholics, Jews, and people of color. One hundred years ago, women had just been given the right to vote. One hundred years ago, an African-American man created a fervor by attempting to run for office. One hundred years ago, our country was deeply divided and far from progressing, yet here we are today. It is always a struggle to unite us instead of untie us.

W.E.B. Du Bois was a voice of reason back in the day. In 1921, he wrote *Manifesto to the League of Nations* that addressed labor issues for Africans:

"The absolute equality of races, physical, political, and social, is the founding stone of World Peace and human advancement. No one denies great differences of gift, capacity, and attainment among individuals of all races, but the voice of Science, Religion, and practical Politics is one in denying the God-appointed existence of superior races, or of races naturally and inevitably and eternally inferior."

Du Bois was a man on a mission, a mission to move us forward.

We do not make progress aiming at something in our rearview mirror. We find strength and greatness when we evolve, enlighten, and enable others to do likewise. Aim here, leader. Push yourself and your team to make progress. Be a bit more like Du Bois, and push us forward, not back. Do not stay in the status quo and seek equilibrium. What, friend, might you accomplish if you made it your mission? Is your strong CORE and authentic OPUS serving as a compass and map for your mission? Unite us, leader. Your job is to unite all of us. Are you doing your job today?

Day 199: Hillary was right...

Tell me—I may listen.
Teach me—I may learn.
Involve me—I will do it.

Remember this ancient, Eastern proverb when it comes to connecting with your teams. Involve them.

Teach, teach, teach.
Teach, teach, listen.
Listen, listen, teach.

Learn from my mom (Marie Logan Scott). When Jordan was born, Mom gave me this advice on the phone upon hearing of his birth. She said, "When he's young, take the time to teach him like his life depends upon it. Teach him about God, the importance of family and friends. Teach him the moral code and to not let the negatives pull him down. Teach him to look up, get up, and never give up." Yes, my mom can preach it out. And she told me to listen. Tune in like an animal being stalked, not like a stalker. "Study him," she said. "The older he gets, the more you listen and observe. As he becomes a young man, listen, listen, and listen some more. He won't want to hear your instruction, so you've got to sneak it in with questions, stories, and keep it short." My mom is one wise woman.

Your teams need more of your ears and less from your mouth. We all listen to our voice more than any other. Help them make theirs more positive without them even knowing what you're doing. Involve them.

Who do you have a hard time hearing? Who has a hard time listening to you? Involve others, friend. Involve them. I guess Hillary was right. It does take a community. Sorry it's taken me so long to hear you.

BUILT to **LEAD** | together we transform

Day 200: Socratic...

Socrates was alive from 470–399 BC. He's one of the few dead dudes that we in Western civilization continue to learn from as a leader. Socrates was wise and didn't compromise much. In fact, his death was his choice. Socrates chose to drink the deadly hemlock juice over recanting or repairing. Socrates believed he was doing what was best for Athens, and the Athenians killed him for caring so much. So, what exactly did Socrates do?

He led with questions.

Socrates riled up the Athenian youth by not answering their incessant questions. Instead of handing out answers from his wise mind, he handed out questions. He greeted questions with questions. One of his favorite go-tos was simple, CCD, and freakin' magic. One of Socrates' favorite responses to thoughtful, difficult questions was, "what do you think?" The student would incredulously respond that he came to Socrates to hear his thinking, not share their own. Socrates would smile and ask them, "Tell me more." (We don't really know this, but let's assume, shall we?) The student would eventually share their thinking, and Socrates would smile again and ask them piercing questions to further their thinking. Socrates believed the best way forward for both him and his students was not for him to be the Shell answer man. He didn't want them queuing up outside his door, awaiting his wisdom. Socrates wanted them to learn to think for themselves. So, he asked better questions.

This methodology scared many Athenian leaders. They didn't like the young people thinking for themselves and, instead, wanted them to simply comply. Socrates was well ahead of his time. His peers killed him for it. Today, we honor him and his methods. We refer to this questioning tool as the Socratic method. I use this tool every day in every practice. All day long, I'm returning good, piercing questions with few answers and lots of thought-provoking Socratic questions. I'm becoming more and more Socratic, I guess. How 'bout you?

Are you a problem solver or a builder of problem solvers?

Day 201: Bounce...

According to most experts, we still only have about ten percent understanding of our ten-pound mass upstairs. One of the latest findings is about our serotonin transporter gene, known as 5-HTT, which helps regulate serotonin in the central nervous system. Serotonin is the feel-good chemical in the brain. Turns out each has two copies of this gene, one from mom and one from dad. The one you want is the long versions of this gene. The long one gives you a bounce. According to research done at the Institute of Psychiatry in London, only 32% of us get the bounce.

Translation. Thirty-two percent of us will see adversity with eyes filled with serotonin and feel good. We'll see the challenge and get after it. You can get tested for this gene, according to Ben Sherwood, in his book, *The Survivors Club*. Whatever your genetic makeup, however, there is much you can do to build resilience. According to Dr. Dennis Charney, the reigning king of resilience studies in America, there's a ten-step prescription for building yourself into a bouncer with or without any help from the gene pool. I've listed his steps and then put the pointer to our framework. The tie-in is amazingly on point.

1. *Practice Optimism.* BTL Essential 7: Build your optimism. The way you talk to yourself in adversity matters a great deal. Learned optimism is all about becoming hard on self without getting down on self.
2. *Identify a resilient role model.* BTL Essential 1: Build your CORE. Become a resilient, CORE-centered role model for your family, friends, and clients. Mass attracts mass, remember.
3. *Develop a moral compass and unbreakable beliefs.* BTL Essential 1: Build your CORE. Discover your Worldview, Identity, and Principles. Live with Passion, Purpose, and according to your Process. This will define your due north and the detailed map toward your OPUS.
4. *Practice altruism.* BTL Essential 2: Build your humility. Nothing makes you want to give back more than when you see yourself in proper perspective. Stop looking down on others and build the habit of looking up with gratitude.

Dang it, that's a lot of good stuff. Let's take a pause for today and reflect about our resilience. Tomorrow, we'll get after this again, picking it up at five.

Day 202: Bouncer...

Let's pick up where we left off yesterday.

5. *Develop acceptance and cognitive flexibility.* BTL Essential 8: Build your commitment to learn. The lifelong learner learns from the past, lives in the moment, and develops the most productive way forward.

6. *Face your fears.* BTL Essential 3: Build your courage. Step one is facing your fears. Step two is acting into them. More love than fear, please.

7. *Build coping skills.* BTL Essential 4: Build discipline. Disciplined courage is a powerful combination. The first coping mechanism is taking responsibility for one's own happiness.

8. *Establish a social network to help you.* BTL Essential 12: Build transforming relationships. The builder's journey requires the aid of true friends. Be one.

9. *Stay fit.* BTL Essential 5: Build your healthy, physical life. A fit mind surrounded by a sick body is silly. We, in America, need to take this one to heart. Pun intended.

10. *Laugh as much as you can.* BTL Essential 9: Build your emotional intelligence. The number one emotion we struggle with is anger. The number one emotion our teams want to see is caring. Once cared for, we find the ability to laugh at our differences. Start by learning to laugh at self instead of others.

Sit with these bouncers for a while. You and I can build our resilience even if we came up short in the genetic pool. In fact, we're learning a ton about our genetic expression and are starting to believe genetic expression is malleable too. We are not victims of our genes, environments, or much of anything. We become more resilient by our choices. Follow this prescription, and you're well on your way. We believe the BTL framework offers all this and more. We are here to help you on the climb. You have what it takes, at least in our minds. What, friend, do you think?

Day 203: Assume less...

Assume less, friend, when you think it's obvious your teammate understands where you're coming from, why you decided whatever you decided, or what TBD means regarding their spot in the starting lineup. Humans don't hear well when hurting, and most humans are hurting most of the time.

Remember, when you say to your team things like "let's just think out loud for a moment," they don't hear those words. They hear the boss has an idea and wants to cram it down their throats and make them think it was theirs. Their fears are triggered even further when it involves anything or anyone their mind views as a loss. We're mostly wired for loss aversion, remember. Any time the brain thinks a loss is coming, it triggers big-time fear, anxiety, and doubt. The ears shut, and the mind gets focused on limiting the damage. The more words you use, the worse it gets.

Assume less.

Every day, we encounter leaders who've assumed too much. So much conflict stems from assuming. Most leaders suffer from the curse of knowledge. Once we know something, we cannot remember what it felt like not to know. Avoid the curse of knowledge, leader. Put the cookies on the bottom shelf, speak CCD, and be disciplined in asking them to play back what they heard. You'll see.

Assume less. Speak CCD. Listen a lot more. Enough said...

Day 204: Like a lobster...

After listening to my client describe his situation in detail, I coached him up very CCD. I told him to be more like a lobster. He looked at me, confused, maybe a lot like you may be feeling upon hearing this. So, I told him a bit more.

You see, friend, lobsters have been around for something like 350 million years. They survived whatever it was that took out the dinosaurs, who've been gone for sixty-some million years. Lobsters live on the ocean floor and protect their turf without often going to war. When they encounter another lobster, they mostly shadow box and shoot hormones to establish their position. They've got a live-and-let-live mindset and don't really want to get into a pinch-off. So, they stand up straight, shoulders back, and rarely fight to the death. If you want to know more, read Jordan Peterson's book, *12 Rules for Life*. So, friend, be more like a lobster. Stand up straight, shoulders back. Like a lobster, you'll know what to do the next time you get in a pinch.

Live hard. Love harder. What are your rules for life? What are your reminders to live them?

Day 205: Hard on self...

One of our favorite BTL teachings is around the notion that the elite are hard on self without getting down on self. This is true. Recently, this truth has taken a turn toward a more complete truth. You see, the truth will set you free but usually only after it makes you miserable for a while (thank you, Richard Rohr). The elite are simply hard on self, not down on self—of course, there is always an "and."

The elite are hard on self, not down on self when the outcomes are not what they wanted. In other words, the elite are hard on self when they lose a game, match, sale, or some teammate/client tells them to get lost. The elite see losses as learning. This mindset is difficult and requires deliberate practice and large doses of courage to maintain.

And surprisingly, the elite are hard on self, not high on self when the outcomes are freakin' magic. In other words, the elite are hard on self when they win big, get promoted, make the big sale, or find that perfect teammate/client who makes their day. The elite see winning as learning. This mindset is difficult and requires deliberate practice and large doses of humility to maintain. Hard on self, not high on self. My struggle is here. I don't tend to get down, but my oh my, can I get high.

Hard on self, not down on self or high on self. Hard on self and filled with hope. Someday, we will know the truth, and the truth will set us free. I'm satisfied knowing my aim is simply to keep loving, keep working, and keep helping a few along their way.

Are you hard on self and soft on others or hard on others and soft on self? Ask a teammate today.

Day 206: More will be received...

Remember, your brain can effectively hold one mess at a time. And as C.S. Lewis taught, "You can't get second things by putting them first; you can get second things only by putting first things first."

Well-meaning teammates and leaders will oftentimes offer strong teammates twelve things to work on, and they'll all be fairly good things. Sadly, this feedback will overwhelm even the best of us. So, leader, think more critically when coaching up your team. Offer one thing. *Stop.* Ask the receiver what they heard. Rinse and repeat until it's squeaky clean. Guidance isn't very helpful if, upon arrival at said corner, it tells you the next twelve turns to make.

Turn right here; I can handle.

Even when given the green light, send less. Even when you are facing a hoarder of bad habits, send less correction. Even when you're invited in after all these years, send less. Send less, my well-intentioned friend. Even when you've mastered telling teammates what to do, send less. Master the art of the question. Master getting your teammate to think more critically and owning their way forward. Make them tell you more. The BTL leader is the master of pushing the tension to its rightful owner. The first step in pushing tension to your teammates is asking great, thought-provoking questions instead of handing out answers like candy.

First things first, my friend. Send less. More will be received. Slow down and write where you want to baby step sending less. ACT...

Day 207: Outward...

We come into the world alike. Every human is born self-centered and other-controlling. As babies, we cry to get what we want (food, water, eye contact, touch, love). We cannot care for ourselves and must control our mother/caregiver, or we die. Our focus is inward, naturally.

As we grow and mature, we learn to self-care, even though we still desire others to care too. We become autonomous or at least aim at autonomy. We also learn to get along with others by crying and screaming less while smiling more. This usually lasts for a while until something difficult jolts us back into fear mode. For some, this happens early with the loss of a loved one or some other obvious obstacle that cannot be overlooked. For others, this jolt comes much later. Whenever it comes, it has a very predictable effect: it draws us further inward, for many, to the point of complete absorption in self. Most adults are not unlike their early childhood selves: self-centered and other-controlling.

The aim of BTL is to build excellence in individuals, teams, and leaders. Together, through awakening, challenging, and the consistency of hard work, we transform from self-centered/other-controlling toward CORE-centered/self-controlling. As we become CORE-centered and self-controlling, we develop the ability to focus our attention beyond ourselves and truly observe the world and other people. We focus outward, and our mind is forever changed. Masters focus outward toward their aim and with their team. Build inner strength now so you can focus outward with ease. Do not wait for the storm to begin building a better nature. The crucible reveals. Simple as that. Where is your focus, friend? Are you primarily self-centered/other-controlling or CORE-centered/self-controlling?

Ask a truth-teller today about your focus. Ask them to tell you more. Wait for it.

Day 208: Don't be nice...

Nice people are a problem. Don't become one. Nice, remember, is love in appearance. Nice people tax the system because we can't trust they mean what they say. You know this is true.

CCD is not nice. Clear, concise, and direct—always with respect—is kind. This is love in action. These people mean what they say and say it in a way you and I can digest. Master this. Becoming BTL requires kindness communicated CCD and acted on consistently. This unleashes a system to work on bigger problems than figuring out what Mr. Nice really meant or what Ms. Nice is actually going to do.

Kind people are the only kind of people who build a culture of excellence. Nice people don't have the stomach for it. Mean folks won't have the committed followers to ignite it. Excellence requires kind men and women who care enough to extrude the high performers with low ethic and the low performer with a high one. Be kind.

Are you Becoming BTL? Are you mastering the art of being kind enough to speak hard truth and do hard things? Slow down and reflect. You're most likely a bit too nice...

Day 209: Autonomy and alignment...

In our study of the human condition, we've discovered lots of truths that are universal, as well as many that are situational. Humans are hardwired, we believe, to both become the original they are and build a sense of belonging with others. Become and belong—we've labeled this condition.

Another way to say this is that humans yearn toward autonomy and alignment. We want to learn to stand on our own, find our way, make our mark, and develop a strong sense of self. Humans want autonomy. And we all want to find a team where we fit in, where we sense some semblance of alignment, and where it feels like home. Autonomy and alignment.

At BTL, our Purpose is creating this weird combination. We build individuals, teams, and leaders who become and belong. Our Purpose oozes this essence:

Together, we Awaken, Challenge, and Transform a few individuals, teams, and leaders from a lone toward becoming all ONE—one 'L of a difference. One, distinct and deeply connecting, Becoming BTL. Together, we transform. Always together.

There are no perfect humans; therefore, no perfect teams, families, companies, or countries. Our aim is not perfection but progress. We aim at excellence. Our country is here because a few founders decided to experiment becoming and belonging with thirteen distinct and deeply connected colonies. We've been figuring it out ever since. Maybe you need to get comfortable with progress, not perfection. Maybe you need to demand more and accept more. Maybe you need more clarity with your Purpose and Passion. Maybe you need more time a lone. Maybe you need more time with others becoming all ONE. Maybe you need to make peace with your place. Maybe you need a push.

Where do you need to get busy? Becoming? Belonging? Working on yourself or working on others? Accepting yourself or accepting others? Demanding more out of you or out of your team? Write what you're thinking. ACT...

Day 210: Betrayal...

We tend to think there can't be much worse than a slow, painful death. There is. And none of us gets out of here without experiencing it, especially if we bear the burden of leading anything and anyone.

Our most prolific president and illustrious founder, George Washington, had Benedict Arnold. Jesus had Judas. Marcus Aurelius had both brother (Lucius) and friend and right-hand man (Cassius). William Wallace had Robert the Bruce. Socrates had his. Homer did as well. You will, too, friend. Nothing stings like betrayal. Nothing. So, friend/leader, do not imagine yourself to be the exception. Expect some of those closest to you to turn against you. Do not be surprised when your Brutus (Julius Caesar was) figuratively stabs you in the back.

Remember, too, that revenge is not the best response. The best response is to use the betrayal and betrayer as the way forward—the obstacle becomes the way. Marcus did not seek revenge against his brother or friend. Jesus demonstrated abundant grace. William won Robert over, and George rallied his remaining officers to better anticipate the Brit's next move. Betrayal stings. Use the sting. "The impediment to action advances action. What stands in the way becomes the way." Thanks, Marcus, for modeling the way. Good.

What are you thinking? Write, please.

Day 211: Experience...

Experience is a great teacher, but only if you learn from it. You are not a victim of your corporate cultures, lifeless marriage, or dysfunctional partnership. You always have the freedom to choose your personal culture. All humans desire a deep reservoir of rewarding experiences, transformational relationships, and a smooth road to the promised land. If you've been blessed with any of these, be grateful. However, don't despair if your history has come up lacking—instead, learn.

We cannot control circumstances, people, and the experiences life thrusts upon us. We choose our response. We choose our deepest-held beliefs. Do not expect coddling when you're Becoming BTL. Expect more challenges to your belief system than consoling. Your builder is not here to make you feel better. Your builder is here to make you better. You will experience acute pain through this experience. Peace, joy, and happiness come along for the ride.

Recently, we challenged a client to embody his beliefs. He said he got it. He wasn't even in the neighboring zip code. I challenged him, as did two of my fellow builders. He didn't get it. I know this because he kept nodding along instead of falling to his knees. He is becoming a master at triple-D—defend, deny, destroy. He is not learning.

"Experience is the greatest teacher" is a half-truth. The whole truth is if you learn from it. What are you learning today? What are you resisting? Are you becoming a master learner or a master of triple-D?

Day 212: Laureates...

I didn't know the term baccalaureate was derived from the bay leaf. I didn't know jeans made it to America with Columbus. I didn't know Peter and Paul were martyred on the same day in June 67 AD. I didn't have any idea way back in the day, 80,000 Romans would proceed through the eighty gates of the Colosseum in less than five minutes. I didn't know Michelangelo painted the Sistine Chapel standing upright. I learned so much walking the streets of ancient Roma with a thirty-two-year-old named Antonio Sorrentino. He's part neuroscientist and part architect. He's currently studying how the brain is changed by architecture. Bk would have loved this.

There is no cure for insatiable curiosity.

In 2018, Miss, Tay, and I invested two days with young Antonio learning about ancient Rome. He was an informative teacher. I asked him how much of his learning came from university vs. his curiosity. You already know the answer, don't you? He told me 90% of his education has been satisfying his own curiosity. The university only teaches us how to learn. Most sticky learning comes from solitary confinement, so to speak. Most of mine has come from this well-worn chair in my crazy, cluttered, and cramped quarters known as our home office. It doesn't look organized to the untrained eye, but it is. I love learning in here so I can apply it out there. Study. Learn. Apply.

If you want to build mastery in your domain, don't forget to follow up on whatever professional development you've had with your sense of curiosity. Ask yourself what you want to know more about and get busy getting after it. I'm currently re-reading *Pioneers,* David McCullough's latest and the story of the early Ohio settlers. We, at BTL, are insatiably curious about the roots of sustained high-performance individuals, teams, and leaders. We've much to learn. We appreciate being beside other curious masters like young Antonio and many of you. Thank you for your insatiable curiosity toward mastering your craft.

Are you insatiably curious about mastering your craft, your life, relationships? Where do you need more? Want more? See you on the climb...

Day 213: Dumbass...

Learn from Aesop's fable of the Ass, the Cock, and the Lion—

An Ass and a Cock were in a cattle-pen together. Presently, a Lion, who had been starving for days, came along and was just about to fall upon the Ass and make a meal of him when the Cock, rising to his full height and flapping his wings vigorously, uttered a tremendous crow. Now, if there is one thing that frightens a Lion, it is the crowing of a Cock: and this one had no sooner heard the noise, then he fled. The Ass was mightily elated by this and thought that, if the Lion couldn't face a Cock, he would be less likely to stand up to an Ass: so he ran out and pursued him. But when the two had got well out of sight and hearing of the Cock, the Lion suddenly turned upon the Ass and ate him up. False confidence often leads to disaster.

Aesop, a former slave, was born somewhere six centuries before Christ. His fables are relevant today. Recently, a BTL practice participant asked me to give them a book that was more contemporary than my previous recommendations from the Civil War era or Friedman from the 1970s. So, if you are like her and need something more contemporary, might I suggest you go back a few thousand years and realize your problems are nothing new? Don't be a dumbass.

Pick up one of your old books, please. Re-read. Rewrite. Study history or repeat it, right?

Don't be a dumbass, friend

BUILT TO LEAD | together we transform

Day 214: How to read and write...

I can remember back in 2004 when Larry Allen told me in very CCD fashion, "Chet, you don't know how to read a book!" My justice thread was tweaked, and Triple-D went into action.

I lost the argument.

Larry was right. So, I agreed to his book recommendation, *How to Read a Book* by Mortimer Adler. Changed my life. Speed reading and consuming data like a man possessed is done. Today, I read and write slowly. BTL builders read and write slowly. We become masters by writing more than we read. You don't need to read another candy-ass book, friend. You need to re-read more. Pick up one of Pressfield's, Friedman's, or C.S. Lewis' beauties and re-read it slowly. Adler said it takes six reads to capture the essence of a good book. He's right. Mastering the art of living requires that we master human nature, namely our own.

Are you on this long, hard climb, friend? Slow down and write your thinking.

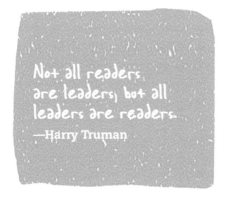

Not all readers are leaders, but all leaders are readers.
—Harry Truman

Day 215: Attention...

Study and dissect the course and form a plan of attack. Match your game to your strategy each day. When you're on, pick the most aggressive targets. When your B or C game shows up, pick conservative ones. When you address the ball, focus attention exclusively on one question and only one question. "What is my target?" Make this your mantra. Always pick a specific target and give it your undivided attention. Make a fearless swing toward your target. Regardless of the flight of your golf ball, when you address it for your next shot, focus your undivided attention exclusively on one question and only one question. *What is my target?*

According to Dr. Gio Valiante in his book *Fearless Golf,* this is the framework for mastering the game. Recently, I re-read this book after first reading it a decade ago. The applications to BTL and mastering this infinite game we call life stunned me. Leaders, if you want a team to run through walls with you, give them more of your undivided attention. We have a shortage of focused leaders. This shortage is growing. We are distracted, divided, and doing too many things at the same time. Multitask things, not people. Focus your undivided attention on the teammate you're with. Become a master at being interested. Be with.

Secondly, know the questions you ask yourself when adversity strikes. For many, these questions need to change. Too many we work with are suffering from anxiety, incessant worry, and unease. Too many are asking the wrong questions. Here are a few examples of questions focused on the wrong target: How did I end up in the weeds again? OMG, it's time to swing for the fences, right? What the hell just happened? Is anybody watching? How can I get outta here with minimal damage to my rep? Why do I keep getting overserved at parties? What is wrong with me? I'm just one hot mess.

Slow down. Pick yourself up. Be hard on self, not down on self. Change your questions. Change your life. Write. What is your target? Focus undivided attention there. Fearlessly swing again. Pick another target. Rinse and repeat. Learn. Pick better targets. Life is a lot like golf, huh?

Day 216: Setting the edge...

Leaders set the edge. BTL builders do too. Here's why it's harder as a BTL builder, friends. BTL builders are outsiders.

At every BTL practice, it's the job of the builder to set the edge. We are not in the coddling business that has become the new American way. We are here to make you less soft. So, when you show up to BTL practice, do not expect it to be entertaining, fun, and all feel-good bullshit. Expect hard OPUS and challenges out of belief. Your builder is going to set the edge, and it's all about performance. Your builder will break glass on their way to building you and your team. Do not be surprised when some of your strong ones receive hard truth from a well-intended challenge. Do not be easily offended. Expect an edge, a performance edge from your builder. Live hard. Love harder. Expect resistance, hurt feelings, sabotage, and misunderstanding among those being built. Set the edge.

Krit, Tay, and I witnessed a 2008 Kansas basketball team practice. I was blown away with how hard it was. I still remember one of the bigs messing up and running the entire Allen Field house steps. I watch elite teams practice now all the time, and it's not the same. I don't see the trash cans lining the court, anticipating there will be those who can't finish the iteration with their stomach filled. I don't see them running suicides, full-court, and screaming at teammates to gut it out, so they don't have to run another one. I don't see the same edge. We are becoming coddlers instead of elite edge setters. Don't believe me—read all about it in Greg Lukianoff and Jonathan Haidt's book, *The Coddling of the American Mind*. See what you think. It's not an easy read, but it spells out in graphic details how good intentions and bad ideas are setting up a generation for failure.

"Our chief want in life is someone who shall make us do what we can." Thanks, Ralph Waldo Emerson. Your job, leader, is to make your team do what they can. Leaders set the edge. Are you?

Day 217: All ears...

Humans do not leave systems; they leave humans. Usually, they leave their leader. Do not miss this. This could be huge. High performers mostly leave because they don't feel they're heard. Nothing frustrates high performers more than feeling they're misunderstood. So, leader, stop the rush to judge and the rush to answer questions. Listen. Ask the high performer, "Tell me more." Keep them speaking while you tune in like an animal being stalked. Listen and give them body language that says you are beginning to get them. You don't need to say a thing. Lean in. Smile. Open your mind by way of your ears. Humans, especially high-performing ones, want your ears. Stop using your damn mouth so much. Stop the word vomit. Stop speaking over them. Stop speaking, period. Listen. Love. Learn. Be all ears. This same truth applies at home.

Who do you have a hard time hearing? Why? Slow down. Write.

> Shut your mouth, open your eyes and ears. Take in what is there and give no thought to what might have been there. or what is somewhere else. That can come later, if it must come at all.
> —**C.S. Lewis,** *Surprised by Joy: The Shape of My Early Life*

BUILT TO LEAD | together we transform

Day 218: Hard on self...

Hard on self, not down on self. This is the mindset required for excellence. Most of us are soft on self, hard on others. This actually builds self-esteem alongside self-delusion. Do not aim at normal, friend. If you want to build a second nature, you must flip your internal script when reacting to the input of life. When a crazy person won't stop texting you late at night, stop telling yourself they are a whack job and begin to own what you've done to cause them to think you're in their circle. When your wife yearns incessantly for connection, stop telling yourself it's her problem. When your business partners don't act like partners, stop getting angry, thinking they've got a screw loose. These are all examples of soft on self and hard on others. Flip this.

Habituate being hard on self, not down on self. Habituate becoming hard on self, soft on others. Hard mind. Soft heart. You cannot control circumstances or people. Control your mind. Control you. Your mindset matters more than your skill level.

Aristotle was right: "Excellence is an art won by training and habituation. We do not act rightly because we have virtue or excellence, but we rather have those because we have acted rightly. We are what we repeatedly do. Excellence, then, is not an act but a habit."

What are you habituating, friend? Are you hard on self and soft on others? Are you high on self and hard on others? Are you hardening your mind for the hard things you want to do while softening your heart for those coming alongside? Are you able to be a warrior with work, kill stuff all day, come home, shut technology down, and simply be with? Slow down and reflect. Write. ACT...

Day 219: Study, learn, apply...

In the history of marathons, only fifty-one men have run the 26.2 miles in under 2:06. Forty-seven of them are from Kenya and Ethiopia. In the London Olympics, British cyclists won twelve medals in road and track cycling—double any other nation. And the British have won six of the last eight Tour de France races and could have made it more if not for Chris Froome's unfortunate accident. Are we to assume Brits are made for cycling, and Kenyans were born to run?

Think about the top performers around your place of work. When you try to explain their performance as compared to yours, don't you do likewise and say something about how they were the lucky gene pool winners or simply better by innate design or demographics? The truth is the high performers—at least where we work and observe in this work called BTL—are better because they are obsessed with getting better, welcome hard feedback, and have a willingness to endure more training, more sacrifice, and more lead bullets. The elite study, learn, and apply. The British sucked at cycling until recent history (2012, in fact), and Finland dominated distance running for decades. The British rise to the top of cycling has been guided by Dave Brailsford, who has boiled down his training philosophy into a singular phrase: "Continuous improvement through the aggregation of marginal gains." In other words, there are no silver bullets, only a lot of lead ones.

The British are focused on lots and lots of lead bullets that, on their own, produce only marginal gains. However, as they pile them on top of another, they add up to measurable distance. Your performance needs lots of baby steps that lead to measurable gains as well. There are no silver bullets. Lots of lead bullets, friend. I'm guessing the Ethiopian/Kenyan connection isn't as much about proximity to mountains or predestination either.

Want better performances? Aggregate a bunch of marginal gains. Focus on lots of lead bullets. Lots and lots of lead bullets. Study, learn, apply. This should be starting to sound familiar. If you want to know more, read *Atomic Habits* by James Clear.

Day 220: Sabotage...

Growth is the good to great disruptor, and oftentimes, so is sabotage.

Let's study some history together, shall we? Meet Benny, one of the greatest saboteurs in American history. You see, Benedict Arnold was George Washington's top general and had the reins at West Point and access to all kinds of intelligence. He betrayed George in one of our darkest hours. Benedict sold us out, and it appeared to be a death blow. It was. You see, when Benedict sabotaged the American Colonial cause, we were losing the war and having one hell of a time getting recruits. Benedict's leaving backfired. Instead of a death blow, it became a call to action, a rallying point, and the catalyst for our cause. The tide turned our way. Oftentimes, sabotage produces unintended consequences. Study history—you'll see.

So, next time somebody betrays you or wreaks havoc on your system, don't freak or fret. Remember history and stay calm. Do not freeze. This is the enemy. ACT. Step into the fear. Speak truth to your teammates. Face the bloody facts and remind yourself and everyone else why we're here, where we're going, and why it matters. In essence, nothing has changed. The obstacle has always been the way. Sometimes, it takes betrayal to bring us together. Your job is to build a high-performing system and disrupt it. You must make the team push beyond the comfort of the status quo. Equilibrium is overrated. Just this side of chaos is the one you want. Sabotage is a part of every system. Be ready. It just might be the MOT your system's been waiting for to break through to the other side.

> "As the saying goes, no good deed goes unpunished...self-differentiation always triggers sabotage."
> —*A Failure of Nerve* **by Edwin Friedman**

What doesn't kill us makes us stronger, right, Nietzsche? What disruption do you want to bring to the most beautiful system in the world, you? Don't wait for Benny to do it for you.

Day 221: Good Will...

Recently, during BTL practice, I helped a client get some clarity. Clarity arrived when I asked him about his favorite movie, *Good Will Hunting*. He related to Will and the humanity of his struggle to figure it out while traveling his Builder's Journey. My client has a hard time giving himself credit for the good that's come his way but no problem blaming himself for what's gone wrong. He's off-the-charts responsible. So, we talked. My normal tendency is to coach people to take more responsibility. Today, the story required flipping the script. So, it was. Your job, leader, is not measured by how much you know.

You're judged by how much the team learns.

Will was led by a brilliant leader who stuck to his disciplines, trusted his gut, and cared enough to let Will know it wasn't his fault. Will's leader was hunting for good and didn't stop until he found it. My client got the message. I hope he realizes he was the one doing the hunting all along. I hope he gives himself some credit for the clarity. He's the athlete; I'm the coach. The same is true for you, leader. Put the cookies on the bottom shelf. Don't tell them what you can ask them. Involve them. Create a team of problem solvers. Talk about goodwill.

What is your team learning? Are you flexible in style while strong in your CORE? Are you curious before challenging? Are you versatile and varied, as are the teammates that make up your teams?

Day 222: Loners to owners...

Do not over operate in another human's space—this is micro-managing. Do not under-operate, either—this is irresponsible. Finding the sweet spot is where teams flourish. Too much operating by another in your space leads to a high performer feeling smothered or a low performer being coddled. Too little leads to high performers not being pushed and low performers not being held accountable. Sometimes, leaders choose to over operate. Sometimes, the very same leader chooses to under-operate. This is wise when done well. This, too, is difficult.

Leaders have to find the sweet spot and keep pushing it out. Systems tend toward equilibrium. Human systems require leadership to maintain healthy equilibrium as they grow. This will lead to more conflict between corporate and field or any other variety of "us vs. them." The leader's job is to somehow remain above yet stay connected. The leader's job is to transform a team from a bunch of loners to owners—from a lone toward all ONE. The leader's job is to orchestrate this somewhat covertly behind the scenes, leaving the lone wolves to think it was their idea to join the pack. This, too, is difficult.

Building a completely self-managed team is delusional. There are no self-managed systems unless you believe the universe somehow manages itself. Everything rises and falls on leadership. Stop looking up, down, and all around for someone else to hold accountable or blame. Be the change. Learn when to over-operate for the health of the system and when to under-operate too. Your system needs leadership to level up. In your system, friend, act as if that leader is you.

Are you a loner or an owner? Tell me more.

Be the change...

Day 223: Chemistry to Concordance...

We are practicing seven good minutes again. We're far from mastering the art of connecting, friend. Teams won't perform at their peak without a sense of safety, shared transparency, and a passionate Purpose. Scientists now have a word for this way of being beyond chemistry. It's called concordances. In concordances, we sense oneness and agreement. Sounds freakin' magic, huh?

The key to creating concordances comes down to the ability to stay curious and listen. No comments, just curiosity. Our bodies are the best tool to communicate deep listening, not our mouths! Here's another recent discovery: it's almost impossible to communicate empathy when speaking. The times when the hair on your neck and arms stand up is when someone is totally consumed understanding you. We are committed to practicing seven good minutes to the point of mastering these moments. You see, nothing matters until we create a culture of safety and belonging. Create concordance, ONEness, and agreement.

Great cultures create belonging, build a sense of shared vulnerability, and unify around a passionate Purpose. Great cultures are led by people who are becoming their own man or woman, who love the work and love the team. Today, practice seven good minutes and create some belonging, agreement, and ONEness. Create concordance.

What does ONEness mean to you? Write about a time you've felt it. Write about a time you've initiated it. More of this, please...

Day 224: Hedgehog and Fox...

I've got a friend Dub who admires Warren Buffett. His OPUS is becoming a master investor like the famous ninety-year-old from Omaha. He's well on his way. So, I've decided to study a little Buffett to broaden my learning in the financial field. Most of my study isn't focused on financials as there are many advisors better equipped than I'll ever be. However, only seven pages into the book *Outsiders* by William Thorndike, and I'm feeling very much at home. The eight top CEOs of all time are highlighted in this read, and it sounds like most of them followed the BTL model unknowingly. All were humble types who avoided the spotlight, believed in decentralized power and authority, defied conventional protocol, and were positive deviants who didn't follow their peers. Yeah, baby.

I'm digging this read. I thought it would be boring like most of my other Harvard Business Review reads. I might need to slow down my judging brain and stop judging the book by its cover. So good to read outside your comfort zone, friend. Sometimes, you study like the hedgehog (who does one thing very, very well) and stay in the lane of your domain. Sometimes, you study like a fox (who is clever, cunning, and creative) and learn about many different things. For me, becoming fox-like involves studying finance. Remember, great leaders are hedgehogs and foxes. Iconic leaders are operators and investors.

What are you studying outside your stated domain?

Day 225: Defining failure/success...

Robert Graves once said, "There is no such thing as good writing, only good rewriting." I believe it was C.S. Lewis who said something similar about reading, hence his urging for all of us to read good books and re-read them six times to gain an author-like understanding.

I recently challenged some of the athletes we practice with to work on changing their mindset and decided to go back for some more study on the subject myself. I went to my library in search of my favorite book among many on this topic and couldn't find it. The book is *Mindset*, authored by Carol Dweck. So, like any good student, I bought a fresh copy of her book and began the re-read without the benefit of my notes. I had read the book twice and had two reads worth of notes scattered in the front/back/ margins. Funny, the book is hitting me differently this time as I'm not at all interested or focused on what I wrote previously.

Her research on mindset is boiled down to belief. Belief in a fixed mindset is defined as someone who thinks intelligence, personality, character, and the like are mostly fixed features brought about through birth and environment. Belief in a growth mindset is defined by one's ability to reach, stretch, fail, and learn. A fixed mindset values winning. A growth mindset values improving. A fixed mindset picks easier targets to avoid the ultimate failure—losing. A growth mindset picks stretch targets to avoid the ultimate failure—not learning. Looks like it matters when it comes to your beliefs, especially those around the definition of failure and success.

Do you believe success is defined by your accumulation of wins and losses or by your growth and learning through both? How do you define failure? How do you define success? Slow way down. Reflect. Write. This matters…

BUILT TO LEAD | together we transform

Day 226: Fighting in fields of fennel...

Marathon is a tiny Greek town 24.85 miles from Athens and means "fields of fennel." The Persians landed there in 490 BC, hoping to crush the last Greek city-states of Athens and Sparta. No bueno.

Fast forward a decade, and Darius' son, Xerxes, came knocking at Thermopylae. The "Hot Gates" were where the Persians ran into a few thousand unified Greeks from many more city-states. You see, after the story of Marathon spread, Greece had become more united, more one. So, when the Persians came back for a redo, they were greeted by a more unified front. The Persians would win the battle of Thermopylae but lose the war in the following sea battle at Salamis. We've mostly forgotten those who died so democracy might live. Our founders studied Athens and Sparta. It gave them courage to take on mighty Britain.

So, leader, set your team free. Teach them responsibility too. Tell them the story of Marathon and the fight for freedom in the fields of fennel. The fight for freedom is truly a marathon. Keep fighting with a marathon mindset. Keep fighting for right, friends. Keep bookending freedom and responsibility. Thanks, Sparta and Athens, for modeling the way.

What history are you studying today, friend? How are you bookending freedom and responsibility in your life? Are you fighting? What are you fighting for?

> "Freedom is in danger of degenerating into mere arbitrariness unless it is lived in terms of responsibleness. That is why I recommend that the Statue of Liberty on the East Coast be supplemented by a Statue of Responsibility on the West Coast."
> —*Man's Search for Meaning* **by Viktor Frankl**

Day 227: Scared up...

Back in 2019, Krit and I scaled the Santorini "hat," as we called it. This 2.5-mile round trip didn't look like much until we got to the final leg, which was straight-up rock climbing. Grabbing hold of the rocks and pulling up on day one, we both felt adrenaline rush through our system as fear grabbed us in the throat. We could feel the shake of truth once we were safely on top. We laughed at how fear scared us up. The second go 'round, or up, really, we had Tay in tow. This time, Krit went up with relative ease as her system knew what was about to be done had already been "done so," as Kit Carson liked to say. Confidently, she climbed, so much so that Tay heard a young dude waiting in worry comment that if she could do it, he had to give it a go.

Life is about learning to do hard things well.

We do this by doing hard things not so well, at least at first. Some things take years to master, and some things not so much. Some things will frustrate you at first and scare you to pieces. Some things will scare you up. The key is not to let fear keep you down. You and I are meant to burn out bright, not slowly flicker, flicker, and waft away. Sometimes, you have to be scared up to go up. Embrace this. Soon, you'll be loving the challenge of the climb and laughing at what once scared you silly. So, today, do something you've been waiting, worrying, and watching others enjoy. Give it a go. It's all right to be afraid. Don't let it keep you down. Grab the first rock, set your right foot, pick a proximate target for your left hand, and pull yourself up. Like Krit, you're going to like what once languished you in fear. Soon, you just might love it.

What fear can you use to scare you up?

BUILT TO **LEAD** | together we transform

Day 228: Leaders launch...

Stumbling into the movie *Hidden Figures*, I couldn't take my eyes off the story of Katherine Johnson and the women manually doing the very complex math necessary to launch our first American astronauts into space back in the early 1960s. After finishing the film, the book by the same title was on its way. A quick conversation with Gurue led to him sharing a clip from the movie *The Right Stuff*, where Chuck Yeager breaks the sound barrier back in 1947. My mind began to surge with excitement over another series of teams to study. Before ordering the book by the same name, however, my eye's caught sight of Scott Kelly and his recently published account of a year in space. *Endurance* would mesmerize me for a week as I learned how hard it is to live in space, even though it appears so easy to just float along. So much learning.

I'm finishing Tom Wolfe's book *The Right Stuff*, which has me blown away by how little we understand about pushing the limits. Early days of space flight were fraught with conflict over the fight for control. Engineers wanted to send monkeys up in a capsule. The seven men wanted to pilot a spacecraft. Engineers didn't design for a window. The astronauts demanded a capsule with a view. Engineers didn't design a way for the seven astronauts to exit on their own. The astronauts demanded a way to blow open the hatch from the inside. Engineers did not design override controls for the astronauts. The astronauts said no bueno. They demanded control of the spacecraft and even wanted control of the re-entry procedure.

All humans, especially the elite, want some semblance of control. Most elite teams' struggles center around someone's unwillingness to let go and someone's attempt to wrestle it away. No easy answer. Some days, we go the way of engineering. Some days, we lean toward the astronauts. Learn to push the right buttons, leader. What kills both engineer and astronaut? Indecision. The problem I see way too often in our modern, data-driven world? Way too much delaying. I mean, come on, man, are we ever gonna launch?

What are you waiting for? Launch...

Day 229: Reality is not broken...

The book *Reality Is Broken* by Jane McGonigal is a worthwhile read. Jane is a leading video game designer, and in her book, she describes why so many of our young people find such great joy playing video games. In the real world of work, friends, we don't level up like we do when playing Fortnite. In reality, we don't level up quickly or in a linear, up and to the right fashion. Life is more fits and starts, right? Many of us have grown impatient, however, and adopted a video game mentality to our professional life. We expect to level up quickly and frequently. We want the dopamine drip and don't want to deal with the mundane reality of long stints on the plateau. Masters understand the real world doesn't work like a video game. Masters understand that the road to mastery is filled with lots of basic stuff.

Basic stuff done really, really well.

Basic training is what led to the creation of one of my favorite core-building tools, the TRX. The SEAL who created the TRX knew the SEALs needed to keep training even when away from their gymnasiums. So, he created a suspension trainer they could take on the road. SEALs do basic stuff over and over and over again. Basic training doesn't end when the SEALs graduate from BUDs. They keep training, keep working, and keep focusing on small, incremental gains. They keep learning basic stuff to the point of uncommon mastery.

Master chefs have the same basic ingredients you and I have. They just know how to put them together to make something magical and memorable. The same is true for you. Find meaning in what others find boring. Reality is not broken. Reality is all we've got. In the real world, it takes time to level up. Sometimes, a long time. Patience. Your expectations may need it.

Keep working in alignment with your CORE and toward the aim of your OPUS. Don't simply do-do. Dream and do. Basic stuff done really, really well. When was the last time you rinsed your CORE, OPUS, and PoP? Done so.

Day 230: Learning about beautiful systems...

You have to learn how to do everything, remember.

During BTL team practice, I challenged a team of two teammates to look back and recognize their growth toward oneness. Teammate two shared he's better at influencing people in writing vs. speaking. Teammate one said she's always had a team, but it's never been a BTL team. I've been the boss, she shared, and created blind followers—they've complied. For the first time, she's allowed a teammate to corral her. "There is a beauty and brilliance in systems," she emphatically declared. This was a huge declaration. You see, this teammate never liked systems and always ran by the seat of her pants, leaving bodies in this very powerful wake. Her transformational learning has been on the power of leaning against one of her signature strengths (strategic clarity) and allowing teammate two to grab the controls. The system is stronger now that both are able to fly. We ended this beauty with me asking them to tell me about the most beautiful system in the world. They both looked at me puzzled and grew silent. Finally, teammate two broke the silence: "Apple's internal system," he blurted out with confidence. You see, this teammate loves systems, process, and control, and he is enamored with how Apple seems to do it all, well, beautifully. Not even close, I boldly proclaimed.

The most beautiful system in the world is you.

You are the most beautiful system in the world. You, your neighbor, boss, brother, enemy, coworker, partner, client, and teammate. You don't serve meaningless men and women. You serve the most beautiful systems in the world: human beings.

What are you learning about the most beautiful systems in your business, leader? What are you learning about the most beautiful system called your bride, brother, or even bully?

Day 231: Talent is overrated...

Talent is overrated. You know this. According to Angela Duckworth's research, covered nicely in her first book, *Grit*, talent is a starting point—nothing more. Her performance formula is as follows:

Talent X effort = skill.

Skill X effort = accomplishment.

This is another partial truth that's good to sell books but not so good in the real world of work. What's true is that effort counts twice. Effort multiplies your talent, and effort multiplies your skill. As you approach mastery in whatever skill you're building, the effort required for incremental gain goes up, and the frequency for gains is elongated. Translation. Masters marry the mundane and keep working on domain-specific expertise for hour after hour after hour. Most of us quit when we reach some comfortable performance plateau. Skills slowly diminish. Fact.

Here's the nuance for building sustained accomplishment, regardless the work. Remember, you can't do it by yourself—you've got to increase collaborative effort. Masters do not work alone. Masters understand the new science: nobody is as smart as everybody. So, today's masters expend effort working collaboratively with teammates, competitors, coaches, and any others who can multiply their performance. Together, we transform, remember, is the BTL tag line because it's true. Together, we transform. This does not mean you don't have to work hard on your own. You do. It's just not enough. You also have to work well with others and have the humility to hear other ideas, criticisms, and critiques. And the humility to give help too. Talent is overrated.

So, friend, if you're aimed at mastery, you've got to expend effort. Lots of effort. You must work on the physical skills as well as the mental skills. You must expend effort collaborating with colleagues. And you must sharpen yourself with iron. Stop running from the tough competitors. Your tough competitors are not to be feared. Your tough competitors are just people striving to get better together. Talent is overrated. Are you?

Day 232: The scientific method...

Sigmund Freud summarized his Worldview into two words: "Grow up." He believed humans are alone in this world and traced most mental disorders to messed up belief systems. He believed religion was delusional. The scientific method, he believed, was to be trusted. C.S. Lewis summarized his Worldview into two words as well: "Wake up!" Lewis was an atheist up until he turned thirty-one years old. He came to faith, according to him, by examining the evidence. His awakening drained his mind of depression and unleashed his creative spirit, as reflected in his broad range of writings.

Grow up. Wake up. You decide.

Where do you do your best work? Where you are free to be who you are or where you are told what to say, how to say it, and play all nice and politically correct with fellow professionals you work alongside but do not know? Let me help you out with some scientific data. According to Gallup, one of the most trusted organizations in one of the most trusted countries in the world suggests 90% of American workers do their best work outside of work. Huh? Yup, it's true. When surveyed by Gallup, workers in our free country confirm they do their best work where they are not paid, namely for charity, community, and family. Why? Because they believe in the purpose of the charity, community, and family; their company, not so much.

What are you building, leader? One where humans open up, share vulnerability, and become ONE, distinct, and deeply connected? Or one where humans shut up, leave their whole selves somewhere else, and just do their job? Wake up, leader. Open up or shut up. You decide. The choice seems obvious, doesn't it? I love the scientific method. Thanks, God, for giving it to us.

Live hard. Love harder.

Day 233: Practice...

Today, I stumbled into an insight that has been seemingly just out of reach but within my grasp all along. Most of life is like this. We work, and we work some more. We practice, and we practice some more. We experiment, and suddenly, the chemicals seem to come together, and just as suddenly, it's there. It's funny how this works. The recipe for Penicillin had always been there. However, Fleming, a holiday, and a forgotten petri dish were required before he stumbled onto the insight.

Today, it hit me why countless teams have made the decision to stop practicing. Teams don't make the decision to stop. Leaders do. Leaders who don't have a vision worth dying for. You see, it doesn't make sense to practice unless you understand it's the only way to find the damn few. The Spartans practiced because King Leonidas believed freedom required the discipline of the Agog. The SEALs practice because their leaders believe elite fighting teams deserve to know only the damn few will be beside them. Bk practices because he is sold out to building communities that reflect his OPUS. Durp practices because he believes in turning debtors into payers by building them up. His collection agency gets people jobs. Who practices with no end in sight? Damn few, it turns out.

Recently, another client gained clarity around her big dream, and her eyes and voice told me real progress is being made. And clarity came to me. It had been there all along, hiding beneath my lab reports and papers. Back from holiday, and suddenly, I see the petri dish and the crazy substance growing. Want more clarity, friend? Practice. Clarity will come. Keep working if you want to be one of the few—the damn few. What do you believe will transform your team? What are your actions telling them?

BUILT TO LEAD | together we transform

Build Your Emotional Intelligence

12 ESSENTIALS OF PERSONAL EXCELLENCE

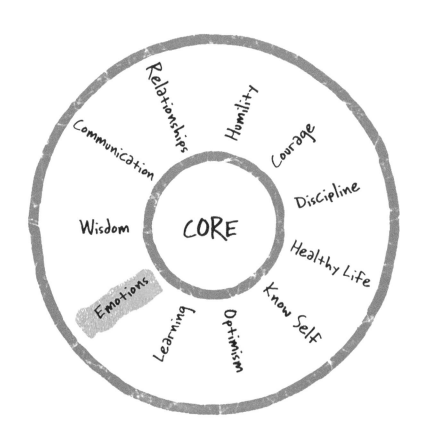

Pete's Builder's Journey

A **BUILT TO LEAD** shaped brick to the head took my thirty professional years and turned it into Passion.

That **BUILT TO LEAD** shaped brick was Chet Scott, my neighbor, friend, coach, and founder of BTL. We both shared a Passion for leadership, team building, and personal development. We took long rides on our bikes and shared what we were learning and our big dreams. For me, Chet was a great sounding board, good listener, and wise, and he always had a little different perspective. Chet had built a world-class team at CompuServe, and he was ready to live his OPUS...his Builder's Journey was about to begin! He made the leap and started **BUILT TO LEAD**. Larry Allen, a former pastor, a man of deep conviction and integrity, would soon follow. I thought I was right behind them in making the leap, but it didn't happen!

Passion:
I clearly had the Passion, reading thirty to forty books a year on anything related to leadership. I had finished a two-year coaching program, and I taught and facilitated personal development classes in the evening...I loved it!

Purpose:
I didn't have the courage nor the conviction to leave the comfort of a job that was clearly not fulfilling the purpose that God had for my life. I hired Chet as my coach, and from day one, he challenged me to define my *why*, my strong sense of purpose for my life! We coached for approximately a year, bringing into alignment my Passions, CORE Principles, and the clarity of my Purpose.

That year of coaching was the beginning of my Builder's Journey. I was ready, convicted, and truly understanding of what I believed to be God's Purpose for my life!

"Encouraging, uplifting, and challenging family, friends, and clients in reaching their goals, big dreams, and their OPUS."

I had found my life's work, my OPUS!

I have never once looked back on my decision to join BTL. I've had fear and doubt at times about the future, but don't we all at times? What I've learned through study and practice is how to manage my personal psychology, something all elite performers must learn with study and practice! Just one of many skills we share with all of our clients.

Thank you, Chet; thank you, Larry; and thank you, John Rue, and the rest of the BTL team who consistently model the CORE-centered strength that we all need in leading others!

Day 234: Emotions 101...

If we are to manage our emotions effectively, we must determine if we should act on what they're calling us to do. This is not easy. As Aristotle said, "Anyone can become angry—that is easy. But to be angry with the right person, to the right degree, at the right time, for the right purpose, and in the right way—this is not easy." Building our emotional intelligence means growing in our capacity to think before we act. Emotions are meant to move us. Reason is meant to route us the right way 'round. When they work in concert, it's a beautiful thing. We feel whole, and the world feels right.

However, when passions suddenly surge, the balance of power shifts and the emotional brain grabs the upper hand. We tilt, and it's the emotional brain doing the tilting. This can be dangerous. The rational brain gets swamped, and we no longer think clearly—we react. We flood. We're hijacked by our emotions and say and do things we oftentimes deeply regret. You and I need to build emotional intelligence skills just like we build technical ones. Here's Emotions 101, if you will.

1. Build emotional self-awareness. Notice when the body signals tilt is coming. Warm extremities and tingling are a couple of early warning signals. Don't ignore them.
2. Know your triggers. Most triggers are specific people and circumstances. Tune in.
3. Control your anger. Breathe. Learn productive ways to let the steam out without blowing up.
4. Care deeply. The number one emotion your family, friends, and teams want is caring.

Think clearly. Preload responses to one, two, and three based on four.

Which one of these needs work, friend? Today, pick one and baby step in.

Day 235: Disasters...

When faced with disaster, the brain goes three places. These three places are tied to your performance. Check it out.

Denial. This first stop is often the last. When something happens we've never imagined possible, most of us stay in denial way too long. We ignore the news reports, the negative performance review, and lack of results, and we continue to do what we've always done. In a real disaster, this leads to quick death most of the time.

Deliberate. Something bad happens, and we begin to process alternatives. Sadly, we keep processing. We wait for one more piece of data, which leads to delays, delays, and more delays. We keep ruminating about alternatives. We send our team back and forth with alternative after alternative. All they want is a decision. Meanwhile, the staircases are blocked, and our room's filling up with smoke.

Decide. When adversity strikes, the brain is flooded with chemicals to prepare us to fight or flight, which always results in less focus toward decision making. We forget what we know works. We swing for the fences. Adversity is not the time for training the brain. Adversity is when we are better off not thinking. You and I rarely rise to the occasion. We fall to the level of our training, right? You must train with tension in your practices to perform under pressure in MOT.

Very rarely do people panic. Most do nothing. Today, there are few lions, tigers, and bears to fake with our attempt at playing dead. Yet it is still the most common response to unbridled fear. We don't actually play dead; we simply become paralyzed, freeze, and stop moving. In my study of disasters the world over, this is the most common reaction.

Denial. Deliberate. Decide. Which one trips you up in crisis, friend? If you want to know more, read *102 Minutes* by Jim Dwyer and Kevin Flynn. This is the story of 9/11 and specifically who survived below the strike zone. Sobering. Come back tomorrow for some more good stuff.

Day 236: Leading through disasters...

The only way to combat these untrained, prehistorically wired brains is to train them. This is one of the big reasons we believe in practicing with your team. The obstacle is the way, leader, assuming you've practiced under pressure and prepared accordingly. The best teams prepare when times are good and when times are not so good. Practice is what leads to performance. Deliberate practice that is.

If you're to lead your team through a sales slump, it will help to have practiced the fundamentals when sales were free and easy. The time to develop and build disciplines is not during the adversity. We perform through adversity because we have been committed to practicing all the while. Are you practicing the fundamentals that drive you and your team's performance?

If we are to survive adversity, we need to train our brains how to respond now. We train our brains to respond without thinking. This is how you and your team will know you are ready—when you can perform under pressure without thinking. This matters when the adversity is a terrorist attack and when it's something as small as losing your biggest customer or losing a couple of games in a row to unworthy competition. Study Rick Rescorla and his deliberate practice with Morgan Stanley executives in the years leading up to 9/11. Google him. Leaders are measured by the quality and quantity of their decisions, especially their decisions during MOT. Train the brain to decide. Train under tension. Make your team deliberately practice "finding the stairwell" so they won't have to think when the unthinkable happens. Please read *The Unthinkable* by Amanda Ripley. We're building emotional intelligence. Wise.

How are you preparing yourself for adversity? How are you preparing your team for adversity?

Aristotle was right. You are what you habitually do.

Day 237: Root or rot...

I recently challenged a few people to write out the conflict between them. They had stopped writing because it hurt to see their stuff in black and white. This is normal. Writing about conflict within and with another is like having a root canal without Novocain—it's gonna hurt for a short while. Prepare for this pain. Root it out, anyway. You would not let a dead root continue to rot in your mouth, would you? Why let diseased, damaging, and deadly thoughts remain rooted in your head?

One reason team chemistry is so rare is because building any trust is hard—the deep stuff, desperately so. Your problem, most likely, is you live in some form of false harmony and have grown accustomed to playing nice. Your problem might be you don't know how far you've fallen from the aim for which you were made. Peace, remember, is found on the other side of acute pain. Get to the root. Stop living in some slow death rot. Remember, for many millennia, humans didn't have the option of going numb. The only option was the one my grandpa Scott liked to remind me of when I came running to him in pain. Grandpa would look at me and make sure nothing was broken. Once certain my pain was temporary, Grandpa laid out some CCD magic that stuck: "Buck up, Chester. Buck up." My tears would cease, shoulders would straighten, and my body would turn 'round to face fears and go play with the big boys again. It wouldn't be long before smiles and laughter replaced all thoughts of pain.

Get it out of your head. Once you see it in black and white, focus your brain on keeping your message simple. CCD (always with respect) is the language of connectors who understand conflict isn't better when it's rotting. Conflict gets better when a leader helps us get to the root and dig out what's causing us chronic pain. Most conflict, remember, is simply a conversation to be had. Most of the anticipatory pain is worse in our heads than in reality.

Write for clarity on your conflict. Learn from the books we've recommended and understand your tendency is to stay in denial too long. Buck up. Root it out.

Day 238: People don't forget...

People will forget what you said, people will forget what you did, but people will never forget how you made them feel.

—Maya Angelou

Today, we practiced giving teammates our esteem. We tried to give them courage with our words. We sincerely complimented those around us. We did not offer flattery or puffery. We chose our words carefully and spoke from our hearts. I esteemed a few teammates. One, in particular, received it well. He let my words in, and it changed his heart—his eyes told me. Remember, the Latin word *cor* means heart. To have courage means to have heart. The word discourage means to take heart. Encourage to give heart. We have an abundance of leaders masterful at taking hearts. Our aim at BTL is building leaders who have and give heart. We need more giving and less taking, right?

Your words matter, leader. The way you choose them matters more. The emotion, tone, and body language leave more of a mark than you think. Everything, and I mean everything, rises and falls on leadership. People don't forget your presence, leader.

Is what you're sending worth receiving? How does your presence leave your people feeling? Slow down, my wordy, worried, and often hurried friend. Slow down and think about your presence. Write. Reflect. ACT courageously...

BUILT TO LEAD | together we transform

Day 239: Fatigue...

Fatigue—what is it, really? For the last hundred years or so, we've believed the research of a guy named A.V. Hill, who, in 1920, coined the term "oxygen debt" when explaining his newfound theory on fatigue. According to Hill, at some point during exertion, your muscles don't get enough oxygen to power them, you go anaerobic, lactic acid builds, and within seconds, muscles stop working. You hit the wall! Exercise physiologists have believed that fatigue is muscular, is mostly linear, and something at the muscular level reaches a point of no return. When an athlete reaches this, they reduce effort or stop completely. Enter crazy scientist Tim Noakes.

To Noakes, fatigue is an emotion.

We propose that fatigue is a combination of the brain reading various physiological, subconscious, and conscious signals and using these to pace the muscles in order to ensure that the body does not burn out before the finish line is reached. I am not saying that what takes place physiologically in the muscles is irrelevant. What I am saying is that what takes place in the muscle is not what causes fatigue. Instead, metabolic and other changes in the muscles provide part of the information that the brain needs to be able to calculate the appropriate pace for events of different distances and in different environmental conditions.

Translation. Your performance is regulated by your brain, not your biceps, buttocks, back, heart, lungs, legs, tri's, traps, toes, or other muscles large or small. Like so much of science, Noakes' or Hill's theories are hard to prove. For me, Noakes makes the most sense. Recently, my alarm didn't go off as expected. My wakeup call was literally a call from PJ. He, jmo, Kevin, downer, and Slo were huddled out in the cold waiting for me. So, instead of my normal routine of coffee and reading prior to the torturefestivus, I brushed my tooth, threw on my gear, and headed down. Everything hurt worse. I was out of sorts. Instead of saying, "Keep working," I caught myself watching the timer and others. I was an emotional wreck. My performance sucked.

What limits your performance, friend? Your mind or your muscles? What do you think? If you want to know more, read *Endure* by Alex Hutchinson.

Day 240: Durp was not dying...

Yesterday, we learned a little science about fatigue. Today, let's learn from another besides me. Enter Durp, example number two. Back in 2014, on our first day cycling in Albertville, France, we traveled new roads for all of us. We wandered over new mountains and around new lakes. It was supposed to be an easy day and ended up being anything but. I was cooked as we headed home and sat in the back, hoping Blondie and Downer would ease us back gently. As they hammered Durp and me into fried mush, I said a few prayers for the finish line. I wasn't sure how far we had to the barn, but it was too far.

Durp was dying beside me, or so I thought. Suddenly, like someone had shot him out of a cannon, Durp pedaled to the front and took a pull from Blondie. My legs burned, my lungs screamed, and my mind said, *No way!* Durp found a way and hammered it home to Albertville. It seemed like five miles at warp speed. *How*, I thought to myself, *had Durp done it?* He found a reservoir of energy, not in fatigued muscles but in his mind. For most of us, remember, fatigue is an emotion.

Want to unleash your performance? Work on your mind. Mentally tough minds keep muscles going. Train. Work. Push. Reach. Do the hard work physically, yes. And work on training your mind to expect adversity, get comfortable being uncomfortable, and fight through the negative emotions raging in your head. The best way is with a meaningful mantra you hammer into your subconscious, so it plays on autopilot when you need it most. Fatigue is a combination of physiological and psychological forces. Don't forget to train both.

Funny, the NCAA only regulates the time we can train our athletes physically. I guess we know what they believe, huh? What do you believe limits your endurance, friend? Slow down and train the brain. Today, do some work to harden the mind as much as you harden muscle.

BUILT TO LEAD | together we transform

Day 241: Facts...

Recently, I reminded one of my clients his focus needed a redirect. He's been feeling tired like he's drowning. He's feeling stupid that he's not built a more sustainable model for his masterpiece. In summary, he's been feeling like a dumb shit (his words). I listened and tuned in to my friend, heard the hurt and the sadness in his tone, and saw it etched across his face and shoulders. So, I did what I tend to do. I challenged him to focus on facts, not feelings.

I encouraged him to write all that is good in work on the left side of a sheet of paper. And on the right, all that is not good. He couldn't come up with much after a few minutes. I told him to keep writing and waited. His pen picked up the pace as I poured more coffee in his cup. I asked him to read what he wrote. Nothing but negatives. So, I asked him to recall the facts of this past year. The facts revealed something quite contrary to his current feelings. You see, he had just dug out of a deep hole. He had been on an adrenaline high as he fought for his work and life. Now that he's out of the hole and standing above ground, his nervous system returned to normal, and the chemical rush subsided. Naturally, he feels down.

This is normal. Fact!

As he let these facts roll over him, his face began to crack a bit of a smile, as did mine. Energy returned as he turned his focus away from how he felt. Feelings, you see, cannot always be trusted. Focus on the facts. Marry your mind to productive action. You and I cannot control circumstances, other people, hellish tumors, and certainly not the future. We can catch our feelings when they go negative and stop them from spreading. We can turn our focus to the facts and choose to act. Productive action doesn't always feel good. Productive action is good.

What feelings do you need to re-evaluate, friend? Choose a baby step. You'll feel better. Fact.

Day 242: Surgeons capable of sermons...

BTL leaders are surgeons capable of sermons. Let me explain. One of our clients is like a heart surgeon (he's not really a surgeon but a CEO), the kind you would want operating on your heart if you had the widow maker valve 90% blocked. He is a master of his craft and knows it. He would cut you in all the right places and sew you together with precision. His communication would be CCD and lack heart. He would communicate facts, make demands, and leave many teammates feeling they're lacking. He would not be mean-spirited or bullying. He would simply be an elite surgeon expecting elite, emotionless excellence around him. His edge and expertise would intimidate. Ever met him?

Here's what he's working on. He's working on continuing to build his technical skills while learning to preach. He's learning to speak from the heart and connect more deeply with his teammates. You see, preachers understand it's not enough to tell the team once or twice a life-giving truth. Preachers are masters at repeating, rinsing, and reminding. Preachers understand the human heart is hurting, regardless how well the teammate/patient appears. So, virtuous preachers, like MLK, just kept repeating the message to a hurting world about something civil and something right. Our client thinks one and done. He's like a surgeon. Precise. Focus on performance. Efficient. Rinsing, repeating, and reminding seems like a waste of time. It's not.

He's becoming a surgeon capable of sermons. Humans want to be led by a leader who is both strategically competent (like a surgeon) and empathetically connected (like a passionate preacher). Surgeons perform under pressure. Preachers act with compassion and perform with feelings. Surgeons are cool. Preachers are caring. Your team wants you to be both surgeon and preacher.

Do you need to master your craft or master your caring? Tough and tender, right? Write...

Day 243: Bend...

There are two mindsets, according to Carol Dweck, the author of *Mindset*. A fixed mindset thinks talent, intelligence, and capacity are fixed. A growth mindset thinks strength, smarts, and capacity are built through training. You're not born with the right stuff; you work to make your stuff right. In our work with athletes, the power of changing mindset toward growth has been huge. Here's an example of what a growth-minded gymnast sounds like as she evaluates a performance. Let this in and extrapolate to you and your team.

Overall, I am happy with the team's performance yesterday. I could see our BTL training helping us. Individually, yesterday's performance has just made me hungry for more. Even though I stumbled on my middle pass, I felt I was mentally and physically prepared to be in the position where my four-minute touch was not what I wanted it to be. I had to try to forget it like we've learned in BTL. During my touch, I fell three times in a row, trying to get in one good turn before the competition. I had to keep reminding myself that I knew how to do it, and I've done the pass well a million times. I was doing a lot of back and forth in my head of "trust your training" and "OMG, you just fell on three middle passes." Thankfully, I was able to have more of the first thought than the second. In years past, I don't think I would have been able to catch myself being negative in those moments before my routine, and I probably would have fallen on my butt instead of fighting to stand up the pass. That being said, I am not satisfied. I changed something in my middle pass, and I want to figure out what was wrong with it so I can change it for my next opportunity on the competition floor. I think I was running too hard and going all out for the first layout, leaving no rotation for the second flip. This is something I can learn to control in practices to come.

Write honestly what you think is limiting your performance. Grab a truth-teller. Talk. Write your plan to close the gap. Work on something in your middle pass. Baby step. Keep reaching. Growth comes when we embrace the fall and bounce back. Growth comes when we say "fail" and figure out what went wrong. You see, the word plasticity describes your mind. Go on: bend it to your will. Bend. Gymnasts do. You can too...

Day 244: Tilt...

Back in the day, I played a fair amount of pinball. It had a nuance I liked and disliked at the same time. As you mastered pinball, one of the tricks was figuring out how to shake the machine without sending it into tilt. Tilt was a four-letter word and signaled complete system shutdown. The flippers wouldn't flip, and the silver ball slid silently away—game over. Masters shook the machine and made it look easy. Novices? Not so much.

Poker players use the word tilt to indicate when the lights have gone out on a competitor. When a player is on tilt, he's not thinking clearly. He may be flipping on a flop, folding on a hold, or betting against probabilities. He may be frozen in place or playing at a frenzied pace. This player is quickly taken out by others unless she has preloaded a response.

You aren't immune to being shaken into a state of tilt. Remember, 9/11 showed us a herd of CEOs frozen in their chairs just below the impact zones. Firemen, literally, shook them to their senses. They were frozen in place—tilt. We have a tilt epidemic today. Edwin Friedman wrote *A Failure of Nerve*, summarizing his life's work as rabbi, coach, and counselor. He saw FON in synagogue, government, and large enterprise and small. Tilt.

Prepare for tilt. Preload your response. There are always warning signals. Most of you must make more decisions to avoid tilt. A few of you need to walk away from the table and get some fresh air. Know your tendencies and learn to lean into them and when to lean away. Push the flipper. Nudge the machine ever so slightly. There will almost always be another silver ball. It helps to have a truth-teller beside you who can sense you bleeding out before the sharks do.

Catch your breath, calm your mind, and choose a baby step of PA. What triggers your emotional system, leader? Who are your triggers? Who illuminates your blind spots even when it's hard truth?

Day 245: Embrace the suck...

So, you want to pour yourself into someone on your team? Good, building another is a worthy aim. However, before you begin the building process with them, take a look in the mirror. Do you love yourself? Do you love your work and your team? Are you disciplined in productively acting toward mastering your craft? If you answer yes to these three with conviction and clarity, you are either self-delusional or self-confident. We're going to assume you're confident. Good. Building another will shake you to the CORE.

Step two is not trivial. Are you and your teammate willing to engage in honest dialogue? Don't mistake this for telling another your thinking is truth. A virtuous builder tunes in like an animal being stalked and guides their teammate toward better thinking of their own. BTL builders ask great questions, both curious and challenging. Speaking truth, you see, takes few words. BTL builders understand their teammates' ideas are the ones they're most likely to act upon. So, they use questions to get their teammates' ideas out in the open.

Step three requires the person you are building into is coachable. This one is really difficult because you have to begin by giving the benefit of the doubt. You cannot know their will to pain until you begin the journey together. No matter how competent you become as a builder, your impact is mostly determined by picking worthy targets. Everybody says they want to get better. Only a few are willing to do the work. Only a few have the courage to speak and listen to truth about themselves and then figure out the best way forward.

Find your few. Love them enough to prepare for practice like your life depends upon it. Expect them to forget what you've done for them. Expect their commitment to wane. Expect most of them to quit or fire you for no reason. Expect them to demand more from you than they give. Expect them to let you down. Give them more. Give them everything you've got and keep finding more to give. Give freely. Expect less. Give more. This is the recipe for building another. Embrace the suck.

Give and take care...

Day 246: Capricious...

In 2019, we toured the island of Capri off the Amalfi coast of Italy. The weather changed capriciously as we boated over in glorious sunshine only to be greeted by thunderstorms upon arrival. As Miss, Jordan, Andrew, Krit, Tay, and I walked the island, it went from sunny to storms as it pleased—nothing was predictable. This two-week trip was enjoyable because it was the opposite of capricious. It's been consistent.

Remember this truth as you lead your team today, leader. Your team does not do well working with someone who is unpredictable and changes mood, style, and behavior like the Capri weather. Teammates value consistency and calm. Teammates look to their leader to regulate emotions, both their own and those around them. Mount Vesuvius, located within eyesight of Capri, blew its top and buried Pompei without warning. Do not be capricious, blow up unannounced, and bury your team in negative emotions from which they cannot recover. Nobody wants to be led by someone unpredictable. Fact.

Calm and consistent, not capricious or Vesuvius. Today, anticipate changes in your emotional state. Preload your response. Enjoy your walk in the park.

BUILT TO **LEAD** | together we transform

Day 247: Illustrators...

The best way to know you're being lied to is not a polygraph test. Polygraph, according to Webster's, is a synonym for "lie detector." This, too, is a lie. A polygraph test measures the autonomic nervous system signs of arousal like blood pressure spikes, sweating bullets, your heart pounding, and stuff like that. It's not very scientific. The problem is it takes too long to train the eye, so we've accepted a cheap substitute.

The best way to know you're being lied to is to study the body language of those in your circle. The best body part to study is the face. The face doesn't lie for a brief second. Problem. It takes too long to master this. Moving down. Illustrators, according to Paul Ekman, the "father of the face" and guru of the science behind body language, are your best bet for detecting lies. People illustrate when they can't find the right word, and all of us develop a habit in how we do it. In other words, if somebody you work with is comfortable with you, they will illustrate by default. Study this. Memorize tendencies and default settings. Most people illustrate with hand gestures, arm crossings, leg shakes, and large body movements away or toward. These are easier to read than the micro-expressions of the face. Study here.

When people get pissed, excited, or enthused, default illustrators go up. If somebody is measuring their words and thinking too much, normal illustrators stop. Study the illustrator patterns of the people closest to you. When you detect a change in their default, you've struck a nerve. This doesn't indicate a lie. Dig. Be CCD and trust your gut when filtering their response. You may dig up a lie or two. Most cultures are not one of truth but of lies. The truth is you're being lied to. Can you imagine the value of detecting a few?

> "When asked, the average person a hundred years ago said the biggest problem in business was stealing. Today, it is lying. People value trust today more than ever before."
> —*Love Is the Killer App* by **Tim Sanders**

If you want to know more, get *Telling Lies* by Paul Ekman. Devour it like your life depends upon it. It just might.

Day 248: Overwhelmed...

One person's challenge is another's chill. One person's comfort zone is another's panic. One person's distress is another's eustress. We are all wired uniquely. Our optimal performance zone is outside what is comfortable and toward the edge of what is challenging. Too easy, and we're bored. Too difficult, and we're overwhelmed. Just this side of chaos does not sound like your optimal performance zone, but it is.

Every day, my aim is to figure out how to put my clients up against theirs. Today, I flooded a friend. I could see his brain go into full tilt. My aim was good, but my execution was ineffective. He's tough, and we're working toward incorporating a bit more tender. He's learning new skills, and we're finding our footing. Together, we're transforming even when it feels like we're on tilt. It is good to experience the feeling of being overwhelmed and realizing you're distressed—nothing more.

Life is a process of learning. Joy is found when learning to do hard things. And nothing beats the mountain top high of learning to do hard things well. Of course, along the climb, there are going to be moments that overwhelm. Anticipate these MOT. Preload your response. You will see the power in this practice. Pretty soon, what once put your system on tilt will have you smiling with satisfaction.

Today, freak yourself out by doing one hard thing you've never done. Embrace failing. Learn. Tomorrow, reach for it again. Preload your response to another fail doing a hard thing you want to do. Mastering the art of living is found here. Tell yourself, "Keep working" instead of "this sucks." Trust the process, do the work, and we'll see you on the climb.

Day 249: Emotions...

Emotions are contagious.

According to Daniel Goleman, author of numerous books on the subject of emotional intelligence, the common cold of leadership is most likely not what you think. Leaders' lack of listening is common and cold. Leaders mostly miss this because they are fixated on the future and overwhelmed in the moment. Most leaders have not mastered the ability to talk about tough topics. Sure, they can speak easily enough—it's the tuning into the contrarian, the productive rebel, the non-conformist, the upset utility player, and others whose opinions grate on the leader's last nerve. The common cold may be an inability to listen, but the problem runs much deeper. The problem is around why the leader would rather speak than listen. Most leaders overvalue their speech and undervalue their team's.

Practice flipping this value system, friend.

You see, leader, your presence is never neutral. Leaders influence the vibe by the way they walk in the room. Leaders either bring up the energy or bring it down. Emotions, remember, are contagious.

Emotions are contagious. The question remains. Are yours worth catching? How do you know? When was the last time you were unproductive with your team and simply listened to whatever they had to say? Master this...

Day 250: Decisions...

All decisions are emotional. Most decisions are framed by fear. This is normal and nothing to hide from. We mostly make decisions based on what we're afraid of. Fact. Our best decisions, however, are laced with love. You see, friend, life is filled with uncertainty. Fear tells us to play it safe and take the sure thing. Love tells us to go for it and take a shot at what makes us tingle with anticipation, lights us up, and fills us up. Choosing to live your OPUS is a choice informed with love, oftentimes the kind that scares you in the depths of your *neshama*, your very being.

Love and fear inform.

Life does not come with any guarantees and is filled with uncertainty and noise. Life is an energy management problem, remember. You know this. Are you making your big decisions filled with fear or tuned into love? Slow down and sit with this thought. Slow down. What's it going to hurt for you to turn your frequency toward love? My bet is not as much as you think. Love informs. Love moves you in your soul. (Neshama, right, Durp?) Love does more. Love does. Good.

Which signal are you most tuned toward? Write. Be honest. What are you afraid of?

Day 251: Dream and do...

A really cute couple who began their dating life over seven good minutes recently shared with me a taste of their wedding vows. One of them made mention of the power of dream and do. Dream and do is so much more powerful than its close cousin of "do or die." Do or die taxes the system. Dream and do is positive and powerful. Dream and do is what kept Viktor Frankl alive through three years of Auschwitz hell. Every day, he told himself that he was not going to be the plaything of the prison guards; instead, he dreamt of his release and rewriting his life's work on logo-therapy. He told himself that these moments in hell were not breaking him; they were building him, so they did.

Replace do or die, friend, with the power of dream and do.

Today, I'm up early riding because I can't wait to get out there and enjoy the beauty and the pain—especially with a few friends. Today, head coaches from OSU will think that BTL practicing with them is the realization of someone's big dream because it is. Two business owners, later that same day, will get my best because it's part of my big dream to give it to them. And come five bells Eastern, my favorite Chicago CEO (ok, you're my only one) will be practicing with me and getting my best because he's now a part of my OPUS too. Today will be another manifestation of dream and do. Yesterday was too.

So, friend, do not delay the authoring of your OPUS. Stop playing small or settling. You are meant to dream and do. Stop settling for bright lights if you dream about countrysides and quiet times. Stop playing another's tune when you know you've got so many songs inside of you. Stop toiling in the soil unless you really love getting dirt under your nails. You are meant to dream and do. Stop delaying the dream because your current situation is hell. Channel some Churchill and keep moving. Hard labor you disdain as you tire. Hard OPUS you sustain as you perspire.

Are you driven by a do or die mindset or inspired to dream and do? Write. Be honest.

Day 252: Margin...

Open a book. What do you see? Well, Captain Obvious, you will see words, sentences, and paragraphs. You will see periods, commas, and other syntax and symbols. You may see illustrations and pictures on some pages. What else? "This is not a trick question," I reminded two clients yesterday. They struggled to see anything else until I primed them to look around. "White space!" they exclaimed, overjoyed they could now shut me up and move things along. So, I asked them if they knew why. Do you?

The reason all books have margins is because our brain gets overwhelmed when it sees nothing but characters across the page. Publishers have understood this and built in margins, so we'll keep reading just a little bit longer before fatiguing. Your brain needs margin to focus fully in the moment.

You cannot do your best work without margin. Too much of a good thing is not a good thing. Create margin. I read and write every day because I schedule time when I'm free to be. I create margin to read, write, hike, or even go for a ride on my bike. I create margin so I can watch Coldplay's concert from Jordan at sunrise and sunset with my Miss. I create margin so I can cry as music moves me to be a better man. I create margin to connect with old friends, sip coffee or tea, or just be quiet and let it be.

Life is an infinite game, and so is love. You don't win at either by scheduling yourself wall to wall. You are not your position. You aren't winning by being the busiest. You don't win in life or love when you have to fit them into your already filled schedule.

Create more margin. Are you scheduling your day with margin? Are you busy in the car, on the plane, and in the train? Live hard. Love harder.

Day 253: De clutter de mind...

David Allen, author of *Getting Things Done,* charges his clients a boatload to help them clean up messes. You see, he believes the key to getting the right things done is decluttering your environment. We agree and charge much less.

Your problem is not the clutter in your office, home, or workshop. Your problem is the clutter in your mind. Every day, we see anxiety-riddled humans lost in their own heads. They are trying to work so many lingering problems they cannot think straight. No matter what you're trying to accomplish in work or in life, you aren't going to go far if you have more than one creative mess in your head. Fact.

So, friend, why don't you start with the most common and consuming mess—a lack of clear Identity? Stop delaying, deleting, or delegating the most important work within. Build your CORE. Gain clarity of your deepest held Beliefs, Identities, Principles, Passions, Purposes, and your Process to tighten it all up. Your self-authored CORE centers you and de-clutters de mind. You're welcome for the awakening.

The clearer your CORE, the cleaner your head. Rinse and repeat, please.

Day 254: Arousal emotions...

The word emotion is derived from the Latin word *motus*. Motus means to move. Emotions are meant to move us. If you want to move toward excellence or the ever-popular best version of yourself, you need to tune your mind to pay attention to your arousal emotions. Your primary arousal emotions are negative and positive. Anger, albeit squarely in the negative camp, has fueled many spectacular performances (thank you, MJ). Use this as fuel when you lose. Use this as fuel in spurts. Use this when you are dissatisfied with your current state. Use anger to your advantage. Do not let anger use you. Anger, unbridled, will burn you out and eventually burn you up. Use with caution.

There's nothing like love to get you up and after whatever is your pursuit. Bathe in love. Love your pursuit. Love the climb, the competition, the building, the practice, and the acute pain. Love the smallest of incremental gains. Love your work and love your team. Use all the positive vibes/emotions that follow love's lead. Use these positive emotions for a lifetime.

The elite know the enemy of excellence is found in the passive emotional states. The elite do not allow contentment or sadness to stay for long. These emotions tell you to sit and feel good about the progress you've made or, worse yet, tell you it's okay to feel sorry for yourself. Normal humans are far too easily pleased, said a very wise C.S. Lewis. Don't be normal. Use your emotions. Use your reason. Figure it out. I mean, come on, man, God gave you both emotion and reason—it makes sense to use both!

Remember, the normal brain defaults to energy-save mode. Don't be normal. Instead, use your arousal emotions and sound reason to keep working toward Becoming BTL. Use motus. Do not let it use you. What are your emotions arousing in you, friend?

BUILT to LEAD | together we transform

Day 255: Elite's underbelly...

High performers are not normal. Rarely do they fit in. Oftentimes, they exclude those they've previously held close. High performers have climbed into some rare, oftentimes unoccupied air and have moved from being distinct to appearing distant. Elite performers are exceptional and oftentimes belong to exclusive clubs. Community comes behind closed doors where elite performers sharpen one another and grow closer in the process. All is good as elite vs. elite strengthen and stretch on the road toward becoming ONE.

Elite's underbelly is exposed here.

SEALs, as an example, suffer a 90% divorce rate. CEOs and presidents are not far behind. Elite performers must learn how to be inclusive with those they hold closest. This seems obvious from the comfort and community found in the valley. Try noticing the nuance when you occupy the corner office, and you'll learn it's not nearly so easy at altitude. Elite have to understand becoming ONE is easier in the locker room than it is at home. Elite performers must keep perspective and not believe their own bullshit or their team's.

Elite's underbelly is subtle. Elite performers have worked really hard to climb to the peak. They've moved from normal to good. Finally, they've mastered their craft to the nth degree and are elite. They stand out in a crowd. Subtly, the creep begins. They begin to allow the accolades in and look down a bit more. It's always a fine line between distinct and deeply connected vs. distinct and disconnected. Elite performers must tune into those close and not in the club. At home, they must toggle from intense to interested. Simple, not easy.

How are you flipping the switch, my elite friend? Slow down. Write. Talk to a loved one. Mostly listen. Replace your underbelly with a strong CORE. Good.

Day 256: Who is your audience?

Most of the world struggles connecting outside their comfort zone.

Most humans are more afraid of connecting with peers than communicating with outsiders, and even huge numbers of unknowns don't cause most to cringe. However, in front of a room full of peers, many melt. Some meltdown. Puddles. As I've studied this up close and personal in my profession, the root reason most humans react differently in front of different audiences is due to the value they've placed on what people think. If you think your audience has more power, prominence, position, or even passion than you, you are in trouble. You can be the head of the system and feel inferior in front of an audience of your own people. Funny, huh?

So, if you want to become a consistent connector regardless the audience—practice. Practice in front of a mirror with nobody around. Study your subject. Build your competence. Practice with a coach or confidant who will be hard on you. Understand all great communicators are nervous before they go on stage. The difference between master connectors and normal ones is the ability to use nervous energy. You've got to harness the power of your nerves and turn this into an emotional edge. This takes a different type of intelligence: this takes emotional intelligence. Build some of this, friend.

And work within. Nothing calms a human like clarity within. When I'm running practice one on one, one on a few, or one on many, I run it the same way. I know my subject matter, tune in like an animal being stalked, speak from the heart, and am either Curious George or "my way IS the Highway"—never mixed. My strong CORE enables me to care but not too much. Here's why. Regardless the size, shape, or city, when I'm in front of an audience, they are all the same. My belief guides me. I believe my audience is always one. As Os Guinness expressed more eloquently than I ever could, "I live before the audience of ONE—before others, I have nothing to gain, nothing to lose, nothing to prove."

What audience are you afraid of, friend? Why? Write.

BUILT to LEAD | together we transform

Day 257: Spartan way

Life has always been hard.

The ancient Spartans built a team that embodied the opposite of fragility. The Spartans were anything but fragile, as Nassim Taleb, author of *Antifragile,* would describe. Spartan antifragility was built in the *Agog*. The young Spartan boy from age seven to eighteen was built into a warrior. In the *Agog,* these young warriors were taught mental and physical toughness. The leaders applied pressure and taught their young how to stand. Here's another lesson from Steven Pressfield and his worthy read, *Gates of Fire.*

This is the Spartan way toward building strong mental habits. I'm not suggesting you try this one on your team—start by applying this lesson to yourself!

The Peers in their messes are encouraged, when they deem it useful for the instruction of youth, to single out one lad, or even another Peer, and abuse him verbally in the most stern and pitiless fashion. This is called *arosis,* harrowing. Its purpose, much like the physical beatings, is to inure the senses to insult, to harden the will against responding with rage and fear, the twin unmanning evils of which that state called *katalepsis,* possession, is comprised. The prized response, the one the Peers look for, is humor. Deflect defamation with a joke; the coarser, the better. Laugh in its face. A mind which can maintain its lightness will not come undone in war.

Mental toughness is built through stress. Do not buy the modern mantra. Leaders are not here to relieve pressure. Never have been. Leaders are here to help the system transmit the tension to its rightful owner. Leaders adapt to strength, so the team evolves accordingly. And leaders pull the weaker ones along as long as they have the will to work. Leaders make the team do what it can. Most limits to today's performers are mind games we're losing before we step onto the pitch, field, court, or mat. BTL practice is a modern rendition of the Agog. We render tougher teammates.

What, leader, are you doing to build mental toughness with your soft team getting softer? What are you doing to become less soft yourself? Slow down. Write.

Day 258: Commitment...

The single greatest predictor of who stays married has much more to do with beliefs than it does adultery, abuse, addiction, or any other adversity the marriage is certain to face. All relationships face an assortment of adversity. The greatest predictor of who stays is whether or not they have an opt-out belief. The same is true if you want to finish anything you've started. When overwhelmed, your preloaded "no opt-out" keeps you pedaling, working, standing, and staying put. The weak mind wants to opt-out when times get tough. You've read your vows; now hard wire 'em into your mindset. No opt-out.

The same is true when we study who makes it through SEAL Buds, West Point, or Green Beret's selection school. All their predictive tests, talent evaluations, and even their whole candidates' CORE don't reliably predict who makes it through. The greatest predictor for making it through Buds, West Point, or the Green Berets? No opt-out.

Want to change a limiting behavior of yours? Set some bright boundaries your brain can't miss. Give yourself no option—none. "Never give up. No opt-out." You can make it through almost anything if you give yourself no option to quit. Need more data? Read Angela Duckworth's book, *Grit*. Read John and Julie Gottman's research. Read Galton's white paper from the 1800s on high performance. Read 1 Corinthians 13 and keep rereading it. Marriage is meant for your holiness more than your happiness. You become more whole when you value commitment more than freedom. Remember, you don't get better by quickly, easily, and frequently changing partners, companies, or other commitments. You get better by committing to the real, hard work of changing yourself. You get better when you build a mindset of no opt-out. Commit to be the change; you'll see.

What are you preloading as your response to your biggest struggles? Ask your team, family, and friends if they see no opt-out in you. Ask them to tell you more...

Day 259: Hard truth...

A few years back, Tay told me how offended he was when his longtime soccer coach called him out for not bringing the ball down to his foot and playing it to a teammate before it touched the ground. "Dad, I thought he was calling me out for something in front of my team. I thought I had made a good play, and he stopped practice to tell me I could have done it in one step instead of two. I thought he was being ridic." As Taylor reflected on his learning from this teaching moment, he told me Coach was right. "I could do it better, and once I tried it on my own, I did."

Tay, like all of us, has a hard time hearing hard truth. All humans must build capacity to hear hard truth if they hope to build capacity for better work. Hearing doesn't mean responding. Hearing simply means letting it in. The strong hear lots of noise and are very selective with what sticks. All of us must get better at hearing and letting in what is offensive to our ears, and I'm not talking about foul language. The elite hear more than most because they seek it out. When was the last time you made someone hit you? When was the last time you spoke hard truth to make another do what they can? Leaders do not shy away from delivering messages the masses don't want to hear. The BTL leader models the way by connecting before correcting.

Develop an appetite for getting better, so hard facts don't make you bitter. Tay took it. His touch went from two to one. Lean against your tendency. Lean into hard truth. My biggest gains have come from some of my biggest pains—my truth-tellers. My bride continues to be my best friend. She connects before she corrects. She loves me and lets me know hard truth without fear of respite. I may not enjoy her words in the moment, but her track record is freakin' magic. Miss makes me do what I can. What a gift.

Who cares enough to correct you? How well are you hearing hard truth? Are you connecting before correcting? Get your ratios right, remember? Slow down and reflect. This is worth a re-read.

Day 260: Twin towers...

The twin towers of your emotional life are the ability to resist impulse and express compassion. Tough mindset. Tender heart. The first tower is built in moments of toughness. The ability to will yourself through something hard and resist the pain messages in your head is a tough mindset. The ability to listen to hard truths from a trusted friend or not so friendly foe is a tough mindset. The ability to stay true to your vows when temptation tickles your fancy is a tough mindset. Poise under pressure reveals a tough mindset. Build this tower, friend.

The twin tower is built in moments of compassion. The choice to help someone who has no way to pay you is tenderhearted. The willingness to offer a hand to a grieving, hurting, or wounded teammate is tenderhearted. Caring enough to lend an ear or a shoulder to that same hurting human is tenderhearted. The ability to love the least and the lost is tenderhearted. Build this twin tower, friend. Build a tender heart.

The twin towers of your emotional life are a tough mindset and a tender heart. Tough and tender. You have to lean against some built-in tendencies to build one of these towers, much less both. They are essential for remaining consistent and calm. You see, your emotional life has to keep pace with your technical life if you are to succeed through the tough tests. Build your twin towers now. Character is who you are. What comes out of you under pressure simply reveals what's been inside all along. If you don't like how you respond when the pressure's on, slow down and think about your twin towers. Resist impulse. Express compassion. Left foot. Right foot.

Which tower is your tendency?

Day 261: Mentally strongest...

The mentally strongest measure progress looking back (root of self-esteem) and dream big about the future (aim of OPUS). Got it. What about the present? What do the mentally strongest do in the moment? Well, that's rather simple: they make the most of it. Whether given much or little, whether enjoying victory or down in defeat, sickness or health, youth or elderly, work or play, labor or leisure, in the company of dear friends or surrounded by mortal enemies, the mentally strongest live hard and love harder. You see, friend, the mentally strongest among us understand this present moment is a gift from God; it's sacred.

The best way forward is making the most of this moment. We all know this, but only the mentally tough actually live like this. Most humans are too mental keeping others happy, fitting in with their team, and keeping up with the chaos to do what it takes in everyday MOT. You see, to make the most of this moment, you've got to preload your response to all the bullshit you can't anticipate is coming your way. You don't want to waste your day. It just gets away from you, right? This is because you're weak in your CORE. Your strong CORE is where you preload your most precious. Simple, not easy.

Life comes at us all at the same rate of speed, just so you know. You are not special, nor are you a victim. Time operates the same. Fact. So, if you want to make the most of the gift of this present moment, it's going to take more than telling yourself to be more present. You must learn to let your yes be yes, and your no be no. You must learn to align behaviors to beliefs instead of rationalizing the other way 'round. You must learn to choose acute pain over chronic. You must learn to resist impulse. You must learn to live hard and love harder. The mentally tough make the most of the present moment as a habit of the heart. Do you?

Day 262: Hard and soft...

I just finished a re-read of David Goggins' book, *Can't Hurt Me*. I'm now finishing my first read of Katrin Davidsdottir's book, *Dottir*. She is the two-time CrossFit Games World Champion. She and Goggins are freaks from hard training. They are both hard bodies with harder minds. Whatever the aim of your OPUS, learn from these two champions and harden your mind while softening your heart.

Hard OPUS requires a hard mind. Hard OPUS is still filled with adversity, obstacles, and a ton of opportunities to opt-out. Hard OPUS is hard. We've grown soft as a society. We think we've got more stressors and less time, and we face more change and obstacles than previous generations. We tend to catastrophize our workload and opt-out at the first feeling of discomfort and pain. We load manage ourselves well below our capacity.

I have a few very self-aware clients who are hardening their minds. These studs are going through hard stuff like the sale of a company, divorce, disease, and rapid, almost runaway growth. They are doing more than they think, and it's fun to build beside them as they respond to hard truth by doubling down on effort. Hard minds are required to stay true to your CORE and aimed at OPUS. Nothing in life is easy. Suck it up.

And don't forget this truth: hard minds, hard bodies, hard CORE, and hard OPUS can callous our hearts too. It's really easy to harden our hearts and look down on those who've not done the work. The aim is to harden the mind and soften the heart. This requires us to look up and be grateful, humble, and filled with more love than fear. This requires us to slow down and remember how fortunate and far we've come since waking up. This requires us to listen to hard truth from our builders, family, friends, and truth-tellers.

Hard mind. Soft heart. Are you building both? Are you looking down or lifting others up? Are you aware of your governor? Are you overriding it or overreacting as you attempt to perform at your peak? What's your mindset—can't hurt me, or can't?

Day 263: Feel and think...

The best things in life follow a distinct pattern. The pattern is feel and think.

Think back to the love of your life. You felt the electricity and then thought about what to do. Think back to your home purchase. You felt something when you walked in the foyer that informed your thinking: *This is the place for us to make our home.* Think back to your favorite restaurant, car, bicycle, boat, friend, or food: it's a feeling that informs your thinking. This is why when it comes to your OPUS, your builder is going to make you get to "hell yeah, that's right" with regard to your O & P before they let you think through the Unifying strategies for living it out. You've got to feel the "O" the same way you've felt any other love.

After you feel love, you've got to think through how to stay connected when you don't feel so much love. We feel our way to the big dream; then, we stick to disciplines we've thought through to live life (Unifying strategies). Do not mix the order. When we get busy doing before we feel the dream with crystal clarity, we get busy on the dreaded do-do trail. It's hard to do-do and then feel like you're living the dream.

Feel and think. Dream and do. Not do or die. Not think and hope the feelings come. Once we get the dream down, we think our way to living it. Feel and think. This is more of the why behind the design of the OPUS. Order matters. A labor of love starts with a feeling. You feel energized, engaged, and ecstatic even at the thought of living the dream. Every morning when I get out of bed, I thank God for the gift of another day. I remind myself of who I am and meditate on my strong CORE. I reflect on my OPUS. I get busy preparing for practice, being with Miss, sport, study, and giving more than I take.

Feel and think. How about you? Are you feeling it? Slow down. Do you have a ritual reminding you who you are, what you believe, where you're going, and why it matters?

Day 264: Elite endurance...

I'm re-reading during this forced isolation, and *The Sports Gene* by David Epstein is this week's tasty morsel. There was a group of athletes I wrote nothing about during my first taste but can't stop writing about on my second. This group of athletes does not respond to negative reinforcement. They are sixteen strong and must work as one. Excellence in their sport is all about VO2 max, which can exceed eight times that of an average man and even four times the women's marathon world record holder!

So, what is the key to this athlete's elite endurance? Well, in a word—love.

"Sled dogs must have the will to forge ahead. To go that distance, it's like a bird dog sniffing down a pheasant, it has to be the one thing in their life that brings them the greatest amount of pleasure. They have to have the innate desire to pull the sled."

From 2007–2011, a former drug addict (Mackey) turned dog trainer won the Iditarod with a team of dogs descended from a single dog named Zorro. Zorro was not a five-star recruit. Zorro was a plodder who loved to run. Mackey fielded a team of plodders with an elite work ethic and a love to run. He flipped the sport on its head with a simple change in recruiting philosophy.

Yeah, in the Iditarod, there were [elite] dogs that weren't enthused about doing it. I want to be out there and have the privilege of going along for the ride because they want to go, because they love what they do, not because I want to go across the state of Alaska for my satisfaction, but because they love doing it. And that's what's happened over forty years of breeding. We've made and designed dogs suited for desire.

What's your most precious, friend? What brings you the most pleasure when you practice it over and over? Do you have an innate desire to pull your team?

> I believe God made me for a purpose, but he also made me fast. And when I run I feel His pleasure.
>
> —*Chariots of Fire* **by Eric Liddell**

BUILT TO LEAD | together we transform

Day 265: Freud and Frankl...

Viktor Frankl is one of my heroes in life. If you haven't read *Man's Search for Meaning*, you've whiffed. Frankl and Freud, alive at the same time, both worked on human personality theory in its infancy. Freud developed a theory of humanity revolving around the pleasure principle. Frankl couldn't have been further removed in reality. Frankl, while working on his theory, was forced to abandon his work and leave his notes behind. He would lose his work, wife, and all he held precious during his three-year survival test in a Nazi concentration camp. His theory had nothing to do with pleasure. His was around man's search for meaning. Frankl believed man woke up wanting a sense of purpose, belonging, and mission. Here's Viktor's recipe for finding meaning regardless your circumstance. I've paraphrased slightly.

1. Find a purpose to work on, some reason to get out of bed in the morning. The more your purpose serves other people, the better.
2. Build a redemptive perspective on life's challenges. When bad stuff happens, recognize the ways it serves you in spite of the pain.
3. Share life with loved ones. Give and receive love unconditionally.

Frankl called this treatment logotherapy or therapy of meaning. It worked back in the day, even with his 30,000 suicidal patients in the Viennese hospital system. In other words, logotherapy worked even when the challenge was phenomenal and the pain acute. At BTL, we believe it still does. This is why we want you to build your CORE, author your OPUS, and do it all fueled by passion (not anger but love). Thanks, Viktor, for modeling the way. Help us to embrace your recipe regardless of our personal pain.

What, friend, are you searching for? Endless pleasure? Purpose? Pursue purpose laced with passion. Pursue the "and." You will get some well-deserved pleasure and meaning on this path of your purposeful choosing. Freud and Frankl would be smiling. Freud and Frankl are worth learning from. Freud and Frankl were right. What do you think? When was the last time you learned from those unlike you? Write...

1

Build Your Wisdom

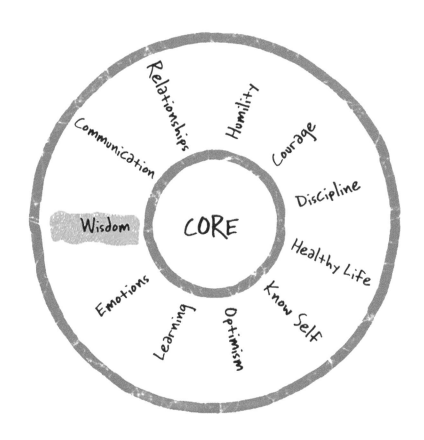

John's Builder's Journey

Born on my paternal grandfather's birthday, December 6, 1958, as the only son of an only son of an only son, I grew up in Cincinnati, Ohio, in a Procter & Gamble household. Spoiled by four sisters and parents who groomed us toward white-collar achievement, I also had the farmer values of my mother's family rooted in Michigan.

Survive and thrive was what my dad learned from his parents, who survived the Great Depression. Get an education. Take the fast-track when you can. So, I was president of the sixth-grade class, captain of the high school baseball team, and graduated summa cum laude. Then, an undergrad at Miami U. and in three years—dorm president. I received my MBA at age twenty-three from U. of Michigan, was editor of the business school newspaper, and had a summer internship in Washington, D.C.

Recruited by up and coming CompuServe in 1982, I competed with this guy named Chet Scott to be the best hot young salesman. Speaking of hot, I also met Connie, the secretary in the Dayton, Ohio, office. My first major *decidre* was a totally non-politically correct move to date in the same office—but ever on the fast track, I married her within a year. Letting her walk away was the best *decidre* I never made!

Chet and I became friendly rivals, but it was clear he was the better salesman, working out of the Columbus sales office. He was the better sales manager too. But we were both promoted on the same fast-track. When Chet won the promotion to regional manager in 1987, I moved my young family to Columbus as the new director of marketing—a D-level junior executive before my thirtieth birthday, deferred comp plan, stock options, and corner office. As I took a slow walk around the block with my dad as he recovered from a quadruple heart bypass, he was so proud that I had arrived. A year and a half earlier, I'd named our first son after him, Jack.

Little did I know how quickly life would change.

BUILT TO LEAD | together we transform

Casting a shadow over our move to Columbus was the diagnosis of lung cancer in Connie's mom, who was forty-nine. While I traveled in my new job around the US, Connie—pregnant with our second son—commuted to be with her mom in Dayton. The following July, Connie called me late one afternoon at work to report her mother was weakening. We needed to get back. I was the starting shortstop for our company softball team, and we'd made the tournament finals. I told her we'd leave right after the game. Somehow, her mom held on a couple more hours, waking up to ask for her daughter. When Connie finally got there, her mom held her hand and died while I was still parking the car.

The rest of 1988 and the next year was a blur. Chuck was born in October. More travel while Connie commuted to help with her surviving dad in Dayton. 1989 ended with Connie and I coming back to Columbus after Christmas to work on our Victorian Village house, leaving Jack and Chuck in Cincinnati at my folks. On the evening of December 28, Connie said her traditional good-night to three-year-old Jack on the phone. The next morning, the phone rang, and a man with a voice I barely recognized woke us up. It was my dad. Little Jack had slept right next to him on the floor in his sleeping bag, but he never woke up. Our son had died inexplicably sometime in the middle of the night.

It's only human nature with young kids of your own to be around someone who's experienced a parent's worst nightmare. We got many wonderful notes, but when I went back to work, there were very few colleagues with kids who could draw near me. Chet was one of the exceptions. Married a year before I was, our two boys had been almost the same age. Perhaps the biggest compliment for a great salesman is he makes you want to know more about his company as the answer to your needs. That day, Chet was a great ambassador for God. He had the courage to draw near me, empathize, and share his faith in Christ. Chet assured me God was not punishing us, little Jack was in heaven (and having the berries of a time with Connie's mom), and Christ could help me and Connie get through this. Chet gave me a book to read called *Investigating Christianity* written by his pastor and invited me out to his church with a strange name, Xenos, to hear more. My boss and mentor, Greg, and his wife, Sue, were also exceptions. Sue was a woman of faith, and even as she wept with Connie, she assured Connie of the hope we could see Jack again. They all joined us at Xenos where we learned about the ultimate Builder's Journey of Jesus Christ, who had died in our place on the cross and rose from the dead and now offered the gift of life to as many as would receive it. He was knocking on the door of our hearts, and if we'd open the door, He'd come in and unite our spirit with the power of His Spirit. Saying yes was the best *decidre* Connie and I ever made together.

For the next several years, we opened our home in Victorian Village to host a Bible study group for eighteen to twenty-eight-year-olds led by one of the pastors, Gary, and his wife, Bev. Our faith deepened in the truthfulness of Scripture and in intimacy with God and each other. We never found out why Jack died, but we became profoundly grateful for the three years he lived and for the good God has brought through his life. We experienced healing as we ministered to others. I became a much better husband, friend, worker, and father to Chuck, and we were overjoyed when Carly was born in 1993.

In 1998, I made another big *decidre* leaving the corporate world to join Gary on the Xenos staff, taking a 60% pay cut and moving to a smaller home. Chet and I reconnected in '03 through a pastor's group he was facilitating, and it's where I found my true life OPUS, which led to joining the BTL band full-time in '08. Once rivals, Chet and I have become life-long allies helping leaders and teams discover and live out their own Builder's Journey.

The irony looking back is the point I thought I had arrived was a time I understood life least. It took suffering to realize how weak my CORE was and to be willing to be built by God and others. "Together, we transform" is truly God's motto—the master-builder of all.

> Praise be to the God and Father of our Lord Jesus Christ, the Father of compassion and the God of all comfort, who comforts us in all our troubles, so that we can comfort those in any trouble with the comfort we ourselves have received from God.
>
> —2 Corinthians 1:3–4

BUILT TO **LEAD** | together we transform

Day 266: Don't be a pro...

There are lots of pros at work. We, in fact, work with a ton of professionals. There are few masters, however, in the art of living. Why?

It's much easier to just settle for being a pro. A master in the art of living integrates work and play, labor and leisure, loved ones and love tos, and hardly knows when she's working or playing. Masters don't let work creep into everything. Masters integrate and stop doing too. Mastering the art of living is only for the few who understand the most important things in life cannot be measured. I mean, come on, man, can you measure love, laughs, or living well?

Are you settling for being a pro or aiming higher? Slow down and sit with this for a while. Write like a master...

Day 267: Meek is anything but weak...

Leaders possess a contagious confidence based on hard-earned competence. BTL leaders are calm in the storm. Like a solid rock, the waves crash all around them, and they appear unmovable. This can lead to arrogance, hubris, self-centeredness, narcissism, and eventually toward self-sabotage. Catch yourself, my strong, CORE-centered, BTL leader. Put a bit in your mouth even though you've earned the right to run free.

Stay curious. Be a bit meeker, and keep your sword in its sheath.

The proud sister looks down on her running mates. The proud man sees others' fatal flaws while ignoring his own Achilles heel. Hell awaits this leader. A fall from grace is simply a matter of time. Do not think this applies to others. This is applicable to you and me. Bathe in intellectual curiosity. Bathe in relational curiosity. Bathe in situational curiosity. Bathe in emotional curiosity. Develop an appetite for consuming hard feedback that comes when we seek feedback like a curious child.

Stay curious. Be a bit meeker, and keep your sword in its sheath.

Someday, the meek shall inherit the earth, the Bible reminds us in Matthew 5:5. The meek are simply men and women who carry their sword with strength and honor and choose to keep it in their sheath. Do not mistake this for weak. Strong women cut a mighty swath when they decide to use their sword. They are capable of cutting a wide swath—they just rarely swing. The strong rarely pull the sword from its sheath. They've learned to stay calm and curious while remaining confident and convicted. They stay curious when others start cutting. These BTL leaders are meek. Don't confuse meek with weak. Real strength is best kept in its sheath.

Becoming BTL is all about becoming a bit meeker—sword in sheath. Slow down and sit with this for a while.

Day 268: Peace with my place...

I tell my clients all the time to control what they can control, stop resulting, and pass the tension to its rightful owner. I suck at taking my own advice. Most of my sleepless nights are a result of being overly responsible. I quote Rich Nathan, "Only speak to those that are turned toward you," yet I get bent about those turned away or turned against. This kind of bullshit drives me nuts. And the funny thing is, I'm the problem.

You, too, may be an overly responsible leader. We see lots of them in this gift we call BTL. Do not make the same mistake as I've made. Lean against owning outcomes, resulting, and blaming yourself for whatever goes down. Focus on your twenty square feet. Make peace with your place. Nothing drains us more than trying to fix people outside our control. Speak to those turned to you. Don't chase those turned away or against you. This takes too much energy and is foolishness. Build wisdom. Control what is controllable. Make peace with your place. Others cannot take your energy unless you let them. Stop this, Chet, you big dumbass. Remember the advice of a powerful, wise eighteen-year-old named Miles. As Miles, dying of osteosarcoma, a soft tissue cancer that wrecks its way inward until it finds bone, told my client just before he passed, "Keep fighting. Stop struggling." He wanted my client to make peace.

God, help me make peace with my place. It is not my job to turn every team into the highest-performance collection of people on the planet. It is my job to model the way, embrace pain and suffering, and embody truth in love. It is my job to give everyone my best and leave it to them to decide what, if anything, to do with it. God, help me keep fighting the good fight and stop struggling.

Where, friend, do you need to make a bit more peace with your place?

Day 269: Pericles...

Pericles entered public life in Athens around 463 BC and, although he came from aristocratic roots, was very much friend of oarsmen, farmers, and craftsmen who were the pride of ancient Athens. He led the city-state to unprecedented prosperity. Unlike his predecessors, he didn't use the surplus to buy favors. Instead, he initiated a massive public building project and commissioned the cities best craftsmen to build like banshees. Over the next decades, he built all sorts of temples, theaters, concert halls, the mighty Parthenon, and statue of Athena, goddess of wisdom. He led Athens through their golden years, known as the Periclean golden age. He was the man, adored, adorned, and much admired. He thought this had bought him loyalty.

Sparta came calling in 432 BC and demanded surrender. Pericles led them through this protracted war using reason and stall tactics strategically. He chose a defensive strategy against a superior foe. It was working until a plague struck, and Pericles found himself at death's door. In his weakened state, his team freaked. Instead of honoring him, they blamed him. He went from enamored to persona non grata in an instant.

I hope you're listening. You most likely believe this team you've taken to dizzying heights will stick with you through the upcoming downturn. You trust those you've done so much for will appreciate your efforts and remain loyal through thin as they benefited through thick. You would be wrong. Humans are not loyal to leaders. Human nature is self-centered and other-controlling. Human nature is to stick it to the man whenever it's in their best interest. Accept this truth. Understand you will be popular during prosperity and a lone when times get tough and profits thin.

Pericles was a stud and dropped like a dud in a New York minute. You will be too. Pay attention to Athena and surround yourself with those who are competent and of good character. Expect sabotage. Don't be surprised when you misjudge character. Learn. Tighten the circle when times are good. Fight the tendency to let the good times tempt you into running fast and loose. Stay lean. Inspect what you expect. Assume less. Don't get caught in the emotional high of your pedestal and prosperity. Athena would call that foolish. Build wisdom. Sucks to lead, doesn't it?

Day 270: Occam's razor...

Some 700 years ago, Friar William of Ockham developed a really simple guiding principle for humans aimed at excellence. We call this Occam's razor: "Pursue the simplest way forward." Simplest, not easiest. French writer Antoine de Saint-Exupery "anded," if you will: "Perfection is finally attained not when there is no longer anything to add, but when there is no longer anything to take away." Not to be outdone, a more modern mortal (Einstein) reminded us yet again: "Make things as simple as possible, never more so."

There are some laws of physics that govern systems as they grow. But most of what complicates and compromises our ability to perform are human decisions, mostly ones we're not even conscious of. Complication creeps in, almost like a thief in the night, and robs us blind. Complexity is a sign of growth. Complication is not. Recently, a few young leaders opened their mouths and opened some eyes. They brought forward ideas to simplify. It helps, oftentimes, to have young eyes look at old problems, leader, if you're willing to listen.

The work of Becoming BTL is a complex process. The 12-8-4 framework is simple, not easy. This work, a lot like life, does not have a clear beginning, middle, and endpoint. I mean, come on, man, does anyone know when they're getting started in pursuit of excellence, when they're halfway there, or if they ever arrive? Don't get overwhelmed by the complexity of Becoming BTL, friend. Start with working on your BTL six-pack, your CORE. Author your BTL OPUS, and you're on your way. This is the simplest way forward.

How can you cull activities to create clarity? How can you put the cookies on the bottom shelf for your team? Are you building wisdom today? Write. Cull. Simplify. Good.

Day 271: Miss makes me...

In 2000, I was diagnosed with squamous cell skin cancer. I remember the call when I first heard the dreaded C-word. I had lost my father to cancer in 1996, so the wound was still fresh. I knew about the need for sunscreen when I was a kid. My dad was a doctor, my mom a nurse. I applied sparingly. I wasn't disciplined, got burned, and didn't think much about it.

The sun damage I've accumulated cannot be reversed. All that can be done is what I'm doing: limit my exposure and apply sunscreen like a banshee. I would love to go back and rewrite my sun's history, but time does not allow us that luxury. I took too long to apply what I knew. I got burned. I tell this story to my clients to make a point. The point has nothing to do with the sun, their skin, or preventative medicine. The story serves as a setup for this question:

What's it going to take for you to deeply change?

It could be they want to stop responding to loved ones in anger, even though they sometimes explode to the point of blind rage. It could be they want to lose thirty pounds, even though they continue to work all the time, entertain clients at the trough, and drink like a fish. It could be any number of things they know they need to change. I ask them if they understand they are playing with fire. The consequences may be delayed for decades, but they're coming. I'm sitting on fifty-nine cuts and counting. I remind them that they, too, will pay for whatever deep change they're delaying. They can either *deeply change* or prepare to be badly burned. I try to pierce them with words.

What behavior do you need to change before you get badly burned? Write it down. Make it specific, concrete, and actionable. Who makes you better?

BUILT TO LEAD | together we transform

Day 272: The end game...

I can remember being fixated on a number back when I was thirty-eight years old. Sitting with my financial planner, we worked backward from the number I needed to feel comfortable taking the leap into the abyss and starting BTL. I was miserable working with WorldCom executives I didn't believe in or grow up with. We'd been acquired and felt like it. The work was no longer anything resembling OPUS, yet I continued to labor, travel, take dumb conference calls, and go through the motions, all because I hadn't hit the number that was somehow going to buy me my freedom. What a dumbass.

BTL is now in her nineteenth year. She began with my dream of building better leaders and has evolved into our dream of building individuals, teams, and leaders from a lone toward all ONE. Money is no longer in the way. Meaningful OPUS ran her over and never looked back in 2002. Freakin' magic, baby. BTL is built to provide meaningful work to masters in the making and to transform those we work with. We're in the transformation business, you could say. We are no longer normal, nor do we care.

You see, friends, I designed BTL to be weird and only reward me for doing the work. I designed her to only pay me for my labor, so to speak. My financial advisors went nuts. "Chet, you are a dumbass, and you're leaving stupid money on the table with this strategy," I heard from old and new financial advisors alike. "Stop giving away your content, stop giving away clients for free to other builders, stop neglecting to franchise this thing. You need to do speaking engagements, books—you know, leverage this creation of yours! What the hell are you thinking, anyway?" And then the best question in the history of business questions would drop: "Have you not thought about the end game?"

The end game! What the hell is the end game for you, leader? Slow down and sit with this for a while. Write about the game you're playing. Are you playing the numbers game or the infinite game? Do you know the difference, dumbass?

Day 273: LA's way...

Larry Allen was my best builder. He left us way too early on May 21, 2009, but he's far from gone. His influence remains. Larry caught me doing something right, something he admired, and he told me. He told me that I was a genius over and over—to the point of embarrassment, and he meant it. LA esteemed me.

Larry was committed to mastering his craft. He and I would read the same books and wrestle over our learnings together. His perspective was always different yet aligned with mine. His commitment to mastery gave him credibility with me. When I asked for feedback, he told me the unvarnished truth. This made us both miserable until we learned each other's language. Eventually, we became truth in love brothers. We were transforming together. Larry would want me to spell it out from A, B, C, and all the way to Z. Me? Not so much. I want you to figure out A, how to nuance B, and reconstruct C, and even throw in a D for good measure.

So, Larry, here's the ABCs of becoming a builder of another. I hope you're happy with the recipe.

A. Get your ratios right. 4:1 positive to negative is the minimum. 9:1 is magic. Find the bright spots and openly esteem another.

B. Master your craft. Your credibility depends on you being committed to excellence.

C. Build your integrity. Building another requires that you aim at a life of integrity first. C.S. Lewis was correct: putting first things first makes second things more.

Thanks, LA, for building me on this journey and bringing structure and order to my mess. Thanks for your patience and for modeling the way. Someday soon, we'll be reunited in perfect truth in love. On that day, I've already got a bike route planned. Side by side, we will ride. Side by side, we'll ride, maybe even LA's way this time. LA's way. Good.

Day 274: Meaningful game...

BTL has gone from Miss and me to LA, Petey, Browny, Gu, Kitty, FD, Rachael, Tay, Andrew, and now Jiggs. We are growing old but not tired together. Money has never gotten in the way. The BTL Builder's earning power is only limited by them. They are given much. Nothing is taken from them. We are a loose confederation who plays together because we love to, not because we have to. There is no end game. There is no 401k, retirement party, or partnership buyout. I'm no longer thinking about numbers. BTL has taught me that meaning matters most. BTL is a labor of love perpetuating a labor of love within you. Weird, huh?

We suggest you focus on building something meaningful to you. Build something that makes humans better, brings people of diverse minds and backgrounds together, and leaves a mark bigger than an estate. Your business is not meant to be a finite thing, like a game of football with a beginning, halftime, and ending. Your business, as Simon Sinek states in *The Infinite Game,* is not meant to go extinct when you do. Build something meaningful and beautiful and design it to play on long after you've gone home. By the way, this is another reason why we don't design BTL one-on-one practice or team practice with an end state in mind. We want to perpetuate the journey, not because of money but because there is no end game to growth. Healthy systems are either growing or dying. We're here to perpetuate growth. We're going to keep giving until we're gone. We're practicing abundance, the most sustainable model on the planet.

Keep building, brothers and sisters. Trust your strong CORE and authentic OPUS. Build wisdom. Today, play with meaning more. What's your focus, leader? The end game or the meaningful game?

Day 275: Exclusion...

Everybody is talking about inclusion today. Our counsel to clients is to focus more on exclusion. The hard part about culture is not coming up with the words to put on walls. The hard part is exiting high performers who don't belong, who are not living your values, and who are unwilling to change. You see, every week, I'm included in conversation around this topic with some client of mine. These are all highly functioning teams that look good and are, in fact, good. These are "best places to work" kind of places. And exclusion is still real, hard work.

Culture, remember, is built by closing the gap between what is said and what is done, what is talked about vs. what is tolerated.

Culture is built by exiting those whose behavior is flat out bad, and performance is freakin' good. Culture is built, not by talk but by what you tolerate. A culture of inclusion is meaningless unless it is combined with the discipline of excluding those unwilling to live it. Inclusion, like so much of life, is easy to say and hard as hell to live. Exiting the excluders is the discipline of inclusive, excellent cultures. Keep working on exiting those unwilling to meet the standard.

What behaviors are you tolerating, leader, from one of your high performers? Have you told them hard truth? Have you passed the proper tension? Are you prepared to exclude them? We're all watching, remember, wondering what the hell you're doing.

Day 276: Mindful...

Mindless is your brain on energy-save mode, your default setting. You see, thinking requires more glucose than you think. So, your brain loves it when you don't. You mindlessly commute from home to work, meeting to meeting, and this to that and the other thing. Mindlessness is a modern epidemic.

Mindful is its opposite. Mindfulness is when a moment in time has your full attention and energy. Mindful moments are the only moments when flow (state of optimal performance) is possible. When in flow, the activity is all-consuming in terms of attention and energy. This is full engagement. We love being in these moments, and our performance peaks, as one would expect.

Mindfulness and flow go together like bacon and eggs. The problem is flow fatigues our brains. Focus frees our performance, declutters the mind, and takes a ton of glucose in the process. This is a good tired, friend. This kind of tired requires rest and recovery. So, thinking comes at a cost—a cost of glucose. Certainly, practicing mindful meditation is a good thing; it's just not the same thing as being mindful in your moments of truth. If you want optimal performance in work and life, you must be mindful. You must align energy and attention and fully engage in what you're doing.

Every day when I practice with one of my clients, I'm in the zone. I'm not thinking about the previous practice or the practice to follow. I'm not thinking about yesterday or tomorrow. My little voice is on mute. Focus is on my OPUS. Energy, attention, and full engagement are pegged.

Are you minding your business or mindlessly distracted with the busyness of your phone, social media, and other bullshit out of your control? My dumb phone minds me. How 'bout your smart one?

Day 277: Shaming works...

Shaming works, just not the way most leaders think. Don't waste your time shaming the bottom feeders. Instead, shame the best. Yes, you read this correctly: shame your best. Parade around your top performers shamelessly. Back when I was at CompuServe, I would do conference calls with the entire sales team and tell them month in and month out how Jay Dinucci and the Atlanta team were killin' it. Everybody wanted to hear their name. I rubbed their nose in the fact that Snuch and team were smoking their sorry-ness. The competitive juices flowed. From 1990–2000, this global team never grew less than 35%—I guess it worked! Tell the truth about the best. Broadcast it. This will shame all the right people.

You see, high performers don't really like to hear about other high performers. High performers like to hear about themselves (few admit this fact). High performers like to see their name at the top of the charts. So, when they keep seeing somebody kicking their butt, they don't like it. This is the kind of shame you want to spread. Play to the competitive nature of your elite. Shame them into setting higher goals. Do not let them settle. Shame the best. Make those near the top want to reach a bit higher to unseat the top dog or dogs. Shamelessly remind them they are not number one, two, or three, but they could be with just a few small, incremental gains. Rub their noses in it as you congratulate the podium finishers for their good work. Smile as you broadcast this. Don't feel bad for highlighting the same people, month in and month out. Shaming works.

Just the other day, we read, don't shame. Today, we're all about shaming. Which is it, you ask?

Both. Embrace paradox. Hey Jmo, Soup, Ferrer, Bunten, Thum, Bobbytheh, Quinner, and Mohaffer, do you want to hear another story about Snuch and Kiely? I didn't think so. Today, have some fun shaming your high potentials, not your bottom feeders. Smart.

Day 278: Wisdom 101...

There are three basic functions our brain performs. Sometimes, they are unconscious and almost instinctive or reflexive. Other times, they are slow and methodical. Regardless, the brain always takes these three steps:

Perceives reality. Oftentimes, we do not see reality clearly due to a variety of mental models that prejudice our thinking (we all have biases, friend). As Anaïs Nin wrote in *Seduction of the Minotaur*, "We don't see things the way they are, we see things the way we are." We will not develop many alternatives if we're suffering from acute tunnel vision. Wisdom comes with the discipline of widening one's perspective. Who do you trust to illuminate your blind spots? Start here.

Processes alternatives. Do not focus only on solutions to the problem. Many times, this is the trap we leaders stumble into without even knowing it. We are problem solvers. Understand why the problem exists in the first place. The best questions lead to the best thinking. The best thinking leads to the best decisions. Remember, we tend to default to either/or thinking when in the crucible. Are you still slowing yourself down enough to consider "anding?"

Deciding and chooses PA. The last step is deciding and taking action. Understand your motives, especially those driven by fear, anxiety, and doubt (the catastrophic creepers). Look for holes in your thinking. We will not grow wise a lone. Do not surround yourself with enablers who perceive reality, process alternatives, and make decisions the same as you. Gain fresh and broader perspectives by seeking people who think differently than you. Do not rush the big decisions of life and stop ruminating and chewing the cud on the daily, weekly decisions of life. Most of our clients struggle being decisive. This is a failure of nerve.

Remember, we judge our best by the quality of their decisions in their MOT. Professional poker players, according to my son Jordan (a pro), make more decisions than amateurs, a lot more. Be a pro. Make more decisions today. Done so...

Day 279: Quality and quantity...

The quality and quantity of decisions plus luck determines the quality of life. Yesterday, we learned our brain perceives reality incompletely, processes limited alternatives, and eventually decides. The natural brain is slow to act. You have to train the brain to build wisdom, friend. The best training comes when you've done the clarifying work on your CORE and OPUS.

The best decisions are ones aligned with your CORE and toward the aim of your authentic OPUS. The best decisions are not always obvious or easy. Sometimes, you speed up and decide quickly. Sometimes, you slow down and take more time. If you believe all virtue is built going against your nature, you'll see the immense value in training the brain. The best training is to gain clarity within and with your aim.

Slow down and write some truth. Do you know who you are? Do you know why you're here? Do you know where you're going? Have you decided to move from your natural state of self-centered and other-controlling to your second nature of CORE-centered and self-controlling? Is your OPUS embedded in your frontal lobe for quick, easy access when distractions or lesser aims come calling? Does your yes mean yes and your no mean no? Becoming BTL is a wise woman's journey of discovery. We all get there, mostly by course-correcting. What course correction are you deciding to make today?

Day 280: Flow...

According to modern science, the first condition to put yourself in an optimal performance state is that goals are clear. If it were this easy, the world would be filled with flow. I mean, come on, man, how many of you out there don't know what you're aiming at? Grappy and I were laughing the other day about what wrestling team doesn't want to win the national championship. The problem with finding flow by starting with goal-setting is it's not high enough.

The first essential for finding and sustaining flow is love. You've got to love your aim. It's not enough to have clear goals. You've got to love them. You've got to love something besides becoming a $5M producer. You can't control that. And once you hit it, you won't have the same energy for going further. It's not enough to aim at winning a national championship, either. You've got to aim higher. You see, flow is found when you fall—fall in love, that is. Flow starts when you fall in love with the work and focus on what you can control.

When you fall in love with mastering your craft and mastering your life, you begin to integrate work and life, labor and leisure, vocation and recreation, and you can't tell when you're doing which. To you, it feels like work and play. Time speeds up and slows down too. The past is ancient history. The future is hopeful. The moment is as God ordained it—the present. This. Is. Flow.

Strong CORE, authentic OPUS, discipline of PA. Is this beginning to make sense? Do you have a big enough dream to find flow? Write.

> Dream no small dreams for they have no power to move the hearts of men.
> —Johann Wolfgang von Goethe

Day 281: No shame in...

Shaming is the enemy of performance. Shaming another is pathetic. This rant, however, is about self-shaming. You see, if you feel like you suck or can't figure it out, you will, and you won't. Healthy humans take responsibility and give themselves a break. They live in this tension. You cannot enter high performance, beating yourself up. Shame is like tying a weight around your waist and trying to run from it. That would fit the definition of a drag, wouldn't it? The recipe for building strength instead of shame is to take responsibility, marry PA, and give yourself the benefit of the doubt.

Your self-shaming sucks the life out of you. Many struggle here, women more so than men. I highly recommend the book *Captivating* by Stassi Eldredge. If, on the other hand, you feel good about you and can't seem to find a partner or a team that measures up, you've got a much bigger problem. You're taking too little responsibility for your problems. You tend to blame others and circumstances. You look out the window and avoid looking in the mirror. You esteem yourself to such an extent it extends beyond healthy confidence. Reading anything from C.S. Lewis might be just what you need to widen your perspective. Clive's writing has a way of humbling the mighty.

Mastering the art of living means living in the tension. Own your stuff and close integrity gaps. This clarity allows you to look out the window and help family, friends, and clients do likewise. Wisdom, turns out, comes from a willingness to work within. Wisdom comes from looking at problems, honestly owning your own, and slowly chipping away without shaming yourself. Wisdom arrives when dizzyingly high performances are married with deep humility. Wisdom comes from living in the tension, slowing down enough to study tendencies, and understanding how to extrapolate your learning into PA for you and yours. The strong, remember, are hard on self without getting down on self. No shame in that.

Day 282: Deviation from default...

A few years ago, I had the opportunity to listen to Patsy Boykin, former CIA operator, and expert on detecting lies. Her ninety-minute presentation was quite entertaining and educational. Most of Patsy and her colleagues' work is based on the groundbreaking work of Paul Ekman, known as the "Father of the Face." We all tell lies. That's another topic for another day. Most lies are best detected not by focusing on the face or the words out of the mouth. Most amateurs are deceived by words and fake smiles. You've got to know the signs of a true smile, a Duchenne smile (named after Doc Duchenne's discovery). Once you've got a mental model of the Duchenne smile, focus your mind on tone and body.

Beware of the "Brokaw hazard."

On page ninety in *Telling Lies*, Ekman describes Tom Brokaw's method of deception detection. "Most of the clues I get from people are verbal, not physical. I don't look at a person's face for signs that he is lying. What I'm after are convoluted answers or sophisticated evasions." Therein lies the hazard. You see, Tom's technique only works where he knows the liar well. He must know the convoluted answers and evasions are not the routine way his target talks. The key in detecting lies is in noticing the deviation from default.

Stop burning energy, trying to figure out if Brokaw is lying about what's her name. Unless you know his defaults, you're grasping for air. Instead, invest energy and focused attention in studying the most important people in your work and life. Understand your family, friends, and clients. Notice the subtle but obvious deviations from default. You may just avoid getting burned as I once did by a good friend whom I took at his word and got taken for a ride. Most sabotage is an inside job. Study history, you'll see. Study your system, both personal and professional. Notice the deviation from default and go deeper. Your system's survival and, at a minimum, its vitality just may depend on your ability to detect the inside job before it's too late.

Slow down and reflect. You've been reminded...

Day 283: Ideas...

Here's an interesting statistic from the Norman Vincent Peale Helpline. The Helpline is set up to help people in crisis who have nobody close to talk to. So, how many incoming calls are crisis?

Forty percent.

The majority are frequent callers who call nearly every day. These callers have chronic pain and have worn out their welcome with family and friends. So, they call the helpline in hope of being heard. Think about this for a while. As leaders, you, too, have very few crisis calls. Most of your frequent meetings are dealing with chronic people who come to you in search of a solution. Here is the training recipe from Norman Vincent Peale's hotline (it might be helpful to you). When teammates come to you for answers, greet them with some curious questions. Ask them what they think as a default. Get them engaged by empathizing with them and labeling their pain/problem. Continue to help them through curious and challenging questions. Do not give them answers or get frustrated and give 'em my favorite "buck up" speech.

Your job is to make your teammates solve more and more of their own problems. Your job is to make them so strong they no longer call on you for chronic pain relief. Once you get teammates thinking and solving problems on their own, they will call with what you've wanted all along—ideas.

Today, monitor frequent callers. Are they calling with ideas or a crisis?

Day 284: Justice thread...

Every human is born with a justice thread. We're wired for justice. This is why something inside of you quivered when you first witnessed a bully shoving a classmate of yours back in elementary school. Most aren't strong enough then to do anything about it. Now, when the same thing happens to you, your justice thread screams for revenge. We hit back (if we think we can get away with it). We make things right—somehow, someway.

All of us have a justice thread, and it's overly tuned to ourselves. Only the strong resist the urge to get even. Masters in the art of living recognize the early warning signals that they're tweaked and slow down their racing, retaliatory brain. They take four square breaths and calm the %$&* down. Wisely, they choose their response. Simple, not easy.

Newsflash. You are not *just*. You have teammates who rub you raw. You have built up biases and a limited perspective. This is a fact of human nature. You have mental models that guide your decisions and have to know when to lean against them and into them. You have to trust your gut, make the obvious, quick calls, and know when to slow it down and ruminate a bit more. Real. Hard. Work.

So, what does the wise leader do? They look in the mirror, not out the window. They build within. The stronger your CORE, the more consistent your reaction to the input of life. Straighten your justice thread, first, before you get busy reacting, retaliating, and enacting revenge. This is wisdom. Master this, and you just saved yourself a bunch of pain, misery, and hours of repair.

Are you aware of your triggers? Are you working on your reaction to people, circumstances, and obstacles that have historically tweaked your justice thread? If your aim is making things right, stop making decisions when you're sideways. Who tweaks your sorry-ness? Who is hard for you to give your ears? Write why. Come clean. Repair. Becoming BTL is becoming a master of repair...

Day 285: Ambiguity...

Ambiguity is the enemy of excellence, isn't it? Clarity is the one we want. This is why we encourage our family, friends, and clients to never stop rinsing their CORE and OPUS. We want 20/20 clarity. If clarity is good, crystal clarity is better. And we believe, paradoxically, that high-performance individuals, teams, and leaders take up residence just this side of chaos. Wait. What?

Clarity is the aim. Embracing ambiguity is the game.

Learn the Ten Commandments and act in alignment if you're a believer. Memorize the beatitudes and build a bit more dangerously. Follow the rules and break them in all the right places. Bookend freedom and responsibility. Understand John 8:32, and someday, the truth will set you free; in the meantime, it just may make you fairly miserable. Thanks, Richard Rohr.

We all love control, don't we, leaders? We love structure and order. We love making sense of things and building systems that scale our individual and collective success. We love hacks and quick fixes. We love E (Event) + R (response) = O (outcome). E + R, however, doesn't equal O. You and I are not in control, are we? Slow down. Life is paradox. The enemy of excellence is not ambiguity; it's your decision to allow ambiguity to stop you short of your best. Clarity is the aim. Embracing ambiguity is the game. Act in ambiguity, you'll see.

Day 286: Reminders...

Early this morning, I reminded a client his divided attention at home is a problem. His bride wants him undivided, and he gives her something less. He keeps his phone on vibrate (even in church) so he can respond to those responsible for his fortune. He says that it's faith, family, and fortune. His behaviors say otherwise. So, I reminded him to look at his CORE and OPUS. Close integrity gaps. Become more whole. He agreed to a baby step of discipline to give his bride undivided attention. We laughed at how many times we've covered this topic and finished off our time with an ancient phrase that guides my practices.

"The greatest moral teachers do little instructing—they mostly remind us."

You and I need reminders, friend. You are best when you are whole and undivided. You cannot split your attention well. Multitask things. Single-task people. What people do you not deem worthy of your full attention? Why do you think it's all right at home but not at work? Slow down and reflect. You may have an integrity gap to close. Write.

Day 287: Reflective ACTionator...

Many of us take forever making simple, everyday decisions. "Why is it taking so long?" those around us ask as they shake their heads. For some, our tendency is to rush to judge, make emotional decisions in the moment, and change directions on strategy and people on the fly. So-and-so doesn't come back after lunch, and everybody hopes they aren't next. Yikes. Neither of these is the one you want.

The first, let's label the ruminator. This leader tends to ruminate too long and delay decisions. High performers head for the highway. The PA here is to finish— sooner. Number two, we'll label the terminator. They tend to react. Emotional moments override their senses. This team lives in fear of their volatile leader, and trust quickly crumbles. PA here is to slow down, reflect, and work a plan everybody understands.

The one we want, we'll label the reflective ACTionator.

This leader understands she's on the hook to make better decisions and has a process for asking piercing questions to get to the root of the problem or person. They understand who they are, what they stand for, where they're going, and why they're going there. No clutter in her head, so she cleans up quickly and consistently. We all want to be led by a reflective ACTionator who thinks, feels, and acts more predictably today than yesterday. Over time and through adversity, this team will perform some freakin' magic. How can you become less ruminator, less terminator, and a little more the reflective ACTionator?

No easy way.

Build within again. Write your thoughts at the beginning/end of each day. Your ruminations will begin to reflect a pattern. It'll start to be enlightening—at least to you. You will more confidently act. As you gain confidence from baby steps, you'll pick up speed. You'll become one who appears to act with little or no hesitation. You'll be the reflective ACTionator. The quality of life comes down to the quality and quantity of your decisions. Write. ACT. Do more than you think.

Day 288: Insatiably Curious...

Charles Darwin was insatiably curious. His priest, a dude named John Stevens Henslow, was incredibly open-minded. Darwin was an outsider to the academic world of research, and John was not your typical priest either. John, it turns out, paved the way to get Charles on the HMS *Beagle*. He didn't stop there. He challenged Darwin to read a controversial new book titled *Principles of Geology* by Charles Lyell. This book would change the way Darwin thought about nature. The rest is history, as they say.

Leonardo da Vinci's first principle for genius was to become insatiably curious. David Epstein, author of *Range,* believes the first principle for building greatness in any endeavor is to be high in active open-mindedness. BTL believes in the power of "anding." We study, learn, and apply. We do not marry what we believe or think we know. We stay curious and open. And we are not easily swayed but are open to well thought out, factual, and logical arguments. We are insatiably curious about the essentials of excellence and remain open-minded to learning more. We've learned a lot over the past twenty-five-plus years of study, but we've only just begun.

What piques your curiosity, friend? What are you reading that is feeding it? Write.

Day 289: Leaders face it...

Healthy, vibrant systems expand. The root reason you don't see the Polynesian people today is because they failed to see the symptoms of slow death until it was too late to reverse the tide. This same root is the reason the fortune 1000 is on average less than forty years old, a system called CompuServe is gone, and countless other companies have come and gone, never to be heard from again. All of them ignored the early warning signals and, like Titanic, slipped from sight suddenly even though their demise was anything but. I didn't have a seat on the Titanic, but I was sitting near the top when both CompuServe and WorldCom disappeared. I saw a failure of nerve in our leaders and in myself. Not good.

So, friend, when you extrapolate this learning to you and your system, remember some history. Healthy, vibrant systems expand. Healthy, vibrant systems calculate the trend before it's too late to reverse. They get busy turning well before the iceberg is upon them. Leaders of these systems don't experience a failure of nerve when facing facts. BTL leaders call them out and ensure their systems course correct. Healthy systems never cut their way to greatness—you've got to read the tea leaves and anticipate the next move before the competition does. You've got to know when to comfort and when to push. Today, we tend to coddle a bit too much. Correction. We coddle way too much.

Your system's longevity depends on your ability to sound the alarm before an iceberg impact is imminent. Your problem, most likely, is you're too worried about what others think and about being too extreme. You're coddling instead of course correcting, and time's getting away from you. I see this every week.

Leaders make course corrections before the iceberg's obvious. Leaders face their fears, feelings, and focus on facts. Leaders understand noise, distraction, and obstacles are just the gig. Leaders lead us through these times by making more decisions when it matters most. They understand the enemy is their feelings, instead of fearlessly facing facts. Leaders focus on facts. Leaders are decisive when it matters most. Are you?

Day 290: Depression...

Depression is part of the human experience. Depression is a natural state of mind. I am depressed, in fact, as I'm writing this. Lead anything and anyone, friend, and you are going to multiply the opportunity for you to feel down. Fact.

This is yet another reason to begin the build within today. Life does not get easier as you age, you don't find more time to work on you, and you do not naturally mature through the process of getting older. Build a strong CORE today. Never stop. Train yourself to stand. MOT are coming whether you want them to or not—they are coming. Some of them are going to kick you so hard, like me, you're going to drop to your knees, fall on your face, or not feel like getting out of bed. As a leader, you are expected to rise to the occasion, anyway. You will learn to play while hurting. The stronger the CORE, the quicker you turn your state of mind. Second nature, remember, is the one you want.

Depression is not the root problem. Staying down too long, burying your feelings, and being too proud to ask for help is getting closer to the root. Life is hard. None of us gets out of here without getting hurt. The best among us bounce quicker, stay up longer, and have a tribe that carries us. The wise build the CORE when the seas are calm. The time to build is not when you're out to sea, and the storm is on the horizon. This was not meant to lift you up or bring you down. Like everything else, this was simply a reflection of what I feel as I live this work. Slow down and sit with this for a while.

How are you feeling? Are you running your feelings through that well-built CORE of yours? Smart.

Day 291: Do more by design...

The world is busy and getting busier. Greatness of any guise takes design. You and I will not live great lives if we simply go with the flow and take life as it comes. It would be freakin' magic if we could live by default and have it turn into gold. Life is not like that. We get better by choosing better because we've designed our way forward, not by defaulting to shortcuts because they're easier. You can do what is easy now, and life will eventually get hard. You can do what is hard now, and life will get easier. You choose. Your choices have consequences.

During BTL practice fifty-four, a team was challenged to go deeper and put first things first. They were each given a mirror and the opportunity to work on their greatest leadership challenge—the challenge of leading self. Some took the challenge and came clean about their habit of looking away. Some played on the surface. Some dove in deep. This team, just like yours, is making progress because individuals are making progress. The most important culture in your company, friend, is the culture in your twenty square feet. When teammates enter your domain, make certain they enter a culture of high design, aligned by your strong CORE, and aimed at an authentic OPUS with your name on it.

Are you living true to your character in your twenty square feet or worrying about your reputation? Are you a different character at home vs. away? Are you awake and oriented times four or sleepwalking through life? We get better by doing more than we think. Are you beginning to understand nothing makes sense without a strong CORE and authentic OPUS? Dream and do, remember. Don't mix the order.

Day 292: Integrity...

According to Merriam-Webster's definition, integrity means "the quality or state of being complete or undivided." None of us has integrity, do we? Are you complete or undivided? To be human is to be a perpetual work in progress, isn't it? So, if this is true, think about this for a moment or two. Are you more tuned in to other people's integrity gaps or your own?

We've all got integrity gaps. Only the strongest see their own. This is how you get better. The norm is to see your family, friends, clients, and competitors. Your own? Not so much. This is how you get bitter. Seeing your integrity gaps requires that you know what you believe so you can do the hard work of aligning behaviors. Have you done the hard work within to know what you believe and see where your behaviors have fallen short? Focus on what you can control—your character. Your reputation is what others think of you. Your character is who you are. Focus here.

Write about one of your integrity gaps. Be honest. What baby step are you taking today to begin to close it down? Choose wisely.

Day 293: Common practice...

The melody line of our work is CORE, OPUS, and PoP. Every time we practice, we are focused on inspiring our clients to do the work within, bring clarity to their big dream, and build the discipline of playing with their playbook of productive action.

The world wants you to do more. We want you to dream more.

Once you get clear on being who you are and your aim, we want you to be you and do you. This is common sense. This is not common practice. Excellence is achieved when you make lots of common-sense kind of decisions. You make them frequently and without thinking. Is this your common practice, friend? Live hard. Love harder. I mean, come on, man, who doesn't know that life is hard and the only logical response is to love harder? Is this your common practice?

Write what is common sense but not yet common practice for you. This is real, hard work. Be honest—it's the hardest job of every human. Common sense, right?

BUILT TO LEAD | together we transform

Day 294: Unite or untie...

I recently stumbled onto something that may be useful. Listening to a client describe a relationship that was not working, suddenly, this thought flew into my consciousness. He must decide to unite or untie. He's been loosely coupled, and the relationship is wobbling. He looked drained. He had chosen to wobble instead of the acute pain to align. We see this wobble every day. It's easy to justify wobbling and accept this is simply the way of the world because it is. Excellence is not built by accepting loose coupling or lowering standards. Fact.

Unite or untie, friend.

Problems, especially relational ones, do not get better with age. Problems, like an open bottle of wine, don't age well—they sour. Unite or untie. Choosing to remain loosely coupled is a choice; it's just rarely a good one. Unite is centered by "it"—intentional transformation. Untie is centered with "ti"—terminate intentionally. Leaders must be in the middle of both. Leaders intentionally transform with the few, and leaders intentionally terminate the toxic and the ones unable to meet performance standards. Leaders cannot be all ONE with everyone. Leaders, if they're building something special, something elite, something united, will have to untie from others along the way. Sometimes, leaders have to untie from the very people who brought them to the dance.

It is time to unite and untie. You need wisdom to know when to choose which. You need a few truth-tellers around to make sense of human messes. Lead anything and anyone, and you're going to have plenty of messes you didn't make, don't want to deal with, and are not sure what to do with. Unite or untie, anyway. Loosely coupled or the acute pain to align. Choose wisely. Done so...

Day 295: Victimhood...

Lew Wallace was a stud general during the civil war. He played a key role at the battle of Shiloh, where he reported directly to Grant and had the chance to work alongside the likes of William Tecumseh Sherman. He got some messy directions when ordered onto the battlefield and led his team up the wrong road. He reversed track. In fact, he spent the entire day going nowhere. His team of 7,000 marched up one road, back to base camp, and up another. In all, they traveled fourteen miles that day and never saw the battlefield. This miscommunication would cost Lew dearly.

He got fired.

Sent home to Indiana and disgraced, there's no doubt he got the short end of the stick. Did he fall into victimhood and call out his injustice? Did he try to salvage his reputation by writing to Lincoln and Grant and screaming out his case? Well, in a word, yes. However hard he tried, he would never, not for the remaining forty-three years of his life, erase the blotch, the stain, the career-ending move of getting lost. He would recover quite nicely. You see, Lew Wallace would go on to write his way out of misery. He would take his sad situation and build upon it. He would pour out his pain onto paper. He would write and write and write. As PJ likes to say, "His pain became his platform." Way before PJ, a dead dude, named Marcus said something similar, "The impediment to action advances action. The obstacle becomes the way."

Lew would choose to write instead of wallow. In fact, Lew would write the best-selling novel of his day and of any day to come. He would write a novel introducing more Americans to the art of reading than any other to date. He would write about fate, justice, revenge, and restoration. His would be the first million-selling novel ever. He wrote the story of Judah Ben Hur. And he would have never started to write if he hadn't felt so wronged. He chose to "work on me" instead of today's favorite, "woe is me."

Want to learn more about the writing of Ben Hur? Read *The Ripples of Battle* by Victor Davis Hanson. Woe is me, or work on me? You choose.

BUILT TO LEAD | together we transform

Day 296: Repent...

Repent, according to Merriam-Webster's definition, is "to change one's mind."

So, friend, you only have two options available if you want to feel more whole, united, and an ever-increasing sense of personal integrity. You can rationalize your behavior to better align it with your deeply held beliefs, or you can repent—change your mind—and decide to deeply change behaviors out of alignment with beliefs. Repent is not a four-letter word. Stop acting like you're whole when you're not. The best among us understand that ever-increasing integrity is the beginning and end of excellence—the alpha and omega if you will.

Repent. Repair. Restore. Renew.

God, help me move from hole to whole. Same sound—one "w" of a difference, and a world of difference it is. And, friend, remember this sad and sobering fact—most sabotage in any system is self-sabotage. We mostly Benedict Arnold ourselves, not our community, country, or company. Repent before you really blow your mind and body up in some sort of self-sabotage that makes no sense.

What hole or holes are you turning away from? What blemish or blemishes are you still covering up? What speck in another's eye is crystal clear, but you cannot see the plank in your own? Repent. Change your mind...

Day 297: Phronesis...

A few years back, Socrates made a bold claim, "The unexamined life is not worth living." I propose a word change. Let's replace "worth" with "great." The unexamined life is not great living. What is?

At BTL, we propose great lives are lived by humans who know who they are (CORE), where they're going (OPUS), and are committed to productive action (PA) toward their aim. Socrates said you must commit to the examined life, and he was right. You've got to commit to quality time reflecting too. I'm proposing the discipline of *phronesis* here. The Greeks referred to *phronesis* as practical wisdom. So, as you get after a life aligned with your CORE and aimed at OPUS, you've got to set aside time to reflect regarding your efforts and aim. We're referring to this as "Sunday discipline."

If you've built your CORE and authored your OPUS, every Sunday night, sit for a few and put a handful of PA on paper. Week two and every week thereafter, rinse and repeat with a twist. Week two, take a few minutes to reflect on what you did the past week. Look at your PA and grade it simply. Remember Yoda here. There is no try. Do or do not translates to pass/fail—next to each PA, write pass or fail.

Phronesis is built here. Think about your PA: *What could make it better?* What PA are you doing that another could do better? What PA do you always put on paper but rarely knock out? Why? What PA felt great and energizing? Why not more here? Over time, the Sunday discipline is going to open your mind to new ideas. You may even change some direction or belief as you reflect on these quiet Sundays in your room alone. Pascal would be so damn proud of you.

The enemy to progress is thinking you've arrived and moved on in search of something novel and new. *Phronesis* reminds us there is nothing new under the sun. The real way forward is clarity within, clarity of aim, and clarity and consistency of "left foot, right foot" as you baby step forward. Rinse and repeat...

Day 298: It's not just business...

"It's just business" is a phrase frequently used to explain away bad behavior. The truth is that it's not—it's not just business. So, friend, the next time you feel the need to use this phrase to explain away the way you've treated another human being or collection of human beings, stop yourself and look inside. You are not simply a businessman or woman. You are a human being with a deep desire for justice, beauty, spirituality, autonomy, love, purpose, accomplishment, and community. The problem is you and I live a divided existence. Whenever you say complicated disclaimers like "it's just business," it's because your ego, mistaken Identity, or greed has separated you from your spiritual self. You're lost and don't yet know it. Wake up.

It's not just business. Every interaction we have with human beings is an interaction with an immortal soul. We either allow these interactions to make us more complex (BTL word would be distinct) and mature, or we choose to feed our ego and make our lives more complicated. You know this is true when you slow down and evaluate the decisions of your life, both personal and professional. It's not just business. It's not just what boys do when they go on boys' trips. It's not just girl chatter. It's not just the way we do things around here either.

You and I choose how we react to the input of life. Complex and mature (the road to distinct and deeply connected). Ego-centric and complicated (the road to a lone and disconnected). If you find yourself offering up disclaimers like "it's just business," you would be wise to slow down and better understand the thinking behind this rationalization. "It's complicated," you might respond. Not really, huh? Which road are you on, friend?

Day 299: Compliant to committed...

Every leader wants a committed team. I mean, come on, man, who doesn't want a team ready to run through walls for them? So, friend, why do we rarely see such an outfit? Why do most teams do just enough to get by, keep their job, keep their heads down, and lay low? Why?

Because most teams are led by motivated leaders. Motivated leaders get, at best, a motivated team—compliant. Whatever level of motivation the leader possesses, you can be assured the team will have a little bit less. Stop trying so hard, leader. You cannot motivate another human, at least not for long. Stop trying to give another what they can only get from themselves. Instead, find more inspiration from the depths of your soul. Know your why and know your way, remember? Breathe fresh air into your lungs and let it manifest into more. Care deeply for your cause. Care deeply for those carrying it out alongside you. Get curious when you notice some not owning their twenty square feet. Committed followers cannot be bought. They must be built.

Ask them what's going on, sit quietly, and hear them. Ask them to tell you more. Ask them. Stop telling them so much of your good shit that they hear as simply more bullshit. Ask them. Meet them where they are and lift them up with good, curious questions. Hit them between the eyes with caring, challenging questions. Sit and listen. When they're thinking is accurate, celebrate with them. When it's not, correct them because you care. Make them write their plan for upping their game. Push the tension to them.

Want to move your team from compliant to committed? Stop telling. Ask them. Are you committed? Are you worth catching? Write.

BUILT TO LEAD | together we transform

Day 300: Thermostat or thermometer...

Emotions move us. Reason protects us. Wisdom is knowing when to lean into which, when to let your emotions take you where they will, and when to take three deep breathes and quiet them. Wisdom is knowing our most rational thoughts are laced with predictably irrational ones. Leaders embrace this ambiguity. Actually, leaders lead us through this ambiguity every day.

Emotions move. Reason calms. Leaders get comfortable with ambiguity. Leaders understand all decisions regardless the reason, data, and logic behind them are laced with emotion. Do you see why it's impossible to lead another without deeply understanding yourself? Do you see why leaders are reticent, reluctant, and only revealed once they've done the deep work within? Do you see why a strong CORE is central to your ability to integrate emotions and reason? Do you see your tendencies? Do you tend to trust your gut or data? Do you tend to wait too long to act? Do you tend to act too often without enough reason? Are you a thermostat or a thermometer when the pressure's on?

Emotions move. Reason calms. Leaders deftly develop both around their CORE. Leaders know when to lean against their tendencies and when to lean into them. How 'bout you?

Day 301: Fight and unite...

During practice forty-two, one of the teammates questioned another on this very topic. It was a very legitimate question from a concerned colleague. It led to a productive fight. As practice wound down and most in the room were satisfied with the result, one very CCD teammate made a sincere and sober observation. She said, "Chet, this wouldn't have happened without you. We would have never had this conversation on our own. How are we going to learn to do this without your help?" Totally legit. Here's what I told her and the rest of the team.

Deliberate practice.

The skill of learning to fight to improve performance is a skill you learn through practice. For a while, we show each client the way, model it, embrace the pain and suffering, and understand many will not like it, or us, for that matter. Welcome to leading anything. Your job, if you're a leader, is to realize you are already *that guy*. Leaders are that guy who brings up hard topics, welcomes hard hits, and doesn't shut down when others get heated. Leaders calmly feel the heat and don't add fuel to the fire. BTL leaders don't automatically shut down hard conversation. Normal humans do. BTL leaders welcome honesty and develop the wisdom to know when to let it go, when to let it go on, and when to step in and shut it down. This takes deliberate practice.

Deliberate practice is also required for teams to learn to push, poke, and prod for performance. Sometimes, it will backfire. Sometimes, fall flat. Sometimes, go too far. Sometimes, it won't go far enough. Over time, you and your team will learn. Few teams master the art of moving the tension to its rightful owner. Good teams do. Fight to improve performance. Stop fighting to prove a point. Fight and unite.

Slow down and reflect on your fights. When was the last time you had a fight that led to unite? Write. Fight. That's right...

Day 302: Falcons...

Falcons are the fastest creatures in the world, capable of hitting speeds up to 240 mph. During a one-on-one practice with Ron, we watched this beautiful bird fly by our beautiful building that afternoon and were mesmerized by its speed and agility. Leaders, at least the good ones, are a lot like falcons—they're decisive. When it comes to ruling the air, speed matters. The same is true on the ground.

Your job, if you're a leader, is to be decisive. Speed and agility matter. Leaders, not unlike professional poker players, are distinguished by the quality of the small bets they make. Amateurs keep waiting for the perfect hand and one more piece of analytics, and they fold frequently. Professionals are more decisive. They don't bet the farm, but they defer and delay less often than they decide. There is nothing wrong with taking your time with big decisions. Just realize your tendency is to take your time with small bets too. Decide more. Move. The best way to stay ahead of the competition is to migrate your value proposition ahead of the competition and your customers.

Falcons only reach Mach speeds when they've decided to go all-in and dive after their prey. When they miss their mark, they pull up before going splat and pick another target. They spend next to no time getting down on their failed attempt. We reward the leader who flies like a falcon. We love being around someone who isn't afraid to go for it, pull the trigger, and take a calculated risk. Every day, I'm around leaders who value smooth flight over speed. Smooth flight is overrated. Speed and agility matter more.

Learn from falcons and take more risks and deep dives. Yeah, baby. Falcons are decisive. Are you?

Day 303: Mustangs, mules, and an ass...

Mustangs run wild. It's hard to pick out the leader amongst a herd of mustangs because they are all on the hunt for green pastures. A team of mustangs is a team on the move, making things happen. You want mustangs on your team, leader.

Mules are sterile. Mules are stubborn. Mules are small. Mules, however, are not stupid—at least not when compared to normal horses. You see, mules have eyes that allow them to see their hindquarters, giving them a much better sense of balance. They are less likely to have trouble with their hooves and are less likely to stumble going down treacherous, uneven terrain. Mules can survive on less water than horses and require less hay or grass. Mules, historically, have gotten a bad rap, especially by me. I recently devoured a book titled *The Oregon Trail*, and it's given me some new learning on the power of being sterile, stubborn, and small. My perspective has changed. I've been a little closed-minded when it comes to these animals and rushed to judge. Turns out there is a place for mules on every team, including yours.

In fact, your team works optimally when you have deep diversity of minds, talents, and types. Turns out, we work best when we've got just the right mix of mustangs, mules, and even some donkeys too. It's really not an either/or choice when it comes to the types on your team. Embrace the "and," especially the ones who are not your type.

Abraham Lincoln, when elected as our 16th president, appointed his chief rivals onto his cabinet. He took his competition, Seward, Chase, and Bates, and brought them closer and learned to collaborate with those very unlike him. His team of rivals came together and kept this country of ours united too.

If you want to learn more, pick up *Team of Rivals* by Doris Kearns Goodwin. Who knows? You just might have a rival (ass) on your team who is the perfect fit for just the right hole. Mustangs, mules, and an ass or two. Good.

Day 304: Bernie's bad...

Way back in the day, PVC and I boarded a plane and made the trip to Jackson, Mississippi, and our day with Scott Sullivan (CFO) and Bernie Ebbers (CEO and cowboy in charge of WorldCom). It was during this visit I would share my one-page presentation with Bernie on the idea of consolidating seven divisions of sales into one. You see, I ran one of those groups, and our biggest competitors were the other WorldCom divisions. We were all selling the same services, and the former carrier groups had no idea how to market the offerings of the old UUNet/CompuServe arms. So, they tended to give it away or, at a minimum, deeply discount it.

We were a mess of fifty-seven acquired companies that had not been integrated. My proposal was not nuts. There were 13,000 folks in seven divisions of sales. My recommendation was the job could be done with 3,000. In essence, WorldCom was paying 10,000 people it didn't need to. Bernie, chewing on some massive cigar as we talked, told me thanks but no thanks. "I refuse to leave the dance without the people that brought me," he remarked with CCD clarity and shoot in his eyes. End of convo. No discussion. Done.

Within twelve months, tens of thousands of WorldCom associates would be laid off. Within two years, WorldCom would be dead. Bernie was responsible for the second-largest corporate loss in the history of these United States (Enron numero uno). Bernie's bad started with not making the hard call to consolidate and integrate his companies. He waited too long and trusted his CFO too much, in my opinion.

Today, I told this story to a client of mine who is facing a hard call with one of his partners. His gut is telling him one thing, his head another, and his heart is hurting. He doesn't want to be responsible for ruining people's lives. He's in a hard spot of bother. Kicking it down the road won't work even though he wants to. Leaders make hard calls. The great ones make them before they have to. Do you?

Day 305: This Is OPUS...

Ever wonder why so few people author and live their OPUS, their labor of love?

It's just a little bit easier to get busy and tell ourselves, "One day, I'll take the time—just not today. I'm too busy, too scared, too poor, too much, or too little." *One day*, we tell ourselves. *One day*. So, we get a job and get busy getting work done. We do. We get more responsibility so we can do more. We get even more responsibility so we can do more on steroids. Pretty soon, without our awareness, we are on the do-do trail, and around every turn, it's no longer sunshine and kittens. We start to step in some do-do, and it stinks. We burn out. We blow up. We can't wait to stop doing and seek distractions to dull us from the chronic pain. We take the third, fourth, and fifth drink. We turn to porn in the late afternoon. We turn to pills when we're on the road. We burnout, and it's not bright. This is not OPUS. This is labor in some form or another, and we can't wait to get to the top of this trail where everything will be better when we finally arrive in control. Sadly, when we arrive at the do-do summit, it, too, stinks—this time to high heaven. Yikes.

The do-do trail leads right where you would expect it to if you ever slowed down enough to think about it. Few take the time because they tell themselves they're too busy to do so. Funny, huh? OPUS is a labor of love, and we can't wait to do what we've dreamed of doing. We dream and do. Dream and do. Dream and do. We catch our breath when we reach the summit of dream and do mountain and look out over the horizon for another target. We can't wait to keep climbing, discover new trails, and try new things on this journey with seemingly no end. This is the recipe for sustained greatness and the fountain of youth.

One word makes a world of difference. Laborers do-do. OPUS practitioners dream and do. Who are you?

BUILT to **LEAD** | together we transform

Day 306: The missing piece toward peace...

I recently stumbled upon another piece of CCD magic. I'm not sure how this stuff develops into crystal clarity in my mind, leaps out of my mouth, and makes the connection to a few other crazy craniums. It just does. And I know it's like speaking a foreign tongue to most. Here's the missing piece for the few of you, if you will.

The number one piece toward lasting peace is patience.

The enabler of patience is clarity of priorities. You cannot master thirty of them. The clarity of your priorities comes from knowing who you are and what your aim is: CORE, OPUS, PoP. Don't forget the clarity that comes when you don't have to think in your MOT. Do you realize how peaceful it is not to think when the pressure mounts? Freakin' magic, friend. Instead of overthinking and getting all caught up in your head, you simply respond to the input of life with internal alignment, toward your external aim, and with an uncommon discipline of your PA. Peace is found on the other side of acute pain. It takes patience to sit in the hard stuff for what seems like forever but, in reality, is only for a short while.

The number one piece toward lasting peace is patience. That, friend, is the missing piece. Have you figured out your missing piece toward peace?

Day 307: Wanna make a bet?

Professional poker players make a ton of decisions—quick ones too (thank you, Jordan). The average hand takes just over two minutes and could have upward of twenty decisions, according to Annie Duke, one of the top professional poker players the past twenty years. I loved her book, *Thinking in Bets*.

Life is more poker than chess. There are finite moves in chess, and everything is in the open. There is no hidden information. The chance of you or me beating a world champion in a game of chess is slim to none. Yet all day long, top professional poker players lose 30–40% of the time, oftentimes to far inferior amateurs who just got lucky. Life is a lot like poker, isn't it?

If you're a leader, you're making more bets, and some of them have big ramifications. You could say the quality of your life comes down to the quality (and quantity) of your decisions and getting more lucky than not. Remember, the biggest difference between professional poker players and amateurs is the quantity of bets. Pros make more decisions. Quality comes as they study, learn, and apply. Pros don't focus on outcomes or resulting (poker word). Pros master the process and understand you can do everything right and still have it all go wrong. Pros just keep working and learning whether they're winning or losing.

Are you a pro, friend? Wanna make a bet?

BUILT to **LEAD** | together we transform

Build Your
Communication Skills

12 ESSENTIALS OF PERSONAL EXCELLENCE

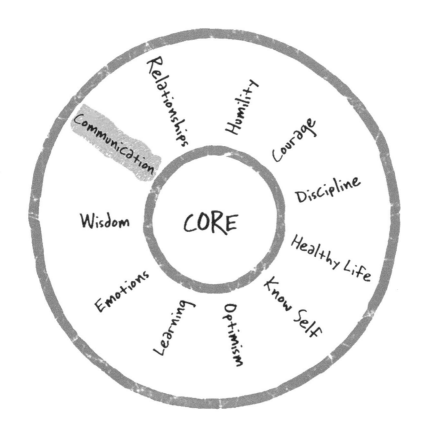

Rachel's Builder's Journey

I grew up in a great family, the oldest of four kids, with two caring and committed parents. Born to lead, contrarian by nature, tender once you get past the tough. Forever a square peg in a round hole. Too fiery, too outspoken (especially as a young girl in conservative circles), too competitive, too willing to call bullshit. Always *too much*. I had a chip on my shoulder and was quick to fight for those in my circle and those not in a position to fight for themselves.

This fiery side served me well as I became a twelve-year college softball coach. I demanded excellence. I believed in building people and building cultures. I crisscrossed the country for the next great job and the next big challenge. When I finally got the dream job, I realized that perhaps the dream job wasn't a dream, after all.

The dream job turned into a vision collision—and fast. I knew what I believed and how I wanted to build a program, and that was at odds with those in power. I chose to walk away from the dream job before I became someone or something I didn't believe in. It would have been either a slow death or a quick-firing had I chosen to stay. Undoubtedly, the right move *and* one that came with a lot of soul searching and second-guessing both before and after. If I wasn't a coach and wasn't climbing to the best job, who was I? I lost my way for a time and never stopped looking.

While lost and looking, I met this crazy guy, DD, and we started on the journey of becoming **BUILT TO LEAD**. Through good, hard work (and play) together, I started to get clarity I'd never had—who I really am, what I really believe, and why it really matters. I became grounded, found my way again, found myself. I embraced the things I'd lost—my instinct to challenge others, my intensity and love for life, and true deep community (thanks, DD). All the pieces fell into place. The ways I'd been *too much*—the instinct to challenge others, for instance—now, I could see so clearly how I could use it in service of my OPUS.

Around this same time, I also met someone who sees the beauty in the magic moments of life *and* in the mundane. And she has a knack for making the mundane magical. She reminded me of the rootedness of family traditions built around shared values, the anchor, the shelter, and the belonging. Life isn't simply work. It's to be lived together and loved together.

I now had the anchor of a strong CORE and a clear OPUS and a partner in life who makes life magical. It was time for the next leap into the unknown. I became a builder. Since the moment I made that decision to relentlessly chase my OPUS, I've woken up alive and on fire. You see, I love the epic, the big dreams, and the deep passions. If it doesn't move me, I won't pursue it. So, my dream is to awaken, challenge, and transform the willing world changers. I want to band together with the few—the few elite coaches, teams, leaders, and entrepreneurs—and I want to challenge them fearlessly out of passion and belief. Together, we transform.

Along this journey, I've had and will have setbacks and hurdles. *And* I've loved each one of them because they've come in pursuit of my OPUS. They've made me better. I've got a lifetime of practicing, growing, loving, and building ahead of me—exactly the way I want it.

Day 308: Seven good minutes...

One of the favorite exercises we practice with BTL teams is seven good minutes. Here's the framework:

Pick one person you want to understand better.

Invest seven good minutes, without any interruptions, asking them questions that lead to understanding. Start easy and go progressively deeper. Maintain eye contact as long as you can. Tune in like an animal being stalked, not like a stalker. Be interested. Do not interrogate. Do not comment. Do not attempt to fix. Do ask curious questions that lead to understanding. Notice how hard this is. Focus your mind exclusively on the other person. Notice the noise that plays in your head. Shut it off.

Switch roles. Seven and seven is my favorite drink. Rinse and repeat. Seven and seven. Good.

Mastering the art of living requires that we master the art of listening. Practice this like a banshee.

Day 309: I don't believe you...

Blaise Pascal, back in the early 1600s, said, "I give you the gift of these four words—I believe in you." Sam Phillips, back in 1954, told Johnny Cash something eerily similar when giving him feedback on his song. He looked young Mr. Cash in the eye and said, "I don't believe you." Recently, I reminded a dear friend and client that "anding" these thoughts is the job of every leader. You've got to let your teammates know you believe in them, and you've got to be honest with those you don't believe.

Do not shy away from telling the truth to the teammate you still believe in but no longer believe. This is where the transformational leader shines. "I believe in you" and "I don't believe you," tells a teammate some hard truth they can use. Most leaders, when they stop believing, make the mistake of keeping it to themselves. They don't open their mouth and deliver tough truth. Hence, one of my favorite catchphrases, "When the leader stops believing, someone will soon be-leaving." The transformational leader gives the gift of belief, and she also gives the gift of "I don't believe you." Most leaders just turn away and let nature slowly lead someone to leave.

I believe in you, and I don't believe you. Powerful words. Stop holding back, biting your tongue, and hoping somehow they'll figure it out on their own. Leaders are believers, remember. Give the gift of belief. Give the gift of I don't believe you: I don't believe you are doing the work. I don't believe your heart is in your work. I don't believe you want to be here. I don't believe you're singing your song. I don't believe you are finishing as strongly as you're starting. I don't believe you're leaving it all on the court.

What gift does each one of your teammates need to receive from you, leader?

Day 310: Shoot in your eyes...

Andrew Jackson was a lowly circuit judge way back in the day, holding court in small, Southern towns, trying to make an honest buck. He would ride his horse into town, don his judicial robe, and handle traffic court, so to speak. It was just a job, you know...

As the story goes, there was a rowdy causing quite a ruckus while young Andrew held court one day. The sheriff couldn't contain him, and an entire posse was unable to take care of business. The rowdy was swinging his pistol and knife and threatening anybody who came near him. The third time the sheriff interrupted Jackson's dispensation of justice, he decided it was time to take matters into his own hands and strode out to meet the rowdy himself. "Surrender now, you infernal villain, or I'll blow you through" were the only words spoken. The rowdy dropped his weapons instantly. Jackson went back to the courthouse, and Hoss went to jail. End of story.

When asked why he held a posse at bay but surrendered to Jackson, the rowdy spoke some CCD wisdom, "I saw shoot in his eyes. I saw shoot in nary any other eyes, so I says to myself, Hoss, it's time to sing small, and so I did." Andrew Jackson was not a man of power, prominence, or in a position of local authority at the time. He was simply someone with conviction—shoot in his eyes. This, friend, is how you become the 7th President of the United States. His story is worth studying. Read *Andrew Jackson* by H.W. Brands.

Strong CORE. Authentic OPUS. Are you beginning to see why knowing who you are, what you believe, and what you stand for are essential to Becoming BTL? Slow down and sit with this for a while. Write. Do you have shoot in your eyes?

Day 311: Clear, concise, and direct...

Leader, please remember this when communicating with your team about your big dream. You can be wrong, and the team will forgive you. You cannot be unclear. Fact.

When reminding the team, challenging the team, casting vision, and communicating what needs to be done now, master CCD. Master connectors are crystal clear. Ambiguity and vagueness are not your friends when communicating where we're going and how to get there. Most leaders suffer from the curse of knowledge—the more we know, the more likely we are to forget what it was like not to. Most leaders assume too much when connecting with the team. Assume less, leader.

Master being CCD instead. Be crystal clear. Ask the team to play back what they heard, what they're thinking, and whatever questions they may have. Embrace the silence, and don't be in a hurry to move on. Sit in silence until somebody says what everybody else is thinking. Ambiguity is the enemy of action, leader, if you want a team baby stepping in alignment toward your big dream. Your problem is you think the team understands as you do. They do not. Don't believe me: try asking them. You'll see. You can be wrong; you just can't be unclear.

Today, be CCD, assume less, and ask the team to play back what they heard. Rinse and repeat...

Day 3l2: Ethos, pathos, logos...

Aristotle believed master connectors followed a simple recipe whenever they attempted to persuade their audience. He believed *ethos, pathos*, and *logos* have power when it comes to persuasion. Let's unpack.

Ethos translates to the English word *ethic* and in the art of persuasion is all about establishing your character as credible. Nobody listens for long to someone whose ethic they question. You are credible when you've deeply answered the big questions in life and live accordingly. You are credible when you're a domain-specific expert in your OPUS.

Pathos translates to the English word *passion*. A credible ethos that persuades on data and analytics alone comes up wanting. All decisions are emotional, remember. Your ethos, laced with real emotion, carries your message from heart to heart. Speaking from the heart is a powerful persuader when the heart is full and the emotion is authentic. The stronger the self-authored, authentic CORE, the more trustworthy the heart and more believable the argument.

Logos comes last, logically. Yes, logos translates literally to *logic*. Your argument needs to follow a flow. If you want to persuade, you must be CCD when it comes to your logos. Many an argument is lost because the logic wasn't failed—it was simply too lengthy and lost them before the punch line. Remember, you need a lawyer's argument without a litigator's longevity.

Clear, concise, and direct is the one you want. *Ethos, pathos*, and *logos* are Aristotle's recipe for persuading your audience. You most likely have invested too much time on logos and too little on your ethos. A little more time on number one, please. Today, invest a little more time on ONE.

Day 313: Psychological safety...

I'm rereading *Smarter Faster Better* by Charles Duhigg. There's a chapter about what makes great teams, so I was especially interested to read his research. Turns out he mostly focuses on the research done by Google, whose deep data dive dictates the common denominator of great teams— whether sport, music, or business—is the level of "psychological safety."

Let's unpack this new term. According to Duhigg, "Psychological safety is a 'shared belief,' held by members of a team, that the group is a safe place for taking risks." Sounds simple. Great teams are safe. This safety creates an uncommon sense of togetherness. What, you ask, are the key behaviors Google identified that build psychological safety? Good question. The answer is BTL practice.

According to Google, a great team's number one behavior is that all team members play, and the best indicator of them playing is how they talk. Google tracks teammates words in meetings and aims for "roughly the same amount." The second behavior that builds psychological safety is looking teammates in the eye, reading body language, and being curious when someone is tweaked vs going turtle. They use the same Simon Baron-Cohen test we've been using for years to measure teammates ability to read emotion. Again, this is why we practice curious questions as the bolted-on habit of BTL practice. This takes time and feels out of control for most. Google is training their leaders to be master listeners. Simple, not easy.

Teaching the art of listening cannot be Googled. You must care enough to want to hear from everyone on your team. You must be patient as a saint. You must learn to listen to those who rub you raw. Practice letting these teammates dominate the airways. Practice disciplining the mind to suspend judgment. Understand it's not the person rubbing you raw. It's your perception that's the problem (thank you, Epictetus). There's your linchpin.

Where do you care less? With whom do you want to care more?

Day 314: The Curse and Cookies...

I remember reading the Heath Brothers' book, *Made to Stick*. It was filled with little, usable nuggets, one of which they called the curse of knowledge—once we know something, we forget what it was like when we didn't. The curse is around communicating with those who know less than you. Masters suffer from this curse more than the mediocre middle. Masters must learn to share less than they know. And to get our best, they do this without making us feel less.

Sitting in Vineyard Columbus, listening to Pastor Rich Nathan, gave me a great "and" to this learning. Rich is one bad ass preacher. He is a lawyer by training and has a handful of associate pastors whose job it is to lawyer him up. He picks a topic, does his research, and has them do theirs. Then, they huddle up and decide what they're throwing out. They toss tons of good stuff out the window. Why would they toss tons of learning away? According to Rich, master connectors put the cookies on the bottom shelf. Imagine you had a child and decided to bake them cookies for a tasty treat. Once the cookies were out of the oven, you invited them to come and get it! Instead of putting them within reach, however, you stuck them up on the top shelf of your cabinets. They would try as best they could, but the cookies would remain out of reach. No bueno.

Put the cookies on the bottom shelf.

You have the curse of knowledge and tend to overshare what you know to those you lead. It's all good stuff, but it's top-shelf knowledge, and the team lives in the real world. Bring it down without putting them down. Bring it down. Make it memorable; make it sticky. You see, friend, masters connect us normal folks to the melody lines. Masters remember what it was like before they knew what they now know. Put the cookies on the bottom shelf. I mean, come on, man, let them have some of your good stuff—just not all of it.

Day 315: Yearning...

I could write this rant every single day. At least three times a week, someone approaches me to talk about this exact problem—their loved one is going nuclear out of nowhere. My client tells me their spouse, girlfriend, boyfriend, partner, or roomie greets them with incessant whining. I always ask them if they remember my most frequent counsel toward this all-too-common malaise. Ninety percent of the time, they can't remember but beg me to give it to them again. Here's what I tell them every—single—time.

Hear the yearning.

Hear the yearning, not the complaining or whining. You see, friend, when you finally return home after a day slaying dragons and conquering the world, your beauty wants to be with you. Slow your sorry ass down. Your beauty yearns to connect. When you don't give your full attention, the lover's response is to amp up the volume. I mean, come on, man, they married you, moved in, and never want to move on. So, of course, they move toward you. All you've got to do is work on transitioning a bit better. When you re-enter your lover's space, forget your battles, big wins, horrific losses, and ass-kissing compliments. Most conflicts start with some kind of harsh setup. Control your piece of the tension and prime yourself to transition with open arms, open ears, and an open heart. Prime yourself to hear the yearning.

Hear the yearning. You'll see. When your loved ones sense you hearing their yearning for connection, they dial it down almost instinctively. They feel your calm presence and know they have you—all of you. They feel more, not less. Together, we transform—as we hear the yearning, transition toward our lover, turn off technology, and tune in like an animal being stalked.

What are you hearing? Remember, you don't hear things the way they're said—you hear things based on what's in your head.

Day 316: Assume less, again...

You are a foreigner in your kingdom. Your name may be on the building, you may have been the head coach for decades, and you may have all the right intentions and off the chart integrity. You are, however, like me here in Positano—a foreigner in a distant land. Your team speaks a different language. When you speak words to them, they don't process them the way you do. Your words carry more weight and inflict worry, lots of worry. So, stop speaking without thinking.

Tune in like a foreigner in a distant land. Catch the tone and body language and stay curious. Shut your judger down and try to remember what it was like when you weren't the one in power. Every leader we work with would benefit from being a foreigner in their own kingdom, if you will. We assume way too much and wonder why we're surprised so frequently when a truth-teller like me comes in and translates what the team has been trying to say for freakin' years.

Speak CCD. Tune in like an animal being stalked. Ask the team to play back what they heard. Stop assuming. Ask them to tell you more. Remember, leaders are believers, and leaders are connectors too. It's your job to lead in the connection business. Act more like a foreigner than a dictator, and more real connections will be coming soon. Every leader gets exactly the team they deserve. Want a better team? Become a better connector. Think of yourself as I do here in Positano. Humbly lead the way to better conversations, better connections, and better outcomes.

Speak less. Say more. Assume less. Question more. Tell me more, friend. Tell me more...

BUILT to **LEAD** | together we transform

Day 317: Ambiguity...

You and I suck at action in ambiguity. Humans can handle all kinds of adversity and get through to the other side. We give up quickly, however, when our mind thinks this thing (whatever it is) doesn't have an end. We stop swimming from Catalina to LA on a foggy morning when we simply cannot see the shore. We ring the bell in SEAL training after the instructor continually moves the finish line iteration after iteration. We can't handle ambiguity, at least not for long.

Remember this when you lead your team through the inevitable transitions that come with mergers, hyper-growth, unexpected loss/ decline, and all kinds of other changes with no end in sight. You know more than your team does. You've been architecting the thing for months, maybe even years. It's no big deal to you by the time it finally happens. Your team has not had your experience. It's a sudden change to their sense of equilibrium. Something small but sinisterly unclear, at least to them, can shut them down. Suddenly, they lose sight of the shore and can't manage another stroke.

Clarity is the job of the leader. You can be dead wrong about the future, and the team will forgive you. You cannot be unclear. Master CCD. Speak from the heart. Tell them the truth regarding the transition and take their questions. Make them ask you stuff and sit silently until they do. Ambiguity is the enemy, and it's everywhere. Nothing lasts forever, and nobody knows what's happening next. Leaders live in the same ambiguity as all of us and realize they've got to keep swimming in spite of the fog. Leaders are believers. They believe the gig is out of their control and may not end when they think it will. Leaders don't stop when clarity's missing. Leaders admit they don't have all the answers but confidently tell us that this PA is what we're doing now. Leaders productively act in ambiguity.

Day 318: Turn right here...

Most clients speak too much and say too little. The transformational leader flips this by mastering the art of listening. When the master listener opens her mouth, a few searing words of wisdom trickle out. She usually offers up one thing, and then, just as we're leaning in to drink more, she stops. Instead of blathering on, the transformational leader is CCD and then asks the receiver what they heard. This is a habit of master connectors. Is it one of yours?

Imagine you're in a new city driving from the airport to one of your prospects. You put the destination in your iPhone and head out of the rental lot. Upon arrival at your first four-way stop, you tune in, awaiting instructions from your phone. Instead of just giving you the next turn, your smartphone decides to be more efficient and spit out the next twelve. Here's what would happen next: your brain would freak and freeze. Too much good information is not good.

"Turn right here," I can handle.

The same is true with your guidance. Even when given the green light, send less. Even when facing a hoarder of bad habits, send less correction. When you're invited in after all these years, send less. Instead, master the art of the question. Master getting your teammate to think more critically and own their way forward. Make them tell you more. Send less. I tell my clients to write narratives and throw up on paper whatever they're thinking. You cannot write too much when it comes to getting clarity. However, when it comes to connecting to your team, master the art of CCD. Speak less. Say more. The greatest speeches in history are short ones. Lincoln's Gettysburg address is two minutes.

Practice "turn right here." Good...

BUILT TO LEAD | together we transform

Day 319: Stories...

Humans do not remember sound bites, snippets, or standalone data, no matter how seemingly significant. Humans hold onto stories. Sadly, many only remind themselves of old, tired, negative stories. So, leader, if you want a team to run through walls beside you, tell them stories of their great work and contribution. Do not make this stuff up—simply observe them doing their thing and remind them why it matters to you and those you serve. Tell your stories and stories from history that inspire them to be more and do more.

Remember, humans are wired to belong and become. We all want to know we belong to another, and we all want to become autonomous—our own man, if you will. We love stories that show us the way toward becoming who we are, and that make us want to do more together too. Recently, during another BTL team practice, I told the team one of my stories, the story of why we go to the French Alps and ride the steepest, longest, and hardest alpine passes we can find. I told them how it started with Larry Allen and me dreaming about doing something hard for my fiftieth birthday. I told them about him dying before we made the first trip and how Downer took his spot, and we put his number 83 on top of the Alps. I told them about Miss and Andrew coming along in 2019 and more wives and children coming in 2022. I told them a story, and afterward, one of them told me it was the best one I've told yet. Who knew?

Tell stories, leader. Make your teammates want to be and do more. Tell your stories. Tell their stories. We remember stories. Make them good ones. The good ones are always from the heart...

Day 320: You are the message...

Leaders are believers. Leaders believe in themselves, their team, their OPUS, and something bigger than themselves. We connect to believers, even when our beliefs are out of alignment. Do not take up residence in a system where you don't believe. If you do, you will soon find yourself saying something very hard to understand, much less believe. You will ask your leaders for better messaging so you can keep the team motivated. You will be on the slippery slope to becoming a bullshit artist. Bullshitters speak a lot but say very little. Not good.

Leaders do not message. Leaders speak from the heart, and we are either drawn in or repelled by their clarity. Leaders are not neutral and don't try to be. Leaders believe. Leaders, at least the ones worth following, have love in their heart, and shoot in their eyes. Becoming BTL is all about belief.

When was the last time you rinsed your CORE and OPUS? What are you reading to widen your perspective? Are you mastering CCD from a full heart? You don't need a speech coach to better connect to your team. You are the message. Trust your CORE, remind them of your OPUS, and be clear about what you're doing right now. What are you waiting for...?

BUILT to **LEAD** | together we transform

Day 321: Got it...

Every day, I have a front-row seat to communication conflict. One person sent a message. Another received it. The conflict came in the silence, in the assumptions that happen when we send and don't receive. Let me attempt to illustrate this by going back to my CompuServe roots. CompuServe built a communications network designed to only carry the communication from computer to computer. The network was comprised of computers (called micro-nodes) distributed around the world. The magic of this data network was it was shared. So, lots of companies were able to share in the cost, which made it economical before the freedom we now know as the Internet.

The basic protocol that kept everybody's data from getting lost was the key. Every node in the network was smart. Every time one node talked to another, it followed a very specific protocol. The receiving node sent "ACK" to the sending node, and they compared bits to make sure what was intended actually showed up. Smart, huh? If the sender got no "ACK," they simply sent it again. No ACK; no go. ACK; we go. The network worked amazingly well because this protocol assumed nothing. The network worked because every node was smart. We humans aren't nodes, but we could learn a little something from the protocol that kept the system together. "Got it" can be amazing. "Got it, and I'm working on it" can be even better. "Got it, and thanks for sending, and here's when you can expect to have your request fulfilled" is better yet. "Got it, and let's talk" can be the convo that keeps conflict from creeping to the surface.

Nothing, however, leaves the sender hanging like a node with no ACK. Today, I heard another story about someone assuming too much. Seems like ACK is really problematic for our young, tech-savvy leaders. Way too many young minds assume too much when it comes to trusting technology. Assume less. Remember, just because you've heard someone or read their text, tweet, or DM, doesn't mean they know this. ACK more. You are smart enough to know this, right?

ACK. Got it. Good.

Day 322: 55, 38, 7...

Talk is cheap. Less is more. According to Albert Mehrabian from the University of California, listeners remember very few of the words you and I speak. Albert's the guy who coined 55,38,7. Here's Albert's research with a few of our thoughts on top.

Fifty-five percent of your message is your body language. The primary source is your face and, most specifically, your eyes. The receiver is looking for sincerity.

The question: Do I believe your eyes and words align? The receiver does not grade on the curve. Anything less than 100% belief is a fail.

Thirty-eight percent of your message is your voice. Tone, quality, variation, volume, and feel. We primarily listen to tone and feel. The receiver is looking for love—truth in love.

The questions: Do I believe you care? Do I believe you believe what you're telling me?

Seven percent of your message is your words. Enough said.

The questions: Do your words *sear* me? Do your words draw me near or push me away in fear?

Who knew talk was cheap? Turns out all our wordiness makes us less believable. Build a strong CORE. Speak from your heart. Lead with love. You will be internally aligned and fully engaged. A few will believe you and remember what you said. CCD from a love-filled heart is the BTL recipe. Duchenne smile, please. Talk is cheap. Less is more. Freakin' magic, baby.

Day 323: Play back what you heard...

Recently, during practice fourteen with another team learning each other's language, the head of the system shared some of his learning with fifteen teammates. It was nothing dramatic, nothing complicated, and his words were CCD magic, or so it seemed. However, I had a feeling. So, without hesitating, I interrupted him and asked him to repeat his previous sentence. He glanced at me like what in the world was I doing, but he repeated himself. I asked for a show of hands if they thought he said XYZ. Most raised their hand. I then asked who thought he said ABC. All ABC'ers raised in unison, including me. Remember, this is your world too. You think you're being CCD magic and handing out compliments while most hear criticisms. You think you're being CCD magic and telling the team how jacked up you are about the new projects, and most think you're beyond pissed off instead of pumped up. You think you're being heard correctly because the room remains silent and heads nod. Rarely is it so.

Yeah, I know it's awkward to ask the team to "play back what you heard" as a safeguard against being misunderstood, but it works. Of course, the body language and tone make all the difference in the world regarding how those five words register in the minds of your teammates. So, leader, remember the aim is to make sure you're delivering a message that is received as you intended.

"Play back what you heard" is freakin' magic when the team knows you're trying to avoid confusion, not catch the confused.

These five words have played a major role in creating positive culture throughout nearly twenty years of BTL team practice. Go on—give it a try. I cannot believe how many times I've used this and been shocked at what the team played back to me and countless leaders in BTL practice. Play back what you heard. Assume less. Done so...

Build Your Interdependent Relationships

12 ESSENTIALS OF PERSONAL EXCELLENCE

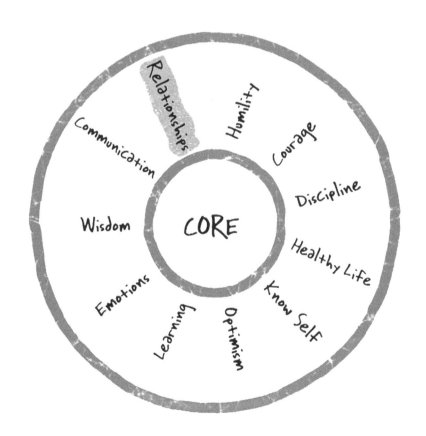

David's Builder's Journey

I began working with **BUILT TO LEAD** in 2010. I was in my late thirties, married to a tender-hearted spitfire, the father to three of the world's greatest kids, and an executive at a major athletic footwear company that had just acquired our family's business. *And* my life had become completely consumed by an anxious mind. My story and struggles are nothing major—most aren't—but because I ignored and/or poorly dealt with my shit, like most, I found myself reaching a breaking point I wish on no one.

I grew up one of four boys who loved to compete in just about everything. Me...not so much. Around twelve, my parents moved to see if a new home, city, community, school—life could save their marriage. It didn't. As my family started breaking apart in an "every man for themselves" kind of way, I went into survival mode. Never a good place for anyone to be, let alone a young person. Over the next four years, I lived in three different homes, changed schools five times, and saw both my parents start new lives. I felt alone, even though I wasn't. Funny, huh? But because I had begun only looking out for myself in a dysfunctional way, I didn't know how to lean on others for help.

This lone wolf mentality was developed (and mastered) over the next couple of decades. It kept me alive *and* kept others from hurting me. You see, even though I had some amazing people in my life, including my blended families, I had become wired to survive, get by, manage through, and hold on. This works in life or death situations, but on a day-to-day basis, it's unsustainable. Under this type of stress-based approach to living, my mind was becoming full of anxiety, and my body was breaking down as well.

On Christmas Eve of 2009, my anxious mind called a time out. We were at the airport getting ready to pick up our daughter from Ethiopia, and I couldn't get on the plane. My thoughts were irrational and scrambled. I was convinced that traveling to a third world country and adding another child to our family was now a bad idea. As I began to cry uncontrollably, my tender-hearted spitfire took over. She managed to contact the agency in Ethiopia (on Christmas morning) and inform them of our situation. They confirmed it was okay for her to come without me, but I wasn't comfortable with that. So, she called my younger brother, and within thirty minutes, he was at the airport with his passport in hand and went in my place.

I was wrecked, embarrassed, and broken. My doctor told me he sees more people for anxiety-related issues than any other by a mile. He assured me I was going to get better *if I did the work*. So, I began going to weekly therapy to learn more about the impact my childhood experiences were having on me as an adult. It was eye-opening and a catalyst for my journey to becoming **BUILT TO LEAD**…enter Chet Scott. On the first day I met him, he told the group of us this was a gift and went on to tell us he "wakes up dead people." I remember thinking to myself, *This guy is pretty pompous, and those are some presumptive statements*. But I was intrigued and curious (if you will), so I played along.

One of the most important things I did during this time (and still do) was write. It forced my brain to slow down and articulate thoughts outside of my anxiety. Chet then challenged what I wrote to make sure it's right. And that is the foundational process of becoming **BUILT TO LEAD**. Together, we hammered on more clearly defining who I am, what I believe, and why it matters. It was incredibly painful *and* transformative. This discipline makes your whole system take pause because words on a paper are more real than thoughts in your mind, especially my anxious ones. And once you get your words on paper right, they are stronger than thoughts by a mile *and* are the source of truth when you struggle to know it.

Over the last ten years, I've continually challenged what I've written to make sure my beliefs and behaviors align—this is the greatest form of integrity and where the most change/transformation has happened. You can't write how much you love your wife for her high standards and grit and then not welcome her challenges and strength. You can't write that you believe all great discoveries have been made from a willingness and ability to not be right and then not be willing to fail. Having a document, a personal source of record rooted in integrity, being driven by passion, and committed to a purpose for all that is true and right in my life *and* someone who helped me along the way has transformed me from a dead man walking to a man becoming fully alive. What a life-changing gift it is.

Day 324: Together, we transform...

"Together, we transform" is not easy. Writing this book has been hard OPUS. Like all Builder's Journeys, it starts alone. I started writing sixteen years ago as a discipline. It's lonely writing. It's work. As Steven Pressfield shared with me and models every day, you have to show up with your lunch pail mentality and slay the keyboard, one word at a time.

Editing is harder. It's your baby, you know, and you have to cut it to pieces. Once you realize it's addition by subtraction, the pain eases but just a bit. It still hurts to cut what you think is art. Culling is hard OPUS. I rewrote this book by myself on two different occasions. Miss thought I had turned mad. I cut it to the bone this last rinse, or so I thought.

Enter Gu and Dosch.

These two Builders turned editors came alongside for a long, long week of culling. We set our aim to begin Becoming **BUILT TO LEAD** by setting the edge. CCD and putting the cookies on the bottom shelf quickly followed. We listened for melody lines and cut bullshit. We attacked our curse of knowledge. We slowed down. Put first things first, just like we do in any BTL practice. Laughter arrived. Joy showed up. Exhaustion was met with OPUS, and we kept going.

The result would be a better day for you, the reader.

Together, we transform is where OPUS resides. Nobody is as smart as everybody, remember. You are not meant to go it alone or a lone. You and I are meant to become all ONE—one 'L of a difference. Start by going at it alone and build your distinct strong CORE. Grab hold of a damn few and become deeply connected. Pull them up and allow them to pull you alongside. Be with.

Learning to do hard things together is where we find ourselves. We are a band of builders at BTL. We hope you are becoming the original you are. We hope you feel a sense of belonging here. We hope you are Becoming BTL and mastering the art of living.

Together, we transform. Always together...

Day 325: Honor the past...

Half of Greece resides in Athens now, and they are not one. They beg you to patronize their establishments and drive you out in the process. The citizens seem to be oblivious to their golden era. The tourists all want to see the Acropolis and Parthenon and hear stories of the Greek gods without understanding why it matters. I will not be back to Athens but will tour Greece again. I want to meet the Spartan, Theban, and the Cretan. I want to go back to Santorini and hang with our friend, George, who knows his OPUS is not flying high but laying low with his TC Villa guests. The golden age of Greece, America, or any other community is not found by living in the past.

Honor the past. Celebrate the present. Build a vision for the future.

These are the big three values of vibrant communities. Performance cultures honor their past. They honor those who paved the way, but they do not live in 500 BC or even 1977. Honor the past, don't live in it. Vibrant communities celebrate the present. They celebrate small wins and love getting tired together doing what matters. They give great service, world-class products, and one of a kind experiences. They dream big and do the little things well. We flock toward them. They cannot serve us all, so they pick a price point that ensures they serve those who value what they do. They make us want to be with them, not because they're begging but because they're better.

Your business is either heading toward being the best or begging. Honor the past. Celebrate the present. Build a vision for the future and go freakin' get it. Are you begging for business or building better?

Day 326: The gift...

The gift of BTL team practice is the gift of time—time to think, time to connect, time to become, and time to sense you belong. Oneness is the heart of performance in work and life. Oneness doesn't come easily within, much less with another or many others unlike you, and unlike me. We know it when we sense it, when we feel it, and when we experience it. We know it when we know who we are, accept who others are, and come together to do something we both think is worthwhile. God ordained this coming together to accomplish something, and He said it was good. God named it labor but not just any kinda labor. God named you and me His labor of love, His great work, His magnum OPUS.

It only makes sense that our journey together as humans is figuring out how to include more humans and welcome them into our homes, communities, companies, countries, and cultures. It only makes sense to do something good for all of us and use our limited time here to be good and do good, right?

BTL team practice is a gift a leader gives to her team. It becomes *the gift* when a leader makes it safe, shows vulnerability, and connects us to her OPUS while creating a sense of shared purpose along the way. Your team wants the gift. Give the gift of getting tired together. Jolt yourself and your team off cruise control and make each other think. So, leader, go on. Be with. Be vulnerable. Make it safe and make it meaningful. Practice. A client and friend of mine recently retired. On his last day at work, he sent me a beautiful thank-you note with a picture of what he was taking home with him: it was a picture of some of his learning from BTL team practices. BTL practice made him think. He got better. We did too. It was a gift.

E Pluribus Unum—out of many, one. This is the gift. Are you giving it?

PRACTICE

Day 327: Becoming BTL...

In 2014, Durp challenged me to say yes to working with OSU wrestling. He wrote me a searing letter and even called me some names. Grappy and I have been building ever since. A year and some change later, Cbear (women's gymnastics) became our second OSU sports team client. In 2015, David Deck (Doscher) took the leap from the corporate world to join the BTL band. He's younger than most of us and brought an energy and unique perspective from the big Lou. He's like a little brother to me and a gifted builder to his clients. Young Rachael, one of David's clients, decided to join the BTL band in 2018, and she makes David look like an old man. As if we aren't undergoing enough of a youth movement, upon graduation, our son Taylor decided to join us too. He had interned throughout college and fell in love with the work. Jiggles came on board in 2019, and Andrew (Dorothy) went from rowing to rocking our boat in 2020. None of it was planned—a perfect mess in the making.

In 2020, BTL turned eighteen, and my sense is that more evolution is coming. The core, however, remains the same. The BTL band will continue to practice one on one and one on a few. We will continue to run the same few plays over and over again. We will not grow tired of CORE, OPUS, or PoP. We will grow and nuance new ways forward. It will be hard OPUS. It will be good to be with whomever God puts in our path.

So, friend, why do I write this for you to read?

We want you to realize you are in the process of Becoming BTL, and you're probably really frustrated with how long it's taking and how nonlinear your progress. We want you to be encouraged and keep climbing. Clarity is coming. We're on our Builder's Journey, and speaking for the BTL band, we really appreciate your help. We're grateful to be working together. I started this experiment a lone. Today, we're a band of ten becoming all ONE.

Are you beginning to see the pattern of Becoming BTL just this side of chaos? Are you trusting the process? Are you mastering your craft? Clarity's coming…

Day 328: Teeks...

We learn more from example than from principle and precept. I learned the most from Bernie Ebbers and our dog Tank (aka Teeks).

Teeks taught me more. Teeks, you might recall, was our little black dog who was rescued from a bunch of drunk fraternity boys. He never trusted men when he first met them, but once he did, he would lick your face off. Teeks was the best guard dog in the history of the planet. His daily routine was to take up his post and scan the side, back, and front yard for any and all outsiders. When anything entered Teeks' territory, he attacked it with no holds barred. He protected his turf and his family. He did his job and did it well. Teeks lived hard.

Leadership lesson—leaders protect their team and turf. Leaders live hard.

Teeks loved harder. He would greet me at the door, ask me about my day, and follow me wherever I went. If I got home and had a call to do with a client, he would lie up against the door listening and waiting for me to come out. When any of his pack came into his home, he would race them to the couch (he always won) and jump from one to another, giving out unlimited kisses and affection. Teeks loved to lie on my chest, next to Miss in bed, and bury himself under the bed just to be near us. Teeks loved everyone who made it into his pack. He gave all of himself when he loved you. You felt his energy, and it was life-giving stuff. Teeks loved harder.

Leadership lesson—leaders love being with their team. Leaders love harder.

Live hard. Love harder. (Leaders learn from everyone. Leaders learn.) By now, you should know my best learning came from my best four-legged friend (thanks, Teeks)…

Day 329: We...

We came. We climbed. We conquered.

Miss, Andrew, Downer, Littlest Fricker, Blondie, Doc Guv, and I climbed mountains together. We departed together, climbed at our own pace, reconvened at the summit, and rinsed and repeated for nine glorious days. Our favorite new climb was Plan du Lac, a 15-km quiet, hairpin-filled beauty and beast. When Littlest and I arrived (him first) at the summit, we decided to descend a few meters down the backside, past the hippie bar, and take in the sights and sounds. For a brief moment, we said nothing as we stared in awe-filled worship of God's great creation.

We heard nothing for a brief moment. We enjoyed silence and beauty together. The flowers were popping out of the rock-filled, grassy slopes as if angels had sprinkled the seedlings in some kind of purposeful arrangement. The snow was quietly melting, sun was shining brightly, and the sky was deep blue. The silence and beauty juiced our weakened COREs. We took it in and smiled at each other as we both were thinking the same thing: gratitude.

We came. We climbed. We conquered. And we realized (again) that we are, in fact, not in control. We came because captains flew us, cars drove us, and bikes carried us. We came because Martine housed, fed, and watered us. We climbed because bikes were geared especially for the endeavor, energy bars fueled us, and signs guided us, and we put in the work prior to taking on the task. We conquered together. None of us is as strong as all of us. When twigs tired, minds weakened, and lungs were left breathless, a cry of "bonjour, pussycats" from across the mountain would inspire a return of "bonjour, Louie." We talked even when we couldn't see each other. Our connection carried us when our wills were weakened. We carried each other, even though we each had to go it a lone. We went home stronger, even though bodies and bikes betrayed us. We went home stronger because of we. Slow down and sit with this for a while.

Day 330: Born to run toward...

I first read Christopher McDougall's book *Born to Run* back in 2009. New Balance was a new client then, and I was learning about minimalist running shoes through working with them. David Deck was a young executive with NB who immediately stood out in our three-day-long BTL retreat kicking off NB team practice. He kept asking questions and was childlike in his curiosity. Something inside me told me we would become fast and forever friends. I was right.

C.S. Lewis was one wise dude. His reading discipline was to re-read two for each new one. I'm beginning to do more rereading of old books that hit me hard the first go 'round. This was one of those books, mostly because I'm not a runner, but I've enjoyed running occasionally. A few months after reading this, Littlest Fricker would hit me with hard truth about my sugar addiction and forever change my relationship with sweets.

Become more disciplined, friend, in going back, not to loathe, linger, or romantically reminisce. Go back to study, learn, and apply. Go back to get better. Here are some learnings from this trip going backward: women crush men when it comes to ultra-running. Take Leadville 100 trail run as an example. Nearly ninety percent of the women entrants finish under the 30-hour limit while less than half of the men do. The longer and more grueling the race, the better the females finish. In my study of human performance in business, sport, and life, over these past twenty-seven years, I've come to discover women are not the weaker ones. Women endure childbirth and, even more painful, marriage/partnership with weak, sorry ass men who can't handle physical pain, much less relational/emotional suffering. We, men, need a wake-up call when it comes to commitments. We are called to be a steadying influence in the storm, a rock that endures crashing, relentless waves, and remains strong. We are born to run toward trouble, not from it. We are born to model the way, embrace pain and suffering, and embody truth in love. We are not born to run away.

You are born to run. Which way you running, friend? This rant kind of took an unexpected turn, huh?

Day 331: Vows and wounds...

A vow, by Merriam-Webster's definition, is "a solemn promise or assertion; specifically: one by which a person is bound to an act, service, or condition."

I made a vow to myself when very young. I was not going to let people push me around like they did my dad. I watched his mom treat his other brothers better, and his physician colleagues disrespect him. I observed his lack of confidence and willingness to play small. I saw his wounded heart and hardened my own. You see, most vows are rooted in our wounds.

I was super small and slight. I made a vow to myself, early on, to make something of myself, no matter the cost. If you beat me at basketball when I was young, we would play again and again and again until I beat you. Driven. Focused. Competitive. These were my early descriptors. My wound, I guess you could say, drove me to accomplish. I was tough. This worked well for a while. You see, being tough and demanding doesn't make for much of a cuddly dad. Kids came early before I understood myself, my wound, and my Miss, much less what it meant to be a dad to little boys. So, I subconsciously lived out my vow to myself when raising Cain, if you will. I made sure my sons were strong and pushed too hard. I was involved and loving, don't get me wrong, and was very committed to being a good, loving dad. I just hadn't learned to modify my approach. Once Krit came along, I had no push in mind; just protect.

It's clear to me I'm a better builder than father. It pains me to admit this. My sons are distant; even Tay, who is still proximate, holds me at arm's length. So, my distant friend, take some time to look within and understand the vows you've silently made to yourself. These vows can be very powerful and cause great good. And they can be very powerful and cause great grief. None of us gets out of here without experiencing deep wounds to our hearts—none of us. The strongest, I've come to discover, do the most repairing.

Becoming BTL means becoming a master at repair. Where, friend, are you repairing today?

Day 332: Food, wine, and fellowship...

Gregg Popovich, head coach of the San Antonio Spurs basketball team, appears to be just another example of a grumpy old man. According to Daniel Coyle in his book, *The Culture Code*, Pop is nothing like the tough dude we so often see portrayed during interviews. And boy, does he win. In the last twenty years, no professional sports team has won more games when they were not the favorite on the Vegas betting line. In fact, no team is even close. Pop's secret?

Tough and tender—love the team, love the work.

Turns out Pop is a love cat. His go-to expression is food, wine, and fellowship. He loves good food, good wine, and his players and their loved ones. He doesn't take the team out for dinner to get them drunk and distracted. He loves getting to know them. And as they enjoy good food and good wine, he's figuring each of them out and figuring out how to get their heart in their work. This is another classic example of the BTL belief around leaders. The transformational ones do this, not once in a while, not as a discipline, not because it's expected, scheduled, or some other obligation. Transformational leaders figure out their favorite way of "being with" to create a culture of belonging. Pop does it with food, wine, and fellowship.

What, leader, is your secret sauce for creating a culture of belonging within your tribe? When we visit your practice facility, would we feel like we've entered a high-performance family oozing truth in love, demanding excellence, tough and tender, real and raw? Or would we get a sense of false harmony, buried resentment, and people on their heels hiding in fear? Good teams require tough and tender leadership. They take on hard topics, and sometimes people's feelings get hurt. These teams have learned the truth will set you free, but it hurts like hell along the way.

Forget looking good. Be good instead. Get real. Tough and tender. Love the work. Love the team. Food, wine, and fellowship (or whatever fits your love tos). I've never really liked the Spurs. Sure is good to know that Pop loves 'em. How do you love your teams?

Day 333: Amos and Danny...

Michael Lewis, in his latest rant, *The Undoing Project,* tells the story of two Jewish psychologists, Amos and Danny, who've changed our minds. Amos Tversky and Danny Kahneman have done more research on what makes us tick than any couple in history. Their life's work has been captured in *Thinking Fast and Slow.* In Lewis' book, he takes you through their story, how they met, where they came from, and what it was like to watch them work.

Amos and Danny are polar opposites. Danny doubts almost everything he thinks, and Amos has no doubt his thoughts are right. Amos was a stud in the Israeli Armed Forces and jumped out of jets without thinking. Danny was in the IAF, too, but he never tasted combat, instead preferring to operate in the background, deciding who best to fly those same jets. The two of them argued famously and laughed hysterically. The most telling trait of their chemistry as scientists was found in one, comically simple thing.

According to Lewis—

Amos would turn up around noon, and the two of them would walk down to a fish and chips place no one else could stand, eat lunch, and then return and talk the rest of the day. "They had a certain style of working," recalls Paul Slovis, "which is they just talked to each other for hour after hour after hour." Whatever Amos and Danny were talking about must be funny, as they spent half their time laughing. They bounced back and forth between Hebrew and English and broke each other up in both.

They talked. There is no substitute in your partnerships for real, honest conversation. So, next time you think about the confirmation bias, actor/observer bias, loss aversion, or even the silly coffee and donut problem from BTL practices, remember, you've got Amos and Danny to thank. Thank God, these two talked.

How about you and your partners at work? When was the last time you talked, laughed, and loved? Take a walk with one of them today. Talk…

Day 334: Wasichu...

Thanksgiving is my favorite Holiday. I've made it a tradition of mine to read more about the Native Americans. Each Thanksgiving, I try to take the time to read a book that widens my understanding of these people who came before us *wasichu*. Wasichu was the Lakota word for "white people." Its alternative meaning was "the one who steals the bacon." I'm re-reading *Sitting Bull* by Bill Yenne. Here's a little taste from Sitting Bull's perspective:

I do not want anyone to bother my people. I want them to live in peace. I myself have plans for my people, and if they follow my plans, they will never want. They will never hunger. I wish for traders only and no soldiers on my reservation. God gave us this land, and we are at home here. I will not have my people robbed. We can live if we can keep our Black Hills. We do not want to eat from the hand of the Grandfather. We can feed ourselves.

Sitting Bull is a well-written story about the Native Americans and the forming of our country. This story and others like it have a humbling effect on me. The wider our perspective, the more we unite with those unlike ourselves. We are still a country trying to figure it out. Look around the world and notice a world still on the road and a long way from the mark. Today, let's be thankful, grateful, and helpful. Tomorrow too. Let's give the world a taste of what makes no sense. Let's not only say grace—but let's give it. We, the BTL band, are thankful for you. Thanks for your attention and trust. Thanks for being iron and sharpening us. Thanks for allowing us to sharpen you too. Together, we transform. Always together.

What's your favorite celebration? Tell me more.

BUILT TO **LEAD** | together we transform

Day 335: Attune...

According to John and Julie Gottman's research the past forty years, women want a man who is tuned toward them. Shocker, I know. Here are the big four questions your woman wants answered in the affirmative: Is he safe? Will he be there for me? Is he dependable? Is he trustworthy? These are solid questions worth further investigation. The Gottman's have us covered with an acronym: A.T.T.U.N.E. Check it out.

Attend. Undivided attention whenever possible. When she enters your space, put away distractions and attend to her or tell her when you will. Attend to her emotional needs, first and foremost.

Turn toward. Talk. Face to face, men. Tune into what's not said but written on her face. Again, read her emotions. You cannot look at your phone and her at the same time. Stop swiping, please.

Understand. Do not fix, don't try to distract her, don't offer solutions, don't make jokes, and don't minimize. It's not about saying anything, men. It's about showing up and sitting in.

Non-defensive listening. Again, don't counterattack, react, justify, or Triple-D. Tune in to all emotions and downregulate your anger. Translation. Stay calm.

Empathize. Open your heart and mind. Try to feel what your woman is feeling.

Attunement is a learned skill most men haven't built. Attuning begins by tuning in to ourselves. I mean, come on, man, if you haven't figured out what frequency you're on, how you gonna possibly find her channel? You must know who you are first. Now you're more than ready to tune in to another with a clear mind, welcoming heart, and open hands.

Your partner wants you tuned in to them. I hope this helps. Attend, turn toward, understand, listen, and empathize. Attune today...

Day 336: Initiate...

Toward the end of BTL team practice eighty, with a team of grapplers, one of the leaders shared a desire of his. He said he wanted this team to be a place where everybody felt cared for. I stopped him mid-sentence. Everybody wants this. Everybody wants to work/live in real community and know they are cared for. The only way it happens, though, is when you get out of your own head and embrace Marcus Aurelius' mantra: "It's up to you." I reminded this strong man that it's up to him to embody what he wants to see in everybody else. If you want any place you take up residence, friend, to reflect a caring, competitive, challenging, and courage-giving culture, it's up to you. Everybody wants this.

Stop wanting a more caring family. Care more for every family member. Stop wanting a more caring work life. Care more for everyone you work with. Recently, I reached out to another long-lost friend. We hadn't connected in forever, it felt. We talked on the phone for twenty-five minutes. He recalled something I said to him at a Starbucks in UA on 11.11.11. He played it back to me verbatim nearly nine years later! He said he thinks about it all the time. I had no idea.

The road toward becoming ONE, distinct and deeply connected, runs parallel to the superhighway titled one, distinct and disconnected. Nobody has time for everybody. Nobody stays connected perfectly. Be one of the few who chooses the road less traveled, the narrow ONE titled distinct and deeply connected. Be the one who cares for others, who people know they can count on when their world goes dark. Take the time to initiate connection. So many people want deeper connections, yet they can't quite be the one to pick up the phone. Be one of the few who chooses the road less traveled, the even narrower one labeled simply "initiate."

Initiate with a loved one, teammate, or forgotten friend. Do it today. Done so...

BUILT TO LEAD | together we transform

Day 337: Regrets...

When you're ninety, you will wish for the three Rs.

Ninety-year-olds, when asked what they would do differently if given a re-do, consistently answer with the three Rs. They wish they had taken more risks. Remember, humans are hard-wired for loss aversion. Ninety-year-olds wish they had invested more time in the relationships that matter. Remember, men are the biggest culprits here. Men tend to over-value metrics and measurement, meaning, not so much—at least till we reach a certain age. And ninety-somethings wish they had reflected more. The untrained brain avoids slowing down and staring at its navel 'cause it tends to go all negative in the process. The normal brain simply gets busy to avoid such uncomfortable conversations with itself. When we're young, our regret is mostly focused on acts of commission. We wish we hadn't done or said something. When we're old and reflect back, however, we mostly regret what we haven't done—acts of omission.

Risk.
Relate.
Reflect.

Hmm. Does your calendar reflect your attempt to do it all, or do you have margin for spontaneity alongside responsibility? Do you sense alignment as you walk through your week, or does it feel like something's a bit out of whack? Maybe you and I would benefit from some RR&R. Take more risks, choose to lose with those you love, and write like a banshee as a habit of your heart. Remember, if it all goes bad beyond your worst nightmare, you can always invoke the fourth R—repair.

Don't wait for ninety, friend. Risk, relate, reflect, and go on—repair—start today. Take a breath and let this one sink in...

Day 338: Sound barrier....

In October of 1947, Chuck Yeager broke the sound barrier flying over the Mojave Desert. Many scientific minds believed this could not be done. Many believed the plane and pilot would disintegrate from the force of the shock waves creating the sound. A few with the right stuff kept pushing the envelope.

BTL team practice is designed to break you and your team's sound barriers. You know, break through how you sound one way when you're around so and so and another way when you're not. Your team is limited by sound barriers. Most teams believe there are certain sounds the boss can't hear, certain sounds top performers don't want to hear, and certain sounds we better keep hidden from those on the front lines. Not unlike many scientists seventy-some years ago, we're afraid of what's on the other side of the sonic boom. We've been told for years what can and can't be said, so we mostly play it safe and fly well below our challenge zone, nowhere near the edges of the envelope, and more or less cruise around in our comfort zone. We play it safe.

I recently read *Hidden Figures* by Margo Lee Shetterly. The book is about the women back in the 1940s, 1950s, and 1960s who broke gender and racial barriers never before thought possible. Nothing was handed to these barrier breakers. As we study history, it never is. You and your team can break through barriers limiting your performance if you can learn to talk about them. We cannot change what we don't address. We cannot address what we keep sweeping under the rug. Go on, friend, break the sound barrier in our next BTL team practice. It's always the shakiest right before we break through. Once we punch through the sonic boom, we discover smoother air, and soon enough, we're flying higher.

What sound barrier do you and your team need to pierce? Do you believe you have what it takes, or it's not your place? Are you ready to fight to improve performance, not prove a point? Slow down and reflect. Now, go break your sound barrier…

Day 339: We are family...

In 2019, we toured the island of Santorini via e-bikes. We strolled four miles in nearly four hours. We rode up to ancient castles and through tiny villages, and we learned why Santorini wines grow in a basket on the ground instead of on vines heading to the heavens. We laughed. We renewed connections with our children—you see, we are family.

We sailed together, literally and figuratively, as best we could. We will grow old but not tired together. It wasn't about the bike, boat, or even the spectacular beauty of the island. It was about being together. The bike was just a tool to get us to another side of the island and learn how to be with again. Our family, maybe like yours, is no longer living under one roof. We live in Florida (Jordan), Berlin (Andrew), Kansas City (Krit), and Columbus (Tay). We work in different worlds too. Jordan is a professional poker player, Andrew, an artist and craftsman, Krit plans world-class events, and Tay works with us at BTL. We are ONE, but we're not the same. We must shut off our judger and learn to celebrate those we cannot control. This is not easy.

You and I are God's children, I believe. God gives us the freedom to choose our way forward and loves us anyway. As I bathe in this truth, it reminds me there is so much I don't know with regard to His world, so why should I get so bent when others are finding their way traveling a different route than me? Why not just view them as one of God's children? I guess that would make *all* of us family. God, help me gain this perspective.

Day 340: Pyramid or Coalition...

A coalition, by Merriam-Webster's definition, is "a temporary alliance of distinct parties, persons, or states for joint action" and comes from the same root word as coalesce, meaning to blend, mingle, mix, and grow together. If you like pyramids, coalitions are messy. Teams form and dissolve as the situation demands. Leadership in coalitions isn't granted by position but by buy-in. Tasks are assigned to leaders who can draw a crowd of the best workers opting into the new assignment. People across coalitions are selected by their peers. The inmates run the asylum.

BTL is a coalition. It takes a special inmate to thrive in our coalition. Someone highly self-authorizing and committed to excellence. Someone looking for meaning in their work. So, what's critical in a coalition? First, the meaning must flow from the clear Purpose of the enterprise. Autonomy is essential. Growing skills from competence to mastery is the norm. The work has impact and makes a positive difference.

The pyramid is all about command and control. A successful coalition is built on a model of engage and evolve. The pyramid moves forward on the *what* of strategic planning; the coalition is based on the *why* of CORE purpose. The pyramid hires for talent and experience; the coalition looks for character, energy, and heart. Pyramids are obsessed with lagging indicators of financial performance; coalitions are obsessed with leading indicators of associate engagement, customer involvement, and referral.

The coalition is about as different from the pyramid as day from night. The pyramid is a formidable, predictable structure. It's messy building a coalition where you give away your positional power to create organizational power. The best coalitions are led by leaders like Durp, who are not Pharaoh-driven but led by a purpose to change their industry and make it better. Coalitions are messier and scarier. They operate just this side of chaos. This is where high performers thrive.

Remember, Becoming BTL, mastering the art of living, is a team sport best played with peers. Does your team see you as a peer or the pharaoh?

"For life, to continue to evolve, all newly developed forms of togetherness ultimately must be in the serve of a more enriched individuality, and not the other way around."
—*A Failure of Nerve* by **Edwin Friedman**

Day 341: 300...

Recently, we celebrated 300 BTL team practices at Choice Recovery. We watched a clip, shared some Worldviews, and drank an adult beverage while telling stories of how far we've come and where we're headed. I almost cried a couple of times as my body shook with emotion thinking about the changed lives in the room. BTL team practice has a beginning. It begins when some leader combines caring with courage and gives the gift to their team. There is no designated halftime, and there is no end game. The aim is to continue failing and learning, loving and learning, winning and learning, falling and learning—for as long as our brain and body are working.

You see, friend, the aim of our OPUS is to grow old but not tired with a few like-minded souls who love ourselves, love each other, love Becoming BTL, and love our teams. Together, we Awaken, Challenge, and Transform from a lone toward all ONE. Together, we are becoming distinctly who we are and deeply connecting with souls very different from our own. This is the ONEness we are building slowly but surely in one tiring team practice after another.

Yesterday, my soul celebrated seven such practices. I was tired at the end of the OPUS day, but it was a good tired. I had been in hard practices, fun practices, loving practices, practices that went personal, and practices that got spiritual. BTL team practice is for the few. It took this team ten years to hit 300. Thanks for all the hard OPUS, Durp. You have done the work within and toward your aims. You have gone through hard labor on your way to hard OPUS. You have carried your smile with grace and goodness through good and not so good. You've inspired me and many others, my friend. By the way, I think we will have a few bottles of Opus One for 600. I'll be seventy and smiling. We'll be a bit older, my friend, but we won't be tired.

What team are you leading toward your 300...?

Day 342: Hit and help...

The level of dialogue determines the level of trust.

Tight teams talk performance-aggressive and hit each other with hard, performance-enhancing truth. Tight teams don't gossip or tell half-truths. Tight teams fight to improve performance, not prove a point. The tightest teams have the best fights, the least fear, and the most love. The tightest teams do not necessarily have the most talent, but they get the most out of whatever they have.

You do not get the team you want, leader. You get the team you deserve. Want a better team? Become a better leader. Trust yourself, not because you're some kinda Pollyanna positive but because you've led an examined life and are discovering you have what it takes. Trust yourself because you've earned it and can rightly esteem yourself. Trust your team. Stop babying/coddling them. Your job, leader, is not to be likable, but it's to be believable. Your job is to make them do what they can. Push more tension toward them and learn to make it feel like it's their idea.

Recently, a client wrote to me that he's stopped hinting. You see, he holds back speaking truth to some of his teammates who he's not quite sure can handle it. So, he hints and hopes they take the hint, so to speak. This is passive-aggressive, not performance-aggressive. This is not good. Move from hint to hit. Hit them with hard truth they can use to get better instead of hoping they pick up on it on their own. Hit, don't hint. Hit because you want to help, not hurt. Hit because it's the right thing to do. Hit because you are kind, not nice. You see, nice people hint and hope. Kind leaders, on the other hand, hit and help. Stop hinting around, faux leader. Hit and help. Write. ACT…

Day 343: Coalitions...

Coalitions operate just this side of chaos because just this side of chaos is where the elite take up residence. Companies, big and small, almost always start as coalitions. Somewhere along the journey, they choose to organize formally. Large companies can operate as coalitions. One of our best clients, Lockton Companies, has over 8,000 associates worldwide, yet they operate more like a coalition than a command-and-control company. How's it done, you ask?

Not easily.

The key comes down to the owner's/leader's willingness to create a culture where freedom trumps absolute control. Freedom, wedded with responsibility, produces a coalition culture. It feels just this side of chaos, but it really, really performs. It attracts the autonomous elite and requires strong leadership that isn't heavy-handed. And it's really difficult to sustain, don't get me wrong. Remember Viktor Frankl's sobering observation in *Man's Search for Meaning* as he looked upon America so many years ago. "The Statue of Liberty on the east coast [should] be supplemented by the Statue of Responsibility on the west coast." You can't build a sustainable coalition, much less country, without bookending freedom and responsibility. Building these kinds of coalitions is foreign to most leaders because most leaders share Lenin's Worldview more than Lockton's. Lenin spoke for the majority of leaders when he said, "Freedom is good, but control is better."

Choose to live like Lockton and take up residence just this side of chaos. Lenin's time is long gone. Choose to build an elite coalition where freedom and responsibility are bookended. Choose to build like Lockton. Choose to build like Choice Recovery, where Durp's big dream is a self-sustaining system. Choose to build like Kaufman Development, where Brett's krazies are just this side of chaos, creating spaces that, well, defy gravity. Choose to build like we do at BTL, where we practice what we preach and play together in ways that make no cents but make perfect sense to us.

You choose. Your choices have consequences…

Day 344: Enlightenment...

The Medici family left a mark. Back in fifteenth century Florence, Italy, this fine family decided we had been dark long enough. So, they put their money where their mouth was and invited scientists, sculptors, poets, philosophers, people of high finance, and even some of those crazy artists like Leonardo to come to their fair city. Florence became a confluence of ideas as painters rubbed up against poets, and philosophers hung out with bankers. Florence is known as the epicenter of the Renaissance, the Enlightenment, if you will, that led to a creative explosion of epic proportions!

Every CEO who wants a creative confine around her company needs to study a little Medici and Leonardo. Turns out history's greatest genius couldn't have done it without being surrounded by diverse minds, diverse disciplines, and diverse cultures. You may not like those nutcases down the hall, and you may not be able to engage your engineers in long conversations about E! News. However, you may need their minds to bring your creative idea into some innovation we can see. Remember, there are no enlightened ones, only those earnestly seeking it.

Stop running your ideas by minds that think like you. Start mixing it up with diverse, different, and even some diametrically opposed. When you least expect it, the idea will become fluent, and your eureka moment will arrive. Medici knew what he was doing. Be one of the few and face your fear and invite some foreigners in for a little idea exchange. Your team's next big idea may be brewing in many a mind, but you've got to get them together so it will go from fool's gold to fluent.

Who do you need to include, leader, into your next brainstorming session? The best way to avoid sabotage from the outsider is to make them one of us. Slow down and sit with this for a while. Seek light. Eureka is coming. Like Medici, you'll leave a mark. Go on—invite some outsiders into the "you're not as open as you think" team. Done so.

Day 345: Sober...

Recently, I called an old friend. We haven't worked together in twenty years. Something nudged me to call him. So, still remembering his mobile number (weird, yes), I called him up to talk. He didn't answer. Within seconds, he texted my dumb dumb (phone) and said he would call me momentarily. We talked as if nothing had changed. We caught up on family and work. We talked sports, and then I made mention of how much I've learned about addiction through the work of BTL. "It's everywhere," I said matter of factly.

Silence.

I sat in it. I've slowly learned that silence isn't simply something to be enjoyed in solitude. Silence is required to transform from a lone toward all ONE. We mostly fill the void with words. Slow down. Listen. Sometimes sitting silently with another, even for a very short while, is required for ONEness. You cannot tune into your team while speaking in their silence. Most humans, remember, are hurting most of the time. They want a leader who is unafraid of this reality, who understands this is the gig, and who wants to know more than just the surface stuff.

After silence came sobs.

My friend apologized profusely as he struggled to share. I sat in my car silently and humbly. You see, I had reached out to an old friend on a very important day to him. He had told nobody what he began to tell me. His words pierced my heart and soul. As I listened intently, my heart softened to his hurt, and my mind changed toward my own. When we hung up a few moments later, we were both feeling better. I'm sure he felt better getting something heavy off his chest. I know I was better hearing his hurt and softening my heart.

Together, we transform, friend, from a lone toward all ONE. One 'L of a difference is love. Love. Who knew a lunchtime spent alone reflecting and reminiscing would lead to changing me? God alone. That's who. At least, that's what I believe. So, next time something nudges you to reach out to a teammate, take the time to talk. You may just get more than you give. Give and take care...

Day 346: Relationships...

We are built by relationships. We are built for them too. We cannot reach our potential without a few friends. True friends help us remove our layers, throw away our masks, and become comfortable in our own skin. They move us from fear into courage and fill in what we perceive as voids with confidence and encouragement. Together, we transform. Always.

Relationships are the essence of life. None of us live in total isolation or independence. We all need people and are needed by people. The quality of our relationships is a great determiner of the quality of our life. Deep relationships bring us satisfaction, peace, and great joy; however, these same relationships can bring us intense, cutting pain and wound us seemingly for life. Bono is right: "Home is where the heart is, and home is where we hurt." For many reading this book, let this serve as a reminder to find flow at work and with your husband, friend, or wife. This is simple, not easy. Let's slow down and listen to what Mihaly Csikszentmihalyi, author of *Flow*, said about family:

If one is serious about family life, however, one must also take on the challenge of transforming it into a flow experience—which means investing as much psychic energy into it as one would in making a business organization work. In many cases, even when our bodies our home, our minds are not. Attention remains focused on work-related problems, and our family quickly notices that we are mentally and emotionally absent.

Slow down. Reflect. Connect. Go home. Mastering the art of living is not found by winning at work and losing in life. Be with...

Day 347: Friends...

You know your close friends, many would say, by what they do when you're suffering. Most of us struggle with suffering and have a hard time being with those in the middle of unchosen suffering. We want to be there for them, but we don't know what to say, don't feel qualified, or are overwhelmed in the moment and freeze. As you are sure to suffer, preload this response: expect few to come closer, be grateful for those who do, and give the benefit of the doubt to those who keep their distance. Give more than you take. Be a friend. You'll have more than enough.

Today, a bunch of my friends suffered together. This was chosen suffering, so much different than the unchosen kind. We suffered over fifty-three miles and 5,600 feet of climbing. We chose to do this. We experienced the camaraderie of suffering and grew closer in the process. Maybe it would be good for you, friend, to find some like-minded folk and develop the discipline and joy of learning to do hard things well. Maybe, just maybe, this would serve to inoculate you from freezing when the bell tolls for one of your friends. It was good to be with you, Littlest Fricker, Governor, Grappy, Downer, and PJ. It was good to suffer alongside each of you and enjoy the beauty of the climb.

Suffering is coming, the unchosen kind. You and I don't control this for ourselves or for those we call close friends. Develop the discipline of being with. Be a friend. Inoculate yourself as best you know how. Model the way. Embrace pain and suffering. Embody truth in love. These are my three CORE Principles that help me live in alignment with my Worldview.

I'm becoming a better friend with fewer regrets. Always a work in process, far from arrived, and more and more grateful for those in close proximity. Slow down and reflect. Count your blessings. Reach out to a friend. Give more than you take. Give and take care.

To the Ancients, Friendship seemed the happiest and most fully human of all the loves; the crown of life and the school of virtue. The modern world, in comparison, ignores it.
—*The Four Loves* by C.S. Lewis

Day 348: Text, tweet, or talk...

Leader, let me practice being CCD. Your words matter, especially the words you communicate electronically. You see, email, text, tweet, and all the emojis in the world cannot communicate context as completely as two humans talking face to face. Too many leaders today rely on the ease of electronic communication instead of the more difficult, time-consuming talk.

Most conflict is simply a conversation to be had. A face-to-face conversation that is. "With all due respect," leader, you have the time. (By the way, this is a bullshit phrase from ancient Parliamentary times, and I recommend you avoid using it electronically. See *Urban Dictionary* for modern interpretations.) Talk. Take bullshit offline and talk.

Of course, you cannot make time for everything and everyone. This is why the work within (BTL CORE) is even more important the higher up the ladder you proceed and why the clarity of aim (OPUS) informs critical conversations like none other. Have you taken the time to build both? Stop building and filling up your day on the busy-ness express. Stop sending passive or passionate electronic communications that leave the receiver reeling. Leaders and their powerful yet peaceful presence regulate the room. Transformational leaders talk. Translation. Transformational leaders mostly listen and let you, their turned-up teammate, do most of the speaking. Text, tweet, or talk. Which one matters the most to you becoming ONE, distinct, and deeply connected, leader? Text, tweet, or talk.

Pick up the phone and talk to someone you've not heard from in a while. Talk.

BUILT to **LEAD** | together we transform

Day 349: What more can the heart desire?

The most-read post on the BTL blog is this one from 2008. It comes courtesy of Tolstoy and his worthy read, *Family Happiness*. You need to read this and sit with it for a while, maybe a long while. The world is not speeding up, but many of you are. Time is not changing, but many sense they have less of it. You and I are not an amalgamation of our successes and fails; we are so much more. Tolstoy wrote better than he lived. Far too many of us seem to be following suit and working better than we're living. I hope you enjoy this short snippet.

I have lived through much, and now I think I have found what is needed for happiness. A quiet secluded life in the country, with the possibility of being useful to people to whom it is easy to do good, and who are not accustomed to having it done to them; then work which one hopes may be of some use; then rest, nature, books, music, love for one's neighbor—such is my idea of happiness. And then, on top of all that, you for a mate, and children, perhaps—what more can the heart of a man desire?

What a great question. What do you think? Write...

Day 350: Bids...

Recently, a young married couple told me they're struggling. Seems they fight all the time about a bunch of nothing, they shared. I listened and observed their body language, words, not so much. They have a bidding problem.

According to the Gottmans' research in *The Relationship Cure,* unless your ratio of positive to negative emotions is at least 4:1, your relationship will not endure. Nothing is more emotional than the bidding process. We all bid to one another all the time: "Would you please take out the trash? Let's go to a show tonight. I'd really appreciate it if you would leave your phone in the garage when you come home, honey."

When a loved one bids, they don't care so much about the answer as the attitude. The bidder wants a turn toward. Even if the answer isn't the one they want, it feels good knowing our request was heard. Too often, busy partners don't hear the bid. The bidder assumes they've been blown off. This is the equivalent of a turn away and sparks negative emotions. Worse still is the turn against. Avoid this one like the Black Plague.

The turn against goes something like this, I told them:

Bride: "Hey, it would be great to go to the Apple store together and pick out my new phone. Can we do this later today?"

Groom: Deep sigh. "The Apple store is a nightmare on Saturday. You take forever deciding on anything, which makes it feel like the nightmare never ends. Besides, why can't you do stuff like that on your own?"

The young couple looked at me and then at each other and started to laugh. It seemed they've both been missing lots of bids because they're busy swiping new phones and looking down instead of toward each other. These two are going to be just fine. They've learned to laugh, not loathe. I told them to practice seven good minutes, figuring out what each other wants first and foremost. Give each other some of what they want and get clear on what ain't happening. We laughed at the simplicity of it all and went our separate ways. You see, friend, most conflict is simply a conversation to be had. Laugh, don't loathe. Turn toward. Talk.

Do you have a bidding problem?

Day 351: Vision Correction...

Your problem is your problem. Your partner, boss, buddy, son, sister, bride, or your brother are not your problem. Your problem is not another person. Your problem is how you respond, react, and relate to another. Your problem is you think you see other's problems with 20/20 clarity. You cannot see another person's problem with 20/20 clarity because you cannot see inside another person's brain. You and I are not God. Assuming we know another person's problem is assuming we are God. Yikes.

Your problem is your problem.

Your problem is not another person. If you are trying to mediate a problem with a teammate, trying to salvage your marriage through counseling, or working on any other relationship in your world, your problem will not get better until you fix your focus. Let's take a simple test. Ask yourself to fill in the blank on a couple of statements. Answer honestly. This will be hard.

1. My partner needs to deeply change _____.
2. I need to deeply change _____.

Which statement was easier to complete? Which statement was filled with concrete examples? Which one was top of mind?

Want better relationships? Focus on you. Even though your problem is your problem, it doesn't give license to your partner's inappropriate behavior. You may be married or partnered with a real problem child. Again, we end up needing to fill in the blank on statement number two. We cannot change another, but we can change how we respond.

The foundational problem is your problem. What do you think about your biggest problems? Would reframing the root and your response be helpful? Slow down. Reflect. Write. Your vision just got better...

Day 352: Exceptions...

This morning I shared a solid truth with a leader. He was wanting to know about holding people to performance standards and when to make exceptions. Here's the truth if you want a high-performance culture. Do not make exceptions based on how much you like the particular performer falling below the bar. Don't make exceptions based on how much over the bar an unethical performer is performing. Don't make exceptions because you simply need bodies now. Exceptions are the enemy of excellence. If you want a sustainable high-performance culture, make exceptions around effort. Effort counts the most. If you have a performer who is missing the mark but putting forth world-class effort, make the exception here.

Make exceptions around effort.

Sustainable high performance is rooted in endurance. Anybody can put forth full thrust for an hour, a day, or even a season. Whenever we study the elite, the melody line is their ability to put forth a full measure, practice after practice, game after game, meeting after meeting, quarter after quarter, and season in and season out. The elite understand effort and endurance are under their control. Talent is overrated. Playing nice is immaterial. Allowing unethical behavior is certain lawsuit city and eventual system suicide. Lowering expectations for those you like is country club cliché. Do not make exceptions here. Make exceptions around effort.

What exceptions are you making?

BUILT TO LEAD | together we transform

Day 353: My way IS the highway...

When I started BTL back in 2002, I decided to do it my way—my way IS the highway. So, when my financial advisor told me I was leaving money on the table not annuitizing my intellectual property, it took me no time to tell him—that's right. When I told other coaches my plan was to travel only to Kansas City and build 90% of the business here in Cbus, they told me I was nuts. It took me two seconds to tell them—that's right, I'm nuts.

But, when Larry Allen and Gurue ganged up on me with their lawyers' argument to change the composition of the BTL CORE, it took me a long, long, long time being curious to finally tell them—you're right.

Here's the learning...master connectors are both Curious George, and my way IS the highway.

When they don't know the way forward, insatiable curiosity is the way. When they do know, my way IS the highway is CCD freaking magic. Masters never mix the two. Do you?

Do you know your highway?

Day 354: Love the outsider...

According to Thomas Cahill in *The Gift of the Jews,* we were not moving much before the Jews taught us how to roll up our tent and shake it up a bit. The Jews also taught us to think about community as a collection of unique individuals, how to think about time differently, and how to understand our individual and collective destinies. The Jewish people are a gift from God, you could say. I, in fact, believe that's exactly what they are.

So, back in October of 2019, I was invited into their world for one beautiful evening. I was an outsider in their celebration of marriage. Brooklyn was no longer a New York City borough; it was a gift of Jewish community. It was about seven circles, seven blessings, and all that is right in this world of seven continents. That night, one of my dear friends and clients, Durp, got married in a traditional Jewish ceremony. It was all done in Hebrew, and my friend Bk wasn't much of a translator. It didn't matter. The room swept me up as if I was one of theirs. A rabbi saw me standing outside their dance circle, grabbed me by the shoulder, and thrust me into the circle. I moved. Another black hatter smiled, grabbed my other hand, and away we went. A few minutes later, the same rabbi pulled me out of the circle and shoved me straightway to the center where Durp had been dancing with his brothers. I hugged Durp and told him, "I didn't know what I was doing, but I loved it." He replied that he didn't either. We laughed, shared a little jig, mostly hugged, and shared some love. It was wonderful. I felt like I belonged. These people were not afraid of the outsider.

You see, friend, the Jewish people are beacons of community; they've had to be to survive throughout history. The world has not been kind to them. That night, the Jewish community loved each other, loved Durp and Shaindy, and even loved me. God, help us learn there really is no us and them. God, help us love those outside our immediate circle. God, help us follow your design and act like we're all ONE. Amen (another gift of the Jews).

BUILT to **LEAD** | together we transform

Day 355: Prepare them for the road...

Back in 1984, CompuServe promoted me into management. I was twenty-five years old and one of the youngest managers in the company. Later that year, Miss and I would welcome our first son, Jordan. My manager told me to make my numbers and not to be afraid to manage those older than me. Good advice—everybody in the office was older than me.

My mom gave me the best leadership advice about raising Jordan. She told me when he's little, it's really simple: teach, teach, teach. You've got to teach him the right way and how to figure things out. As they grow, she told me, you migrate a bit in your approach: teach, teach, listen. Once they start to speak, you better listen up. You still teach more than you listen, but you tune in and make sure they know it. When they get into double digits, you better be ready. The recipe is flipped on its ear. Now, it's listen, listen, listen. You only teach by sneaking it in and making them think it's their idea. She called this "a little bit here, and a little bit there." I remember this stuff she said back in 1984. I don't remember anything from CompuServe's introduction to management training course.

Most of my learning as a leader came from my fails, and I had plenty. As a husband, father, and CompuServe manager, I seemed to go from one mistake to another. I didn't have a roadmap. I had plenty of confidence, conviction, and desire to become more competent. My parents had prepared me for the road, not the other way around. My mom, I recall, when I was leaving for college, told me to enjoy myself, get a good education, and realize I wasn't coming home. Oh, she wanted me to come home, but she wanted me to stand on my own. She prepared me for the road. Whether you're leading family, friends, or teammates, your job is to prepare them for the road, not prepare the road for them.

Thanks, Mom, Dad, Coach Crank, Coach Odle, Greg Tillar, Miss, and many, many more for preparing me for the road. Lord knows I was not easy for any of you. I'm doing my best to pass it along and still learning mostly from my mistakes. Leader, are you preparing your team for the road or preparing the road for them?

Day 356: Affirmation vs information...

Most people, when they ask for feedback, want affirmation, not information. Most coaches in the business world understand this and give their clients exactly what they want: a cheerleader. They want somebody who affirms the goodness in their strengths and takes their eyes off bad habits. The world is full of coaches, leaders, and associates who are all playing this game. Not good.

The truth is that the higher up you get in whatever system you're in, the more desperately you need information, not affirmation. And the less likely you are to even sniff it. Today, I gave one of my client's information he can use. I spoke CCD. I asked him to tell me what he heard and why he thought he was hearing it. I didn't let him off the hook until he thought his way through it—until it had become his idea. He converted this feedback into his new PA.

Recently, a couple of teammates were given the chance to give their leader some information. One chose to do so, and one took a pass. This leader has work to do to make it safe for all to speak truth, especially hard truth. Always work to be done to hear more truth from your teammates. And always work to be done, teammate, to stop taking a pass when the opportunity arrives to speak truth to your leader. Come on, man, give your leaders some information they can use. Tell them something they can't see from their perch, but you see with clarity from your position. Truth in love is always the aim. Stop asking folks questions that lead to affirmation. Ask them tough questions in safe environments that prime them to tell you the truth. This will make you both stronger.

Don't seek affirmation, friends. Seek information to make you stronger. Which one are you seeking? Which are you sending?

BUILT TO **LEAD** | together we transform

Day 357: Hands on, America...

Mary Katherine Goddard knew exactly what she was doing when she told fifty-six men she would gladly print their parchment. She wasn't asked to sign. She chose to stamp her name anyway. The fifty-six men and Mary did something rare in the history of humankind: they risked it all when they had easier options. These were mostly rich, powerful men of means. Mary was a business owner. These were not terrorists or desperate rebels. Far from it—they were farm owners, plantation owners, and lawyers. These were men with plenty to lose. Rarely do these people lead rebellions. And they didn't just organize the rebellion; they personally led it. The last line in the Declaration of Independence is worth memorizing. Memorizing this will help you take personal responsibility. Our founders understood personal responsibility, as demonstrated in Jefferson's last lines.

"And for the support of this declaration, with a firm reliance on the protection of divine Providence, we mutually pledge to each other our Lives, our Fortunes, and our sacred Honor."

Most lost their fortunes. Some lost their lives. They chose liberty over security. Freedom is not free.

Five were captured and tortured before being put to their death. Twelve had their homes sacked and burned. Many loaned their fortune to the government and died bankrupt as a result. Nine died fighting in the war. They chose liberty over security. We have been given a great gift, and like the third generation of a family business, we're taking it for granted.

Today, choose to take responsibility instead of residence in victimhood. Our founders fought for liberty and gave up their lives of security, so the least we can do is honor this hard-earned liberty without expecting handouts as our newfound heritage. Our heritage comes from having our hands-on. And while you're at it, help another get their hands-on too.

Liberty or security. Responsibility or victimhood. Hands-on or hands out. If you want to know more about America's strong women like Mary, read *Founding Mothers* by Cokie Roberts. Be like Mary...

Day 358: Extra ordinary...

U2 continues to give us a sterling example of extra ordinary (I know it's technically one word). There is nothing normal about this team of four. Teamed together now for over forty-two years, their identity has evolved while remaining anchored to a Worldview that appears dug into depths seemingly unimaginable. Way back in 2014, the band allowed themselves to be distracted. They were flowing and right in the middle of finishing their album *Songs of Innocence* when Nelson Mandela went and died. They took no time to decide to drop everything and write "Ordinary Love" to honor Mandela. Listening to Larry Mullen Jr. (drummer) describe the U2 decision-making process is particularly illuminating to who they are. "It was hard to stop what we were doing. We were on a roll. It was clear where we were going. And a decision was made to abandon ship, more or less, to focus on this."

So, they did.

U2 dropped everything and focused all their creative energy toward making a single for a friend. The track is extra ordinary. Another track is titled "Invisible" and is described by Bono as the way they as a band felt when they were starting out years ago. Funny, regardless what you or I may think about this team of four, one thing we almost certainly share is simply this: we see them.

Remember, our aim is not to be normal. We want you to discover the depths in you and author an OPUS worth striving toward. We cannot predict the size or scope of your audience. A few will be with U2. All it takes is a few to make something extra ordinary. Stop worrying about winning over the masses or taking giant leaps for mankind. Extra ordinary comes through the accumulation of marginal gains. Now, that may not sound sexy, but it's truth. There are no hacks to leapfrog forward. No silver bullets, remember, just lots of lead ones.

U2 is a great example. You, too, are as well. I see you. Keep working…

BUILT TO LEAD | together we transform

Day 359: Articules...

No, this isn't some ancient stoic we just read about. You see, Articules (pronounced like the combination of articulate and Hercules) first came to my attention in the shower. Nope, I wasn't singing or daydreaming—just cleaning. Miss bounded into the bathroom with a big smile and muttered something I couldn't understand. Putting aside the soap, I leaned toward the shower door and asked her to repeat herself.

"Articules, Articules," she exclaimed with joy and a playful sense of glee.

"I just thought of your new name, and it's perfect. I wasn't even thinking about what am I gonna call Chester now, and then it just popped in my head: Articules." My bride, whose been battling Mercury toxicity for years now and just recently fell head over heels and busted up some ribs, was back playing the name game with me. A Duchenne smile creased my face as my heart accepted her admiration and fondness. Nothing heals a heart like admiration and fondness from a loved one. Costs nothing. Takes little effort. Delivers. Every. Time. Funny, Jesus got another human condition 100% right: the more you give, the more blessed you become. Miss gave and received more as she did.

I did nothing to deserve her admiration or fondness. I did nothing. She did it anyway. She's filling better. A sure sign she's feeling better too. Who could use some filling from you, friend? Who knows? You may just be the one to not only fill 'em up but feel fulfilled as you do. Thanks, Missi, for filling me. Articules is, well, in a word—speechless.

Who, friend, could use a little admiration and fondness from you? What are you waiting for? Fill them...

Day 360: Hole to whole...

Most reading this rant reside in these United States of America. We aim to be a place where all are welcome, and it's a really big OPUS, isn't it? In fact, it's impossible, as is our motto: *E pluribus unum*. (Out of many, one.) We are far from united, and we've come a long way. Our biggest struggle, regardless of where we're from, what we've got, what we've done, or haven't for that matter, is the struggle within—the struggle to go from hole to whole.

All humans are attempting to go from filled with holes to whole. One dub of a difference, huh? Work on your Worldview, friend, your dub, if you will. Accept others, especially those with different dubs. This is *E pluribus unum* in action. Our country, like each of us, is always a WIP—a work in process. What makes you whole, friend? What are you doing to fill your hole? Are you awake or sleepwalking through life?

Hole to whole, one w of a difference.

I believe none of us is whole. We're all leaking vessels in need of constant filling. What, friend, fills you these days? Do you know what you believe about the big questions of life? Have you taken the time to rinse your Worldview—the deepest held beliefs through which you make sense of your world? Distinct and deeply connected is BTL's version of "out of many, one." You're Becoming BTL when you leak less, accept more dubs, grab a hand, and unite us. Slow down and sit with this for a while.

What are you doing to become more whole? What are you doing to unite us? Do you see why your Worldview matters most? Slow down and write, please...

BUILT to **LEAD** | together we transform

Day 361: ONEness...

C.S. Lewis, in *The Chronicles of Narnia,* challenges his readers to understand the story we believe we're in determines what we think of ourselves and, consequently, the way we live. For Lewis, Christianity doesn't just make sense of stuff, but it invites us to play in a bigger story. Every day in BTL team practice, individuals, teams, and leaders get more clarity around their individual stories and their role in the bigger story of their team. They wake up to the fact that their work is more than a job; it's a chance to find their voice, sing their song, and sing along with souls very distinct and deeply connected.

This is the ONEness you know you want, even though many have never tasted it. We catch glimpses of it and are drawn toward it. You and I are made in ONEness and made for ONEness. Your life is a story. Make it one worth living, friend. Connect your individual story to your team stories and to an even larger one in your community. You are not meant to go it alone, and you know this. Grab a hand. Give and take care. Give more than you take. The more you give, the bigger the story you're in, and the more likely you are to think of yourself as much more than just your role.

Write your definition of ONEness, friend. Pick a person you want to give courage to and make it a done so. God, help me see your meta-story and play my part to the best of my ability. God, help me...

Day 362: ONE...

We're getting closer and closer to the end of our first way round this journey called Becoming BTL. How have you liked it so far? You, my friend, are looking good and growing stronger. Fear has taken a severe hit, and your face looks a bit brighter, and your words a bit more believable. You seem like you're falling in love with your work and life. Let's slow down and reflect. Read these words Sheldon Vanauken wrote in *A Severe Mercy*:

But why does love need to be guarded? Against what enemies? We looked about us and saw the world as having become a hostile and threatening place where standards of decency and courtesy were perishing and war loomed gigantic. A world where love did not endure. The smile of inloveness seemed to promise forever but friends who had been in love last year were parting this year. The divorce rate was in the news. Where were any older people in love? It must be that, whatever its promise, love does not by itself endure. But why? What was the failure behind the failure of love?

Mastering the art of living is not an either/or game. Becoming BTL isn't either. As you gain strength and clarity, friend, remember to grab the hands of those you love and remain ONE, distinct, and deeply connected. Do not cheat one in service of the other.

Are you ONE, distinct, and deeply connected, Becoming BTL? Are you winning in life and losing at work? Are you losing in life and winning at work? Integrate around love. Slow down and reflect. Write. Love...

BUILT TO LEAD | together we transform

Day 363: Becoming BTL...

During practice with a really cool client, we talked about the why behind our business. He was beginning to get the why behind our name, BTL. He had focused on the Purpose of BTL being leadership training and the end state of becoming a leader. He missed the emphasis on building, on the depth of this particular process. Building humans is a lot different than building a house. It's universal, transcendent, and informative; my client had concluded. He's right.

The aim is to build. It's an intrinsic process. The name BTL and the visual of two people on a climb are more than our brand image—it's who we are. We focus on participation in the process. People are naturally focused on the end game: the finished product. There is no end. The process is incremental, accumulative, and transformational. This is why "keep working" is one of my mantras.

I reminded him of the BTL Purpose. We talked for a great while about each of the words and why they matter. I had never explained to him the reason behind the words Awaken, Challenge, and Transform being capitalized. It's because those three first letters, A, C, T, transform to the word ACT. BTL is all about productive action. I could see his brain light up on this one. Very cool.

There is no end state, friends.

The name **BUILT TO LEAD** is more than a catchy name for our company; its emphasis is on building. Building ourselves. Building individuals, teams, and leaders. Building strong CORE alongside authentic OPUS. Building relationships where we become more, not less. ONE, distinct and deeply connected, Becoming BTL. God willing, we'll be here a while, and you can bet we'll be looking for you on the transformational, hard climb of Becoming BTL. Keep working, my friend…

Day 364: Love...

Love.
Love God, yourself, and people.
Love your work and love your team.
Love the pursuit and passion of following your dream.
Love the falling and the failing.
Love recovering and the healing.
Love the breaking and the building.
Love the storms and savor the smooth sailing.
Love seasons and the changes.
Love what is not common and makes no sense.
Love God, love people, and remove your fence.

This is my poem. Write your interpretation.

Day 365: Caught, not taught day...

Becoming BTL cannot be taught, only caught.

We, the BTL Band of Builders, are not coaches or teachers. We're obsessed with learning and mastering this crazy process we passionately believe. Kiesha, Joe, Brian, Durp, Littlest Fricker, Dan, Dub, Tommyc, Robert, Cbear, Wierema, Rich, Slo, Brookethehippie, Bk, Jiggles, Grappy, Nick, Lori, and many more you read about (and many more you didn't) caught this wonderful bug called Becoming BTL. We hope you're beginning to believe in the power of practice and our framework. We hope you are dreaming and doing while living aligned. We hope you are becoming CORE-centered and self-controlling while taking dead aim at your authentic OPUS. We hope you are mastering your PoP with baby steps of PA. And we hope you are waking up and becoming the CEO of Y.O.U. (Thanks, Larry.)

We're all a perpetual work in process. Come on, friend, grab my hand. Let's go back to Day ONE. Becoming BTL is not one (year) and done. Becoming BTL and mastering the art of living is a daily practice we're grateful for, energized by, and joy-filled as we share it from a place of love. We're conduits, not cul-de-sacs, remember. Together, we transform. Always together. Becoming BTL cannot be taught. Are you worth catching?

Rinse and repeat...

Magnum OPUS

We started with Chateaubriand. We will end with him. Mastering the art of living is about integrating who we are with what we do. It's about working and playing and not knowing the difference. It's a romantic thought and needs a robust framework. Becoming BTL is the Atlas, as Steven Pressfield so aptly described.

We are not made to be in balance. We are made to become whole. We cannot find our true selves until we live integrated. How do we do this? Let me remind you and go a bit deeper.

CORE. OPUS. PoP.

We began with CORE work. Never stop this clarifying work within. Never. We introduced OPUS and the basics behind your labor of love. Continue to adapt your aim as you work and live. Your PoP is your way forward. You've been given the tools. You now must do the real, hard work of integrating.

Here's how.

If you were attending Juilliard School in NYC and learning to play Beethoven's Fifth, how would they teach you? They would not have you start playing the piece and correct you as you played it. They would have you "chunk" it out. A master would make you play a small part of it until you could play it with perfection. You would be taught to chunk it out, first, and eventually put it all back together. It would be a beautiful piece when played following this practice.

Becoming a master in the art of living is our aim. CORE, OPUS, and PoP are the melody line for Becoming BTL. Here's the magic. Trying to author and live an integrated OPUS is like trying to play Beethoven's Fifth for the first time. It's best when done in chunks. Start again by writing a work OPUS. This is easier, actually. Write your OPUS with only mastery of your work as your aim. Apply it with a PoP and get your footing. Feel the progress that comes when you work in a labor of love. Once you've established a labor of love in your work, bring it home, so to speak. Write your life OPUS and PoP it out alongside. Over time, your strong CORE will integrate around love. Your love tos will inform work and life. Your CORE will hold it all together. Your great work is coming to life. This is your Magnum OPUS. This is why we're here.

We, your BTL Builders, are living the dream. I dress in T-shirts. Petey does khakis. Gu's gone all black. Rachel lives in athletic wear. Jiggles is high fashion. Doscher is not. Browny is a fashion statement. Dorothy is not wearing ruby slippers. Kitty is classy, and Tay is, well, Tay. We are ONE, but we're not the same. This is what we mean by distinct and deeply connected. I know, I know, this is just our dream when it comes to dressing ourselves. We are living the dream when it comes to how we present ourselves too. We are comfortable saying yes and no and meaning it. We do not do what drains us. We play to each other's strengths, and it's a perfect mess as best it can be. We are a Band of Builders learning to play together. We've been chunking it out for years, and it's starting to produce some really great notes—namely you.

So, friend, chunk it out. Strengthen your CORE. Author an authentic work and life OPUS. PoP them out until you can't tell which is which, when you're working, and when, in fact, you're playing. Integrate work and life. For me, that means trips to KC to see Krit and clients. It means working in the 3PP building core strength among friends. It means being with Miss, taking her with me wherever I go, and going to her favorite farms whenever she wants. It means saying no to speaking engagements around the world and yes to small, private businesses right around the corner. It means awakening, challenging, and transforming me and whomever I'm with. It means integrating labor and leisure. It means accepting that I'm Toto, and you're the star, Dorothy. This is our Magnum OPUS. This is why we're here.

We're here to support, encourage, and push you to do what you can. You're here because you know you want more. We hope you are beginning to find what you've been looking for deep within the reservoirs of your soul. We have high hopes for you. Keep working. Live hard. Love harder. Integrate. Great lives are integrated. God, help us all become whole. God, help us all figure it out on the climb.

Live hard. Love harder. (Thanks, Teeks…)

Endnote

1   Duckworth, Angela. *Grit: The Power of Passion and Perseverance.* New York, NY: Collins, 2016.

2   Dendy, Sim, et al. *Only the Brave.* Derby, CT: Monarch Books, 2018.

3   History.com Editors. "Leonidas." The History Channel. June 7, 2019. https://www.history.com/topics/ancient-history/leonidas.

4   Friedman, Edwin H. *A Failure of Nerve.* New York, NY: Seabury Books, 2007.

5   Goggins, David. *Can't Hurt Me.* Austin, TX: Lioncrest Publishing, 2018.

6   Taleb, Nassim Nicholas. *The Black Swan.* London, England: Penguin, 2008.

7   Bilas, Jay. *Toughness.* New York, NY: Berkley, 2014.

8   Snyder, Dave. "Great Grains: How Ancient Einkorn Became the New 'It' Wheat." *JSTOR Daily.* May 18, 2016. https://daily.jstor.org/einkorn-the-new-it-wheat/.

9   Luke 6:38.

10   United States Olympic & Paralympic Museum. "Matt Biondi | Swimming | Olympic Hall of Fame." Accessed September 17, 2020. https://usopm.org/matt-biondi/.

11   Caspi, A. "Influence of Life Stress on Depression: Moderation by a Polymorphism in the 5-TT Gene." *Science 301,* no 5631 (2003): 386–389. https://doi.org/10.1126/science.1083968.

12   Lewis, C.S. "First and Second Things." *God in the Dock.* Grand Rapids, MI: William B. Eerdmans Publishing Co., 1970.

13   Aurelius, Marcus. *Meditations.* Mineola, NY: Dover Publications, 1997.

14   Aesop. *Aesop's Fables.* Hertfordshire, England: Wordsworth Editions Ltd., 1998.

15   Hutchinson, Alex. *Endure.* New York, NY: William Morrow, 2018.

16   Harrell, Eben. "How 1% Performance Improvements Led to Olympic Gold." *Harvard Business Review.* October 30, 2015. https://hbr.org/2015/10/how-1-performance-improvements-led-to-olympic-gold.

17   History.com Editors. "Leonidas." The History Channel. June 7, 2019. https://www.history.com/topics/ancient-history/leonidas.

18 Hill, A.V., and H. Lupton. "Muscular Exercise, Lactic Acid, and the Supply and Utilization of Oxygen." *Qjm-os-16*, no. 62 (1923): 135–71. https://doi.org/10.1093/qjmed/os-16.62.135.

19 McClusky, Mark. *Faster, Higher, Stronger.* New York, NY: Plume, 2015.

20 Goleman, Daniel. "Curing the Common Cold of Leadership: Poor Listening." LinkedIn. May 2, 2013. https://www.linkedin.com/pulse/20130502140433-117825785-curing-the-common-cold-of-leadership-poor-listening/.

21 Voss, Chris and Tahl Raz. *Never Split the Difference.* New York, NY: Harper Business, 2016.

22 Duhigg, Charles. "What Google Learned From Its Quest to Build the Perfect Team." *The New York Times Magazine.* February 25, 2016. https://www.nytimes.com/2016/02/28/magazine/what-google-learned-from-its-quest-to-build-the-perfect-team.html.

23 The British Library. "Albert Mehrabian: Nonverbal Communication Thinker." Accessed September 26, 2020. https://www.bl.uk/people/albert-mehrabian.

24 Gottman, John M. Ph.D. *The Science of Trust: Emotional Attunement for Couples.* New York, NY: W.W. Norton & Company, 2011.

25 Strathern, Paul. *The Medici: Godfathers of the Renaissance.* London: Vintage UK, 2004.

26 Espen, Hal. "U2 Interview: Oscar Hopes, That Unfinished Album, Anxiety About Staying Relevant." *The Hollywood Reporter.* February 12, 2014. https://www.hollywoodreporter.com/news/u2-interview-oscar-hopes-unfinished-679321.

Glossary

Names:
Bk: Brett Kaufman, owner of Kaufman Development
Browny: Doug Brown, Builder
Cbear: Carey Hoyt, The Ohio State University Associate AD, Sport
  Administration and Student-Athlete Development
Dorothy: Andrew Teitelbaum, Builder
Dosch / Doscher: David Deck, Builder
Dub: Jeff Wilkins, Deputy Chief Investment Officer at Hamilton Capital
  Management
Durp: Chad Silverstein, owner of Choice Recovery / [re]start
Grappy: Tom Ryan, Head Men's Wrestling Coach at The Ohio State
  University
Gu / Gurue: John Rue, Builder
Jiggles: Mike Schott, Builder
Kitty: Kitty Allen, Larry Allen's wife and Builder
Krit: Kristi Scott, Chet's daughter
LA: Larry Allen, Builder
Miss: Missi Scott, Chet's wife
Peteboy: Pete Kunk, Builder
PJ: Kary Oberbrunner, Publisher
Rachel: Rachel Hanson, Builder
Slo: Jeff Loehnis, CFP®, President at Hamilton Capital Management
Tay: Taylor Scott, Chet's son and BTL Apprentice
Teeks: Chet's dog

Words & Acronyms:
3P: Represents the last three elements of your CORE (Passions, Purpose,
  Process)
3PP: Plank, Push-up, Pull-up Palace aka Chet's basement
BTL: **BUILT TO LEAD**
CCD: Clear, Concise and Direct
CORE: a written document that lists out the following:

- Worldview: I believe... statements
- Identity: I am... statements
- Principles: I will... / I won't... statements
- Passions: I love... statements
- Purpose: your 'why'
- Process: your Playbook of Productive actions

MOT: Moment(s) Of Truth

ONE / ONENESS: distinctly strong and deeply connected

OPUS: a written document that contains the follow:
- Overarching vision
- Purpose
- Unifying strategies
- Scorecard of Significance

PA: Productive Action

PoP: Playbook of Productive action

Triple-D: Defend, Deny, Destroy

WIP: Work In Process, represents the first three elements of your CORE (Worldview, Identity, Principles)

About the Author

Chet Scott is the founder of **BUILT TO LEAD**—a band that believes creating sustainable high-performance teams is not only possible but also worthy of the effort. The BTL band knows what builds sustainable, high-performance individuals, teams, and leaders in work and life. Together they awaken, challenge, and transform a few individuals, teams, and leaders.

He and Missi live in Powell, Ohio, and have four adult children: Jordan, Andrew, Kristi, and Taylor.

Connect at BuiltToLead.com.

Got a story inside you?

Author Academy Elite could be the right choice for helping you write, publish, and market your book.

Discover more at:

AuthorAcademyElite.com

the elite full-service branding experience
that increases your credibility & authority

ethoscollective.vip

To stay connected with Chet,
please visit **BuiltToLead.com**

CPSIA information can be obtained
at www.ICGtesting.com
Printed in the USA
BVHW090137100121
597411BV00004B/4/J

9 781636 800103